Communication Theories

D1384356

Communication Theories

Origins, Methods, and Uses in the Mass Media

Fourth Edition

Werner J. Severin

James W. Tankard, Jr.
The University of Texas at Austin

 LONGMAN

An imprint of Addison Wesley Longman, Inc.

New York • Reading, Massachusetts • Menlo Park, California • Harlow, England
Don Mills, Ontario • Sydney • Mexico City • Madrid • Amsterdam

Communication Theories: Origins, Methods, and Uses in the Mass Media, Fourth Edition

Longman, 10 Bank Street, White Plains, N.Y. 10606

Executive editor: Pamela A. Gordon
Associate editor: Hillary B. Henderson
Production editors: Linda Moser and Ann P. Kearns
Production supervisor: Edith Pullman
Cover design: Wanda Kassak
Compositor: ExecuStaff

Library of Congress Cataloging-in-Publication Data
Severin, Werner J. (Werner Joseph)
    Communication theories : origins, methods, and uses in the mass
  media / Werner J. Severin, James W. Tankard, Jr.—4th ed.
        p.   cm.
  Includes bibliographical references and index.
  ISBN 0-8013-1703-7
  1. Mass media 2. Communication. I. Tankard, James W.
II. Title.
P90.S4414 1997
302.23—dc20
                                 96-9609
                                   CIP

3 4 5 6 7 8 9 10-MA-009998

Contents

Preface

In preparing this fourth edition of *Communication Theories*, we have attempted to respond to the changes in the field of communication and in the area of mass communication theory that have taken place since the third edition. We have also tried to respond to suggestions for improvements made by a number of teachers using the book.

One of our goals is to discuss the radical developments in communication technology, multimedia, and the Internet that are essentially redefining mass communication.

We have updated the sections dealing with the important theoretical areas of agenda setting, the knowledge gap, cultivation theory, the spiral of silence, and the uses and gratifications approach by bringing recent research studies into the discussion. Our revision also includes expanded chapters on scientific method and models, an updated chapter on media ownership, and more recent examples throughout.

Other new sections deal with the New News, public journalism, the visual rhetoric of pictures, media framing, and the social construction of reality.

To stimulate thought about each area of research and theory, we have also added a set of discussion questions at the end of each chapter.

As with the first three editions, the book is aimed primarily at undergraduate students who intend to pursue careers in the mass media—journalism, advertising, public relations, radio, television, film, and electronic publishing—and who need an introduction to the theories, foundations, and research methodology of mass communication. The book is also appropriate for courses introducing graduate students to mass communication theory.

ACKNOWLEDGMENTS

We would like to thank the reviewers of this edition:

C. Thomas Draper—University of Nebraska at Kearney
Kathy Merlock Jackson—Virginia Wesleyan College
Shawn W. Murphy—Midland Lutheran College
Russell F. Proctor II—Northern Kentucky University
Ron Rich—University of Southwest Louisiana
H. Allen White—Murray State University

Communication Theories

part I

The Changing Media Landscape

A_s we move into what is being called the "information age," the challenges facing the field of mass communication seem greater than ever before. Does the content of mass communication have an effect on society's values? If so, what kind of effect? How does it take place? How do people learn from the mass media? How do people develop their basic attitudes toward the world around them? Does mass communication play a role in this process? How is mass communication changing in the face of the new developments in the media—the Internet, the coming Information Superhighway, multimedia?

It is undoubtedly possible to use several different methods to attempt to answer these questions and others. In this book, we recommend approaching questions about mass communication through the scientific method. Science—based as it is on empiricism and logic—offers powerful tools for understanding, predicting, and controlling the world around us, especially as that world becomes increasingly made up of information.

Basic to scientific method is the building and testing of theory, and Chapter 1 discusses the nature of theory as it is used in the field of mass communication. It describes some of the problems communication researchers are attempting to study in the 1990s; in so doing, it also gives an overview of the changing media landscape we are facing as the result of the rapid development of new communication technology. Those changes, in turn, affect mass communication theory itself.

chapter **1**

Introduction to Mass
Communication Theory

We live in a rapidly changing media environment. Only a few years ago, most people had never heard of multimedia or the Internet. Now you can hardly pick up a newspaper without seeing a reference to one or the other, or both.

The changes taking place in the media environment are numerous and, in some cases, breathtaking. Newspapers have been declining in circulation and readership for some time. Television is changing from a five-network (ABC, CBS, NBC, Fox, and public broadcasting) structure to cable systems with 50 channels, and talk of 500 or more. Videocassette recorders make movies available for viewing in the home and allow viewers to time-shift recorded television programs. Some magazines are publishing through pages on the World Wide Web or through CD-ROMs. Older approaches to news are being replaced with what is being called the New News. Advertising is grasping for its role in the new communication landscape. People spend hours visiting with other people in computer "chat rooms," and "virtual reality" games give new dimensions of experience to participants.

The term *cyberspace,* coined by science fiction writer William Gibson, has become a popular way to refer to the metaphoric space where electronic communication takes place. The United States recently reached the point where more computers were sold than TV sets (Powell, 1995). In addition, research shows use of personal computers is starting to take time away from television viewing (Lieberman, 1995).

We seem to be moving rapidly into a new user-active, multimedia, communication environment.

One characteristic of the new media environment is the recognition that all information is the same—it is digital (Powell, 1995).

Of course, it remains to be seen just where all these changes are leading us. Will people really be willing to give up a newspaper with their morning coffee or the chance to browse through a stack of their favorite magazines on their living room couch at the end of the day? One possibility is that the new media, whatever they are, will take their place beside the old media, which may not go away. A common pattern in the past has been that new communication technologies have not nudged out old technologies completely but have caused the old technologies to take on new roles. For instance, television did not eliminate radio but led to new types of radio programming, including talk shows and specialized music formats.

Whatever form mass communication takes, it will continue to fulfill a vital role in our lives. Mass communication provides the eyes and ears of society. It provides the means by which society makes up its mind and the collective voice by which society comes to know itself. It is a major source for the transmission of society's values.

THE CONCEPT OF MASS COMMUNICATION

One of the changes the new technologies are bringing about is that the very definition of mass communication is coming into question.

The definition of mass communication used to be fairly clear. Mass communication could be defined by three characteristics:

1. It is directed toward relatively large, heterogeneous, and anonymous audiences.
2. Messages are transmitted publicly, often timed to reach most audience members simultaneously, and are transient in character.
3. The communicator tends to be, or to operate within, a complex organization that may involve great expense. (Wright, 1959, p. 15)

But Internet newsgroups and mailing lists, radio talk shows that invite calls from listeners, the World Wide Web, multichannel cable television, and such hybrids as books with enclosed computer disks or coupons to be mailed in for updates cannot be pigeon-holed easily as to whether or not they are mass communication.

Some of the characteristics of the new media environment are the following (McManus, 1994):

1. Previously distinct technologies such as printing and broadcasting are merging.
2. We are shifting from media scarcity to media abundance.
3. We are shifting from content geared to mass audiences to content tailored for groups or individuals.
4. We are shifting from one-way to interactive media.

Journalism educator Richard Cole has noted, "The differences between media are blurring. Newspapers are becoming much more like magazines and broadcast" (Fonti, 1995, p. 16).

The boundaries between media are becoming less rigid. Before the movie *Batman Forever* was released, Internet users could sign on to the Time-Warner "Pathfinder" site on the World Wide Web and download a preview they could watch on their home computers.

THE NEW MEDIA ENVIRONMENT

It is difficult at this time to predict the form that our new communication system might eventually take. One possibility is the Information Superhighway, a system that would deliver information, entertainment, and shopping services provided by communication corporations. A model for a somewhat different form is provided by the Internet, a system for networking computers with one another developed primarily by universities and the federal government.

The Information Highway

The term *Information Superhighway* was apparently coined by Vice President Al Gore.

It is currently not clear just what an "information superhighway" is going to look like. One model of the Information Superhighway under consideration by big corporations (most of them entertainment corporations) is the 500-channel television model (Levy, 1995). But this model might have already been rendered obsolete by the Internet. The Internet has developed apart from big corporations, whose power is based on monopoly of information. The Internet has quickly moved into the position of being an important communication tool for many individuals, educational institutions, and businesses. The Internet is developing in such a way that anyone can set up a site, provide a service, and collect appropriate fees.

Another problem with the Information Superhighway is that the heavy emphasis the corporations are putting on entertainment may be misguided. There is some evidence that there is little public interest in a service that would provide "video on demand"—a wide selection of movies or entertainment programs available at any time—which is often touted as part of the Information Superhighway (O'Connor, 1994). In a public opinion poll of 600 U.S. adults, respondents indicated greater interest in using the information highway for voting in elections, getting reference material, or going to school, than for entertainment.

Another poll also indicated little public interest in interactive television (Van, 1994). Interactive television would allow viewers to order customized programming, including movies or other entertainment, and would provide more advanced forms of home shopping.

It is not clear yet exactly what we will get from the information super-highway. As communication scholar Jorge Schement has noted, it might be a "crucible for democracy or an electronic Walmart coast-to-coast" ("Digital age," 1995).

Online Services

One form of information network that already exists is the online services such as Prodigy, Compuserve, and America Online.

The number of subscribers to these services grew during the first half of 1995 by 37.3 percent to reach a total of 8.5 million. The number was projected to grow to 11 million by the end of the year (Husted, 1995).

The Internet

The Internet is basically a network of many computers hooked together. This network is continuously available for electronic messages, including e-mail, file transmission, and two-way communication between individuals or computers.

The Internet had been around for 20 years as a network for Defense Department and scientific communication. What made the network suddenly appealing to ordinary users was the invention in 1993 of Mosaic, a browser for the World Wide Web that made the resources of the web much more accessible (Maney, 1995c). Mosaic let the user tap into web materials by simply pointing an arrow and clicking a mouse, and it made it easy to view online graphics. Netscape, by providing even easier and quicker access, soon replaced Mosaic as the most popular Web browser.

At about the same time that user-friendly web-browsing software was being developed, the World Wide Web itself was showing a phenomenal growth in the number of sites (see Figure 1.1).

Levy describes the Internet as being based on "unlimited channels of communication, community building, electronic commerce and a full-blown version of interactivity that blurs the line between provider and consumer" (Levy, 1995, p. 58).

The three most popular features of the Internet are e-mail, newsgroups and mailing lists, and the World Wide Web.

1. E-mail. Millions of people now communicate by electronic messages, or e-mail. It is not necessary to be a sophisticated Internet user to send e-mail messages—many ordinary people do so through online services such as American Online and Prodigy.

2. Newsgroups and Mailing Lists. Newsgroups and mailing lists are electronic message sharing systems that let people interested in a common topic exchange information and opinions. There are currently 20,000 newsgroups covering all kinds of topics. Some people feel that they get news quicker and better from newsgroups than they do from newspapers and magazines. Perhaps

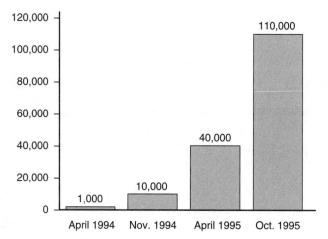

FIGURE 1.1 Number of sites on the World Wide Web by year

SOURCE: Data from "Energizing the 'Net," *USA Today,* October 30, 1995, p. 1B.

more importantly, newgroups allow a kind of immediate response to messages by the news consumer that newspapers and magazines do not.

3. The World Wide Web. The World Wide Web, also known as the WWW or the Web, is a system by which information on many computers can be rapidly and conveniently accessed by many other computers. Currently, the Web uses the metaphor of the page, and users can move from page to a different page by merely clicking a mouse on a highlighted word or spot on a page. These different pages can be on different computers all over the world. Moving about on the Web was made much simpler for users with the development of user-friendly Web-browsing software such as Mosaic and Netscape.

Attention to web sites is usually measured in terms of "hits," or the number of times the site is accessed by a user. Time Warner's Pathfinder service is reported to receive more than 1 million hits per week. Penthouse magazine's web site claims 2 million hits a day, and the site promoting the movie *Showgirls* claimed 1 million hits a day. But the number of visits, in which people actually spend some time and access some information, may be 1 percent of the number of hits (Chao, 1995).

Many businesses are setting up Web pages, often without a clear idea of how they might be most useful (Maney, 1995a). The feeling seems to be, "You gotta have a Web site." The problem, partly, is that Web sites are being looked at as places for advertisements—showing the tendency to look at new media in terms of the old media. But the best Web sites do more than push the sponsor's message—they are interactive, offering the user a number of ways to get involved with online activities and resources.

Political candidates have also been rushing to set up web sites (Maney, 1995b). During the 1996 presidential campaign, these included candidates such as Bob Dole, Lamar Alexander, Pat Buchanan, Phil Gramm, Richard Lugar, and Arlen Specter.

The Internet also has its critics. Essayist Sven Birkerts has suggested that the change from print culture to electronic culture will lead to impoverishment of language. He says electronic communication is leading to a telegraphic kind of "plainspeak" (Birkerts, 1994, p. 128). He predicts that we will see a decrease in subtle forms of language such as ambiguity, paradox, irony, and wit.

Another disadvantage of the Internet and the World Wide Web is the power they have to draw people away from the real world of terra firma—earth, trees, flowers, and sunshine. Clifford Stoll, the author of several books on the Internet, says the problem is that "three or four hours spent behind a computer is not time spent with family, spouses or the community" (Haring, 1995, p. 7D).

University of Texas President Robert M. Berdahl has suggested that the term *virtual community* is an oxymoron (Berdahl, 1994).

Rock musician Mick Jagger expressed similar reservations: "Life's a bit short for the Internet, but when you have a slow social program, it's a substitute" (Gunderson, 1995, p. 6D).

Many questions of taste, ethics, and legality in using the Internet still need to be resolved. Many people sending messages to newsgroups or posting Web pages seem oblivious to the possibility that they might be libeling someone. Ruth Walden, a communication law expert, said, "People on the Net take the attitude that what they say doesn't count. But libel is libel. It doesn't matter if it's published on the Internet or painted on the side of a barn" (Gelder, 1995, p. 17).

Many users of networks and online services are also learning that they may need to become more skeptical about the information they are receiving. Users of the Internet and the commercial online services should be concerned about the accuracy of information from these channels. Messages posted by individuals may contain reliable information, but they may also contain rumors, speculation, deliberately misleading statements, and outright deception. The kind of information one might pick up from newsgroups or mailing lists differs from the information published in a newspaper or magazine in one important respect— it has not been checked for accuracy by an editor.

This situation actually lends itself to an increased need for journalists and other professional communicators—people who have the skills to assess information, verify the accuracy of statements, and perhaps most important, give some guidelines about what is important and useful and what is not.

Another concern about the Internet has to do with the availability of access to all kinds of people. John Perry Barlow writes that Internet users tend to be white males under 50 with plenty of computer time. Users are less likely to be women, children, old people, poor people, the blind, the illiterate, and people from the continent of Africa (Barlow, 1995).

Agents

As the flow of information and the number of channels available to individuals increase, it seems highly likely that people will need some assistance in sorting out all the available information. As MIT Media Lab Director Nicholas Negroponte has suggested, channel surfing does not become an efficient search strategy when you are faced with 1,000 or more channels (Negroponte, 1995).

Help in sorting out information is likely to come in the form of *computerized robots, agents,* or *digital butlers.* These entitles will have some degree of artificial intelligence and will be programmed to do various tasks for us. Some of them will spend time while we are away from our computers searching for information that we have instructed them to look for. They will probably also be capable of learning the information needs of their masters as they work. For instance, they will be able to present us with pieces of information and then make note of which ones we use and which we don't. This knowledge could then be used to modify subsequent searches. Over a period of time, our agents could get to know our preferences very well and search for content that would fit those preferences.

These agents might take some kind of anthropomorphic form to make it easier for us to interact with them. One possible form would be happy or sad faces, with various expressions giving us information about how a search was going (Maes, 1995). Another possible form—and this is probably some distance in the future—could be 8-inch tall holographic figures on our desktop that we would communicate with through speech (Negroponte, 1995). It is also likely that we will have a number of different agents that specialize in accomplishing various tasks for us. Some agents may even delegate tasks to other agents.

The New News

The concept of the New News developed during the 1992 presidential election. In part, it referred to the appearances of presidential candidates on talk shows, on MTV, and in extended interviews on network shows such as the "Today" show.

Jon Katz, the *Rolling Stone* writer who appears to have introduced the term, said, "The New News is a heady concoction, part Hollywood film and TV movie, part pop music and pop art, mixed with popular culture and celebrity magazines, tabloid telecasts, cable and home video" (Katz, 1992, p. 39).

Examples of the New News in operation would include Ross Perot announcing his candidacy for president on "Larry King Live," or the well-known saxophone-playing visit by Bill Clinton to the Arsenio Hall show, or the appearance of President Bush on MTV, or the two-hour interview of Perot on the "Today" show. The Old News is represented primarily by the three television network evening newscasts, the three major newsmagazines, and the ordinary daily newspapers.

One aspect of the New News is the blending of information and entertainment, as we can see in Bush's MTV appearance and Clinton's saxophone playing. Part of the idea seems to be to make news about politics more palatable, particularly to younger audiences. Katz argues that "younger viewers and readers find conventional journalism of no particular use in their daily lives" (1992, p. 40).

Another aspect of the idea of the New News is to get the candidate directly into contact with the public without the interference of a journalist. Sound bites of candidates speaking as presented on the network evening news shows have become shorter and shorter, decreasing to a length of 7.3 seconds in the first five months of the 1992 campaign (Taylor, 1992).

As Jay Rosen notes, "Call-in shows, talk radio, C-Span, 800 numbers, videos and pamphlets produced by candidates for voters—all promise information and political dialogue without intervention by journalists" (Rosen, 1992, p. 20).

In fact, it does appear that the New News formats and the Old News formats present candidates with different kinds of questions. Michael Kinsley, a writer for *The New Republic,* examined questions asked at a White House press conference with President Bush and those asked by viewers calling the *Today* show when Perot appeared (Kinsley, 1992).The White House press corps focused primarily on the process of the campaign, while the viewers calling in asked Perot mostly about substantive issues that affected citizens. In this case, the viewer questions may have produced information more useful to the citizen attempting to follow the campaign.

Some writers suggest that the New News extends beyond election campaign coverage. Katz presents Oliver Stone's movie JFK as one of his primary examples of the New News. He says the film dealt with "passionate and sometimes frightening undercurrents in American life" that the Old News was not addressing (Katz, 1992, p. 38).

In some cases, the Old News seems to be losing out to the New News in those qualities the Old News used to claim as its major strengths—speed of delivery and vividness of reporting. Messages on the Internet concerning Tiananmen Square and the *Exxon-Valdez* oil spill were thought by some observers to be "much more vital and immediate than traditional news stories" (Fillmore, 1993).

Katz suggests that the New News will eventually replace the Old News. He wrote, "Straight news—the Old News—is pooped, confused and broke. Each Nielsen survey, each circulation report, each quarterly statement reveals the cultural Darwinism ravaging the news industry" (p. 39).

But it may be that the Old News and the New News both have something to contribute and that they will end up coexisting.

Along these lines, one study looking at the impact of the Old News and the New News found that the use of New News does not appear to lessen the use of conventional news sources (Miller, Chew, & Yen, 1993). The study also found that Old News sources have higher correlations than New News sources with knowledge of a political campaign and with the belief that the campaign is exciting.

Changes in Advertising

The field of advertising is in a state of transition, primarily because of the large changes taking place in the media environment. Traditional mass media advertising aimed at large, anonymous audiences may be a dying communication form.

If people begin to scan information networks with information agents or, as they are sometimes called, *knowbots* (knowledge robots), advertising may have to find a different role for itself (Rust & Oliver, 1994).

A shift is already under way from mass media advertising to database marketing, in which potential purchasers are identified through information in databases and then targeted with direct advertising appeals (Fox & Geissler, 1994).

Some writers have suggested that marketing in the 21st century will be centered on interactive multimedia, and that advertising departments must find a new mission of transferring information on the information highway (Rust & Oliver, 1994).

The new area of Integrated Marketing Communications can be seen as a reaction to the changes in the communication field and an attempt to define a field broader than advertising.

THE ROLE OF THEORY

Theory is the ultimate goal of science. Theories are general statements that summarize our understandings of the way the world works. In the field of mass communication, much of our theory in the past has been implicit. People have relied on folklore, traditional wisdom, and "common sense" to guide much of the practice of mass communication. Sometimes these assumptions are never even stated or written down anywhere. Other times they take the forms of oversimplified aphorisms or maxims. Many of these assumptions would benefit from being tested through research. The result might be that the maxims are confirmed, disconfirmed, or confirmed only partially (within certain limits). In any of these cases, the media practitioner will have a firmer ground for taking action.

In developing theory, we are often trying to explain something that is difficult to understand. Basically, the goal of theory is to formulate statements or propositions that will have some explanatory power. These theoretical statements can take various forms:

1. An *if-then* statement. For example: "If a young person watches a great deal of violent television, then he or she will commit aggressive acts."

In the study of communication, there are not many propositions that hold so absolutely that they can be stated as *if-then* statements. A more common form of statement is the *is more likely to* statement.

2. An *is more likely to* statement. For example: "A person who watches violent television is more likely to behave aggressively than a person who watches nonviolent television."

3. The greater the X the greater the Y (see Hage 1972). For example: "The greater the violent television viewing, the greater the aggressive behavior."

4. Statements using phrases like *leads to.* For example: "Watching violent television leads to more aggressive behavior than watching nonviolent television."

The communication scientist argues that since we have some theory operating all the time anyway, why not try to make it the best possible theory? The scientist believes that the greatest faith should be placed in those statements about the way things work that have been tested and verified and that have some generality and predictive power. These are the kinds of statements that make up scientific theory. And these statements are useful. As social psychologist Kurt Lewin said in an often-quoted remark, "There is nothing so practical as a good theory" (1951 p. 169).

Communication theory is aimed at improving our understanding of the process of mass communication. With better understanding, we are in a better position to predict and control the outcomes of mass communication efforts.

THE GOALS OF MASS COMMUNICATION THEORY

The more specific goals of mass communication theory include the following:

1. *To explain the effects of mass communication.* These effects can be intended, such as informing the public during an election, or unintended, such as causing an increase in violence in society.

2. *To explain the uses to which people put mass communication.* In many cases, it is more useful to look at the uses to which people are putting mass communication rather than the effects. This approach recognizes a more active role on the part of the communication audience. Several factors are combining to give greater emphasis to audience activity and the uses of mass communication rather than its effects. One of these is the field of cognitive psychology and information processing. The other is the changes in communication technology which are moving toward less centralization, more user choice, greater diversity of content, and more active engagement with communication content by the individual user.

3. *To explain learning from the mass media.* One important question still not fully answered is how do people learn from the mass media. As we shall see, the concept of schema may be part of the answer. Also, Albert Bandura's social learning theory (see Chapter 14) can be helpful.

4. *To explain the role of the mass media in shaping people's values and views.* Politicians and members of the general public often attribute an important role to mass communication in shaping people's world views and values. At times, they probably overstate the case and engage in criticisms of particular programs or movies that are based mostly on speculation. Nevertheless, their basic instinct that mass media content is influencing society's values undoubtedly has some validity. The area is an important one in which further research is needed.

THE EFFECTS OF MASS COMMUNICATION

Even with the changes taking place in the media environment, the effects of mass communication are still a major concern of mass communication researchers and theorists.

The effects of mass communication have been a major concern for much of the 20th century. Some of the earliest motion pictures, including *Birth of a Nation,* were greeted by public questioning of their possible effects on audiences. The golden age of comic books, the 1950s, was marked by a great concern about the possible corrupting effects of comic books on youth (Lowery & DeFleur, 1995). The apparent power of propaganda during World War I also represented an early concern about the effects of mass communication.

As we shall see in Chapter 14, thinking about the effects of mass communication has moved through a number of stages. Some of the earliest thinking attributed great power to mass communication to influence its audiences. This kind of conceptualization of the effects of mass communication is sometimes known as the "bullet theory" or the "hypodermic needle" model of mass communication effects. Under this conceptualization, audience members were isolated from one another and were vulnerable targets easily influenced by mass communication messages. It is difficult to find communication scholars who advocated the "bullet theory" as an accurate picture of the effects of mass communication, but it is clearly a view held by members of the public at various times. One example of "bullet theory" thinking would be a fear of the power of propaganda that was fairly widespread after World War I.

After a period of years and some research on how mass communication was actually working, thinkers about mass communication decided the "bullet theory" or the "hypodermic needle" model was not accurate. This new conceptualization grew primarily out of election studies during the 1940s reported in the books *The People's Choice* (1944/1968) and *Voting* (1954). The new view attributed much less power to mass communication messages. A major statement of this view, often called the "limited effects" model, was presented in Joseph Klapper's (1960) book *The Effects of Mass Communication.* People were seen as ordinarily having a great deal of resistance to mass communication messages. This resistance was due to a number of factors, including support for opinions that individuals received from other people and various kinds of psychological filtering that took place when people received messages.

More recent research has led to further revision of the thinking about mass communication. This newer research restores some of the power to mass communication messages, although not as much as they had under the "bullet" theory. Approaches such as the agenda-setting hypothesis or cultivation theory attribute to mass communication what might be called *moderate effects.* And other theories such as the spiral of silence suggest, under certain circumstances, what we might call powerful effects of mass communication. Not only can effects due to mass communication be large or small, but there can be a number of different kinds of effects. To put it in social science language, there are a number

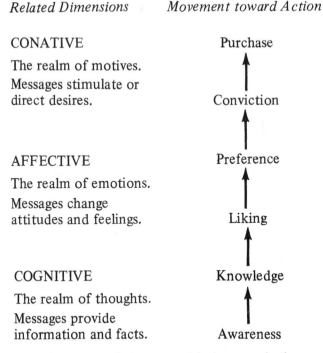

Related Dimensions   *Movement toward Action*

CONATIVE   Purchase

The realm of motives.
Messages stimulate or
direct desires.   Conviction

AFFECTIVE   Preference

The realm of emotions.
Messages change
attitudes and feelings.   Liking

COGNITIVE   Knowledge

The realm of thoughts.
Messages provide
information and facts.   Awareness

FIGURE 1.2 Stair-step model of communication effects

SOURCE: Adapted from R. Lavidge and G. A. Steiner, "A Model for Predictive Measurements of Advertising Effectiveness," *Journal of Marketing* 25 (1961): 61, published by the American Marketing Association.

of different dependent variables that can be examined in the quest for possible effects of mass communication.

Some effects—such as the effects of newspaper reading on levels of knowledge about political candidates—are probably intended by communicators. Other effects—such as the effect of television violence on tendency toward aggressive behavior—are probably not intended. In general, communication theorists are interested in both types of effects—intended and unintended.

It can be useful to organize the possible types of effects into some kind of framework, or scheme. One such framework, developed by Lavidge and Steiner (1961), is presented in Figure 1.2. The model presents six steps, each of which must be accomplished before the one above it can be attempted. The six steps are grouped into three dimensions or categories: the cognitive, the affective, and the conative. The cognitive deals with our knowledge of things, the affective with our attitudes toward things, and the conative with our behavior toward things. Some media practitioners might be interested in only a portion of the effects specified by the model. The reporter, for instance, might be interested only in achieving the cognitive effects. A creator of an advertisement, in contrast, would probably be interested in achieving the full range of six steps. So, in fact, might an editorial writer attempting to get readers to vote for a certain candidate—if we replace purchase in the model with vote.

CHANGES IN MASS COMMUNICATION THEORY

Mass communication theory is changing—and probably needs to change even more—to keep up with the changes in the media. Among the noticeable changes are the following:

1. There is a greater emphasis on uses of mass communication than there used to be. The important role of audience activity has become even clearer with the moves to newer forms of media.
2. There is a shift to cognitive science or information processing approaches (Beniger & Gusek, 1995). This involves at least three aspects:
   a. A shift in independent variables from the variables of persuasion (for instance, source credibility) to concepts such as discourse (the nature of language used) and framing (how an event is packaged and presented in the media).
   b. A change in dependent variables from attitudes (pro and con evaluations of an object) to cognitions (knowledge or beliefs about an object).
   c. A shift in emphasis from change as a result of communication (for instance, changes in attitude or behavior) to restructuring (including changes in our schemas or models of an event, or the social construction of reality).

One result of the changes in technology is that it is no longer possible to think of television as a uniform or monolithic system, transmitting essentially the same message to everyone. This realization has consequences for a number of theories of mass communication that assume to some extent a uniform television message, or a uniform media message (Webster, 1989). These theories include Gerbner's cultivation theory and Noelle-Neumann's spiral of silence (Chapter 14), as well as, to a lesser extent, the agenda-setting function (Chapter 12). Essentially, it appears that the fragmented or segmented audience that is characteristic of the new media probably leads to a lessening of the impact of the mass media suggested by cultivation theory, the spiral of silence, and the agenda-setting function.

In general, the rapid changes in communication technology suggest that researchers should try to formulate communication theory in terms that go beyond the details of a specific medium or technology. For example, we probably should avoid phrasing our theories in terms of newspaper reading or television exposure, and instead phrase them in terms of variables like public affairs information seeking, the need for companionship, degree of user control, and so forth. In doing so, we would be making the shift from what sociologist Jerald Hage called specific nonvariables to general variables (Hage, 1972).

Also, students of communication might want to shift some of the emphasis on effects to thinking about the social impacts of communication. Rogers (1986) suggests that some important social impacts of new communication technology are unemployment, an increasing information gap between the rich and the poor, increased gender inequality in use of media, information overload, increased invasions of privacy, decentralization of power in society, and segmentation of mass media audiences.

THEORETICAL QUESTIONS RAISED BY CHANGES IN THE MEDIA ENVIRONMENT

Some important but difficult questions are raised by the changes in the media environment. They include:

1. How are the new communication media changing the nature of knowledge? Knowledge doesn't just rest in books on library shelves, as it once did. It now exists in interlinked pieces of information in cyberspace where people can jump around from one to another in an instant. This form of Hypertext changes the basic structure of knowledge in ways that probably have important consequences.

2. How are the new communication media changing the nature of human thinking? Derrick de Kerckhove of the McLuhan Program in Culture and Technology has suggested that networked communication is having some subtle but important effects:

> New media are transforming us into a very intelligent society. Instead of being homogenized by the control of our tastes, as happens when we passively watch TV, we are invited to contribute the work of our minds to that of others in a direct and collaborative way. Thus networked, human intelligences multiply their own production rate by the rate of the others with whom they network. (de Kerckhove, 1995, p. 68)

3. What are the uses (and purposes) of print that we might be losing as we move away from exclusively print media such as newspapers and magazines? As essayist Sven Birkerts has suggested, our ability to express ourselves in verbal language may be suffering.

4. What form should online (or electronic) newspapers take? While some writers suggest that online newspapers are not the right direction for newspapers to move in (Katz, 1994), it seems like a natural and unavoidable development. But finding the right form for the new online media may not be easy. Ralph Lowenstein, journalism educator, has suggested that the challenge is to develop

a form that will be usable and useful to the 8-year-old child as well as the business executive (Lowenstein, 1994). Present online newspapers tend to be difficult, cumbersome, and time-consuming (Katz, 1994). One of the more successful efforts seems to be *Time* Magazine Online on America Online. One of its strongest features is the intense back-and-forth discussion between *Time* Online subscribers and *Time's* writers and editors (Katz, 1994).

CONCLUSIONS

This book deals with the scientific study of mass communication. The end product of scientific research is theory. Mass communication theory is aimed at improving our understanding of how mass communication works. Mass communication theory attempts to formulate and test scientific explanations of various phenomena in mass communication. Basically, mass communication theory attempts to provide the best possible answers to questions about how mass communication works. Some of the more important of these questions deal with the effects of mass communication. Others deal with how people use mass communication for their own purposes.

Mass communication theory can be used to help the media practitioner communicate better. It can also be used to inform consumers, and other interested parties, about the effects of mass communication.

The field of communication is in a state of dramatic flux. As new media technologies give more control to the user, the very concept of mass communication is undergoing challenge. Communication theory needs to adapt and adjust to these changes. Some existing theories may hold up in the new communication environment, but others may need modification in order to fit the new circumstances.

DISCUSSION

1. What are the advantages of a scientific approach to the study of mass communication?
2. What are some of the characteristics of the "new media environment"?
3. What are some indications that we are moving to a more user-controlled kind of communication system?
4. As we move into a new user-controlled, multimedia communication environment, what happens to the concept of "mas communication"? Has it lost its meaningfulness or usefulness?
5. Will online newspapers replace paper newspapers that you can hold in your hands? Why, or why not?
6. What are "agents"? How might they change the way we think about mass communication?

7. What is the New News? What are some examples of the New News? What does the New News do that the Old News does not?
8. What are some of the various types of effects that mass communication can have?
9. What are some of the possible effects of mass communication that the public has expressed concern about?
10. Throughout the history of mass communication theory, the thinking about the size of the effects of mass communication has changed. Describe these changes.

REFERENCES

Barlow, J. P. (1995). Is there a there in cyberspace? *Utne Reader,* March–April, pp. 52–56.

Beniger, J. R., and J. A. Gusek (1995). The cognitive revolution in public opinion and communication research. In T. L. Glasser and C. T. Salmon, eds., *Public Opinion and the Communication of Consent,* pp. 217–248. New York: The Guilford Press.

Berdahl, R. M. (1994). "The University in the New Information Age," speech presented to the Tenth Annual Leadership Institute for Journalism and Mass Communication Education, sponsored by the Freedom Forum Media Studies Center, June 20.

Birkerts, S. (1994). *The Gutenberg Elegies: The Fate of Reading in an Electronics Age.* Boston: Faber and Faber.

Chao, J. (1995). What's in a Web 'hit'? *Austin American-Statesman,* July 3, p. E2.

de Kerckhove, D. (1995). A very intelligent society, or what are the new media doing to us? *Multimedia Online,* premier issue, Oct., pp. 62–69.

Digital age media heralds hope and hype (1995). *Communiqué,* June, p. 3.

Fillmore, L. (1993). Online publishing: Threat or menace. Speech presented at Online Publishing Conference, Graphic Communications Association, March.

Fonti, N. (1995). Exploring the school's role in the information explosion. *The UNC Journalist,* Summer.

Fox, R. J., and G. L. Geissler. (1994). Crisis in advertising? *Journal of Advertising* 23 (no. 4): 79–84.

Gelder, A. (1995). Cybernauts beware: The law still applies in technospace. *The UNC Journalist,* Summer.

Gunderson, E. (1995). Stones 'stripped' to basics. *USA Today,* Nov. 14, p. 6D.

Hage, J. (1972). *Techniques and Problems of Theory Construction in Sociology.* New York: John Wiley.

Haring, B. (1995). Internet vet wary of superhighway's direction. *USA Today,* April 6, p. 7D.

Husted, B. (1995). Consider source when judging Net information. *Austin American-Statesman,* Sept 16, p. D6.

Katz, J. (1992). Rock, rap and movies bring you the news. *Rolling Stone,* March 5, PP. 33–40, 78.

Katz, J. (1994). Online or not, newspapers suck. *Wired,* Sept, pp. 50–58.

Kinsley, M. (1992). Ask a silly question. *The New Republic,* July 6, p. 6.

Klapper, J. T. (1960). *The Effects of Mass Communication.* New York: Free Press.

Lavidge, R., and G. Steiner (1961). A model for predictive measurements of advertising effectiveness. *Journal of Marketing* 25 (no. 6): 59–62.

Levy, S. (1995). How the propeller heads stole the electronic future. *New York Times Magazine,* Sept. 24, pp. 58-59.

Lewin, K. (1951). *Field Theory in Social Science: Selected Theoretical Papers.* New York: Harper & Row.

Lieberman, D. (1995). Home PCs draw viewers away from TVs. *USA Today,* Nov. 16, p. 1B.

Lowenstein, R. L. (1994). The electronic newspaper and journalism education. Speech to the Association for Education in Journalism and Mass Communication, Atlanta, Aug. 12.

Lowery, S. A., and M. L. DeFleur. (1995). *Milestones in Mass Communication Research: Media Effects,* 3rd ed. New York: Longman.

McManus, J. H. (1994). *Market-Driven Journalism: Let the Citizen Beware?* Thousand Oaks, Calif.: Sage.

Maes, P. (1995). Intelligent software. *Scientific American,* Sept., pp. 84-86.

Maney, K. (1995a). Fear, loathing mark rush to Internet. *USA Today,* April 28, p. 2B.

Maney, K. (1995b). How about, "It's the Internet, stupid"? *USA Today,* Oct. 16, p. 2B.

Maney, K. (1995c). It's big, it's confusing—so why all the fuss? *USA Today,* Nov. 13, p. 1E.

Miller, M. M., F. Chew, and X. Yen (1993). The impact of "old news" and "new news" on young people's campaign knowledge and attitudes. Paper presented at the annual meeting of the Communication Theory and Methodology Division, Association for Education in Journalism and Mass Communication, Kansas City, Missouri, August.

Negroponte, N. (1995). *Being Digital.* New York: Knopf.

O'Connor, R. J. (1994). Info highway might be headed in wrong direction. *Austin American-Statesman,* Sept. 5, p. C5.

Powell, A. C. (1995). Diversity in cyberspace. Address presented to the Association for Education in Journalism and Mass Communication, Washington, D.C.

Rogers, E. M. (1986). *Communication Technology: The New Media in Society.* New York: Free Press.

Rosen, J. (1992). Politics, vision, and the press: Toward a public agenda for journalism. In J. Rosen and P. Taylor (eds.), *The New News v. the Old News: The Press and Politics in the 1990s,* pp. 1-33. New York: The Twentieth Century Fund.

Rust, R. T, and R. W. Oliver. (1994). The death of advertising. *Journal of Advertising* 23 (no. 4): 71-77.

Taylor, P. (1992). Political coverage in the 1990s: Teaching the old news new tricks. In J. Rosen and P. Taylor (eds.), *The New News v. the Old News: The Press and Politics in the 1990s,* pp. 37-69. New York: The Twentieth Century Fund.

Van, J. (1994). Interactive TV enthusiasm dims. *Austin American-Statesman,* July 11, p. C2.

Webster, J. G. (1989). Television audience behavior: Patterns of exposure in the new media environment. In J. L. Salvaggio and J. Bryant (eds.), *Media Use in the Information Age: Emerging Patterns of Adoption and Consumer Use,* pp. 197-216. Hillsdale, NJ.: Lawrence Erlbaum.

Wright, C. R. (1959). *Mass Communication: A Sociological Perspective.* New York: Random House.

part II

Scientific Method and Models of Mass Communication

Scientific theory has the great advantage of being solidly grounded in observations. It is easy to spin out many different theories of mass communication effects, some quite grandiose (and some quite menacing). But stating at the beginning that our theories should be scientifically testable means that they ultimately have to be verifiable through observations. This not only cuts out a lot of lengthy debate over matters that can never be resolved, but it also means that our theories are more likely to be related to the real world, and thus, are more likely to have some practical applications.

Communication scientists also develop models of communication. A scientific model is not quite the same as a scientific theory. A model is more limited, and is usually an attempt to identify the crucial parts of a process or phenomenon. Theories are ordinarily constructed to explain communication phenomena, while models usually do little more than describe. Nevertheless, the process of communication is so complicated that models can do a great deal to help us understand it.

Chapter 2 describes the scientific method as it is used to develop and test communication theories, and Chapter 3 presents a number of models that have been found useful for detailing the communication process.

chapter 2

Scientific Method

Science serves as a guard against untested assumptions about the world we live in. The scientific method differs from other methods of obtaining knowledge in that it is based on observation and the testing of our assumptions (hypotheses) against the evidence of the "real" world (empiricism).

Methods of establishing truth that were commonly employed before development of the scientific method included intuition, authority, and tenacity (Cohen & Nagel, 1934).

Tenacity accounts for many of the beliefs that we have always held to be true. Reinforcement by family, community, and peers and frequent repetition support our beliefs, even when we have no verifiable evidence and when our beliefs may be false. Many of the things we believe in were handed down to us and remain unchallenged because there appears to be common agreement about them. As early as 270 B.C. the Greek astronomer Aristarchus of Samos had proposed the heliocentric theory (that the planets revolve around the Sun), but several centuries later the Roman Catholic Church adopted the Ptolemaic theory (that the earth is the center of the universe) which fit its theology and which it sanctioned for more than a millennium. The burning of the Great Library at Alexandria in 391 A.D. was considered an attempt by Christians to destroy the records of Aristarchus' work.

We seldom question our economic or political systems, or our beliefs about family, community, institutions, race, or religion. Few communication students ever question the free use of public airwaves by commercial broadcasters, the federal government's reluctance to apply antitrust laws to media conglomerates, or commercial influences on media content.

As Tan (1981, p. 11) points out, when we no longer find agreement about our beliefs we often turn to authorities for support. We can rely on "experts" whom we consider to be more "competent" or "credible" than ourselves or almost anyone else. These authorities (doctors, lawyers, professors) may be "professionals" whose competence has been certified. Other authorities become sources on questions of politics, morals, and religion because they hold postions which invest them with the power to make such decisions, and because we respect the positions they hold.

As mentioned, Roman Catholic authorities once held that the earth was the center of the universe. Such a view fit their theology, since according to one Bible verse, "God fixed the Earth upon its foundation, not to be moved forever."

Often the sources we turn to disagree, no matter how competent or authoritative they appear. Then we sometimes turn to our intuition, which is based on our personal values, early socialization, or "common sense." Many of our beliefs, which we hold so tenaciously, are based on intuition. Frequently intuition argues for what is "self-evident." For example, for many it was "self-evident" that the sun revolves around the earth.

Unfortunately, the methods of intuition, authority, and tenacity are often used today, although they are more subject to error and bias than the scientific method. This is because scientific beliefs (theories) are verified objectively (tested against real world phenomena). We can analyze the contents of a newspaper both before and after the demise of a local competitor and measure any differences in the amount and variety of its contents, first as a competing daily and then as a monopoly daily. We can draw a random sample from its readership and survey its readers for their opinions of the newspaper, giving us a good idea of what its readers think of the publication. We can devise an experiment to learn which of several methods of presentation will be most effective with a given topic for a specific audience.

In every case we have relied on "real world" data rather than on authority, tenacity, or intuition. If we use research methods which are unbiased, if our measures are reliable and valid and if our findings are replicable, we have probably come closer to "truth" than trusting our intuition, relying on authority, or resorting to tenacity.

This book deals with the findings of research from a number of disciplines or fields. Nearly all of the findings are derived, however, from the application of scientific method, in this case in what have come to be known as the social or behavioral sciences. There are some qualities characteristic of science that we should consider before exploring its basic nature and usefulness for communication theory.

IMAGINATION IN SCIENCE

Thomas H. Huxley, a great 19th-century scientist, once defined science as "trained and organized common sense" and added that theory building is something you engage in "every day and every hour of your lives."

Albert Einstein, the father of the relativity theory, said, "The whole of science is nothing more than a refinement of everyday thinking."

This is not to imply that first-rate science does not require large quantities of imagination—in identifying significant areas of inquiry, in the ability to perceive unrecognized relationships and causes, in the ability to translate abstract hypotheses into real world variables (operational definitions) that can be measured, in the ability to devise measuring instruments to "get a handle" on elusive data, and in many other aspects of science.

Certainly it took imagination for Nicolaus Copernicus to visualize the sun at the center of our solar system and to break with the astronomy of Ptolemy, which for 15 centuries had asserted that the Earth was central and principal and that all other objects in the universe orbited it. It also took imagination for Galileo to see the possibilities of applying a new instrument, the spyglass, to the heavens and to disprove the Ptolemaic theory. In doing so, Galileo created the modern scientific method: he built the apparatus, did the experiment, and published the result.

Galileo's work left the Copernican theory of planets orbiting the Earth as the only credible one, which the Roman Catholic Church had ordered Galileo to neither "hold or defend" (Kane, 1992). As is so often the case with new ideas, many people felt their authority threatened by Galileo's findings and they did everything within their power to suppress his new notions of the universe. (Bronowski, 1973, gives an excellent brief account. A recent and more detailed account can be found in James Reston's book *Galileo: A Life*.)

The Church condemned Galileo, threatened him with torture by the Inquisition, forced him to recant his discoveries as "false and erroneous" and to say that he "abjured, cursed and detested" the errors of his work. The 69-year-old Galileo, eyesight failing, was forced to live the last eight years of his life under house arrest. After 359 years, the Church formally admitted its error (Cowell, 1992; Montalbano, 1992).

Every scientist assumes an approach or a particular orientation when dealing with a subject or issue. This approach determines the concepts, questions, perspectives, and procedures the scientist applies. It also shapes the hypotheses tested and eventually the theory generated. The approach, then, is the framework within which a theory is tested.

As has often been observed, the business of science is theory. Put another way, theory is what science is all about; it is the product of scientific research. A theory can explain, predict, or help discover systematic relationships between facts. The scientist uses theory to make generalizations (abstract representations) about the nature of reality. In our field we wish to be able to make generalizations about the way people communicate. Verified theory then enables us to make predictions about the outcome of certain events. In this case, the goal is to make predictions concerning the process and effects of communication.

THE CUMULATIVE NATURE OF SCIENCE

Science, as all scholarship, is also cumulative; that is, it builds on the work that preceded it. Sir Isaac Newton summed this up three centuries ago when, in one of the most important aphorisms in the history of science, he said, "If I have seen further, it is by standing on the shoulders of giants."

Robert K. Merton, a pioneer in the sociology of science, has pointed out that Newton's aphorism "does not only apply to science. In its figurative meaning it explains the growth of knowledge and culture in virtually every area of learning you can mention." Merton adds, "Newton's aphorism means that no investigator starts out with a tabula rasa, or clean slate. It denies the great man notion" (Whitman, 1976).

The cumulative nature of scholarship and science is made possible by its transmissibility, its ability to overcome barriers of geography, language, and social, economic, and political systems. Transmissibility is possible in part because science, like all knowledge, deals with abstractions about reality. The special language of any discipline is composed of these abstractions.

For cumulation to take place, scholars must share an approach or orientation, or at least a system of scholarly values. Some people believe that if scholarship is to be transmissible across social classes and political systems, it must, to a great extent, be "detached, objective, unemotional and nonethical" (Westley, 1958, p. 162).

The findings of science can be verified objectively through observation in the real world. However, a hypothesis is never proved beyond any doubt; it is only confirmed as the most probable outcome, or effect, of a given cause. For example, we can say that individuals with more education will probably spend more time reading newspapers than those with less education. This will not be true in all cases, but will hold true over a large population.

To test a hypothesis's abstract or conceptual definitions it must first be operationally defined in terms of how the variables will be observed or measured. To continue the above example, we can define amount of education in terms of years spent in formal education and newspaper readership in terms of time spent on the average day with a daily newspaper. Comparisons can then be made of the average time spent daily reading a newspaper for groups of people with high levels of education and time spent daily reading a newspaper for groups of people with lesser amounts of education. More will be said later about operational definitions.

The nonethical nature of science has been the cause of much concern in recent years. Well known is the debate, which continues among atomic scientists, concerning the development of the atomic and hydrogen bombs. At the height of the Vietnam War a Harvard University scientist defended the development of napalm, the jellied gasoline used in warfare that had devastating effects on civilian populations. He said that he would do it again and added that the moral issues were outside his realm (*New York Times*, Dec. 27, 1967, p. 8).

There are, on the other hand, scholars who feel that "value-free research is a delusion." In its theme, an October 1989 Nobel Conference stated, "We have begun to think of science as a more subjective and relativistic project, operating out of and under the influence of social ideologies and attitudes—Marxism and feminism, for example" (*New York Times*, Oct. 22, 1989).

"Legally your researchers are free, but they are controlled by the passions of the day," observed Alexander Solzhenitsyn in a 1974 speech at Harvard University.

The history of science is filled with attempts to impose philosophical and political positions on scientific findings and to make scientific findings conform with untested preconceived notions (often held on the basis of intuition, authority, or tenacity), or to fit current political policies. Well known and already mentioned was the reaction of established authority to Galileo's verification of Copernicus's hypothesis, which placed the sun and not the earth at the center of our solar system. In the 20th century Soviet agriculture and genetics had Marxist dogma imposed on it by Trofim Lysenko. He rejected conventional theories of heredity and asserted that the basic nature of plants and even animals could be radically affected by changes in environment. Discussion and experimentation related to opposing views was forbidden, and it is claimed that Soviet agriculture was set back 25 years (Salisbury, 1976). More recently a top U.S. government scientist charged that the White House's Office of Management and Budget had changed the text of testimony scheduled to be delivered to Congress. He said the changes made "his conclusions about the effects of global warming seem less serious and certain than he intended" (Shabecoff, 1989).

SCIENTIFIC GENERALIZATIONS ABOUT REALITY

Scientists seek to make generalizations about the nature of reality. They accomplish this by repeatedly testing (replication) generalizations (hypotheses) about reality until sufficient confirmations are obtained to warrant calling these generalizations tentative laws. In science the tests of generalizations are accomplished through controlled observations. A scientist must be able to demonstrate that any variables that could provide an alternative explanation for the findings of an experiment have been controlled. This must be accomplished in such a way that it can be repeated by another investigator. The replicability and verifiability of science serve as its guard against fraud and bias.

SCIENTIFIC HYPOTHESES

Once a researcher recognizes that a problem needs a solution, either practical or theoretical, a search of previous knowledge which bears on the problem is made (often a question of "why" about some aspect of the environment, e.g.,

Why are some people early adopters of new media technology, while others are comparative laggards?). After reviewing the existing "literature" (previous knowledge) in the specific area, a hypothesis is formulated. The hypothesis ensures that the search for a solution is not random but rather serves as a guide to the problem's solution.

As has been pointed out, the end product of science is theory that enables the making of predictions. A hypothesis (or scientific proposition) is usually framed in what is known as a conditional form ("if . . . , then . . ."). Although usually unstated, it is assumed that this statement is preceded by ceteris paribus (Latin for "all other things being equal"). A scientist who establishes a conditional relationship is dealing with cause and effect. The cause is called the *independent variable,* while the effect, the phenomena we wish to explain, is the *dependent variable.* It is these causal relations that science ultimately seeks. Scientists assume that the subjects they deal with are natural phenomena or a part of nature, ordered in a natural way, and not a result of supernatural ordering. This implies that the objects of investigations are determined and that causal connections can be found to account for them.

As a scientific discipline develops, it works toward the explanations that are the most parsimonious. As one writer aptly put it, "The parsimonious explanation is the one that accounts for the most variance with the fewest propositions" (Westley, 1958, p. 167). In other words, science tries to explain as much as possible with the fewest generalizations. A twin goal of science, along with parsimony, is a striving for closure. If the scientist works with lawful, ordered, or natural data, it is assumed that eventually the universe is knowable. The sciences work toward understanding the areas that remain unknown—in pursuit of the goal of closure.

Whereas every scientist assumes an approach or orientation when dealing with an issue, science concerns itself with what is, what exists, or what happens when, not with questions of what is right or what should be. This is not to say that social sciences do not deal with ideologies, attitudes, and value systems, but that social scientists, in selecting or framing their methods of inquiry, must take into account the observers' or investigators' biases in these areas. Questions of values, or what should be, are dealt with by the fields of religion, ethics, and philosophy rather than science.

SAFEGUARDS AGAINST BIAS AND FRAUD

As two famous authors in the area of logic and scientific methods have said, "By not claiming more certainty than the evidence warrants, scientific method succeeds in obtaining more logical certainty than any other method yet devised" (Cohen & Nagel, 1934, p. 396).

The scientific method requires that findings be submitted to others working in the field (usually through publication or presentation at scholarly meetings) so that findings can be replicated in different circumstances. This allows for close scrutiny of the objectives, methods, and results used. It also allows for other scientists to conduct investigations which can be used to build theory (the cumulative aspect of science).

As mentioned, the safeguard of science against bias or fraud lies in the publication of findings and the replication of results. Researchers bear in mind a number of questions:

> Can colleagues in the discipline agree that the hypotheses have been put to a valid test?
>
> Are the conclusions that are drawn from the data reasonable?
>
> Are the generalizations made from the data within the bounds of the phenomena examined, or do the conclusions go beyond the data?
>
> Can the findings be replicated?

Unintended Findings and New Directions

In 1940, researchers from Columbia University's Bureau of Applied Social Research set out to investigate the effects of mass media on political behavior. They selected four groups of registered voters from Erie County, Ohio, a typical county in that in every presidential election it had voted as the nation had voted up to that time. These voters were then interviewed at intervals throughout the campaign to determine what factors had the greatest influence in their decision making regarding the election.

The 1940 Erie County study was designed to demonstrate the power of the mass media in affecting voting decisions. Two of the researchers said, "This study went to great lengths to determine how the mass media brought about such changes."

What the researchers found was that "personal contacts appear to have been both more frequent and more effective than the mass media in influencing voting decision." The researchers proposed that messages from the media first reach opinion leaders, who then pass on what they read or hear to associates or followers who look to them as influentials. This process was named the *two-step* flow of communication. (See Chapter 11 for greater detail.)

Because the design of the study did not anticipate the importance of interpersonal relations, the two-step flow concept was the one least well documented by the data. As a result, a number of other studies were later done to verify and refine the concept. In the history of science many studies have produced unintended findings, resulting in entirely new directions of inquiry.

Since its very beginning science has questioned existing findings and laws. Because only repeated testing establishes new principles, the very process of science results in new findings which often raise doubts about what is currently accepted. As new evidence is discovered theories are modified and sharpened. Scientists believe that no theory is final or beyond question.

An example of a check on bias in mass communication research is an article by the noted Columbia University professor of sociology Herbert J. Gans. He examined the findings of three other researchers, reported in two widely published surveys, that contended that U.S. journalists impose a liberal or left bias on the news and mislead the American people (Gans, 1985). Gans questioned the way the researchers analyzed their data and reported their findings. He said that their approach often diverges sharply from scientific methodology and that the researchers have not published or released detailed information about their methods, despite repeated requests (p. 30). Gans argued that, based on what the researchers have published, both studies

1. hide a political argument behind a seemingly objective study, highlighting the data which support that argument;
2. report findings about journalists which do not accurately reflect the answers they gave to the survey questions they were asked;
3. violate basic survey methodology by first inferring people's opinions from answers to single questions, and then treating their answers as strongly felt opinions in a way that makes the journalist appear militant and radical;
4. violate scientific norms by forgetting an explicit promise to their respondents;
5. present a mass of data on the personal backgrounds and alleged political opinions and values of the journalists without any evidence that these are relevant to how the journalists report the news. (Gans, 1985, pp. 29-33)

ETHICS AND FRAUD IN SCIENCE

Recently ethics in science has become a major issue (Comstock, 1994; Hilts, 1994a; Willwerth, 1994). Nuclear exposure experiments by agencies of the U.S. government, and its contractors, on pregnant women, soldiers, convicts, mental patients, and the general population, without their informed consent, have all been uncovered in recent years. Gallagher (1993) and Udall (1994) have written of the use of "down winders" who were nuclear testing victims of Nevada and Utah. Willwerth (1994) writes of the ill-informed consent of mental patients used in psychological experiments, Braffman-Miller (1995) tells of the illegal use of Americans as guinea pigs in medical experiments on radiation.

Mashberg (1994) writes of the use of Nevada residents, described in government memos as "a low-use segment of the population," who were invited to "participate in a moment of history." Actually that "moment of history," consisting of 126 above-ground nuclear tests, lasted for twelve years. Each test resulted in fallout comparable to that from Chernobyl. When Nevada cows' milk contained radioactivity three times the permissible level, the government tripled the permissible levels of radiation in milk.

In the stage of scientific method involving publication of findings, several critics have charged laxity in the peer review process and the publication of erroneous and fraudulent scientific papers. They have made several proposals to make scientific journals more accountable (Altman, 1989; Broad, 1989; Goleman, 1988; Maddox, 1988; Stagner, 1989; Wade, 1988).

With increasingly fierce competition for research funding and ever-greater academic demands to publish, it is not surprising that instances of scientific fraud, and its detection, have become major topics in both the academic and popular press (Altman, 1994; Hilts, 1994b; Levy, 1994; Whitely, Rennie, & Hafner, 1994; Crewdson, 1993; Angier, 1993). Publication of scientific findings and their replication remains as the guard that science has against fraud, and a number of fraudulent findings have been uncovered in recent years.

Recently growing numbers of people have begun to reject the Western scientific tradition. A professor of physics points out that this is a romantic rebellion, "led not by the religious fundamentalists who are the traditional foes of science, but by serious academics and writers who regard themselves as intellectuals" (Park, 1995). He comments on their profound hostility to modern science and asks what century they would have preferred to have lived in. He points out that "there is also a resurgence of belief in magic and psychic phenomena which has spread to all levels of society," and concludes:

> But it is science that uncovers the problems and it is to science that we turn to solve them. This is not because scientists have any claim to greater intellect or virtue, but because science is the only means we have to sort out the truth from ideology or fraud or mere foolishness. (p. 15)

THE PROCESS OF SCIENTIFIC INQUIRY

Scientific inquiry employs both induction and deduction. Induction uses particular or specific instances as observed by the scientist to arrive at general conclusions or axioms. This is the use of data or evidence to arrive at generalities, often called *empiricism*. The mathematical expression of induction is found in statistical inference: the scientist examines many cases and arrives at a conclusion. Deduction, in contrast, begins with what is general and applies it to particular cases; this is often called *logic* or *rationalism*. Deduction is employed by the scientist in making the leap from a hypothesis (a generalization) to an operational definition so that the hypothesis can be tested with specific real-world phenomena or cases.

Several definitions will assist us in summarizing what we have learned thus far. Two authors of a well-known text in comparative politics provide these reasoned and, for our purposes, highly useful definitions (Bill & Hardgrave, 1973, p. 24):

Generalization: A statement of uniformities in the relations between two or more variables of well-defined classes.

Hypothesis: A generalization presented in tentative and conjectural terms.

Theory: A set of systematically related generalizations suggesting new observations for empirical testing.

Law: A hypothesis of universal form that has withstood intensive experimentation.

Model: A theoretical and simplified representation of the real world.

It is important to remember that a model is neither a generalizing nor an explanatory device. (Chapter 3 deals with models, especially communication models, in greater detail.)

A model is a theoretical and simplified representation of the real world. It is an isomorphic construction of reality or anticipated reality. A model, by itself, is not an explanatory device, but it does play an important and directly suggestive role in the formulation of theory. By its very nature it suggests relationships. . . . The jump from a model to a theory is often made so quickly that the model is in fact believed to be a theory. A model is disguised as a theory more often than any other concept. (Bill & Hardgrave, 1973, p. 28)

ACQUIRING EMPIRICAL DATA

In mass communication research several methods are frequently employed to acquire empirical data in a systematic fashion. The most common are survey research, content analysis, experimental design, and case studies.

Survey Research

The sample survey is used to answer questions about how a large number of subjects feel, behave, or are, especially with regard to variables that change over time.

Survey research is the study of a portion or sample of a specific "population" (magazine subscribers, newspaper readers, television viewers, the population of a community or state). If done according to statistical principles, generalizations can then be made from the sample to the population with a certain degree of assurance or confidence. A sample is less costly than a census, which is an enumeration of all the members of a population. A census allows statements to be made about actual population parameters. However, the sample forces the researcher to make generalizations about the population within a degree or range of probability (called the "confidence interval"), which can be calculated statistically for any given sample.

Sample surveys can also compare relationships between variables by correlation (moving toward answers to questions of cause and effect). Often variables of interest to the researcher cannot be manipulated in an experiment (e.g., age, race, occupation). The survey allows for comparisons between people who differ on a given characteristic and also for differences in their behaviors (e.g., how individuals of various ages, occupations, or educational levels differ in their perceptions of media credibility or in their media use).

A Survey to Check News Accuracy.   An example of the survey technique is the use of mail questionnaires to check on news accuracy.

Tankard and Ryan (1974) clipped articles dealing with science news over a three-month period from a random sample of 20 newspapers taken from 167 newspapers with a circulation exceeding 50,000 in the 26 states east of the Mississippi. Cover letters, questionnaires, clippings, and return envelopes were mailed to 242 scientists involved in the news articles. The scientists were asked to indicate possible types of errors in the articles on the checklist of 42 kinds of errors, to express their attitudes toward science news coverage in general, and to provide information regarding their recent activities with representatives of the press.

The survey resulted in 193 usable returns (only 2 scientists refused to cooperate, and 13 mailings were returned as undeliverable).

The investigators were able to specify the types of errors the scientists perceived as made most often, the scientists' agreement or disagreement with nine short statements regarding science writing in general, and the relationship between nine "predictor" variables and perceived error rate (such things as content category [medicine, biology, social sciences, etc.], origin of the report [staff, wire service, etc.], circulation of the newspaper, whether or not a story was bylined).

Tankard and Ryan reported that the mean number of kinds of errors was 3.50 when the scientist read the story before publication and 6.69 when the scientist did not read the story before publication. The attitude items indicated strong criticism by scientists of the accuracy of science news reporting in general. Large majorities of the sample indicated that headlines on science stories are misleading and that information crucial to the understanding of research results is often omitted from news stories (Tankard & Ryan, 1974, p. 334).

Surveying Voters' Attitudes.   More recently, the University of Colorado at Denver's Graduate School of Public Affairs surveyed 900 registered voters in a "Mind of Colorado" telephone poll. They found that:

> Coloradans have little confidence in their government, school systems and local news media and nearly half can't name one public official in the state who exemplifies honesty and integrity. (Roberts, 1994)

Content Analysis

Content analysis is a systematic method of analyzing message content. It is a tool for analyzing the messages of certain communicators. Instead of interviewing people or asking them to respond to questionnaires, as in survey research, or observing behavior, as in the human experiment, the investigator using content analysis examines the communications that have been produced at times and places of his or her own choosing. It has been described as the "objective, systematic, and quantitative description" of communication content (Bernard Berelson, cited in Budd, Thorp, & Donohew, 1967, p. 3).

A sophisticated use of content analysis couples it with additional information about source, channel, receiver, feedback, or other conditions of the communication situation, such as attitude, personality, or demographic characteristics. This allows predictions to be made about the communication process. In such cases content analysis is a tool used with other methods of inquiry to link message content with other parts of the communication setting. It allows the investigator to deal with larger questions of the process and the effects of communications.

After selecting a question to be investigated or a hypothesis to be tested, the content analyst must define the population he or she will work with (publications, newscasts, time span, etc.). If the population is large, a sample is drawn, as in survey research. Categories must then be defined for classifying message content (a crucial step) and the content of the sample is coded according to objective rules. The coded content may be scaled or differentiated in some way to arrive at scores. If the content is to be related to other variables, these scores can then be compared with them.

As with all quantitative research, these scores must then be analyzed (usually using the data reduction techniques of statistical analysis) and the findings interpreted according to the concepts or theories that have been tested.

Newspapers and Television Compared.   A January 1995 content analysis of the *New York Times, Atlanta Constitution,* and *Des Moines Register* and the evening newscasts of ABC, CBS, and NBC concluded that in coverage of many top news stories television is comparable and sometimes superior to daily newspapers. However, with lesser stories newspapers were found to devote much more space to a broader range of topics than did broadcasts. The study, "Headlines and Sound Bites—Is That the Way It Is?" by the Freedom Forum Media Studies Center at Columbia University, contradicted the long-held assumptions that newspaper coverage is superior in quality and quantity to that of broadcast news (*Editor & Publisher,* 1995).

Content Analysis on the Information Superhighway.   With the exponential growth of the Internet it was inevitable that commercial firms would offer "clipping services" of its content. One service retrieves every qualified reference in more than 45,000 messages posted on the Internet every day, using a "predetermined list of client criteria" (Newsbytes, 1995). Content analysis "allows the client to assess their Internet image to determine strengths and weaknesses, opportunities and vulnerabilities in terms that are 'measurable, actionable, and scientific'."

Experimental Design

Experimental designs are the classic method of dealing with questions of causality. An experiment involves the control or manipulation of a variable by the experimenter and an observation or measurement of the result in an objective and systematic way. When it is possible to use the experimental method, it is the research method most apt to provide answers of cause and effect. The classic experiment will answer questions of whether and to what degree a variable (the experimental or independent variable) affects another variable (the dependent variable).

In the simplest form of the classic experiment, two matched groups are randomly selected from a population (defined by and of interest to the experimenter), and one is given the experimental variable (in communication research it may be a news story, a documentary film, a piece of propaganda, etc.). After the experimental group has been exposed to the variable in question, both groups are observed or measured and any differences between them are construed as effects of the experimental treatment.

Many experiments modify the classic design, for reasons such as practical difficulties or costs. Some experiments are made far more complex in order to provide answers to additional questions (e.g., how long the effects of a message will last, the effects of various types or combinations of messages, the effects of a number of different independent variables that may interact).

An Experiment of Communicator Credibility.   A classic experiment in communication research, conducted by Hovland and Weiss (1951), dealt with the effects of communicator credibility on acceptance of the content of a message. Identical messages were presented to two groups, one from a source with high credibility and the other from a source with low credibility. Opinions were measured before and after the messages were presented and also one month later. Four different topics were used (each in affirmative and negative versions) and presented to some subjects by trusted sources and to other subjects by sources held in much lower esteem.

Each subject received one article on each of the four topics, with the source given at the end of each article. Before reading the articles the subjects indicated their trust in each of a long list of sources, including those used in the experiment. The four high-credibility sources used in the experiment were judged so by 81 to 95 percent of the subjects; with the low-credibility sources the scores were only 1 to 21 percent.

The initial attitudes held toward the sources clearly affected how the subjects evaluated the presentations. Those from low-credibility sources were judged "less fair" and conclusions "less justified" than those by high-credibility sources, even though the articles were identical. The researchers concluded that "judgments of content characteristics, such as how well the facts in a given communication justify the conclusion, are significantly affected by variations in the source" (Hovland, Janis, & Kelley, 1953, p. 29).

The researchers found greater opinion change in the direction advocated by the message when the source was of high credibility than when it was of low credibility. However, when opinion data were obtained four weeks later, the differential effectiveness of the sources had disappeared. There was less acceptance of the viewpoints of high-credibility sources and greater acceptance of the positions advocated by low-credibility sources. At that time measures were also obtained of the subject's memory of the sources for each communication.

After ruling out other explanations, the researchers concluded that there exists a "sleeper effect" for subjects who showed increased belief in messages attributed to sources of low credibility; in the investigators' words, "There is decreased tendency over time to reject the material presented by an untrustworthy source" (Hovland, Janis, & Kelley, 1953, p. 256).

The main advantages of the experimental method are the control it allows the investigator and the inherent logical rigor it offers. However, many experiments are "artificial" or oversimplified in their settings and the findings must be translated to the "real" world. For this and a number of other reasons, often seemingly conflicting results are obtained from experimental designs and survey research. Carl Hovland, a pioneer in communication research, addressed this problem as it applies to studies of attitude change and suggested methods for its resolution. He concluded by noting the virtues of each method and the need for both methods in communication research (Hovland, 1959).

"Natural" Experiments.   Often "natural" experiments can be set up outside the laboratory. An example of a planned natural experiment in communication is the "split-run" technique, whereby two versions of an advertisement or other message are run and the relative effectiveness of each is assessed. This may be done through follow-up questions asked over the telephone or in personal interviews, through tabulation of responses from coupons coded to identify which version has resulted in the response, or through other means.

Sometimes the experimenter may be interested in a theoretical question or in the test of a hypothesis and can design a study for an appropriate natural event. The experimenter then "follows up" the event with fieldwork. Such is the case involving the question of the effects of price advertising on the sales of beer and ale. This is a question of considerable controversy in many parts of the United States and an issue of concern for brewers, for the advertising industry, and for consumer groups concerned over alcohol consumption, its negative health aspects, and drunk driving.

In the state of Michigan price advertising of beer and wine was prohibited, allowed, and again prohibited between May 1981 and April 1984. The researcher (Wilcox, 1985) examined total sales of brewed beverages (beer and ale) as reported by a sample of 65 retail outlets in lower Michigan in A. C. Nielsen in-store audits every two months over the three-year period. The researcher also examined data showing the number of surveyed retail outlets engaging in local advertising during the period of no restrictions on price advertising (March 1982 to May 1983).

Examination of the data indicated that a significantly higher percentage of retail stores engaged in local advertising during the nonrestrictive period. However, the presence of price advertising appeared to have no significant effect on sales of brewed beverages (Wilcox, 1985, p. 37).

Case Studies

While a survey examines one or a few characteristics of many subjects or units, a case study is used to examine many characteristics of a single subject (e.g., a communicator, newsroom, newspaper, news syndicate, television station, ad agency). The case study usually tries to learn "all" about the area the investigator is interested in for the specific case over a period of time.

A Case Study of Television News Using Content Analysis.   Berkowitz (1990) did a case study combining observational research with content analysis to examine the selection of local news items for a network-affiliated television station in Indianapolis. He refined the metaphor of the news "gate" and reshaped the notion of gatekeeping to fit the local television situation. Working in the newsroom, he coded a total of 391 potential stories during a four-week period.

Berkowitz found that news selection decisions were based on several considerations besides news values, including information that was easy to explain, that would draw an audience, and that could be assembled with efficiency of effort. As a result of 220 hours of newsroom observation and later interviews, Berkowitz concluded that rather than use textbook news values, newsworkers used their instincts, citing interest, importance, and visual impact, although the latter was rarely mentioned during story conferences.

The structure of the newscast format, which called for an approximate quota of stories from various categories, had almost as much to do with story selection as did the news merits of potential stories. Berkowitz says that "this helps explain why gatekeepers do not always agree on specific stories, but they do tend to agree on the kinds of stories that constitute a balanced news mix" (p. 66).

Berkowitz concludes:

> . . . this study found that decision-making didn't fit the traditional mold of a lone wire editor sitting next to a pile of stories and making decisions based on either newsworthiness or personal preferences. . . . First, decision-making seemed to be a group process; content, therefore, was shaped by group dynamics. . . . Second, the keys to the lock—interest, importance, visual quality—were different than the keys searched

for by past studies of newspaper wire editors or those taught in journalism classes. Whether these keys could even be used was partly dictated by organizational demands such as resource constraints and newscast formats. . . . Stories that passed through one gate faced still other gates on their way toward being broadcast. Spot news closed the gate on planned event stories. Resource constraints and logistical problems sometimes closed the gate on spot news stories. (p. 66)

Histories as Case Studies. Most histories of media institutions can also be classified as case studies. An exception in communication research is an investigation of three centuries of the British press and its regulation by Siebert (1952). In this nonquantitative study, hypotheses are formulated and tested and conclusions drawn, giving it some of the properties of scientific research. A later example is a test of one of Siebert's propositions in North Carolina by Shaw and Brauer (1969), using the historical method in focusing on one editor and the Newcomb ABX model of symmetry from the field of social psychology to make predictions. Case studies usually cannot be generalized to other similar situations. Most often the results are based on a single example and rarely are hypotheses formulated and tested, making it difficult, if not impossible, to generalize to other situations. The method does provide a great many observations, ideas, and insights that can be followed up with other types of investigations to yield results that can be generalized.

REASONING ABOUT THE DATA

Statistics

Scientific investigators rely on statistics to aid them in making inferences from the object of their studies to the populations about which they seek to generalize. Statistics are a tool used in the process of reasoning about the data gathered.

Statistics can be used in a number of ways. One of the most common uses is in data reduction, in bringing large quantities of data to manageable form by providing summaries. These are known as descriptive statistics, which provide information such as the mean, median, variance, and percentiles for a body of data.

Perhaps even more important for our purposes is the use of sampling or probability statistics to enable scientists to make estimates of population characteristics. This use of statistics enables scientists to draw inferences from data at specific levels of confidence. A scientist using the sample survey method can make inferences from the sample data to the population from which the sample was drawn. This is done within parameters that can be calculated after specifying the confidence level (the "odds" of being in error) that the scientist is willing to accept. For example, the range of the mean daily television viewing of a population can be predicted from a random sample from that population once the chances of error are stated (a 5 percent level of confidence would indicate 1 chance in 20). As scientists increase the degree of confidence they expect in the prediction, the interval within which they can make the prediction (confidence interval) also increases.

The investigator who employs the experimental method randomly assigns subjects to various groups. Random assignment assures that there will be no systematic bias in subject assignment. After the experimental group or groups have been exposed to the variable under investigation, observations and measurements are made about the effects of the variable. The resulting data are analyzed with statistical methods to determine if any differences between groups in the effects of the experimental variable could have been by chance and at what level of probability. For example, what is the probability that the group that received a specific message and scored higher on an attitude measure following the message did so only by chance? If the probability is very low, and if other basic requirements of the experimental method were observed, the scientists can then infer that the difference between the groups is due to the different treatment (in this case, the message).

Validity, External and Internal

When evaluating scientific findings and the generalizations made from them, scientists ask questions regarding validity and reliability. Did the experiment, survey, or content analysis measure what the investigator claims it measures?

More specifically, *external validity* deals with the question of whether the phenomena observed and measured by an investigator are representative of the real world phenomena the scientist wishes to generalize about.

The work of Shere Hite, author of three books dealing with male and female sexuality, has been challenged for the representativeness of the samples upon which her conclusions are based. Her third book, *Women in Love*, is based on 4,500 responses to 100,000 questionnaires she mailed out, largely to women's groups. Critics have argued that sampling members of women's groups, and a return of only 4.5 percent, does not provide a valid sample of the population of women in general, to which she projects her findings. An earlier book, *The Hite Report on Male Sexuality*, was described as "social science fiction" by the then-editor of the *New York Times Book Review* (McDowell, 1987).

Internal validity is required in experimental research if conclusions are to be drawn from the data. It raises the question of whether the differences obtained resulted from the experimental treatment or whether they can be explained by other factors. Internal validity deals with extraneous or alternate variables that must be controlled in the research design to rule out their being a cause of any effects that may be observed. Put another way, the experimenter wishes to rule out any explanation for the results or findings other than the experimental or independent variable.

Operationally Defining the Hypothesis

As observed earlier, the act of translating abstract hypotheses to real-world phenomena is called "operationally defining" the hypotheses. For example, the hypothesis "If an individual is a social isolate, then that individual is less apt to use the mass media than one who is socially integrated into his or her community" needs to be defined in terms that can be measured.

The investigator can define social isolate and socially integrated in terms of frequency of visits with neighbors, relatives, coworkers, and others, media use can be defined in terms of reported time spent with the mass media. A comparison can then be made between individuals who report little social interaction with others and those who report considerable social interaction with others, and subgroup reports of time spent with various mass media can be analyzed. The question of validity then becomes whether the measures of social integration actually measure what social integration is, as defined for that study.

Reliability

Reliability deals with the consistency of measurement. *External reliability* is the ability of a measure to provide the same results time after time, within acceptable margins of error, if applied to the phenomena under the same conditions. *Internal reliability* refers to the question of whether various subparts of a test provide comparable data.

CONCLUSIONS

As a scientist in any field of investigation develops and tests hypotheses about the nature of the world in a particular area of interest, the process of observation, testing, replication, cumulation, and closure continues. All of this contributes to the building of a theory that will provide explanations and make possible predictions.

In communication research there has been a gradual and long-term shift from applied research to basic research (sometimes, with unfortunate connotations, called "pure" science). The field of mass communication research, like so many other fields, is moving from answers to specific questions dealing with immediate problems toward theory building to provide the general explanations of how humans communicate.

DISCUSSION

   1. Discuss methods of establishing truth other than the scientific method.
   2. Why, from a scientific viewpoint, are these methods lacking?

3. What areas of inquiry are beyond the scientific method and why?
4. How does imagination play a part in the scientific method?
5. What is the goal of scientific inquiry?
6. What is meant by the cumulative nature of science?
7. What is a hypothesis? How is it used?
8. What safeguards science from bias and fraud?
9. What is inductive reasoning? What is deductive reasoning?
10. How does a model differ from a theory?

REFERENCES

Altman, L. K. (1989). Errors prompt proposals to improve "peer review" at science journals. *New York Times*, June 6, p. 20.

Altman, Lawrence K. (1994). Researcher falsified data in breast cancer study. *New York Times*, March 14, p. A1.

Angier, Natalie (1993). White coats with dirty hands. *New York Times.* Oct. 17, p. 12.

Berkowitz, D. (1990). Refining the gatekeeping metaphor for local television news. *Journal of Broadcasting & Electronic Media* 34: 55-68.

Bill, J. A., and R. L. Hardgrave, Jr. (1973). *Comparative Politics: The Quest for Theory.* Columbus, Ohio: Charles E. Merrill. Especially pp. 21-40 dealing with the scientific method.

Braffman-Miller, Judith (1995). When medicine went wrong: How Americans were used illegally as guinea pigs. *USA Today* (magazine), March, p. 84.

Broad, William J. (1989). Question of scientific fakery is raised in inquiry. *New York Times*, July 12, p. 7.

Bronowski, J. (1973). *The Ascent of Man.* Boston: Little, Brown. See especially Chapter 6, "The Starry Messenger," dealing with Copernicus, Galileo, and the birth of the scientific method.

Budd, R., R. Thorp, and L. Donohew (1967). *Content Analysis of Communications.* New York: Macmillan.

Cohen, M. R., and E. Nagel (1934). *An Introduction to Logic and the Scientific Method.* New York: Harcourt Brace and World.

Comstock, Gary (1994). Ethics and scientific research. *SRA Journal*, 26, no. 2 (Sept. 22), p. 33.

Cowell, Alan (1992). After 350 years, Vatican says Galileo was right: It moves. *New York Times*, Oct. 31, p. A1.

Crewdson, John (1993). When scientists, lawyers argue, justice is the loser. *Chicago Tribune*, Nov. 14, Perspective Sec., p. 1.

Editor & Publisher (1995). TV scores well when compared to newspapers. April 29, p. 20.

Gallagher, Carole (1993). *American Ground Zero: The Secret Nuclear War.* Cambridge, Mass.: MIT Press.

Gans, H. J. (1985). Are U.S. journalists dangerously liberal? *Columbia Journalism Review*, Nov.-Dec., pp. 29-33.

Goleman, D. (1988). Test of journals is criticized as unethical. *New York Times*, Sept. 27, p. 21.

Hilts, Philip J. (1994a). Scientists lament inaction on abuse. *New York Times*, Feb. 6, p. A23.

————. (1994b). Inquiry decides researcher faked experimental data. *New York Times*, Nov. 27, p. A15.

Hovland, C. (1959). Reconciling conflicting results derived from experimental and survey studies of attitude change. *The American Psychologist* 14: 8-17. Reprinted in W. Schramm and D. Roberts (eds.) (1971), *The Process and Effects of Mass Communication*, rev. ed., pp. 495-515. Urbana: University of Illinois Press.

Hovland, C., I. L. Janis, and H. H. Kelley (1953). *Communication and Persuasion*. New Haven, Conn.: Yale University Press.

Hovland, C., and W. Weiss (1951). The influence of source credibility on communication effectiveness. *Public Opinion Quarterly* 15: 635-650.

Kane, Julian (1992). What Galileo actually proved and disproved. *New York Times*, Nov. 17, p. A14.

Levy, Doug (1994). Medical research/fighting fraud/science only as strong as its integrity. *USA Today*, March 16, p. 1A.

Maddox, J. (1988). A too-polite silence about shoddy science. *New York Times*, Sept. 26, p. 27.

Mashberg, Tom (1994). When radiation drew no fear. *Boston Globe*, Jan. 2, National/Foreign Sec., p. 1.

McDowell, E. (1987). Agent for Hite resigns amid a controversy. *New York Times*, Nov. 13, p. 45.

Montalbano, William (1992). Catholic Church clears Galileo of heresy charges. *Houston Chronicle*, Nov. 1, p. A29.

Newsbytes (1995). eWorks, Medialink to offer Internet clipping service. *Newsbytes News Network*, Aug. 15.

New York Times (1967). Napalm inventor discounts guilt. Dec. 27, p. 8.

————. (1989). Does ideology stop at the laboratory door? A debate on science and the real world. Oct. 22, p. 22.

Park, Robert L. (1995). The danger of voodoo science. *New York Times*, July 9, p. E15.

Reston, James, Jr. (1994). *Galileo: A life*. New York: HarperCollins Publishers.

Roberts, Jeffrey A. (1994). Sad state of affairs: Colorado, Residents frustrated, cynical, poll finds. *Denver Post*, Dec. 1, p. 1A.

Salisbury, H. (1976). Trofim L. Lysenko is dead at 78; Was science overlord under Stalin. *New York Times*, Nov. 24, p. 36.

Shabecoff, P. (1989). Scientist says U.S. agency altered his testimony on global warming. *New York Times*, May 8, p. 1.

Shaw, D., and S. Brauer (1969). Press freedom and war constraints: Case-testing Siebert's Proposition II. *Journalism Quarterly* 46: 243-254.

Siebert, F. S. (1952). *Freedom of the Press in England 1476-1776*. Urbana: University of Illinois Press.

Stagner, R. (1989). Bogus research shows experts to be embarrassingly human. *New York Times*, Apr. 23, Sec. 4, p. 22.

Tan, Alexis S. (1981). *Mass Communication Theories and Research*. Columbus, Ohio: Grid Publishing.

Tankard, J., and M. Ryan (1974). News source perceptions of accuracy of science coverage. *Journalism Quarterly* 51: 219-225.

Udall, Stewart (1994). *The Myths of August*. New York: Pantheon.

Wade, N. (1988). Looking hard at science's self-scrutiny. *New York Times*, Aug. 21, Sec. 4, p. 9.

Westley, B. (1958). Journalism research and scientific method. *Journalism Quarterly* 35: 161-169; 307-316. Reprinted in R. O. Nafziger and D. M. White (eds.) (1963),

Introduction to Mass Communication Research as "Scientific Method and Communi-cation Research" (Chapter 9). Baton Rouge: Louisiana State University Press.

Whitely, William P., Drummond Rennie, and Arthur W. Hafner (1994). The scientific community's response to evidence of fraudulent publication. *JAMA* (The Journal of the American Medical Association), 272, no. 2 (July), p. 170.

Whitman, A. (1976). Newton's other law is hailed on its tercentenary. *New York Times*, Feb. 6, p. 21.

Wilcox, G. (1985). The effect of price advertising on alcoholic beverage sales. *Journal of Advertising Research* 25 (Oct.-Nov.): 33–38.

Willwerth, James (1994). Madness in fine print. *Time*, Nov. 2, p. 62.

chapter 3

Models in Mass Communication Research

Whether we realize it or not, we are using models every time we try systematically to think about, visualize, or discuss any structure or process, be it past, present, or future. The effectiveness of such activity depends in large measure on how well our model fits the thing we are supposedly modeling.

In Chapter 2 we discussed the nature of the scientific method, the role of theory, and the advantage of being able to make predictions. We gave a definition of a model as a "theoretical and simplified representation of the real world" and quoted two authors who observed that models are often confused with theories.

If a model is not a theory, what then *are* models, why use them, how does one evaluate them, and what are some of the important models in communication research? The answers to these questions make up this chapter.

A model is not an explanatory device by itself, but it helps to formulate theory. It *suggests relationships*, and it is often confused with theory because the relationship between a model and a theory is so close.

Deutsch (1952) points out that a model is "a structure of symbols and operating rules which is supposed to match a set of relevant points in an existing structure or process." Models "are indispensable for understanding the more complex processes." This is a form of selection and abstraction, which, as we shall see later, is used far more often than most of us realize. Because we select the points we include in a model, a model implies judgments of relevance, and this, in turn, implies a theory about the thing modeled. Of course, abstraction carries with it the danger of oversimplification.

A model provides a frame within which we can consider a problem, even if in its early versions it does not lead to successful prediction. A model may also point out important gaps in our knowledge that are not apparent, and it may suggest areas where research is needed (the goal of closure). Failure of a model when it is tested may lead to an improved model.

The use of theoretical models unites the natural and social sciences, as does the scientific method itself. In nearly all areas of scientific endeavor, symbols are used to describe the essential aspects of reality on which a particular scientist wishes to focus.

The structures and processes we are interested in modeling have to do with how humans communicate, especially with the mass media. This can be the way one individual deals with reality within his or her own mind; how a newspaper, television network, advertising agency, or information office is structured and functions; how information flows in a society; or how innovations are adopted or rejected in a social system.

FUNCTIONS OF A MODEL

Deutsch (1952, pp. 360–361) has discussed the uses of communication models in the social sciences. He cites four distinct functions of models: organizing, heuristic, predictive, and measuring.

The *organizing* function of a model is seen in its ability to order and relate data and to show data similarities and connections that had not previously been perceived. If a new model explains something that was not understood, it almost always implies *predictions* that can be made. If it is operational, a model implies predictions that can be verified by physical tests.

Predictions, even if they cannot be verified at the time for lack of measuring techniques, can be *heuristic* devices that may lead to new unknown facts and methods. Models also allow a range of predictions, from the simple yes-or-no type to completely quantitative predictions dealing with when or how much.

When a model allows us to make completely quantitative predictions with a degree of precision about when or how much, it becomes related to *measurement* of the phenomena we are interested in. If the processes that link the model to the thing modeled are clearly understood, the data obtained with the help of a model constitute a measure, whether it be a simple ranking or a full ratio scale.

EVALUATION OF A MODEL

Each of these functions, in turn, forms a basis for evaluating models.

1. How *general* is a model? How much material does it organize, and how effectively?
2. How *fruitful* or *heuristic* is the model? How helpful is it in discovering new relationships, facts, or methods?

3. How *important* to the field of inquiry are the predictions that can be made from it? How *strategic* are they at the stage of development a field is in?
4. How *accurate* are the measurements that can be developed with the model?

Deutsch (1952) also adds the following criteria for the evaluation of models:

1. How original is the model? Or how improbable is it? How much new insight does it provide?
2. What is the model's simplicity, economy of means, parsimony? (This is linked to the model's efficiency or its attainment of an intended goal with the greatest economy. An unsurpassed example is Einstein's theory that energy and matter are interchangeable, expressed as $E = mc^2$.)
3. How real is the model? To what degree may we rely on it as a representation of physical reality? (pp. 362-363)

SOME EARLY COMMUNICATION MODELS

Lasswell's Model

An early verbal model in communication is that of Lasswell (1948):

Who
Says What
In Which Channel
To Whom
With What Effect?

Lasswell's model allows for many general applications in mass communication. He implies that more than one channel can carry a message. The "who" raises the question of the control of the messages (e.g., the "gatekeeper" study cited in Chapter 2). The "says what" is the subject of content analysis (e.g., the analysis of information on the Information Superhighway). Communication channels are studies in media analysis. "To whom" deals with the receiver and audience analysis (e.g., the Colorado voter's attitudes in Chapter 2). The diffusion study and communicator credibility studies cited in Chapter 2 can be viewed as effect studies.

Lasswell's model has been criticized because it seems to imply the presence of a communicator and a purposive message. It has also been called over-simplified, but, as with any good model, it focused attention on important aspects of communication.

Norbert Wiener published *Cybernetics* in the same year (1948). This book emphasized two important concepts, the statistical foundation of communication and *feedback,* one of the most frequently borrowed concepts in communication.

The Mathematical Theory of Communication.   Shannon and Weaver's *Mathematical Theory of Communication* (1949) has been the most important and influential stimulus for the development of other models and theories in communication. The Shannon model is based on the statistical concept of signal transmission, which was first emphasized by Wiener. In the second part of *The Mathematical Theory of Communication,* Warren Weaver presented a schematic diagram of communication that resulted in many other models of the communication process. In this model (Figure 3.1) the information source produces a *message* to be communicated out of a set of possible messages. The message may consist of spoken or written words, music, pictures, and so on. The *transmitter* converts the message to a signal suitable for the channel to be used. The *channel* is the medium that transmits the *signal* from the transmitter to the receiver. In conversation the information source is the brain, the transmitter is the voice mechanism producing the signal (spoken words), transmitted through the air (the channel).

The *receiver* performs the inverse operation of the transmitter by reconstructing the message from the signal. The *destination* is the person or thing for whom the message is intended.

Other major contributions are Shannon and Weaver's concepts of a message composed of *entropy* and *redundancy* and the necessary balance between them for efficient communication while offsetting noise in a channel. Briefly, the more

FIGURE 3.1   A schematic diagram of Shannon's general communication system

SOURCE: From C. Shannon and W. Weaver, *The Mathematical Theory of Communication* (Urbana: University of Illinois Press, 1999), p. 98. Copyright © 1949 by the Board of Trustees of the University of Illinois. Reprinted with the permission of the University of Illinois Press.

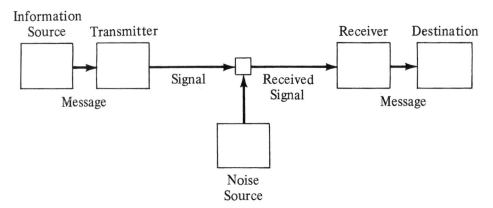

noise in a channel, the greater the need for redundancy, which reduces the relative entropy of the message (e.g., the wireless telegrapher transmitting in a noisy channel repeats key portions of the message to ensure their reception). By using redundancy to overcome the noise in the channel, the amount of information that can be transmitted in a given time is reduced.

Origins of Information Theory. Claude Shannon developed the mathematical theory of signal transmission while he was a research mathematician at Bell Telephone Laboratories and a professor of science at the Massachusetts Institute of Technology.

A direct result of Shannon's information theory is digital communication technology, which became commonplace in the 1980s. We now have digital audio recording on compact disk and tape (Pollack, 1990), and the technology is rapidly spreading over the entire field of telecommunications, including the telephone, radio, and television.

One writer (Fantel, 1989) said:

> What we have witnessed is more than a shift in technology. It is a shift in mentality. We have developed new ways of seeing and representing certain natural phenomena. . . . But by the middle of the 20th century— in 1948, to be precise—a new General Theory of Information had been formulated by Dr. Claude Shannon of Bell Laboratories. This theory, expressed in elegant mathematics, enabled us to break down the analog entities of our normal perceptions (such as sight and sound) into separate digital bits. The advantage was that the bit language would be intelligible to machines and, through computers, could be manipulated very quickly and with virtually no distortion or loss in the process. (p. 28)

The theory also has important and far-ranging applications outside the engineering field for which it was developed, including the social sciences and communications theory. Warren Weaver, then a consultant on scientific projects at the Sloan Foundation, summarized the main concepts of Shannon's mathematical theory and suggested important applications of the theory to the whole problem of communications in society. *Philosophical Review* called it "a beautiful example of a theory that unifies hitherto separate branches of physical science, and Dr. Weaver makes important suggestions as to how this unity may be extended" (Burks, 1951).

Information theory, as the mathematical theory of communication has become known, is described as "exceedingly general in its scope, fundamental in the problems it treats, and of classic simplicity and power in the results it reaches" (Shannon & Weaver, 1949, p. 114). Weaver suggested that the theory is general enough that it can be applied to written language, musical notes, spoken words, music, pictures, and many other communication signals. The term *communication* is used in a "very broad sense to include all of the procedures by which one mind may affect another" (Weaver, 1949, p. 95). The purpose of communication is defined as an attempt to influence the conduct of the destination with a broad definition of conduct (p. 97).

The concepts of information theory provide insight, and they have been applied to mass communication situations. As has already been noted, the theory has provided the impetus for many other models of the communication process. The theory gives insights into relationships within many forms of communication. Weaver says it is so imaginative that it deals with the core of communication—relationships that exist no matter what form communication may take.

Information theory is essentially a theory of signal transmission. At first it may seem disappointing to the student of the mass media because it has nothing to do with meaning and it may even seem a bit bizarre because information theory equates information with uncertainty. As we shall see, these are two of the theory's greatest assets in that they provide a new and fruitful way of viewing the communication process.

The communication process (see Figure 3.1) begins with the source selecting a message out of all possible messages. This message can be in the form of spoken or written words, musical notations, the music itself, pictures, mathematical notations, symbolic logic, body movements, facial expressions, or a host of other forms we have available. The transmitter operates on the message to produce a signal suitable for transmission over a channel. The message exists only between the source and the transmitter and between the receiver and the destination. Only a signal travels between the transmitter and the receiver.

When we use the telephone, the channel is the wire, the signal is the electrical current passing through the wire, and the transmitter (mouthpiece) transforms the sound pressure of the spoken word into varying electrical current. In oral speech the source is the brain, the transmitter is the human voice mechanism or vocal system, the channel is the air, and the signal is the varying pressure passing from the vocal system of one person to the ear of another. The transmitter functions to encode the message; and when it is received, the receiver (in this case, the ear) must decode the message (convert the varying sound waves coming through the air into neural impulses for the destination, the brain).

The *signal,* of course, takes different forms, depending on the communication system we are examining. We have seen that in speech the signal is varying sound pressure traveling through the air (the channel). In radio and television the signal is an electromagnetic wave, while newspapers, magazines, and books use the printed word and illustrations as the signal on a page (the channel). The channel is, as implied, the medium used to transmit the signal from the transmitter to the receiver.

Channel capacity, in information theory terms, is not the number of symbols a channel can transmit but rather the information a channel can transmit or a channel's ability to transmit what is produced out of a source of information (Weaver, 1949, p. 106). Of course, all channels, be they electronic, mechanical, or human, have an upper limit of capacity. For example, the human eye can resolve and transmit far more information in a period of time than the brain can process and store. As we shall see, all communications are composed of chains of systems, and as with any chain, they are no stronger than their weakest link. Channel capacity is also limited by the space or time available to the editor or newscaster and by the time available to the destination to spend with the media.

Once a transmitter has encoded a message for transmission over a channel, a receiver must reconstruct the message from the signal transmitted. Ordinarily the receiver's operation is the inverse of the transmitter's; that is, the receiver changes the transmitted signal back into a message and passes this message on to a destination. In broadcasting the receiver is, as the term implies, the radio or television set. In speech the receiver is the ear and its part of the nervous system. With print material it is the eye and its associated nervous system.

The *destination* is the person or thing for whom the message is intended. With the mass media the destination is, of course, a member of the audience— the reader, listener, or viewer. The destination can also be a thing. A thermostat communicates with a heating or cooling system; a governor communicates with a motor or the fuel supply to an engine. Computers can be programmed to communicate with one another.

The thermostat or governor provides feedback to allow a system to make corrections in its own operation. The concept of *feedback* was first introduced by Norbert Wiener of MIT in his book *Cybernetics* (1948). In the mass media we have many forms of feedback from the destination to the source to help the communicator correct subsequent output. Letters and telephone calls from readers and listeners are a form of feedback, as are responses to advertising campaigns, audience ratings in broadcasting, and increases or decreases in newsstand sales or subscriptions. Feedback in the classroom can take many forms, including puzzled looks or signs of boredom, which inform the instructor that a point needs to be clarified or that it is time to move on to another topic.

THE DELIVERY OF USEFUL INFORMATION

So far you have probably had little difficulty with information theory. But its most unique feature and most valuable contribution to our understanding of the communication process may be harder to grasp: its approach to what constitutes information. As defined by Weaver, the term *information* is used in a very special way. It is most important that you not confuse information with meaning, as is commonly the case (1949, pp. 99–100). Each one of us adds our own meaning to the information we receive, as we shall see in subsequent chapters. Information, in terms of the mathematical theory of communication, or information theory, according to Weaver, "relates, not so much to what you do say, as to what you could say" (1949, p. 100). Information becomes a measure of our freedom of choice in selecting a message to transmit. In information theory terms, information is very similar to *entropy* in the physical sciences— it is a measure of the degree of randomness. Entropy is the uncertainty or disorganization of a situation. In information theory it is associated with the amount of freedom of choice one has in constructing a message.

A highly organized message does not have a high degree of randomness, uncertainty, or choice. In such a case the entropy or information is low because any parts of the message that are missing when it is received have a high probability of being supplied by the receiver. For example, because of the organization (entropy) of the English language, a receiver who is familiar with it can correct most misspellings. Individuals familiar with a given subject can provide missing elements in a passage. We shall see how this has been applied to measure the "readability" of a passage.

The part of the message that is not entropy or information is called, as we might expect, *redundancy.* Redundancy is defined as the portion of the message that is determined by the rules governing the use of the symbols in question or that is not determined by the free choice of the sender. Redundancy is unnecessary in that if it were missing, the message would be essentially complete or could be completed (1949, p. 104). When we use the English language, about half of our choices are controlled by the nature of the language and the rules for its usage.

Redundancy can be used to offset noise in a communication channel. The fact that English is about 50 percent redundant makes it possible to correct errors in a message that has been received over a noisy channel. However, key or important items are often repeated in transmission (a form of redundancy) to ensure their reception when transmitting through a noisy channel ("will arrive Tuesday, repeat Tuesday").

Redundancy is a measure of certainty or predictability. The more redundant the message, the less information it is carrying. Sometimes, however, increased redundancy will increase the efficiency of a communication system.

Noise is defined as anything added to the signal that is not intended by the information source. Noise can take many forms. The example that comes most readily to mind is that of static on the radio. In information theory terms, noise can also be distortions of sound in telephony, radio, television, or film; distortions of shape or shading in a television image; a smudged reproduction of a printed photo; or errors of transmission in telegraphy. Noise can also take the form of a speaker's distracting mannerism—added to the signal, but not intended by the information source.

Noise increases uncertainty and, both paradoxically and technically, in an information theory sense, noise increases information. According to Weaver (1949, p. 109), information as used in information theory can have good or bad connotations. Noise is spurious information. For the sender or source, a high degree of uncertainty or freedom of choice (entropy) is desirable, but from the destination's point of view, uncertainty because of errors or noise is undesirable. To get useful information, the destination must subtract the spurious information (noise) from the received message.

From the standpoint of the destination, noise can also be competing stimuli from outside the channel. Obvious examples are a low-flying airplane that blocks out the sound of a newscast, a crying baby, a barking dog, or quarreling children. Noise can also take the form of whisperers at the cinema or the woman who habitually arrives late for class wearing revealing attire. The woman is obviously communicating information, but from the standpoint of the lecturer it is information not intended by the communicator. The communicator must then increase the level of redundancy in the lecture (usually by repeating a point) to offset the noise introduced by a competing source.

The mass communicator usually tries to reduce noise as much as possible in his or her own transmission and expects noise to be present when the message is received. As has been pointed out, this noise can be offset through increased redundancy. The art of the right balance between entropy and redundancy is much of what makes a good editor—striking a balance between predictability and uncertainty. This, in turn, becomes a function of how an editor defines what an audience wants, what it can absorb, and what the editor feels it should have, all, of course, within the limits or constraints of the medium used to communicate.

When *rates of transmission* are at less than channel capacity, noise can be reduced to any desired level through improved coding of the message. However, if the rate of transmission of information exceeds channel capacity, noise cannot be reduced below the amount by which the rate of transmission exceeds channel capacity. In most communication situations, the capacity of the individual to process information is the limiting factor. If the channel is overloaded, error increases dramatically. A major decision for any communicator when encoding a message becomes that of finding the optimum level of redundancy.

Information Theory and the Digital Future

Information theory forms the basis, of course, for modern electronic computers and the transfer of information by the Internet. Nicholas Negroponte (1995), founder of the famous Media Lab at the Massachusetts Institute of Technology, argues that we still value things in terms of their material worth (atoms), rather than their information worth (bits). He says being digital will cause our copyright laws to be rewritten because we will be shipping information around far more than shipping around physical objects. This, according to Negroponte, will flatten organizations, globalize society, decentralize control, and harmonize people. He predicts that nation-states may go away, overly hierarchical and status-conscious societies will erode, and people will compete with imagination rather than rank. Huge communication corporations will no longer be needed for delivery of information because do-it-yourself publishing is now possible on the Internet.

INFORMATION THEORY APPLIED

Any human communication consists of a series of systems coupled into chains. A *system* is defined as any part of an information chain that is capable of existing in one or more states or in which one or more events can occur (Schramm,

1955, p. 132). A communication system can be the telephone wire, the air, or a human optic nerve. Systems include the channels of information but also include sources, transmitters, receivers, and destinations. Systems must be coupled with one another in order to transfer information, and the state of any system depends on the state of the system adjoining it. If the coupling is broken, information is not transferred (e.g., when a student's attention wanders while reading an assignment).

Human communication contains many coupled systems. This coupling or "interface" between two systems is a gatekeeper point. A gatekeeper determines what information is passed along the chain and how faithfully it is reproduced. This principle applies to reporters, photographers, editors, commentators, and all others who decide what information to use in the media from the vast array of information available. How much do they filter out? How much emphasis is changed? How much distortion is there, both systematic distortion through bias and random distortion through ignorance or carelessness? A newspaper or a broadcasting station is a gatekeeper, deciding what to present to its audience. It must select from all of the local, state, national, and international news available. The human destination (reader, viewer, or listener) also acts as a gatekeeper by selecting and interpreting material according to his or her own individual needs.

Human communication systems, however, are *functional systems*, as opposed to Shannon's structural system—that is, they can learn. When we say that the human central nervous system is a functional system because it is capable of learning, we mean that its present state depends on its own past operation. As Schramm (1955) pointed out very early, the mathematical formulas of information theory are based on probabilities, and learning alters those probabilities (p. 132). This prevents the direct application of Shannon's mathematical theory to human communication.

Communication systems may be corresponding or noncorresponding. *Corresponding systems* can exist in identical states. The telegraph transmitter or key and the telegraph receiver or magneto coil accept and repeat the same series of dots and dashes (minus any noise introduced in transmission). *Noncorresponding systems* cannot exist in identical states. For example, the information given the telegraph operator does not correspond to the message transmitted, nor is the message transmitted identical to the current on the wire or the radiation transmitted through the air in the case of radiotelegraphy.

In information theory terms, communication takes place "when two corresponding systems, coupled together through one or more noncorresponding systems, assume identical states as a result of signal transfer along a chain" (Schramm, 1955, p. 132). In human communication we have very long chains (e.g., foreign reporting). The material of a reporter or photographer on the scene in the Middle East or Asia passes through a great many gatekeepers before it is offered to a potential audience member in the United States. At each step it can be edited, discarded, distorted, reorganized, or changed.

The mass media are usually characterized by a relatively high output compared with a low input; or to state it differently, the mass media are *high amplifiers*—relatively few people produce the news, entertainment, advertising, and public relations that are seen, heard, or read by millions. This is simply another aspect of the industrial revolution whereby, through the application of modern technology, a relatively small number of workers in an industry produce commodities for a much larger number of consumers. This reflects the application of corporate and industrial economic efficiency in creating and distributing the commodity called "information."

The mass media themselves are made up of groups of people, and as with any group, *communication networks* must be established and maintained if a group is to function. Communication networks are equally important in all groups in society as well as in electronic and mechanical communications. Schramm (1955) cites a number of measures derived from information theory that suggest new ways of studying communication activity in small groups (p. 143). Some of them are: *traffic,* or who does most of the talking and how much talking is done; *closure,* or how open is the group to outsiders and ideas from the outside; and *congruence*, the question of whether members are equal participants in group communication or whether some are primarily originators of communications while others are primarily recipients.

Information Theory Applied to Readability

A direct and practical application of information theory's concepts of entropy and redundancy to message content is the *cloze procedure*, developed by Wilson Taylor in 1953. This procedure (examined in greater detail in Chapter 7) provides us with a useful way of estimating the entropy or redundancy of a passage of writing for a given audience. Taylor's procedure deletes every nth word in a passage and then asks readers to supply the missing word. The frequency with which words are provided for the various deletions and the number of different words provided for a particular deletion indicate the predictability of the passage for a given audience or for one individual. Here the concepts of entropy and redundancy in messages are put to work to measure a specific audience's familiarity with a specific content and also the difficulty of the level of writing for a specific audience.

Paisley (1966) demonstrated how the measurement of entropy can be used to determine the authorship of various samples of English prose and verse. He used letter redundancy to identify numerous biblical and classical passages that varied in topic, time of composition, structure, and authorship.

In a series of studies (Krull, Watt, & Lichty, 1977; Watt & Welch, 1982), information theory has been applied to measure television program complexity as related to viewer preferences. One finding was that static complexity has a negative impact on visual attention but dynamic complexity is positively related to attention.

Successful Application of Information Theory

Finn and Roberts (1984) have argued that few researchers have used Shannon's concepts in their research because of a failure to distinguish between two fundamental orientations in Shannon's theory: the relationship between source and destination and the technical characteristics of transmission channels.

These researchers say that communication researchers have had success applying information theory to their problems when they

> have been sensitive to Shannon's entropy formula as a probabilistic measure of information and his realization that communication requires that source and destination be intimately linked by a shared set of messages . . . the assumed linear flow of the diagram obscures what we believe is Shannon's most fundamental notion—that the communication process presumes the existence of a set of messages shared by both information source and destination prior to signal transmission. (1984, pp. 454-455)

Finn and Roberts argue that

> Shannon's conceptualization suggests a reorientation of our approach to such perennial concerns of communication research as selective perception and message comprehension. The focus of such research may need to shift from such topics as channel characteristics and noise in the system to more basic questions regarding the initial degree of correspondence between message sets held by the source and the destination. (p. 460)

Shannon's entropy measure can be applied beyond the technical problems of signal transmission. It makes possible the analysis of categorical (nominal) data as continuous data, which allows the use of more sophisticated and powerful quantitative statistical methods (McMillan, 1953, p. 17; as cited in Finn & Roberts, 1984, p. 459).

One researcher (Ritchie, 1986) raises serious questions about Weaver's interpretation of Shannon's mathematical theory and the way the model has been applied in three decades of communication research. Ritchie concludes that

> Shannon's . . . theorems may serve as the basis for theorizing in our own field in three different ways. First, where our problems can be broken down into subproblems, and where any of these subproblems satisfy the assumptions of Shannon's theorems, the theorems can be applied straightforwardly. Second, where our problems resemble Shannon's transmission problems, but do not seem to satisfy his assumptions, we might strive to develop a theory somewhat parallel to Shannon's theorems, but based on a set of assumptions that we can

justify with our own data. Third, we can consider how Shannon's assumptions might apply to our field, taking the assumptions themselves as problematic, and develop a line of inquiry based on exploring the hypotheses suggested by Shannon's assumptions. (p. 295)

OSGOOD'S MODEL

Osgood (1954) contended that the technical communication model of Shannon and Weaver, developed for application to engineering problems, was never intended for human communication. His own model is developed from his theory of meaning and from psycholinguistic processes in general.

Osgood provides for both the sending and receiving functions within one individual, and he takes into account the "meaning" of symbols. (We have seen that the Shannon and Weaver model specifically excludes meaning from the definition of information.) The Shannon and Weaver model implies separate sources, destinations, transmitters, and receivers. While this is usually true of mechanical systems, it is not true of human communication systems. An individual functions as both a source and a destination, as both a transmitter and a receiver by decoding the messages he or she encodes through a number of feedback mechanisms.

In this model the "input" is some form of physical energy or a "stimulus" coded in a form that is converted (decoded) to sensory impulses.

In Osgood's view, each person in a "speech community" is viewed as a complete communicating system corresponding to the Shannon and Weaver model. Osgood has rearranged the Shannon model into what he calls a "communications unit" to send and receive messages.

Osgood stresses the social nature of communication and says:

Any adequate model must therefore include at least two communicating units, a source unit (speaker) and a destination unit (hearer). Between any two such units, connecting them into a single system, is what we may call the message. For purposes of this report, we will define the message as that part of the total output (responses) of a source unit which simultaneously may be a part of the total input (stimuli) to a destination unit. When individual A talks to individual B, for example, his postures, gestures, facial expressions and even manipulations with objects (e.g., laying down a playing card, pushing a bowl of food within reach) may all be part of the message, as of course are events in the sound wave channel. But other parts of A's total behavior (e.g., sensations from B's own posture, cues from the remainder of the environment) do not derive from A's behavior—these events are not part of the message as we use the term. These R-S message events (reaction of one individual that produces stimuli for another) may be either immediate or mediate—ordinary face-to-face conversation illustrates the former and written communication (along with musical recordings, art objects, and so forth) illustrates the latter. (1954, pp. 2-3)

THE SCHRAMM MODELS

Schramm does not make the sharp distinction that Shannon and Osgood make between technical and nontechnical communication, but he does acknowledge that many of his ideas are inspired by Osgood.

In an early series of models, Schramm (1954) proceeded from a simple human communication model to a more complicated model that accounted for the accumulated experiences of two individuals trying to communicate and then to a model that considered human communication with interaction between two individuals (Figure 3.2). The first model bears a striking similarity to that of

FIGURE 3.2   Three of the Schramm models

SOURCE: From W. Schramm, "How Communication Works," Chapter 1 in W. Schramm (ed.), *The Process and Effects of Mass Communication* (Urbana: University of Illinois Press, 1954). Copyright © 1954 by the University of Illinois. Reprinted with the permission of the University Illinois Press.

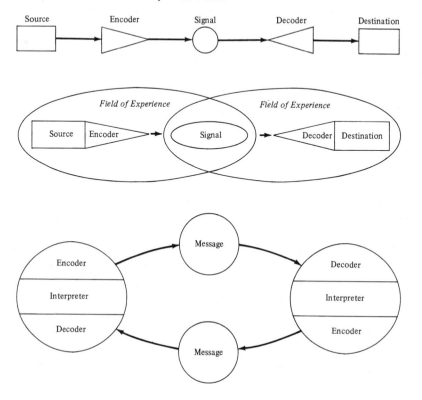

Shannon. In the second model Schramm introduces the notion that only what is shared in the fields of experience of both the source and the destination is actually communicated, because only that portion of the signal is held in common by both source and destination.

The third model deals with communication as an interaction with both parties encoding, interpreting, decoding, transmitting, and receiving signals. Here we see feedback and the continuous "loop" of shared information.

NEWCOMB'S SYMMETRY MODEL

Theodore Newcomb's (1953) approach to communication is that of a social psychologist concerned with interaction between human beings. His model (Figure 3.3) is reminiscent of the diagrams of group networks made by social psychologists and is one of the early formulations of cognitive consistency.

In its simplest form of the communication act, a person, A, transmits information to another person, B, about something, X. The model assumes that A's orientation (attitude) toward B and toward X are interdependent, and the three constitute a system comprising four orientations (pp. 393–394):

1. A's orientation toward X, including both attitude toward X as an object to be approached or avoided (characterized by sign and intensity) and cognitive attributes (beliefs and cognitive structuring)
2. A's orientation toward B, in exactly the same sense (For purposes of avoiding confusing terms, Newcomb speaks of positive and negative attraction toward A or B as persons and of favorable and unfavorable attitudes toward X.)
3. B's orientation toward X
4. B's orientation toward A

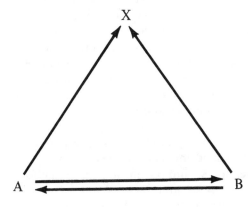

FIGURE 3.3 The basic Newcomb A – B – X model

SOURCE: From T. M. Newcomb, "An Approach to the Study of Cummunicative Acts," *Psychological Review* 60 (1953): 393. Copyright © 1953 by the American Psychological Association. Reprinted with the permission of the American Psychological Association.

In the Newcomb model, communication is the common and effective way in which individuals orient themselves to their environment. This is a model for intentional, two-person communicative acts. Newcomb derives the following postulates from his model:

1. The stronger the forces toward A's coorientation with respect to B and X, (a) the greater A's strain toward symmetry with B with respect to X and (b) the greater the likelihood of increased symmetry as a consequence of one or more communicative acts. (p. 395)
2. The less the attraction between A and B, the more nearly strain toward symmetry is limited to the particular Xs toward which coorientation is required by conditions of association. (p. 399)

Newcomb's model implies that any given system may be characterized by a balance of forces and that any change in any part of the system will lead to a strain toward balance or symmetry, because imbalance or lack of symmetry is psychologically uncomfortable and generates internal pressure to restore balance.

Symmetry has the advantage of a person (A) being readily able to calculate the behavior of another person (B). Symmetry also validates one's own orientation toward X. This is another way of saying we have social and psychological support for the orientations we hold. When Bs we hold in esteem share our evaluations of Xs, we tend to be more confident of our orientations. It follows that we communicate with individuals we hold in esteem about objects, events, people, and ideas (Xs) that are important to us to try to reach consensus or coorientation or, in Newcomb's term, symmetry. Asymmetry is also included in Newcomb's model when people "agree to disagree."

THE WESTLEY-MACLEAN MODEL

Westley and MacLean, in the process of reviewing and classifying research in journalism and mass communications, felt the need for a different model (Westley, 1976). Because of their interest in news they realized that the communication process can be started by an event as well as by an individual. The linear and noninteractive nature of both Shannon's and Lasswell's models were also sources of concern. Although neither of these models was satisfactory for their purposes, they do acknowledge the influence both had on their own model.

Westley had been influenced by the Newcomb model while a student of Newcomb at Michigan. Newcomb's model provided a starting point for the Westley-MacLean (1957) model of the mass communication process. Westley and MacLean took the Newcomb model, added an infinite number of events, ideas, objects, and people (Xs from X1 through Xa), which are "objects of orientation," placed a C role between A and B, and provided for feedback (Figure 3.4).

The Westley-MacLean model provides for As and Xs outside the immediate sensory field of B. The new role, C, allows these additional As and Xs to contribute to B's orientation of the environment. The C role has three functions:

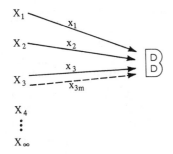

(a) Objects of orientation ($X_1 \ldots X_\infty$) in the sensory field of the receiver (B) are transmitted directly to him in abstracted form ($x_1' \ldots x_3'$) after a process of selection from among all Xs, such selection being based at least in part on the needs and problems of B. Some or all are transmitted in more than one sense (x_{3m}', for example).

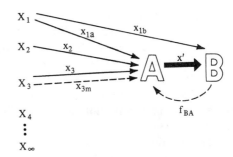

(b) The same Xs are selected and abstracted by communicator (A) and transmitted as a message (x') to B, who may or may not have part or all of the Xs in his own sensory field (X_{1b}). Either purposively or nonpurposively, B transmits feedback (f_{BA}) to A.

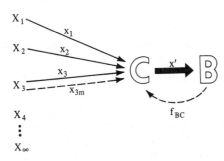

(c) What x'_s B receives may be owing to selected abstractions transmitted by a nonpurposive encoder (C), acting for B and thus extending B's environment. C's selections are necessarily based in part on feedback (f_{BC}) from B.

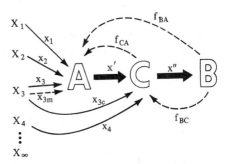

(d) The messages C transmits to B (x'') represent his selections from both messages to him from As (x') and C's selections and abstractions from Xs in his own sensory field (x_{3c}, x_4), which may or may not be Xs in A's field. Feedback not only moves from B to A (f_{BA}) and from B to C (f_{BC}) but also from C to A (f_{CA}). Clearly, in the mass communication situation, a large number of Cs receive from a very large number of As and transmit to a vastly larger number of Bs, who simultaneously receive from other Cs.

FIGURE 3.4 Steps in the progression of the Westley-MacLean model

SOURCE: From B. H. Westley and M. MacLean, "A Conceptual Model for Communication Research," *Journalism Quarterly* 34 (1957): 35–38. Reprinted with the permission of The Association for Education in Journalism and Mass Communication.

1. To select the abstractions of object X appropriate to B's need satisfactions or problem solutions
2. To transform them into some form of symbol containing meanings shared with B
3. To transmit such symbols by means of some channel or medium to B.

Westley and MacLean acknowledge their indebtedness to Newcomb for his emphasis on the shared symbol system.

In effect, C observes, selects, encodes, and transmits a limited portion of Xs to fulfill B's information needs. This is the "gatekeeper" role played by the media. In this model B can be a person, a group, or an entire social system.

Unlike the Newcomb model, in the Westley-MacLean model messages can be purposive (with the intent of modifying B's perception of X) or nonpurposive (without any intent on the part of the communicator to influence B). Feedback can also be purposive (e.g., a letter or call to the editor) or nonpurposive (e.g., a purchase or a subscription that becomes a part of a statistic that indicates the effect of a commercial or liking for a publication).

In the Westley-MacLean model, roles become advocacy roles ("the communicator") and can be a personality or a social system that selects and transmits messages purposively.

Bs (behavioral system roles, to use the authors' term) are what is usually meant by the "destination" or the "public." These are individuals, groups, or social systems that need and use information about their environment to help satisfy needs and help solve problems.

Cs (channel roles) serve as agents of Bs by selecting and transmitting nonpurposively the information Bs need, especially information that is not readily available to Bs.

Xs are the objects and events "out there," in message form (abstractions of X in a form that can be transmitted).

Channels are the means by which Xs (messages) are transmitted through As to Bs. Channels include C who may alter messages (acting as "gatekeepers").

Encoding is the process by which As and Cs abstract from Xs the messages (X') transmitted in channels. Decoding takes place when Bs receive the message and interiorize it.

Feedback provides As and Cs with information about the effect of their messages on Bs.

Westley and MacLean took the Newcomb model and extended it to include mass communication. For this reason, we shall return to this model in our summary chapter as a means of organizing the contents of this book.

THE GERBNER MODEL

Gerbner (1956) elaborated on Lasswell's model and provided a verbal model that implies 10 basic areas of communication research (see also Figure 3.5):

Verbal Model	*Areas of Study*
1. Someone	Communicator and audience research
2. perceives an event	Perception research and theory
3. and reacts	Effectiveness measurement
4. in a situation	Study of physical and social setting

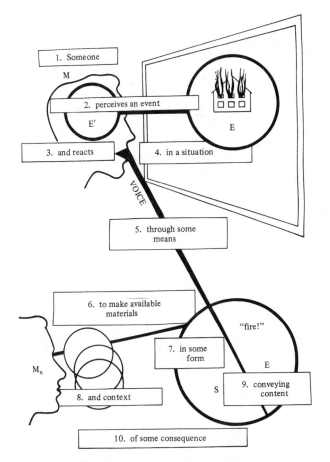

FIGURE 3.5 Steps in the construction of the graphic model

SOURCE: From G. Gerbner, "Toward A General Model of Communication," *AV Communication Review* 4 (1956): 175. Reprinted with permission of the Association for Educational Communications and Technology, 1126 16th St., NW., Washington, D.C. 20036.

5. through some means	Investigation of channels, media, controls over facilities
6. to make available materials	Administration; distribution; freedom of access to materials
7. in some form	Structure, organization, style, pattern
8. and context	Study of communicative setting, sequence
9. conveying content	Content analysis, study of meaning
10. of some consequence	Study of overall changes

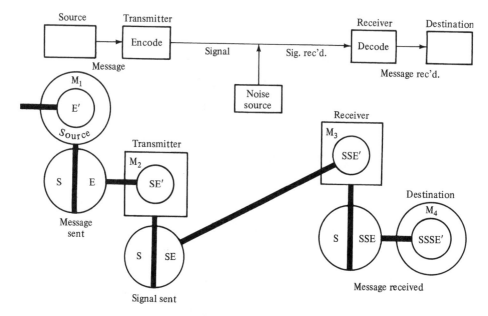

FIGURE 3.6 Shannon's diagram of a general communication system compared with the progress of a signal in the same system as illustrated on Gerbner's graphic model

SOURCE: From G. Gerbner, "Toward A General Model of Communication," *AV Communication Review* 4 (1956): 175. Reprinted with permission of the Association for Educational Communications and Technology, 1126 16th St., NW., Washington, D.C. 20036.

These 10 aspects represent shifts in emphasis only, rather than tight compartments for the study of communication.

Gerbner also provides a pictorial model (Figure 3.5), which he discussed in detail. Gerbner's model appears to be an extension of the Lasswell model, but Gerbner includes a comparison with the Shannon model (Figure 3.6). Once again we see the influence of Shannon.

A SCHEMA THEORY OF INFORMATION PROCESSING

Robert Axelrod (1973) provides a model (Figure 3.7) for what he calls a schema theory of information processing.

Doris A. Graber, in her excellent book *Processing the News*, explains the Axelrod model this way:[*]

> First comes reception of the message. Next, the integration process starts the series of questions to determine whether and how the new

---

[*] From Doris A. Graber, *Processing the News: How People Tame the Information Tide,* pp. 125–127. White Plains, NY: Longman, 1984. Copyright © 1984 by Longman. Reprinted with permission.

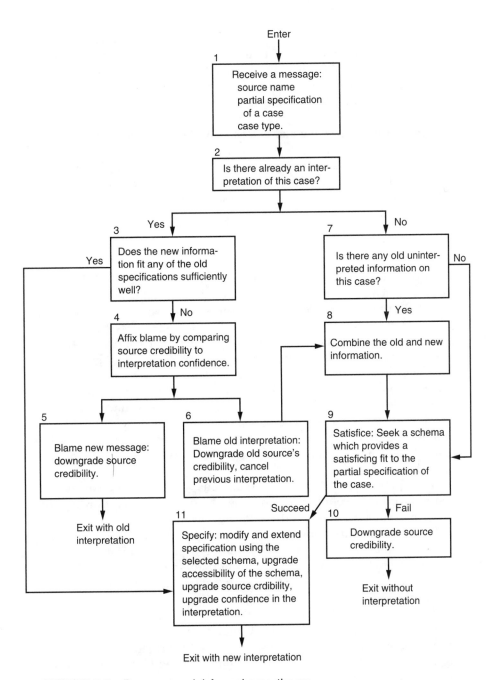

Enter

1
Receive a message:
source name
partial specification
of a case
case type.

2
Is there already an interpretation of this case?

Yes

3
Does the new informa-
tion fit any of the old
specifications sufficiently
well?

Yes

No

7
Is there any old uninter-
preted information on
this case?

No

4
Affix blame by comparing
source credibility to
interpretation confidence.

No

Yes

8
Combine the old and new
information.

5
Blame new message:
downgrade source
credibility.

6
Blame old interpretation:
Downgrade old source's
credibility, cancel
previous interpretation.

9
Satisfice: Seek a schema
which provides a
satisficing fit to the
partial specification of
the case.

Exit with old
interpretation

Succeed

Fail

11
Specify: modify and extend
specification using the
selected schema, upgrade
accessibility of the schema,
upgrade source crdibility,
upgrade confidence in the
interpretation.

10
Downgrade source
credibility.

Exit without
interpretation

Exit with new interpretation

FIGURE 3.7 Process model for schema theory

SOURCE: From Robert Axelrod, "Schema Theory: An Information Processing Model of Perception and Cognition," *American Political Science Review*, vol. 67, Spring 1973, p. 1251. Copyright © 1973 the American Political Science Association. Reprinted with permission of the
American Political Science Association.

information relates to stored concepts and whether it is worth processing. Does it cover a topic about which the receiver already has information? Is it a familiar or predictable consequence of familiar knowledge? Does it make sense in light of past experience? Does it convincingly contradict past experience? Is it worth considering? Is it unduly redundant? If answers to such questions indicate that the information is worthwhile and is reasonably well related to established thought schemas that can be readily brought to mind, it is integrated into them. If not, the new information or its source, may be discredited or rejected or the new information may alter or replace the previous schema that has been called into question. (1984, p. 125)

She adds:

In the process of integration, information becomes substantially transformed to make it a plausible complement to existing knowledge. Some aspects of the story are leveled and others are sharpened. Through this encoding process, elements of the story that seem essential to the perceiver are separated from non-essential details. (p. 125)

Stories always lose detail and become more abstract during processing.

During processing, information may acquire distinct slants that may make it more or less accurate. People are apt to distill information into true or false meanings and inferences and store only the distillation. Specific episodes usually become part of general concepts, with or without the loss of memory for the specific incident. This is especially true when many incidents resemble each other, as happens with routine political events.

This type of processing is a parsimonious way of dealing with information overloads. People want to know the gist of a story; they do not want to memorize it. Since the ultimate purpose of most information gathering is the extraction of meaning, so that the significance of the story becomes apparent, it makes sense to process information for meaning right away. This saves the trouble of storing details and background information. But the price that is paid is vagueness of memories, inability to recall details, and inability to separate various incidents.

The fact that people tend to store conclusions drawn from evidence, rather than the evidence itself, explains why they are frequently unable to give reasons for their opinions. They may, for example, say that they agree with the views of a particular politician without being able to give a single example of shared views. Consequently, social scientists have often erroneously concluded that the opinions were unfounded. In fact, these opinions may rest on careful earlier deliberations that have been long forgotten. (p. 127)

CONCLUSIONS

Shannon's mathematical theory of communication, or, perhaps more accurately, signal transmission, is the most important single contribution to the communication models in use today. It not only has stimulated much of the later thinking in this area, but his schematic diagram of the communication process has also been the impetus for many subsequent diagrams of communication models.

Shannon provides a concept of information as entropy or uncertainty. Messages are composed of entropy and redundancy; the latter can be used to offset noise that may enter the channel during transmission. The theory is very general in its scope, treats fundamental problems, and attains results with a classic simplicity and power.

As we have seen, this concept of information, which has nothing to do with meaning, is not only not disappointing but is highly fruitful in the paths it leads to. On close inspection, a concept of information that is identified with uncertainty is hardly bizarre.

If we evaluate information theory according to the criteria given we find that it does allow one to organize, order, and relate data and shows similarities and connections that had previously not been perceived. It implies predictions that can be verified with physical tests. It has been heuristic in that it has led to new, unknown facts and methods. It provides formulas for the measurement of phenomena of central interest to communication researchers.

Information theory is general enough to organize a great deal of material, much of which is strategic or central to the concerns of communication researchers. It is a model of simplicity or parsimony, yet it is highly original and provides many new insights.

The student who wishes to examine the theory more fully, especially its mathematical bases, is directed to the end-of-chapter references.

In addition to the models discussed in this chapter, there are a number of other models used in communication research and theory building. Several of them will be introduced in other chapters of this book.

As we said earlier, each model emphasizes certain points its creator feels are relevant in the communication process or structure. By selecting certain aspects of communication to be included in a model, the originator of a model implies judgments of relevance, and a theory about the process or structure that is modeled.

No one model can "do it all." Even if it could, it would defeat the purpose of a model—a simplified representation of the real world. Therefore, we select the model that best fits our purposes for the immediate problem at hand. If none is available to do the job required, the researcher might well be forced to modify an existing model or even invent a new one, as we have seen in this chapter.

DISCUSSION

1. How have you in your own mind recently modeled some process or structure?
2. What is a model?
3. How does a model differ from a theory?
4. In what way does a model imply judgments of relevance?
5. Are there any dangers in using models?
6. Can a model ever be a total failure? If not, why not?
7. What are some of the functions of a model?
8. How does one evaluate a model?
9. What insights did Claude Shannon give us into the communication process?
10. What do you think of Nicholas Negroponte's predictions for the digital future? Will organizations flatten, society be globalized, control be decentralized, and people live in greater harmony? Will nation-states and overly hierarchical and status-conscious societies disappear? Will people compete with imagination rather than rank? Will huge communication corporations no longer be needed?

REFERENCES

Axelrod, Robert (1973). Schema theory: An information processing model of perception and cognition. *American Political Science Review* 67 (Spring): 1251.

Burks, Arthur W. (1951). The mathematical theory of communication. *The Philosophical Review* 60 (July): 398–400.

Deutsch, K. (1952). On communication models in the social sciences. *Public Opinion Quarterly* 16: 356–380.

Fantel, H. (1989). The advance was digital, and it's just a beginning. *New York Times,* Dec. 31, Sec. 2, p. 28.

Finn, S., and D. Roberts (1984). Source, destination, and entropy: Reassessing the role of information theory in communication research. *Communication Research* 11: 453–476.

Gerbner, G. (1956). Toward a general model of communication. *Audio Visual Communication Review* 4: 171–199.

Graber, Doris (1984). *Processing the news: How people tame the information tide.* New York: Longman.

Krull, R., J. H. Watt, and L. W. Lichty (1977). Entropy and structure: Two measures of complexity in television programs. *Communication Research* 4: 61–86.

Lasswell, H. D. (1948). The structure and function of communication in society. In L. Bryson (ed.), *The Communication of Ideas.* New York: Harper & Bros. Also reprinted in W. Schramm (ed.) (1960), *Mass Communications,* pp. 117–130. Urbana: University of Illinois Press.

McMillan, B. (1953). Mathematical aspects of information theory. In B. McMillan et al. (eds.), *Current Trends in Information Theory,* pp. 1–18. Pittsburgh: University of Pittsburgh Press.

Negroponte, Nicholas (1995). *Being Digital*. New York: Knopf.

Newcomb, T. M. (1953). An approach to the study of communicative acts. *Psychological Review* 60: 393-404.

Osgood, C. E. (ed.) (1954). Psycholinguistics: A survey of theory and research problems. *Journal of Abnormal and Social Psychology* 49 (Oct.). Morton Prince Memorial Supplement.

Paisley, W. J. (1966). The effects of authorship, topic, structure, and time of composition on letter redundancy in English texts. *Journal of Verbal Learning and Verbal Behavior* 5: 28-34.

Pollack, A. (1990). 2 stereo makers promise digital tape in 1990. *New York Times,* Jan. 8, pp. 1, 25.

Ritchie, D. (1986). Shannon and Weaver: Unravelling the paradox of information. *Communication Research* 13: 278-298.

Schramm, W. (ed.) (1954). How communication works. In *The Process and Effects of Mass Communication,* Ch. 1. Urbana: University of Illinois Press. Also in rev. ed., 1971, W. Schramm and D. Roberts (eds.).

Schramm, W. (1955). Information theory and mass communication. *Journalism Quarterly* 32: 131-146. Also in B. Berelson and M. Janowitz (eds.) (1953), *Reader in Public Opinion and Communication,* 2nd ed. New York: Free Press. Also in A. Smith (ed.) (1966), *Communication and Culture*. New York: Holt, Rinehart and Winston.

Shannon, C., and W. Weaver (1949). *The Mathematical Theory of Communication.* Urbana: University of Illinois Press.

Taylor, W. (1953). Cloze procedure: A new tool for measuring readability. *Journalism Quarterly* 30: 415-433.

Watt, J. H., and A. Welch (1982). Visual complexity and young children's learning from television. *Human Communication Research* 8: 133-145.

Weaver, W. (1949). Recent contributions to the mathematical theory of communication. In C. E. Shannon and W. Weaver, *The Mathematical Theory of Communication,* pp. 95-117. Urbana: University of Illinois Press.

Westley, B. H. (1976). MacLean and I and "The Model." In L. Manca (ed.), *Journal of Communication Inquiry* (Spring): 26-34. Essays in Honor of Malcolm S. MacLean, Jr.

Westley, B. H., and M. MacLean (1957). A conceptual model for communication research. *Journalism Quarterly* 34: 31-38.

Wiener, N. (1948). *Cybernetics*. New York: John Wiley.

part III

Perception and Language Issues in the Mass Media

$\mathbf{V}$iewing communication from the point of view of the receiver—the person who is exposed to countless messages—raises some important questions regarding how individuals receive and process messages, how they assign meaning to those messages, and what kinds of factors can increase or decrease understanding.

The starting point for the processing of messages is the individual act of perception. Chapter 4 discusses scientific research on the process of perception and relates it to the act of communication.

Messages are often, although not always, encoded in language. Chapter 5 focuses on what perspective the area of general semantics provides for the study of encoding and includes some important information on the ways language can be used and misused in the process of communication.

Messages can be put together with different strategies, and some of these are basic and well known. Among the strategies for message creation are the propaganda devices identified in the 1930s by the Institute for Propaganda Analysis. These devices, which are still relevant to communication in the 1990s, are discussed in Chapter 6. Analysis of propaganda led to early theories of how we are affected by mass communication.

Clarity and ease of communication are goals that are shared by both sources and receivers of communication. We know that some pieces of writing are easy to understand and others are difficult. Some of the factors most related to the readability of writing for various media have been identified by research, and these are discussed in Chapter 7.

chapter 4

The Role of Perception in Communication

How do people make sense of the words and images they get in messages? Scientific research on perception and information processing can help us answer this question.

Mass communicators want audiences to pay attention to their messages, learn the contents of the messages, and make appropriate changes in attitudes or beliefs or make desired behavioral responses. Perceptual theory tells us that the process of interpreting messages is complex and that these communicator goals may be difficult to achieve.

Perception has been defined as the process by which we interpret sensory data (Lahlry, 1991). Sensory data come to us through our five senses. Research has identified two types of influences on our perception: structural and functional.

Structural influences on perception come from the physical aspects of the stimuli to which we are being exposed—for instance, the closer together a series of dots, the more they are seen as forming a line. Functional influences are the psychological factors that influence perception, and therefore, introduce some subjectivity into the process.

Selective perception is the term applied to the tendency for people's perception to be influenced by wants, needs, attitudes, and other psychological factors. Selective perception plays an important role in communication of any sort. Selective perception means that different people can react to the same message in very different ways. No communicator can assume that a message will have the intended meaning for all receivers or even that it will have the same meaning for all receivers. This complicates our models of mass communication. Perhaps mass communication is not just a matter of hitting a target with an arrow, as some models suggest. The message can reach the receiver (hit the target) and still fail to accomplish its purpose because it is subject to the interpretation of the receiver.

The process of receiving and interpreting a message is referred to in many communication models as *decoding*. The process involves perception, or the taking in of stimuli through the senses and the subsequent processing of that information. Before we consider the operation of perception in the decoding of a mass communication message, we will discuss some of the research findings about perception in general.

Modern psychology has shown perception to be a complex process, rather different from the naïve view that many people held a century ago. The old view—which we might refer to as the commonsense view—saw human perception as largely a physical or mechanical process. The human eye and the other sense organs were thought to work much like a camera or a tape recorder. This view of perception held that there was a quite direct correspondence between an "external reality" and a person's perception, or what was in the mind. This view would hold that everybody perceives the world in essentially the same way.

Psychologists have found perception to be a more elaborate process than that. One definition (Berelson & Steiner, 1964) states that perception is the "complex process by which people select, organize, and interpret sensory stimulation into a meaningful and coherent picture of the world" (p. 88). Bennett, Hoffman, and Prakash state that "perception is notably active: It involves learning, updating perspective, and interacting with the observed" (1989, p. 3). Scott states that "seeing is a learned behavior that involves cognitive activity" (1994, p. 260). Perception also involves making inferences (Bennett, Hoffman, & Prakash, 1989). In the typical act of perception, a stimulus is assigned to a certain category on the basis of information that is incomplete. As a result, these inferences are not always valid.

INFLUENCES ON PERCEPTION

As we have noted, perception is influenced by a number of psychological factors, including assumptions based on past experiences (that often operate at an almost unconscious level), cultural expectations, motivation (needs), moods, and attitudes. A number of experiments have demonstrated the effects of these factors on perception.

Assumptions and Perception

Much of the research showing that perception is influenced by assumptions has come from a group of researchers working at one time or another at Princeton University. These researchers, who have included Adelbert Ames, Jr., Hadley Cantril, Edward Engels, Albert Hastorf, William H. Ittelson, Franklin P. Kilpatrick, and Hans Toch, have presented what has been called the *transactional view* of perception. The concept is abstract and somewhat philosophical, but essentially it means that both the perceiver and the world are active participants in an act of perception (Toch & MacLean, 1962).

The transactional thinkers have developed a number of convincing demonstrations that perception is based on assumptions. One of the most striking, invented by Adelbert Ames, Jr., is called the *monocular distorted room.* This room is constructed so that the rear wall is a trapezoid, with the vertical distance up and down the left edge of the wall longer than the vertical distance up and down the right edge of the wall. The rear wall is positioned at an angle so that the left edge is farther back than the right edge. This angle is carefully selected so that the room will appear to be an ordinary rectangular room to an observer looking through a small hole at the front of the room. If two people walk into the room and stand in the rear corners, something interesting happens. The one on the right appears to a viewer looking through the hole to be very large because he or she is closer to the viewer and fills most of the distance from the floor to the ceiling. The one on the left appears to be very small because he or she is farther away and fills less of the distance from the floor to the ceiling. This illusion occurs because the mind of the viewer is assuming that the rear wall is parallel to the front wall of the room. This assumption is based on prior experience with other rooms that looked similar. The illusion is so strong that if the two people in the corners switch places, one will appear to grow larger and the other will appear to get smaller, right before the viewer's eye.

Cultural Expectations and Perception

Some of the most striking evidence for the influence of cultural expectations on perception comes from research on binocular rivalry (Bagby, 1957). It is possible to construct a device that has two eyepieces like a pair of binoculars, but can be used to present a different picture to each eye. When this is done, people seldom see both pictures. They more often see one picture and not the other or one picture and then the other. Sometimes they see a mixture of some elements of each picture, but this usually occurs after seeing one picture alone first. Bagby used this instrument to investigate the effect of cultural background on perception.

Subjects were 12 Americans (6 males and 6 females) and 12 Mexicans (6 males and 6 females). Except for one matched pair made up of a person from each country, the subjects had not traveled outside their own country. Bagby prepared ten pairs of photographic slides, each pair containing a picture from the American culture and a picture from the Mexican culture. One pair, for instance, showed a baseball scene and a bullfight scene. Subjects were exposed to each slide for 60 seconds and asked to describe what they saw. The assignment of the Mexican or the American picture to the left or right eye was randomized to eliminate the effect of eye dominance. The first 15 seconds of viewing for each slide were scored for which scene was dominant—the Mexican or

TABLE 4.1 Perceptual predominance in 10 pairs of pictures for Mexican and American subjects

	Trials Where Mexicans Dominated	Trials Where Americans Dominated	Total Number of Trials
Mexican males (6)	44	16	60
Mexican females (6)	45	15	60
American males (6)	7	53	60
American females (6)	12	48	60

SOURCE: From J. W. Baby, "A Cross-cultural Study of Perceptual Predominance in Binocular Rivalry," *Journal of Abnormal and Social Psychology* 54 (1957): 333. Copyright © 1957 by the American Psychological Association. Reprinted by permission.

the American. Dominance was determined by the scene that was reported first or was reported as showing up for the longest period of time. The results (Table 4.1) indicate a strong tendency for subjects to see the scenes from their own culture rather than the scenes from an unfamiliar culture.

Motivation and Perception

One of a number of experiments that shows the effect of motivation on perception was done by McClelland and Atkinson (1948). The type of motivation being investigated was hunger. Subjects were Navy men waiting for admission to a submarine training school. One group had gone 16 hours without food, a second 4 hours without food, and the third 1 hour without food. All subjects were told they were participating in a test of their ability to respond to visual stimulation at very low levels. The men went through 12 trials in which a picture was supposedly projected, but actually nothing was projected at all. To make this realistic, during the instructions they were shown a picture of a car and then the illumination was turned down until the car was only faintly visible. In some of the trials subjects were given clues such as: "Three objects on a table. What are they?"

The results (Table 4.2) showed that the frequency of food-related responses increased reliably as the hours of food deprivation increased. Furthermore, in another phase of the experiment food-related objects were judged larger than neutral objects by hungry subjects but not by subjects who had recently eaten.

Mood and Perception

An experiment using hypnosis demonstrated that mood has an effect on perception. Leuba and Lucas (1945) hypnotized subjects, suggested to them that they were experiencing a certain mood, and then asked them to tell what they saw

TABLE 4.2 Food-related responses

Hours of Food Deprivation	Mean Number of Food-Related Responses (maximum: 14)
1	2.14
4	2.88
16	3.22

SOURCE: Adapted from D. C. McClelland and J. W. Atkinson, "The Projective Expression of Needs: I. The Effect of Different Intensities of the Hunger Drive on Perception" *Journal of Psychology* 25 (1948): 212. Preprinted with permission of the Helen Dwight Reid Educational Foundation. Published by Heldref Publications, 4000 Albemarle St. N.W., Washington, D.C. 20016. Copyright © 1975.

in a picture. Each subject was put in a happy mood and then shown six pictures. Then the subject was told to forget the pictures and what had been said about them and was put in a critical mood and again shown the same six pictures. Finally, the subject was given the same treatment once more except that the suggested mood was anxious. The descriptions of the pictures were drastically different depending on the mood the person was in. They differed not only in the train of thought the pictures suggested but also in the details noticed.

One picture showed some young people digging in a swampy area. Here is one subject's description of that picture while in a happy mood:

It looks like fun; reminds me of summer. That's what life is for; working out in the open, really living—digging in the dirt, planting, watching things grow.

Here is the same subject describing the same picture while in a critical mood:

Pretty horrible land. There ought to be something more useful for kids of that age to do instead of digging in that stuff. It's filthy and dirty and good for nothing.

Here is the same subject describing the same picture while in an anxious mood:

They're going to get hurt or cut. There should be someone older there who knows what to do in case of an accident. I wonder how deep the water is.

Attitude and Perception

The effects of attitude on perception were documented in a study of perception of a football game by Hastorf and Cantrii (1954). The 1951 football clash between Dartmouth and Princeton was an exciting and controversial one. Princeton's star player Dick Kazmaier was taken out of the game in the second quarter with a broken nose. In the third quarter, a Dartmouth player received a broken leg. Discussion of the game continued for weeks, with editorials in the two campus newspapers charging the other school with rough play. Hastorf and Cantril took advantage of this situation to conduct a study in perception. They showed a film of the game to two groups: two fraternities at Dartmouth and two undergraduate clubs at Princeton. Students from both schools saw about the same number of infractions by the Princeton team. But Princeton students saw an average of 9.8 infractions by the Dartmouth team, while Dartmouth students saw an average of 4.3 infractions by the Dartmouth team. That is, the Princeton students saw more than twice as many violations by the Dartmouth team as did the Dartmouth students. Hastorf and Cantril state, "It seems clear that the 'game' actually was many different games and that each version of the events that transpired was just as 'real' to a particular person as other versions were to other people" (p. 132).

PERCEPTION AND MASS COMMUNICATION

So far this discussion of research has shown that perception in general is influenced by assumptions (often unconscious), cultural expectations, needs, moods, and attitudes. The same kinds of forces are at work when people respond to mass communication messages, as the following cases show.

U.S. Army TV Spots

Mass media messages are often misunderstood. Keck and Mueller (1994) conducted a study of U.S. Army television commercials to see whether viewers were perceiving the intended messages, and if not, what messages they were perceiving.

The study focused on two 30-second TV spots. One spot, titled "Dear Dad," was intended to show that Army service builds personal growth, maturation, and character development, and to portray the Army as exciting, adventurous, and challenging. The second spot, titled "Basic Excellence," portrayed basic training as a means to discover one's ability and to overcome personal fears and inhibitions. The target audience for the ads was white males between 18 and 24 years of age.

A group of 396 respondents drawn from the target audience was then shown the spots and asked to fill out a questionnaire. Results showed that some of the intended messages were being perceived by the audience. For instance, 61 percent of the respondents agreed that the activities portrayed in "Basic Excellence" were exciting and challenging. Also, 68 percent agreed that a sense of personal accomplishment could be gained from engaging in the activities highlighted in the spot.

But large percentages also perceived unintended messages. For instance, 39 percent perceived that the drill sergeant was not portrayed realistically in the advertisement. And 66 percent perceived that engaging in the activities portrayed in the commercial would not lead to a good job.

There were also systematic relationships between misperceiving the ads and various characteristics of the audience. For instance, 54 percent of the black respondents felt that the drill sergeant in "Basic Excellence" was accurately portrayed, while only 26 percent of the white respondents and 32 percent of the Hispanic and Asian respondents felt that he was.

In addition, 84 percent of those with no college education thought that "Dear Dad" was a true representation of life in the Army, while only 27 percent of those with some college and 9 percent of the college grads felt that it was.

Antiprejudice Cartoons

Satire is a familiar journalistic device. It has been used in works ranging from Jonathan Swift's *Gulliver's Travels* to Garry Trudeau's "Doonesbury" comic strip. But how is satire perceived?

The American Jewish Committee was interested in studying the effects of satire in reducing prejudice. It sponsored a study by Eunice Cooper and Marie Jahoda (1947) that investigated the effects of antiprejudice cartoons. The cartoons featured an exaggerated figure named "Mr. Biggott," who appeared in situations designed to make prejudice appear ridiculous. For instance, one cartoon showed Mr. Biggott lying in a hospital bed and dying. He is saying to the doctor, "In case I should need a transfusion, doctor, I want to make certain I don't get anything but blue, sixth-generation American blood!" The intention was that people looking at the cartoon would see how ridiculous prejudice is and would lessen their own feelings of prejudice.

Cooper and Jahoda tested the cartoons on 160 white, non-Jewish working-class men. About two-thirds of the sample misunderstood the cartoons. Some said the purpose of the cartoons was to legitimize prejudice. These people explained that the cartoons showed that other people had attitudes of prejudice, so the viewer should feel free to have those attitudes also. The cartoons were most likely to be understood by respondents low in prejudice and most likely to be misunderstood by respondents high in prejudice. Cooper and Jahoda suggested that fear of disapproval by a social group was one of the factors leading to this evasion of propaganda. They argued that accepting the antiprejudice message threatened the individual's security in groups the individual valued.

This study suggests that making fun of prejudice is not an effective way of reducing it. People tend to view satiric cartoons differently, depending on their own attitudes. Both prejudiced and unprejudiced people tended to see elements in the cartoons that confirmed their existing attitudes.

"All in the Family"

When the television program "All in the Family" appeared in 1971, some television critics began immediately to suggest that the program might have a harmful effect of reinforcing bigotry. They pointed out that the main character, Archie Bunker, was portrayed as a "lovable bigot," and that this condoned and perhaps even encouraged bigotry. They also pointed out that the program was teaching racial slurs such as "coon," "chink," and "wop," some of which might have been fading from the American scene at the time.

Producer Norman Lear replied that the program actually reduced prejudice by bringing bigotry out into the open and showing it to be illogical. He said the program showed Archie to be a fool, and that the program was a satire on bigotry. He claimed that the program showed Archie losing at the end to Mike, who made more sense. Carroll O'Connor, the actor who played Archie, also defended the program. He stated in a *Playboy* interview that the effect of the program was to help reduce prejudice. The Los Angeles chapter of the NAACP agreed with this favorable evaluation and gave the program an award in 1972 for its contribution to racial relations.

Neil Vidmar and Milton Rokeach (1974) conducted a study to determine how the program was being perceived by viewers. They conducted surveys of a sample of U.S. adolescents and a sample of Canadian adults. Contrary to the opinion of Lear, neither sample indicated that Archie was the one seen as being made fun of. U.S. adolescents were most likely to pick Mike as the one most often being made fun of, and Canadian adults were most likely to pick Edith as the one most often being made fun of. In another question, respondents were asked whether Archie typically wins or loses at the end of the program. People low in prejudice were most likely to say Archie loses, but people high in prejudice were most likely to say Archie wins. The Vidmar and Rokeach study shows the operation of selective perception in viewing "All in the Family." Viewers high in prejudice and viewers low in prejudice were likely to perceive the program in line with their existing attitudes.

Producer Norman Lear later changed his opinion about the effects of "All in the Family." "To think about what the show might accomplish is to defeat the creative process," Lear has said. "I seriously question what a half-hour situation comedy can accomplish when the entire Judeo-Christian ethic has accomplished so little in the same area (Gross, 1975).

OTHER SELECTIVE PROCESSES

Three other processes that are similar to selective perception sometimes come into play in mass communication. These are selective exposure, selective attention, and selective retention.

Selective exposure is the tendency for individuals to expose themselves to those communications that are in agreement with their existing attitudes and to avoid those communications that are not. The notion of selective exposure follows nicely from Festinger's theory of cognitive dissonance (Chapter 8), which suggests that one way to reduce dissonance after making a decision is to seek out information that is consonant with the decision. Nevertheless, the research findings show that under several conditions people will expose themselves to dissonance-producing materials (see Chapter 8).

However, individuals often cannot judge the message content beforehand. *Selective attention* is the tendency for individuals to pay attention to those parts of a message that are consonant with strongly held attitudes, beliefs, or behaviors and to avoid those parts of a message that go against strongly held attitudes, beliefs, or behaviors (see Chapter 8).

Selective retention is the tendency for the recall of information to be influenced by wants, needs, attitudes, and other psychological factors. Some evidence for selective retention comes from studies of rumor transmission by Allport and Postman (1947), in which they found that details were frequently left out when people passed on stories or descriptions of pictures. In another study supporting selective retention, Jones and Kohler (1958) found that people in favor of segregation learned plausible prosegregation and implausible antisegregation statements more easily than they learned plausible antisegregation and implausible prosegregation statements. The reverse was true for antisegregationists. Both groups learned most easily the information that would be useful in protecting their own attitudinal positions. In a third study supporting selective retention, Levine and Murphy (1958) found that subjects confronted with pro- or anti-Soviet material learned it more slowly and forgot it more quickly when it conflicted with their own attitudes.

The selective processes can be thought of as four rings of defenses, with selective exposure as the outermost ring, followed by selective attention, then selective perception, and finally selective retention. Undesirable information can sometimes be headed off at the outermost ring. A person can avoid those publications or programs that might contain contrary information.

If one expects a mix of information in a message, a person can pay selective attention to only the parts of the message that are agreeable. If this fails, the person can then exercise selective perception in decoding the message. If this fails, the person can then exercise selective retention by simply failing to retain the contrary information.

Sometimes one of these selective mechanisms will be more appropriate or more possible to use than the others. For instance, in watching a televised debate between two presidential candidates, you might not want to practice selective exposure, avoiding the message entirely. If you want to see and hear the candidate you agree with, you may watch only that candidate, practicing selective attention. If you do see and hear the opposition candidate and are exposed to contrary material, you can always fall back on selective perception and hear only what is agreeable, or on selective retention and forget all but the points that reinforce your original point of view.

Earlier reviews of the research relating to selective exposure tended to cast doubt on the validity of the phenomenon (Scars & Freedman, 1967), but later research has found more support for selective exposure. Cotton and Hieser (1980) required subjects opposed to nuclear power plants to write essays that favored locating such plants near populated areas. They manipulated the amount of dissonance by putting some people in a low-choice (low-dissonance) condition and others in a high-choice (high-dissonance) condition. After writing the essays, subjects were given the opportunity to indicate on rating scales how much they would like informational pamphlets dealing with four issues, one of which was nuclear power. The high-choice (high-dissonance) subjects expressed a greater desire for consistent information than did the low-choice (low-dissonance) subjects. They also expressed less desire for inconsistent information than did low-choice subjects. This latter finding of an active avoidance of dissonant information provides stronger support for selective exposure than many early studies were able to do.

Cotton reviewed a number of studies from 1967 to 1983 and concluded that "the later research on selective exposure, generally more carefully controlled, has produced more positive results. Almost every study found significant selective-exposure effects" (1985, p. 25).

MODELS OF INFORMATION PROCESSING

Researchers have come to realize that it is basically impossible to separate the process of perception from the process of information processing. To a certain extent, research that focused on perception has been replaced by research that focuses on cognitive information processing. Human information processing appears to take place in stages, and a number of models have been suggested to identify the key components and stages of the process. Many of these models are based on the workings of the computer. The following paragraph by psychologist John F. Kihlstrom (1987) presents a useful example of an information-processing model:

> The classic information-processing conception of human cognition, modeled after the modern high-speed computer, includes a set of structures for storing information, as well as a set of processes by which information is transferred from one structure to another. In this model, information from the environment, transduced into a pattern of neural impulses by the sensory receptors, is briefly held in the sensory registers, one for each modality. Information in the sensory registers is then analyzed by processes known as feature detection and pattern recognition. By means of attention, information that has been identified as meaningful and relevant to current goals is then transferred to a structure known as primary or short-term memory where it is subject to further analysis. At this stage perceptual information is combined with

information retrieved from secondary or long-term memory. Primary memory, which has an extremely limited capacity to process information, is considered the staging area of the cognitive system, where processes such as judgment, inference, and problem-solving take place. Information resides in primary memory only so long as it is rehearsed. On the basis of an analysis of the meaning of the stimulus input, some response is generated; and finally, a trace of the event is permanently encoded in secondary memory. (p. 1445)

Numerous models of information processing have been developed, each to suit a slightly different purpose. Much of this work is taking place in the interdisciplinary field of cognitive science.

SCHEMA THEORY

One concept that might add to our understanding of how people process information from mass communication is the idea of schema. Although scholars do not agree about exactly what a schema is, the following definition is useful: "In a nutshell, a schema is a cognitive structure consisting of organized knowledge about situations and individuals that has been abstracted from prior experiences. It is used for processing new information and retrieving stored information" (Graber, 1988, p. 28). The concept of schema has become widely used by psychologists, cognitive scientists, political scientists, and communication researchers because of its apparent usefulness in understanding how people process information.

Fiske and Kinder describe schemas as "serviceable although imperfect devices for coping with complexity" (1981, p. 173). They suggest that people are "cognitive misers" whose limited complexity for dealing with information forces them to practice "cognitive economy" by forming simplified mental models (p. 172).

Doris Graber (1988) has done research that indicates that people use schemas to process news stories from newspapers or news broadcasts. She found that people processing news stories choose from a number of strategies, including straight matching of a news story to a schema (interpreting a political candidate as "another Nixon"), processing through inferences (deducing that a cease-fire in Lebanon would not work well because cease-fires had not worked well in Northern Ireland), and multiple integration of a story with several schemas or schema dimensions (a story on school busing can be related to schemas about political participation, the disruption of public education, or the achieving of a multicultural society). Graber found that in processing news stories, people tend to store the conclusions drawn from the evidence, rather than the evidence itself. She argued that processing news through schemas is an effective means of dealing with information overload.

Finally, Graber points out that the matching of news stories with schemas is influenced by cueing, and notes that the mass media are a major source of cueing information. Thus, in the preceding example concerning school busing, the news media themselves can, by means of headlines, pictures, captions, and so forth, help determine whether the story is seen as dealing with disruption of education or achieving a multicultural society. This kind of cueing can also influence schema development, so that when the next story on school busing comes along it is more likely to be related to either the "disruption of education" schema or the "achieving a multicultural society" schema.

In summary, the notion of schema can help us to understand how people may process many news stories. It appears that they attempt to match the information in a news story to some existing schema through a number of different matching strategies. If a match can be found, some part of the information or inferences from the information is likely to be stored in the form of a modified schema. If a match cannot be found, the information is likely to pass by without being assimilated.

SUBLIMINAL PERCEPTION

One other topic involving perception and mass communication is the controversial and rather dubious technique known as *subliminal perception.* This is the notion that people can be influenced by stimuli of which they are not aware.

Subliminal perception first came to public attention in 1957 when James M. Vicary of the Subliminal Projection Company began attempting to sell a special projector. The machine was reported to flash a message on a motion picture screen every five seconds at the same time that a regular motion picture projector was showing a film on the same screen. The message flashes were very brief in duration—1/3,000 of a second.

Vicary reported that he had conducted an experiment in a New Jersey movie house in which subliminal messages stating "Eat popcorn" and "Drink Coca-Cola" were flashed on the screen. He said he achieved a 57.5 percent increase in popcorn sales and an 18.1 percent increase in Coca-Cola sales. Vicary said subliminal advertising would be a boon to the consumer because it would eliminate bothersome commercials and allow more entertainment time ("Persuaders," *Advertising Age,* Sept. 16, 1957, p. 127).

Vicary's claims provoked quite a negative reaction. Norman Cousins (1957), editor of *Saturday Review,* wrote an editorial that began with the sentence "Welcome to 1984." Some people were worried that subliminal ads would be used to force people to drink alcohol against their will. Subliminal advertising was banned in Australia and Great Britain, and in the United States it was prohibited by the National Association of Broadcasters. Since Vicary's original report, the notion of subliminal perception or subliminal persuasion has reappeared in a number of different forms.

Wilson Bryan Key presented a variation of the old idea in his books *Subliminal Seduction* (1972) and *Media Sexploitation* (1976). Key claims that many advertisements contain within them subtle printings of the word *sex* as well as disguised representations of male and female sex organs. These hidden words and symbols are called *embeds*. According to Key's theory, which is loosely based on Freudian theory, the viewer perceives these embeds unconsciously and is influenced by them to desire the advertised product, whether it is a bottle of perfume or an automobile tire. Key's books contain little in the way of scientific documentation. His proof rests more on the reproduction of advertisements supposedly containing embeds. Most of these are ambiguous at best.

In keeping with perception theory, one begins to wonder if the fact that Key sees these pictures as filled with sexual references does not tell us something about Key rather than something about the advertisements!

Another variation on the subliminal perception idea is the subliminal message self-help (SMSH) audiotape, a business with sales that are estimated to range between $50 million and $1 billion a year. The typical SMSH audiotape contains audible classical music or sounds of the ocean with therapeutic messages recorded below the threshold of conscious hearing. Different tapes are available for various therapeutic benefits: stopping smoking, losing weight, building self-esteem, or improving memory. The purchaser of the tapes is supposed to receive these therapeutic benefits if he or she listens to the tape repeatedly over an extended period of time.

Vicary's movie theater study was never described fully enough that re-searchers could evaluate it. Other researchers began to look into the phenome-non, however. Much of the research on subliminal perception was undertaken by the advertising industry. The industry was concerned that the controversy about subliminal perception was giving it a bad name. Researchers who attempted to study subliminal perception immediately ran into some problems. Subliminal perception is supposed to be perception that takes place below the threshold of awareness. One of the first problems is that there is no distinct threshold of awareness (Wiener & Schiller, 1960). At one moment a person might need 1/25 of a second to be able to identify a stimulus, but a short time later the same person might be able to identify a stimulus shown for only 1/100 of a second. Psychologists have typically solved this problem by defining the threshold as the point where the subject identifies the stimulus 50 percent of the time. But this is essentially an arbitrary definition. Also, thresholds differ from person to person and for the same person depending on fatigue and other factors. It is not clear which of the various thresholds should be used.

A number of studies of subliminal perception have shown that people can respond to a stimulus below the threshold of awareness. For instance, a person who has been given a shock when exposed to certain nonsense words will sometimes show a galvanic skin response reaction indicating fear when these nonsense words are flashed so briefly that the person still cannot recognize them (Lazarus & McCleary, 1951).

The results of research on subliminal persuasion have been mixed, but the preponderance of the evidence has been against any significant persuasive effect. For instance, in one experiment Beatty and Hawklns (1989) investigated the possible effect on thirst of presenting the word *Coke* subliminally. Subjects were randomly divided into three groups. All three groups were given the cover story that the purpose of the experiment was to establish recognition thresholds for names of brands of automobiles. The automobile names were presented 15 times, with the exposure time starting below the threshold of awareness and becoming slightly longer each time. In between these exposures, the subjects in two groups were exposed to two different subliminal stimuli. One group received the word *Coke* at an exposure time below the threshold of awareness. A second group received the nonsense syllable *NYTP* at an exposure time below the threshold of awareness. A third group was shown the word *Coke* along with the automobile brand names, so that it became increasingly visible as the presentations continued. Subject thirst was measured with a Perceptual Health Inventory, which also contained other measures aimed at disguising the purpose of the experiment. Statistical analysis showed no difference in thirst ratings for the three groups.

Other researchers have carried out a field experiment to investigate the effectiveness of subliminal self-help tapes. Spangenberg, Obermiller, and Greenwald (1992) decided to focus on tapes dealing with weight loss, memory enhancement, and building self-esteem. In the experiment, labels were switched around on tapes so that some people who thought they were using memory enhancement tapes were actually using weight loss tapes, and so forth. The experiment was double-blind in that neither the subjects nor the experimenters knew what tapes the subjects were really getting. After about a month of exposure, participants reported listening to tapes an average of 42 times.

Measures of weight, self-esteem, and memory ability taken before and after the exposure showed no effect of the tapes on the variables they were designed to influence. But there was some tendency for tapes to have slight effects or to be perceived by subjects as having slight effects corresponding to the labeled purpose of the tape. The researchers said these "placebo-like" effects were the result of subjects processing information in such a way as to support their expectancies. And indeed, that may be a way that SMSH tapes are having a slight beneficial effect—through a placebo-like process of self-deception.

Pratkanis and Greenwald (1988) sum up the research on subliminal perception:

> There continues to be no reliable evidence in support of the more sensational claims for the power of subliminal influence. Further those subliminal findings that appear to be replicable (a) tend to involve only low levels of cognitive processing, levels that are of little value to the marketer, (b) are difficult to implement in mass media settings, and (c) might just as (or more) easily be implemented using supraliminal techniques. (p. 349)

PERCEPTION OF PICTURES

The mass media frequently employ pictures as part of messages. What do we know about how people interpret these pictures? Scott (1994) has argued that we need a theory of visual rhetoric to help us understand how people process pictures, and has offered some thoughts to move us forward in developing such a theory.

Scott suggests that much research on images in advertising has dealt with pictures either as transparent representations of reality or as conveyors of an emotional appeal. She argues for a third possibility—that pIctures can act as symbols and can be used to construct rhetorical arguments. She states that visual elements are capable of representing concepts, abstractions, actions, metaphors, and modifiers, and that they can be assembled into complex arguments. Furthermore, this conceptualization of images means that pictures need to be processed cognitively like other forms of information.

Scott's article brings out three ways of thinking about pictures in the mass media—as transparent representations of reality, as conveyors of affective or emotional appeal, and as complex combinations of symbols put together to make up rhetorical arguments. Different types of pictures in the mass media may be used in these three ways to varying degrees. For instance, news photos may be higher in use as transparent representations of reality than pictures in advertisements, while pictures in advertisements may be used as parts of rhetorical arguments more than news photos. Both types of images may be at times high in conveying affective or emotional appeal (see Table 4.3).

To illustrate the rhetorical use of visual images, Scott analyzes a Clinique ad that shows tubes of lipstick and makeup immersed in a glass of soda water garnished with a slice of lime.

The image is not intended to be taken literally—the message is not that the lipstick and makeup tubes are waterproof, for instance. Scott says we can restate the message of the image in verbal terms in this way "Clinique's new summer line of makeup is as refreshing as a tall glass of soda with a twist." The ad is essentially a visual simile. It is an example of a *visual trope,* an argument presented in a figurative form in order to break through a viewer's skepticism, boredom, or resistance.

Perceiving the Clinique ad correctly requires some rather complex information processing on the part of the perceiver. The viewer must compare two rather dissimilar things—soda water and cosmetics—and deduce what they have in common. Of several things they have in common, the correct one must be selected ("refreshing" but not "tasteless") in order to arrive at the simile. The

TABLE 4.3 Comparison of advertisements and news photos in terms of the type of communication in the picture or image

Type of Picture	Type of Communication in Picture or Image		
	Transparent Representation of Reality	*Affective or Emotional Appeal*	*Rhetorical Argumentation*
Advertisements	Low to High	Often High	Usually High
News Photos	High	Often High	Usually Low

perceiver must also reject the literal message of the image—that someone would try to drink a glass of soda water with lipstick in it.

Scott argues that the field of information processing has been biased toward the processing of verbal information, and that it needs to be expanded to also deal with the processing of visual images. Furthermore, some tropes also involve interaction between images and text, and this kind of interaction needs further study. Scott's notion of the rhetoric of pictures gives us a richer and more realistic way to look at the use of pictures in the mass media. Scholars can add depth to their analysis of advertisements, news photos, and other pictures in the mass media by building on Scott's ideas of visual rhetoric. Likewise, consumers of the mass media can use Scott's ideas to add to their understanding of the use of pictures in the media.

CONCLUSIONS

Perception is a complex process that involves structural factors, or influences from physical stimuli, and functional factors, or psychological influences from the perceiving organism. Among these psychological influences are the perceiver's needs, wants, moods, attitudes, and assumptions.

Psychologists and cognitive scientists have found it difficult to distinguish perception from information processing. Models of information processing typically demonstrate that it is an operation involving stages, with various kinds of cognitive work being done at each of the stages. Some of these stages involve inferences and pattern matching, with room for various kinds of errors.

Schema theory suggests that people processing information from the mass media may act as cognitive misers, throwing out a great deal of the information they are exposed to as irrelevant.

The processing of images or pictures from the mass media raises some additional important questions about perception and information processing. Much of the research on mass communication has treated pictures as either transparent representations of reality or as sources of affective or emotional arousal. But images and pictures are obviously used to communicate in more complex ways. The theory of visual rhetoric suggests that pictures and images can be used to construct subtle and complicated arguments, adding a powerful dimension to communication through the mass media.

DISCUSSION

1. What are some of the psychological factors that influence perception?
2. Does basic research on perception indicate that "we see what we want to see"? Why, or why not?
3. What are some ways for communicators to overcome the barriers of selective exposure, selective perception, and selective retention?

4. Why are techniques of subliminal persuasion so popular when the scientific evidence suggests that they are ineffective?
5. What role do *schemas* play in the receiving of mass communication messages?
6. What does it mean to say that a person is a "cognitive miser"?
7. In advertising, how common is the use of what Linda Scott has described as the visual rhetoric of pictures?
8. Discuss the statement that "a picture doesn't lie."

REFERENCES

Allport, G. W., and L. Postman (1947). *The Psychology of Rumor.* New York: Henry Holt.

Apple, R. W (1976). Voter poll finds debate aided Ford and cut Carter lead. *New York Times,* Sept. 27, p. 1.

Bagby, J. W. (1957). A cross-cultural study of perceptual predominance in binocular rivalry. *Journal of Abnormal and Social Psychology* 54: 331-334.

Beatty, S. E., and D. I. Hawkins (1989). Subliminal stimulation: Some new data and interpretation. *Journal of Advertising* 18: 4-8.

Bennett, B. M., D. D. Hoffman, and C. Prakash (1989). *Observer Mechanics: A Formal Theory of Perception.* San Diego, Calif.: Academic Press.

Berelson, B., and G. A. Steiner (1964). *Human Behavior: An Inventory of Scientific Findings.* New York: Harcourt, Brace & World.

Cooper, E., and M. Jahoda (1947). The evasion of propaganda: How prejudiced people respond to anti-prejudice propaganda. *Journal of Psychology* 23: 15-25.

Cotton, J. L. (1985). Cognitive dissonance in selective exposure. In D. Zillmann and J. Bryant (eds.), *Selective Exposure to Communication,* pp. 11-33. Hillsdale, N.J.: Lawrence Erlbaum.

Cotton, J. L., and R. A. Hieser (1980). Selective exposure to information and cognitive dissonance. *Journal of Research in Personality* 14: 518-527.

Cousins, N. (1957). Smudging the subconscious. *Saturday Review,* Oct. 5, p. 20.

Fiske, S. T., and D. R. Kinder (1981). Involvement, expertise, and schema use: Evidence from political cognition. In N. Cantor and J. F. Kihlstrom (eds.), *Personality, Cognitions, and Social Interaction,* pp. 171-190. Hillsdale, NJ.: Lawrence Erlbaum.

Graber, D. A. (1988). *Processing the News: How People Tame the Information Tide,* 2nd ed. New York: Longman.

Gross, L. (1975). Do the bigots miss the message? *TV Guide,* Nov. 8, pp. 14-18.

Hastorf, A. H., and H. Cantril (1954). They saw a game: A case study. *Journal of Abnormal and Social Psychology* 49: 129-134.

Jones, E. E., and R. Kohler (1958). The effects of plausibility on the learning of controversial statements. *Journal of Abnormal and Social Psychology* 57: 315-320.

Keck, G. L., and B. Mueller. (1994). Intended vs. unintended messages: Viewer perceptions of United States Army television commercials. *Journal of Advertising Research* 34 (no. 2): 70-78.

Key, W. B. (1972). *Subliminal Seduction: Ad Media's Manipulation of a Not So Innocent America.* Englewood Cliffs, N.J.: Prentice-Hall.

———. (1976). *Media Sexplotation.* Englewood Cliffs, N.J.: Prentice-Hall.

Kihlstrom, J. F. (1987). The cognitive unconscious. *Science* 237: 1445-1452.

Lahlry, S. (1991). A blueprint for perception training. *Journal of Training and Development* 45 (no. 8): 21-25.

Lazarus, R. S., and R. A. McCleary (1951). Autonomic discrimination without awareness: A study of subception. *Psychological Review* 58: 113-122.

Leuba, C., and C. Lucas (1945). The effects of attitudes on descriptions of pictures. *Journal of Experimental Psychology* 35: 517-524.

Levine, J. M., and G. Murphy (1958). The learning and forgetting of controversial material. In E. E. Maccoby, T. M. Newcomb, and E. L. Hartley (eds.), *Readings in Social Psychology*, 3rd ed., pp. 94-101. New York: Holt, Rinehart and Winston.

McClelland, D. C., and J. W. Atkinson (1948). The projective expression of needs: I. The effect of different intensities of the hunger drive on perception. *Journal of Psychology* 25: 205-222.

"Persuaders" get deeply "hidden" tool: Subliminal projection. (1957). *Advertising Age* 28 (no. 37): 127.

Pratkanis, A. R., and A. G. Greenwald (1988). Recent perspectives on unconscious processing: Still no marketing applications. *Psychology and Marketing* 5 (no. 4): 337-353

Scott, L. M. (1994). Images in advertising: The need for a theory of visual rhetoric. *Journal of Consumer Research* 21 (no. 2): 252-273.

Sears, D. O., and J. L. Freedman (1967). Selective exposure to information: A critical review. *Public Opinion Quarterly* 31: 194-213.

Spangenberg, E. R., C. Obermiller, and A. G. Greenwald (1992). A field test of subliminal self-help audiotapes: The power of expectancies. *Journal of Public Policy & Marketing* 11 (no. 1): 26-36.

Toch, H., and M. S. MacLean, Jr. (1962). Perception, communication and educational research: A transactional view. *Audio Visual Communication Research* 10 (no. 5): 55-77.

Vidmar, N., and M. Rokeach (1974). Archie Bunker's bigotry: A study in selective perception and exposure. *Journal of Communication* 24 (no. 1): 36-47.

Wiener, M., and P. H. Schiller (1960). Subliminal perception or perception of partial cues. *Journal of Abnormal and Social Psychology* 61: 124-137.

chapter 5

Problems in Encoding

Encoding is the translation of purpose, intention, or meaning into symbols or codes. Often these symbols are the letters, numbers, and words that make up a language such as English. But of course encoding can also take place through photographs, musical notes, or images on motion picture film.

Encoding is in many ways a mysterious process. How do the "preverbal tensions" (or whatever you want to call the feelings that precede words) become converted into words? It is not an easy process even to describe.

Some help in understanding encoding is provided by the work of a group of students of language called *general semanticists*. These thinkers have not explained all the mysteries of encoding, but they have identified some characteristics of language that make encoding (at least in language) difficult.

CHARACTERISTICS OF LANGUAGE

The general semanticists were first led by Alfred Korzybski, a Polish count who emigrated to the United States. His seminal work, *Science and Sanity*, was popularized by Wendell Johnson. These scholars have been concerned with language and how it relates to our success in everyday living and our mental health. They argue that we run into many of our problems because we misuse language. They say we would misuse language less if we used it more the way scientists use it—so that it constantly refers to the realities it represents.

The general semanticists point out several characteristics of language that make it difficult to use it carefully. These characteristics cause difficulty in encoding and make communication difficult.

Language Is Static; Reality Is Dynamic

Words themselves do not change over a period of time, yet the world around us is full of change. Modern science has shown that matter is ultimately made up of small particles moving very rapidly. A wooden table that appears to be solid is actually decaying and oxidizing. Twenty years from now it might not be a table at all, but a pile of firewood. Einstein's formula $E = mc^2$ brought out that even matter and energy are not distinct but can be converted one into the other.

Modern biology shows the same pattern of constant change. The caterpillar becomes a butterfly. The hard shell crab loses its shell and temporarily becomes a soft shell crab so that it may grow bigger. The theory of evolution brought out that even the species are not permanent and distinctive but are changing and developing through time.

Reality is a process, yet the language we must use to describe it is fixed and static. Another example of the process nature of reality is the cycle of the day. The sun is constantly moving, and its position in the sky changes throughout the day. The words we have to describe that ever-changing process are primarily two: night and day. Anyone who has watched a sunset and tried to say exactly when it has become night recognizes the difficulty of fitting those two words to reality in an exact way. People have invented a few other words to help deal with that problem: twilight, dusk, dawn. But we still have only a handful of words to refer to an ever-changing process.

The Greek philosopher Heraclitus said, "One cannot step in the same river twice." *The Way of Practical Attainment* in the teachings of Buddha puts it this way: "Everything is changeable, everything appears and disappears." George Bernard Shaw is supposed to have said, "The only man who behaves sensibly is my tailor: he takes my measure anew each time he sees me, whilst all the rest go on with their old measurements and expect them to fit me." T. S. Eliot in *The Cocktail Party* wrote, "What we know of other people is only our memory of the moments during which we knew them. And they have changed since then . . . at every meeting we are meeting a stranger."

The Chinese 13th-century classic *Romance of the Three Kingdoms* in the opening, "All Under Heaven," begins, "Such is the grand scheme of all under heaven, things that are separated will eventually come together, things that are together will eventually break apart."

Towns and people change, yet the words (names) we have to refer to them usually remain the same. The fact that the word does not change over time can blind us to the fact that the reality is changing. A man might spend 20 years dreaming of retiring in Pleasant Valley, a town he visited as a young man, only to go there and find that it has become a busy city. The name stayed the same; the place changed drastically. The general semanticists recommend a technique of dating to help remind ourselves of this kind of change. Putting a date after the name would help remind us which Pleasant Valley we are referring to: Pleasant Valley 1975 or Pleasant Valley 1995.

A professor of urban planning, discussing the growth of suburban communities which, while situated in major metropolitan areas, have become powerful economic centers themselves, has said (Suro, 1991):

> We are in the midst of a new urbanization process that is very different from anything that we have known in the post-war period. It is hard even to use the old terms like cities and suburbs, center and periphery, and we haven't created a new vocabulary yet. (p. A1)

Alvin Toffler, author of *Future Shock* and *The Third Wave*, said (1989):

> We felt the metaphor of waves offers a powerful way to characterize periods of fundamental change in society. . . . The emphasis on process that Korzybski stressed is present in all the intellectual work my wife and I have done over the years. (p. 197)

The world changes much faster than words do. We are always using verbal models that are somewhat out of date and no longer describe the world we live in. The survival of civilizations and individuals depends on their ability to adapt to change. Failure to recognize change with time leads to generalizations like "If Tom said it, it's a lie. He's lied to me before" or "Once a failure, always a failure."

Language Is Limited; Reality Is Virtually Unlimited

Wendell Johnson (1972) points out that there are 500,000 to 600,000 words in the English language and that they must represent millions of individual facts, experiences, and relationships. The vocabularies that people ordinarily use are much smaller. In telephone conversations, people typically use a vocabulary of about 5,000 words, and the average novel uses a vocabulary of about 10,000 (Miller, 1963, p. 121). This might suggest that our vocabularies are normally sufficient for everyday communication, but it is not difficult to think of cases in which our vocabularies begin to appear limited.

Suppose someone were to place a dozen oranges on a table before you and randomly pick one of them and ask you to describe it in words. Could you describe it in such a way that someone else who had not been present could later pick that orange out of the dozen? Unless by luck the orange had some obvious deformity, the task would probably be difficult. The point is that we can make more distinctions in reality than we have words to describe them with easily.

The same kind of problem shows up on a more practical level in giving physical descriptions of people. Sometimes it seems as if people are only a little easier to describe than the oranges in the example just given. The problem shows up frequently in law enforcement work, where people have to describe another person so exactly that the person can be recognized by other people. Many people often are not very good at this, partly because they do not observe carefully but also because only a limited number of words exist for describing people.

Or think of the problem of describing in words some continuous process, such as playing a violin, riding a bicycle, or tying a shoe. Most people would find these acts difficult to convey in words, and they are the kinds of things that are typically taught by one person showing another. Something as simple as the correct way to hold a guitar might be almost impossible to express in words, and a guitar book for beginners will usually contain a picture to get the message across. The writer of a beginner's guitar manual has a similar problem in communicating what certain guitar effects are supposed to sound like when they are done correctly. Such a writer might be forced to describe a certain rhythm pattern by inventing words such as "boom-chicka, boom-chicka." Even these invented words would only approximate the desired sound.

Because of the limited nature of our knowledge and our language, general semanticists stress that you can never say all about anything. Thomas Edison said, "We don't know one millionth of one percent about anything." General semanticists recommend a technique of putting *etc.* at the end of any statement to remind yourself that more could be said about anything. (If you don't actually say or write the *etc.,* you can at least think it.) The general semanticists named their journal *ETC.* to stress the importance of this idea.

Language Is Abstract

Abstraction is a process of selecting some details and leaving out other details. Any use of language involves some abstraction. And indeed, abstraction is one of the most useful features of language. It allows us to think in categories, and this gives us the ability to generalize.

In classifying a number of fruits into categories—apple, pear, orange, and peach, for instance—we are selecting some details, such as their color, shape, and texture, and ignoring others, such as their weight. We could classify them another way, into categories such as six-ounce fruits, seven-ounce fruits, eight-ounce fruits, and so forth; in this case we would be selecting a different detail, their weight, and ignoring the details we paid attention to at first.

Much human knowledge is intimately bound up in the process of categorizing or classifying; we learn that certain red, round objects are good to eat, and giving those objects a name makes it easier to remember that knowledge and pass it on to others.

Abstraction is a useful characteristic of words, but it is also one that can lead to problems, particularly when people are not aware of abstraction.

All words involve some abstraction, or leaving out of details, but some words are more abstract than others. And as words become more and more abstract, their correspondence to reality becomes less and less direct. S. I. Hayakawa (1964, p. 179) developed a useful diagram to show the way words can have differing degrees of abstraction. His diagram, called an "abstraction ladder," is based on a concept developed by Korzybski (1958, p. 397) called the "structural differential." An example of an abstraction ladder appears in Figure 5.1.

Verbal Level

8	transportation
7	land transportation
6	motor vehicle
5	car
4	Honda
3	Severin's Honda Accord

Nonverbal Levels

2	the maroon Honda Accord that we can see and touch
1	the car as atomic process

FIGURE 5.1 Example of an abstraction ladder

The abstraction ladder in Figure 5.1 takes a particular object, an automobile belonging to one of the authors of this text, and shows how it can be referred to at different levels of abstraction. The lowest level of abstraction, at which no details are left out, is the process level, the level at which scientists using instruments can observe the car. The second level is the car as the object that we can experience with our senses. Notice that even at this level, the level of everyday observation, some details are being left out. This is partly because the eye can process more information than the brain. But it is also because we can observe from only one point at a time. When we observe the car from the front, we do not see the details at the back. And we see only the surface, not the internal structure of the car. Even in observation, some abstraction or leaving out of details takes place. The third level is the first verbal level, the first level involving the use of words. At this level there is one word or phrase that refers uniquely to the one car being described. This could be the phrase *Severin's Honda Accord.* At this level, the word being used refers to the one particular object. At the fourth level, we can use the word *Honda* to refer to the same object. We have then assigned the object to a category, the category of all Hondas. We have left out the detail that would distinguish that particular Honda from all other Hondas. At the next level, that of the word *car,* we would be including not only Hondas but also Volkswagens, Fords, Cadillacs, and all other makes, so still more distinguishing detail would be left out. At the sixth level, we could refer to the car as a *motor vehicle,* putting it into a category that also includes trucks and jeeps and leaving out still more detail. At the seventh level, we could use the term *land transportation,* categorizing the car with railroad trains and snowmobiles. And at the eighth level, we could refer to the car with the word *transportation,* putting it in a class that would also include airplanes and ships. Notice that at each level more detail is left out until at the eighth level we come to a very abstract word, *transportation.* This word does not suggest a particular picture to the mind the way the word *Honda* does. Some people might hear the word *transportation* and visualize a boat, while others might visualize a truck, and many others would have no clear picture of anything.

That is one of the characteristics of abstract words: they do not suggest a clear picture of something in reality, and people often have very different meanings in mind for them.

Because our language is limited and because we abstract and categorize, language compels us to emphasize similarities but permits us to ignore differences. We see similarities by ignoring differences. There are similarities among different things, just as there are differences among similar things.

A well-known historian and philosopher of science, J. Bronowski (1951), said,

> The action of putting things which are not identical into a group or class is so familiar that we forget how sweeping it is. The action depends on recognizing a set of things to be alike when they are not identical. . . . Habit makes us think the likeness obvious (p. 21).

With the exception of proper nouns, our language has no words for unique events, feelings, and relationships. We speak, perceive, and think of the world in categories. These categories are in our language and in our heads; they are not in nature.

We can use language to group together any two things (categorization). We can use language to place anything in more than one category. We can use language to treat things as identical (through categorization) when, indeed, they are unique. Language is sometimes used in this way to imply "guilt by association." What we call a person depends on our purpose, our projections, and our evaluations, yet the person does not change when we change the label.

Assumptions Built into Languages

The structure and vocabulary of every language contains many assumptions about the nature of reality. Many are so ingrained that we are no longer aware of them. Wendell Johnson observed that the language we use not only puts words in our mouths, but it also puts notions in our heads. Benjamin Lee Whorf put it this way (1952):

> And every language is a vast pattern-system, different from others in which is culturally ordained the forms and categories by which the personality not only communicates, but analyzes nature, notices or neglects types of relationships and phenomena, channels his reasoning, and builds the house of his consciousness. Each language performs this artificial chopping up of the continuous spread and flow of existence in a different way. (p. 173)

One example of hidden assumptions in the English language is the many instances of sexism, often unperceived. The women's movement has made us aware of many of them. Other languages face the same problems. For example, the Chinese language is built of ideograms (characters, symbols, or figures that suggest the idea of an object without expressing its name). The ideogram representing woman is often combined with other ideograms for other meanings. The combination of woman and child means good; woman and eyebrow means flattery; and woman repeated three times means treachery. The ideogram woman is also used in many other combinations, including adultery and lustful.

As Wendell Johnson observed, the language we use not only puts words in our mouths, but it also puts notions in our heads—a major point mass communicators need to be aware of.

MISUSES OF LANGUAGE

Because of the static, limited, and abstract nature of language, certain misuses of language are likely to occur. One of the great contributions of the general semanticists has been to identify some of these for us. Four common misuses are dead-level abstracting, undue identification, two-valued evaluation, and unconscious projection.

Dead-Level Abstracting

This concept, described by Wendell Johnson (1946, p. 270), refers to getting stuck at one level of abstraction. The level could be high or low.

High-level abstractions are words like *justice, democracy, freedom, mankind, Communism, peace with honor,* and *law and order*. When words like these are used in a message that does not also contain words at lower levels of abstraction, it is difficult to know what the message is saying. Words at a high level of abstraction that are not accompanied by more concrete words have been referred to as "words cut loose from their moorings" (Hayakawa, 1964, p. 189). They are not anchored to lower levels of abstraction.

Much political rhetoric gets stuck at a high level of abstraction. When the expression *law and order* was used in a presidential campaign, what it referred to at a less abstract level was not clear. It was hard to know, because we were given the high-level abstraction but no translation at a concrete level.

The motion picture *Cabaret* contained an example of the way high-level abstractions can be baffling. In one scene some Germans are sitting around a living room at the time the Nazis were rising to power, and one of them says, "If all the Jews are bankers, how can they be Communists too?"

Language can also get stuck at a low level of abstraction in one message, and this is another type of dead-level abstracting. An example of this might be someone recounting every detail of his or her day. A message that stays at a low level of abstraction usually does not come to a general conclusion, and it is often difficult to see the point of what is being said. Receiving a message stuck at a low level of abstraction can be something like reading a mail-order catalog.

The general semanticists say that the most effective communication *ranges up and down* the ladder of abstraction. An effective message contains generalizations at a high level of abstraction, but there are also specific details at a low level of abstraction. One effective technique for doing this that many skilled teachers use is to give lots of examples.

Undue Identification

This is the failure to see distinctions between members of a category or class. The term points out that different members of a class are seen as identical, or identified. Another term for this is categorical thinking. In everyday discourse, it is sometimes referred to as overgeneralization. One common kind of undue identification is stereotyping.

The following statements all show a failure to see distinctions between members of a class:

> "If you've seen one tree, you've seen them all."
>
> "I'll never trust another woman."
>
> "You can't believe a thing you read in the newspapers."
>
> "Statistics don't prove anything."

The stereotyping of mothers-in-law as interfering and critical or of Italians as great lovers are other examples of undue identification.

Often such categorization with language and failure to recognize differences between individuals leads to *stereotyping*, which makes some subgroup out to be greedy, stupid, lazy, cowardly, or the like. Sometimes this is reflected in cultural jokes. For example, so-called Polish jokes ignore the fact that Poles like Frederic Chopin, Marie Curie, Joseph Conrad, and Nicolaus Copernicus are recognized for major contributions to civilization.

Several generations of Americans have viewed the German boxer Max Schmeling as vehemently pro-Hitler and a willing model for the Third Reich. Schmeling beat Joe Louis in 1936, and Hitler extolled Schmeling as a model of the new Aryan Superman.

The truth about Schmeling is quite different. He refused to join the Nazi party or to be used to support Nazi propaganda. He refused, over Joseph Goebbels's (the Nazi propaganda minister) personal protest, to fire his American Jewish manager or to stop associating with German Jews. After the war Schmeling became quite wealthy and he quietly and regularly gave Joe Louis (then living in near poverty) gifts of money, and after Louis's death, gave Louis's widow $5,000. Schmeling never told anyone, nor even mentioned it in his own memoirs. He also never told anyone of the two teenage sons of a Jewish friend (David Lewin) that he hid in his Berlin hotel apartment and later escorted to safety. It was only when Henri Lewin, who became a successful hotel owner in California and Nevada, told the story in 1989 did the world learn of Schmeling's courage. When asked why he had not told anyone, Schmeling said, "It was my duty as a man" (Weisbord & Hedderich, 1993).

Journalistic overgeneralization was the topic of an op-ed article by Mohamed Kamal, the Jordanian ambassador to the United States (1987). He said, in part,

> I am perturbed by the continuing tendency of the American media to utilize the simplistic equation "Moslem-terrorist-Arab."
>
> There are almost 200 million Arabs and close to a billion Moslems in the world. Is it honest or fair that they be blanketed with the "terrorist" label through the indiscriminate use of an identifying "Moslem" or "Arab" adjective in media coverage of terrorist actions emanating from the Middle East?
>
> Journalists, even those who pride themselves on objective reporting, are curiously selective in their descriptions. They never refer to the Baader-Meinhof Gang as "Christian terrorist." The Japanese Red Army Faction is never called "Shinto terrorist." The obliteration of camps and towns in Lebanon is not called "Jewish terrorism.". . . The press would not think of writing "black thief" or "Christian murderer." Why then does a qualifying racial or religious adjective become acceptable when it is "Arab" or "Moslem"?
>
> Moreover, the American media apparently found it convenient to ignore a resolution at the Islamic summit that unanimously condemned terrorism in any form as contrary to the teachings of Islam. Such a failure is but another form of the discrimination I have defined here. (p. 17).

General semanticists sometimes recommend the use of index numbers to prevent undue identification. If we were to attach an index number to a word like *student* each time we use it, we might be less likely to think of all students as alike. This would remind us that student1 is not student2, or to take another example, that Arab1 is not Arab2. Of course, the important thing is not so much actually to use index numbers in our writing and talking but to think them—to be aware that members of a class share some characteristics but are different in terms of many others. Each classification tells us something about the way an object is considered similar to other objects, but it also tells us about the way it is considered different from certain other objects. No two things are identical.

Two-Valued Evaluation

This misuse is also known as *either-or thinking* or *thinking with the excluded middle*. It involves thinking that there are only two possibilities when there are actually a range of possibilities. Language contributes to this tendency because often only two words that are opposites are available to describe a situation. Familiar examples are words like *night* and *day, black* and *white, right* and *wrong.* As we discussed earlier, *night* and *day* are two words that do not begin to reflect the many different states that occur during the cycle of the day. Many people would say that the same is true of the other pairs of opposites. This is reflected in the commonplace statement when referring to moral questions: "It's not a matter of black and white; there are shades of gray."

Consider the bumper sticker reading "America—Love it or leave it." This excludes the existence of other possibilities, such as "staying and changing it." In times of confrontation it is also common to hear people speaking of "them" and "us," another example of either-or thinking.

Psychologist Earl C. Kelley (1947) has said, "When we take in our surroundings, we select from them, not at random, but in accordance with our past experience and our purposes" (p. 48). William Shakespeare said, "Nothing is good or bad, but thinking makes it so" (as cited by Brown, 1988, p. 16). Contemporary writer, H. Jackson Brown, Jr., in a compilation *A Father's Book of Wisdom*, writes, "We do not see things as they are. We see things as we are" (p. 106). It is the *I* behind the eye that does the seeing. Seeing goes on inside of our heads and inside of our nervous systems. What we see is our response to what we look at.

The general semanticists suggest that a cure for unconscious projection is to add "to me" at the end of any statement you make. Again, it might not be necessary to write or say the words but it would help at least to think them.

THREE KINDS OF STATEMENTS

A major debate in journalism concerns objectivity—whether it is good or bad and whether it is even possible to achieve it. Some well-known journalists, including Hunter Thompson, Bill Moyers, and David Brinkley, have described objectivity as a myth, while other well-known journalists, such as Clifton Daniel and Herbert Brucker, have defended objectivity as essential to reporting.

Some concepts introduced by S. I. Hayakawa can help the journalist to make some sense out of the controversy over objectivity. Hayakawa (1964) discusses three kinds of statements people can make—reports, inferences, and judgments— and the related issue of slanting.

A *report* is a statement that is capable of verification and excludes inferences and judgments. An example is the statement "The low temperature last night in Durham, North Carolina, was 47 degrees." This statement is capable of verification, of being checked out. You could go to the weather station in Durham and examine the records or interview the meteorologist there. Other examples of reports would be these statements:

"The City Council approved a budget of $237 million for the fiscal year 1995." (Either they did or they didn't, and the action can be verified by checking with council members, eyewitnesses attending the meeting, and the official minutes of the meeting.)

"Robbery suspect Larry Joe Smith was seen at Municipal Airport Saturday afternoon." (This would be more difficult to verify, and it might not be verified until Smith is apprehended and identified in court by an eyewitness or in a lineup, but the statement is still capable of verification.)

An *inference* is a statement about the unknown made on the basis of the known. Any statement about another person's thoughts or feelings is an example of an inference. You might observe a person pounding a fist on the table, raising her or his voice, and becoming red in the face. These would be the known aspects. If you then made the statement "Chris is angry," you would be making a statement about the unknown, the person's emotions. You would be making an inference. In many cases, the safest course is to stick to what is known and report it—the pounding of the fist, the raising of the voice, and the reddening of the face. Statements about these observable characteristics are verifiable and are reports.

Any statement about the future is an inference, since the future is unknown. The statement "The president will enter the hospital Thursday for a checkup" is an inference, since it deals with the future. The safer statement in this case would be "The press secretary said that the President will enter the hospital Thursday for a checkup." That is capable of verification—a report.

A man who was mugged said of his assailant: "He must have been six-feet-two and probably high on something." The conclusion that the mugger was "high on something" was an inference, although it might be most accurate to refer to it as a labeled inference since the word *probably* was used.

In another example of a labeled inference, a television correspondent describing Congress's failure to override a presidential veto of an emergency job bill said: "The Democrats seemed bewildered by what happened."

A *judgment* is an expression of approval or disapproval for an occurrence, person, or object. For example, students sometimes use words like *great* (approval) or *terrible* (disapproval) to describe a teacher.

Letters to the editor of a newspaper sometimes contain judgments. Consider the letter describing the television series "Roots" as an "ethnic hate-mongering diatribe" and "overdone fiction."

Sometimes the source of a news story will state a judgment, and it might be necessary for an alert journalist to challenge it. During some textbook hearings in Texas, a feminist critic of sexism in books told a television interviewer: "This year there are some books we almost like, and there are a lot of bad books." The interviewer asked, "What's a bad book?" The critic was ready with an answer, however: "A bad book is one that shows 75 percent or more of males in the working roles." This shifted the interview out of the realm of judgments into the realm of reports.

A journalist can do a great deal toward being objective by eliminating inferences and judgments and sticking as much as possible to reports. But this alone will not guarantee objectivity. Another factor must be considered, as Hayakawa points out. That factor is slanting. *Slanting* is selecting details that are favorable or unfavorable to the subject being described.

In describing large outdoor demonstrations, for example, a newspaper often has several estimates of crowd size from which to choose. Leon Mann (1974) studied coverage of an antiwar rally in Washington, D.C., in October 1967 and found that antiwar newspapers were more likely to choose a large estimate of the crowd size and prowar newspapers were more likely to choose a small estimate.

Absolute objectivity might not be possible, but in fact a journalist (or any other communicator) can go a long way toward being objective by sticking as much as possible to reports (and excluding inferences and judgments), and by making a conscious effort to avoid slanting. Furthermore, these concepts provide some specific terms for discussing the ways in which reporting might or might not be objective.

STUDIES OF OBJECTIVITY

Journalism professor John Merrill (1965) used general semantics concepts as well as concepts of his own in his study "How *Time* Stereotyped Three U.S. Presidents." He set up the following six categories of bias: attribution bias (for example, "Truman snapped"), adjective bias (Eisenhower's "warm manner of speaking"), adverbial bias ("Truman said curtly"), outright opinion (equivalent to Hayakawa's judgments; for example, "Seldom has a more unpopular man fired a more popular one"), contextual bias (bias in whole sentences, whole paragraphs, or the entire story; six judges had to agree), and photographic bias ("What overall impression does the photograph give? How is the president presented in the picture—dignified, undignified; angry, happy; calm, nervous; etc.? What does the caption say/imply?").

Merrill examined a sample of 10 issues of *Time* for each president—Truman, Eisenhower, and Kennedy—and counted the occurrences of bias in each of the six categories. The results, summarized in Table 5.1, showed a strong negative bias toward Truman, a strong positive bias toward Eisenhower, and a rather balanced portrayal of Kennedy. The portrayals of Truman and Eisenhower are good examples of *slanting*—over a period of time the details selected almost overwhelmingly added up to either a favorable or an unfavorable impression of these presidents.

TABLE 5.1 Instances of bias shown by *Time* magazine in 10-issue samples for each of three presidents

	Truman	Eisenhower	Kennedy
Total Bias	93	82	45
Total Positive Bias	1	81	31
Total Negative Bias	92	1	14

SOURCE: Adapted from J. C. Merrill, "How *Time* Stereotyped Three U.S. Presidents," *Journalism Quarterly* 42 (1965), p. 565.

Fourteen years after the publication of Merrill's study, three other researchers replicated it to find out if things had changed (Fedler, Meeske, & Hall, 1979). They said:

> Since Merrill's study was published in 1965, the editors of *Time* have insisted that their magazine has become fairer, and the *Wall Street Journal* has reported that "even critics concede that *Time's* political coverage now is more balanced than in its anti-Truman and pro-Eisenhower days." (p. 353)

The authors added that observations about the magazine's growing impartiality are contradicted by its coverage of the war in Vietnam and other developments. They also observed that since the Merrill study the magazine's circulation had grown by nearly 40 percent and that a survey showed that even the nation's journalists rely heavily on *Time*.

The replication (done as similarly as possible to the Merrill study for consistency) examined *Time*'s treatment of presidents Johnson, Nixon (both before and after Watergate), Ford, and Carter. The three investigators, all experienced journalists, working separately, read copies of all the articles about the presidents that *Time* published during randomly selected 10-week periods and independently recorded instances of apparent bias.

After a detailed analysis of the data they concluded (Fedler et al., 1979):

> *Time* continues to use most of the bias techniques reported by Merrill, although the manner in which some are used seems to have changed. *Time* continues to use a series of devices that guide readers' opinions of the news and that enable *Time* to editorialize in its regular news columns. (p. 335)

The 1979 data indicated that *Time*'s news columns were neutral toward Johnson, favored Nixon before Watergate and were critical after Watergate, supported Ford, and opposed Carter. Note that the data were drawn from news columns of *Time*, not from editorials. The researchers said:

> This study indicates that *Time* continues to weave facts into semi-fictionalized language patterns that are designed to lead the reader's thinking. While this produces a style of writing that is interesting to read, it obscures the preferential positions taken by the magazine. . . . The reader who enjoys a clever and racy style will undoubtedly enjoy *Time* because the style is entertaining. However, the careful and thoughtful reader who does not expect to find the opinions of the magazine in its unsigned articles may not find *Time* very satisfying. *Time* has never claimed to be objective. It is still not. (p. 359)

A few years later Fedler, Smith, and Meeske (1983) examined how *Time* and *Newsweek* treated the Kennedy brothers, John, Robert, and Edward, in their coverage of the 1960, 1968, and 1980 campaigns. Following the example of the two earlier studies, they examined 10 different types of statements in the stories as well as six issues frequently associated with the Kennedys: age, appearance, personalities, families, religion, and wealth (p. 490). They then analyzed 1,896 statements (92 percent of the total statements published) in which there was agreement (positive, negative, or neutral) between the three coders involved.

They found the percentage of favorable, neutral, and unfavorable statements published about the Kennedys by the two magazines was surprisingly similar. Both magazines also published proportionately more favorable statements about John Kennedy than about either of his brothers (p. 496).

In what is essentially a case study of news bias, Herman (1985) used content analysis to examine the treatment of similar new stories. The researcher hypothesized that the mass media often treat similar events differently, depending on their political implications for U.S. interests. He contends that the effectiveness of the mass media as normally cooperative dispensers of official or establishment views is enhanced by the credibility the media acquire in their occasional tiffs with established institutions, like corporations or government. Mass media credibility also derives from the fact that their frequently homogeneous behavior arises "naturally" out of industry structure, common sources, ideology, patriotism, and the power of the government and top media sources to define newsworthiness and frameworks of discourse. Self-censorship, market forces, and the norms of news practices may produce and maintain a particular viewpoint as effectively as formal state censorship.

In one of two case studies, Herman compares the *New York Times*'s coverage of the 1984 elections in El Salvador and Nicaragua, the former openly sponsored and supported by the U.S. government, the latter openly opposed by the U.S. government.

He argues that the mass media would be expected to "disregard unfavorable human rights conditions as irrelevant to elections in the client state but would feature them prominently in covering an election in a disfavored state."

He content-analyzed 28 articles about the Salvadoran election and 21 articles about the Nicaraguan election that were published in the *New York Times* during 1984.

Herman says that from a propaganda framework one would predict that where the United States supports the government in power, the apparent "democratic aspects" of the election would be stressed over any aspects that might detract from the election's legitimacy, which would be downplayed or ignored. One would also expect the media to downplay the foreign sponsor's role in organizing and funding the election, the public relations purpose of the election from the sponsor's viewpoint, and a number of other major factors.

In the case where the United States opposes the government in power, Herman says the same framework would lead to the prediction that coverage would reveal a total reversal of topical emphasis.

Herman argues that the human rights violations were, in many cases, far more extreme in the election the United States supported than in the election the United States opposed, yet the data from the content analysis indicated that the news coverage ignored most of the former while emphasizing most of the latter.

He concluded, "In sum, although basic electoral conditions were far more compatible with a free election in Nicaragua in 1984 than they were in El Salvador in either 1982 or 1984, U.S. news coverage gave El Salvador a triumphant vindication of democracy and Nicaragua an electoral experiment discredited by Sandinista intransigence and totalitarian controls" (Herman, 1985, p. 145). The researcher's generalization from a case study of the *New York Times* to "U.S. news coverage" would be considered unwarranted by most, lacking further data about U.S. news coverage on these topics. Nevertheless, the researcher has provided data on how one of the most prestigious newspapers in the United States covered these two elections and has provided a framework for further investigations of similar events.

The author adds:

The media campaigns . . . embody sharply dichotomous manipulations of symbols and political agendas. These media campaigns were quite successful in scoring political points and making important ideological statements to the general public and the world at large. In these cases dissident voices in the United States were not available in any of the major media, even when those voices might have suggested relevant information that had been "overlooked" or "selected out." These two case studies are offered as illustrations that a propaganda framework is frequently applicable to the performance of the U.S. mass media and that in such cases meaningful diversity of opinion may be absent from media coverage of important news issues. (p. 145)

The Merrill and the Fedler, Meeske, and Hall studies are good examples of the application of principles from general semantics and content analysis applied to an examination of one of the major media in the United States. The follow-up is also a good example of the cumulative nature of science discussed in Chapter 2.

Another journalism professor, Dennis Lowry (1971), used the Hayakawa categories of reports, inferences, and judgments as the basis for a study of whether Vice President Spiro Agnew's famous Des Moines speech had an intimidating effect on television newscasters. Lowry notes the following major criticisms of the media made by Agnew:

1. The fact that "a little group of men . . . wield a free hand in selecting, presenting and interpreting the great issues of our Nation"; these men are the "anchor men, commentators and executive producers" of the TV newscasts

2. The "slander" and attacks which emanate from "the privileged sanctuary of a network studio"
3. "Whether a form of censorship already exists when the news that 40 million Americans receive each night is determined by a handful of men responsible only to their corporate employers and filtered through a handful of commentators who admit to their own set of biases." (*New York Times*, Nov. 14, 1969, p. 24, cited in Lowry, 1971, p. 205)

Lowry studied a random sample of network newscasts before and after the Agnew address. He looked only at statements dealing with the presidential administration, and he sorted them into these nine categories: attributed reports, unattributed reports, labeled inferences, unlabeled inferences, attributed favorable judgments, attributed unfavorable judgments, unattributed favorable judgments, unattributed unfavorable judgments, and others. Lowry found an increase in the percentage of attributed reports, the safest kind of statement, after the Agnew speech. There were hardly any judgments in the newscasts before or after the Agnew speech, indicating that critics who accused the networks of being biased against the Nixon administration were apparently not noticing judgments. The critics may have been objecting to unlabeled inferences, the category with the highest percentage before and after the Agnew speech (49 percent each time). The critics might also have objected to slanting, but that would be difficult to study since it involves omission of material.

IMPLICATIONS FOR ENCODING

Now we can return to our original question of what general semantics can tell us about *encoding,* the translating of purpose, intention, or meaning into symbols or codes. The lesson from general semantics is that encoding is a difficult task often fraught with pitfalls. There are only a limited number of words available in the English language, and often these words correspond to the real world in only a rough way. Any writer facing the common problem of trying to find the "right word" to express an idea is aware of the difficulty of encoding.

Alvin Toffler recalls an experience he had while working as a journalist covering a Senate disarmament hearing in Washington and trying to condense several hours of testimony into 500 words. He says (1989):

I knew that I couldn't capture the full reality . . . since then I have regarded page one of the newspaper as a kind of fiction, a distorted map of a territory, too complex and too fast-changing to map. Nevertheless it is a fiction that we live by. (p. 198)

Furthermore, it is possible to encode in such a way that one is actually saying very little about the real world. This is true when language stays at a high level of abstraction.

Finally, the concept of projection makes us aware of the difficulty of being objective. Any statement is to some degree a statement about the speaker and is thus subjective. The best way to overcome the problem of subjectivity is to stick to verifiable statements, or reports.

CONCLUSIONS

General semantics deals with the relationship between language and reality and with the ways in which language influences our thinking.

General semantics has a number of implications for the practitioner of mass communication. First, it points out the difficulty of encoding, of expressing meaning in symbols or codes. Second, it provides a basis for analyzing and talking about objectivity—a major communications concept. Third, it can help the mass communicator—or anyone else—in sorting out information and misinformation. The general semanticists have identified some misuses of language—dead-level abstracting, undue identification, two-valued evaluation, and unconscious projection—that are widespread. Knowledge of these misuses could be very beneficial to the reporter interviewing a news source. Such knowledge could also help the consumer of mass communication—the ordinary citizen trying to cope with the daily barrage of information and misinformation from the mass media.

DISCUSSION

1. Our world changes faster than our language does. Name a change for which we do not yet have an adequate term.
2. Can you give a recent example from the media of "guilt by association"?
3. Name a hidden assumption in our language.
4. Give an example of dead-level abstraction (at either a high or low level) from a recent speech.
5. Undue identification and stereotyping is frequent in our society. Can you give a recent example from the mass media, your school publications, or one of your classes?
6. We tend to think and speak in polar opposites, or in either-or terms while excluding degrees of possibilities. Give a recent example of either-or thinking.
7. We often tend to project our views when we make statements or evaluations. Give a recent example of your having done so.

REFERENCES

Bronowski, J. (1951). *The Common Sense of Science*. London: William Heinemann.
Brown, H. (1988). *A Father's Book of Wisdom*. Nashville, Tenn.: Rutledge Hill Press.
Fedler, F., M. Meeske, and J. Hall (1979). *Time* magazine revisited: Presidential stereotypes persist. *Journalism Quarterly* 56: 353-359.

Fedler, F., Ron Smith, and Mike Meeske (1983). *Time* and *Newsweek* favor John F. Kennedy, criticize Robert and Edward Kennedy. *Journalism Quarterly* 60: 489-496.

Hayakawa, S. I. (1964). *Language in Thought and Action.* 2nd ed. New York: Harcourt, Brace and World.

Herman, E. S. (1985). Diversity of news: "Marginalizing" the opposition. *Journal of Communication* 35: 135-146.

Johnson, W. (1946). *People in Quandaries: The Semantics of Personal Adjustment.* New York: Harper & Row.

————. (1972). The communication process and general semantic principles. In W. Schramm (ed.), *Mass Communications*, 2nd ed., pp. 301-315. Urbana: University of Illinois Press.

Kamal, Mohamed (1987). Why tar Arabs and Islam? *New York Times*, Feb. 16, p. 17.

Kelley, E. (1947). *Education for What Is Real.* New York: Harper.

Korzybski, A. (1958). *Science and Sanity: An Introduction to Non-Aristotelian Systems and General Semantics.* 4th ed. Lakeville, Conn.: The International Non-Aristotelian Library Publishing Co.

Lowry, D. T. (1971). Agnew and the network TV news: A before-after content analysis. *Journalism Quarterly* 48: 205-210.

Mann, L. (1974). Counting the crowd: Effects of editorial policy on estimates. *Journalism Quarterly* 51: 278-285.

Merrill, J. C. (1965). How *Time* stereotyped three U.S. presidents. *Journalism Quarterly* 42: 563-570.

Miller, G. A. (1963). *Language and Communication.* New York: McGraw-Hill.

Suro, Roberto (1991). Where America is growing: The suburban cities. *New York Times*, Feb. 23, p. A1.

Toffler, A. (1989). The relevance of general semantics. *ETC. et cetera* 46: 197-199.

Weisbord, Robert, and Norbert Hedderich (1993). Max Schmeling: Righteous ring warrior? *History Today* 43 (Jan.): 36.

Whorf, B. (1952). Language, mind, and reality. *ETC.* 9: 167-188.

chapter 6

Analysis of Propaganda: First Theories of Decoding and Effects

$\mathbf{P}$ropaganda was the topic of a number of books between the world wars. When Harold Lasswell's doctoral dissertation on the use of propaganda in World War I was published as a book in 1927, one reviewer called it "a Machiavellian textbook which should promptly be destroyed" (Dulles, 1928, p. 107). The reviewer's reaction indicates the kind of fear with which the techniques of propaganda were viewed following World War I. One book on American propaganda in World War I even had the title *Words That Won the War* (Mock & Larson, 1939). In this climate, it is no wonder that people were concerned about the effects of propaganda as World War II drew near.

Propaganda was thought to have great power. For our purposes its significance is that some of our first theoretical thinking about the effects of mass communication came out of the various analyses of propaganda. As we look back on it now, much of it appears to be rather primitive theory. Nevertheless, two important areas of communication theory have their roots in this early thinking about propaganda. One of these is *attitude change*, traditionally one of the major areas of communication research. What are the most effective methods for changing people's attitudes? The study of propaganda provided some tentative answers to this question. The second area is theoretical thinking about the *general effects* of mass communication. What effects does mass communication have on individuals and society? How do these effects take place?

WHAT IS PROPAGANDA?

The term *propaganda* comes from the *Congregatio de propaganda fide,* or Congregation for the Propagation of Faith, established by the Catholic Church in 1622. This was the time of the Reformation, in which various groups were breaking away from the Catholic Church, and the Congregation was part of the Church's Counter-Reformation. One of the great issues of this period was the struggle between science and religion as the source of knowledge about the world. One of the principal figures in this struggle was Galileo, who argued on the basis of observations through a telescope that the earth revolved around the sun. This idea ran directly against the teachings of the Catholic Church and was in fact one of the Church's forbidden propositions. Galileo was tried and convicted by the Inquisition in 1633 and was made to renounce his statements that the earth revolved around the sun. The Church was left in the position of defending an indefensible idea. Perhaps the term *propaganda* picked up some of its negative associations or its connotations of untruth from this major incident in which the Church was left arguing for a position that was scientifically demonstrable as false. In 1980 the Church undertook a new study of Galileo to determine if he had indeed been guilty of heresy. It was reported that the move was part of a new effort to give the Church a central and credible role in culture and science (Fleming, 1980).

Lasswell's classic work, *Propaganda Technique in the World War* (1927), presented one of the first careful attempts to define propaganda: "It refers solely to the control of opinion by significant symbols, or, to speak more concretely and less accurately, by stories, rumors, reports, pictures and other forms of social communication" (p. 9).

Lasswell (1937) presented a slightly different definition a few years later: "Propaganda in the broadest sense is the technique of influencing human action by the manipulation of representations. These representations may take spoken, written, pictorial or musical form" (1937, pp. 521–522).

Both of Lasswell's definitions would include most of advertising, and in fact, would appear to include all of what is often referred to as *persuasion*. In fact, Lasswell has stated that "both advertising and publicity fall within the field of propaganda" (1937, p. 522).

Lasswell's definitions would include a teacher influencing a class to study, an act many people would not want to call *propaganda*. Thus Lasswell's definitions may be too broad for some purposes.

Psychologist Roger Brown (1958) attempted to deal with this problem by making a distinction between propaganda and persuasion. Brown defined *persuasion* as "symbol-manipulation designed to produce action in others" (p. 299). He then pointed out that persuasive efforts are labeled *propaganda* "when someone judges that the action which is the goal of the persuasive effort will be advantageous to the persuader but not in the best interests of the persuadee" (p. 300). In other words, there are no absolute criteria to determine whether an act of persuasion is propaganda—that is a judgment someone makes. And as far as the techniques used are concerned, persuasion and propaganda are identical. Only when it is perceived that an act benefits the source, but not the receiver, can such an act or message be called *propaganda*.

As defined by both Lasswell and Brown, propaganda would include much of advertising (where the aim is not the good of the receiver but greater sales for the advertiser), much of political campaigning (where the aim is not the good of the receiver but the candidate's election), and much of public relations (where the aim is often not the good of the receiver but the most favorable image of a corporation).

Lasswell (1927) also discussed four major objectives of propaganda:

1. To mobilize hatred against the enemy
2. To preserve the friendship of allies
3. To preserve the friendship and, if possible, to procure the cooperation of neutrals
4. To demoralize the enemy (p. 195)

These are obviously wartime objectives that would not apply to advertising or other peacetime types of persuasion.

Wartime Propaganda

Wartime propaganda can be traced back to *The Art of War,* a book written by Sun Tsu before the birth of Christ (Read, 1941). But it came into its own in World War I, when it was used on a scale and with an effectiveness that had never been seen before. This was in large part because people were naïve about propaganda. One expert has pointed out that the 1913 edition of the *Encyclopaedia Britannica* did not even have an article on "propaganda" (Read, 1941). One of the most effective techniques, particularly in achieving Lasswell's first objective of mobilizing hatred against the enemy, was the use of atrocity stories, which were spread by both sides. The Allies were very successful in whipping up hatred for the Germans with a widely reported story that German soldiers in Belgium were cutting the hands off Belgian children. Atrocity stories were often part of speeches given in movie theaters in the United States by "four-minute men," speakers with talks carefully timed to four minutes (Mock & Larsen, 1939). Most of these atrocity stories were false, but they did a great deal to make World War I propaganda effective because people believed them.

Propaganda Education

Propaganda education became a major concern in the United States in the period prior to World War II. Perhaps some Americans were worried that the techniques the United States had used so effectively in World War I were about to be used against them.

Social psychologist Hadley Cantril (1965) described how sometime during the 1930s he gave a radio talk over a Boston radio station on the subject of propaganda. The next day he received a telephone call from Edward A. Filene, the successful merchant who organized the credit union movement in the United States and founded the Twentieth Century Fund. Filene wanted to finance an undertaking to teach people how to think, and he asked Cantril to spend an evening with him talking over the idea. They finally decided that they might not be able to teach people how to think but that they might have some success in teaching people how not to think. The result was the establishment in 1937 of the Institute for Propaganda Analysis, with Cantril as its first president. The advisory board of the institute included names of several other people who later made various contributions to communication theory, including Edgar Dale and Leonard Doob.

The institute was concerned about the rise of the Nazis to power in Germany and the effects that Nazi propaganda might have in the United States. Hitler and his propaganda minister, Joseph Goebbels, seemed to be having great success with propaganda in Germany. The institute was concerned about the possibility of a Hitler figure rising to power in the United States. This may seem unlikely now, but we should remember that Nazi rallies were being held in Madison Square Garden and across America in the 1930s. Furthermore, there was even a fairly likely candidate to become the American Hitler. This was Father Charles E. Coughlin, a Catholic priest who was broadcasting over a 47-station radio network and became known as the "radio priest." Coughlin's radio program every Sunday was reaching 30 million listeners, as many as some television programs reach today. This audience was proportionately much greater than most audiences reached by mass communication today. Coughlin was apparently a colorful individual: his church in Royal Oak, Michigan, was called the Shrine of the Little Flower, and he had set up on the corner of the property the Shrine Super-Service and Hot Dog Stand. His radio talks, however, seemed to present a fascist philosophy. In fact, his magazine, *Social Justice*, was eventually banned from the U.S. mail because it mirrored the Nazi propaganda line. Coughlin's radio career finally came to a stop when he was reprimanded by the Church.

Perhaps the most famous publication of the Institute for Propaganda Analysis was a book edited by Alfred McClung Lee and Elizabeth Briant Lee (1939) called *The Fine Art of Propaganda.* The book presented seven common devices of propaganda, and it used examples from Coughlin's speeches to illustrate the devices. These devices were given catchy names and were simple enough to be taught in the public schools.

THE PROPAGANDA DEVICES

The seven propaganda devices are *name calling, glittering generality, transfer, testimonial, plain folks, card stacking,* and *band wagon.* Each will be defined and discussed with examples from contemporary society—political campaigns, advertisements, newspaper columns, and statements by extremist groups.

Name Calling

"Name calling—giving an idea a bad label—is used to make us reject and condemn the idea without examining the evidence" (Lee & Lee, 1939, p. 26).

Name calling doesn't appear much in advertising, probably because there is a reluctance to mention a competing product, even by calling it a name. Its use in politics and other areas of public discourse is more common, however.

Terrorism. Two current examples of name calling are *terrorist* and *terrorism.* As the old maxim goes, "One person's terrorist is another person's freedom fighter." General semanticists point out that what we call a person will depend on our purposes, our projections, and our evaluations, yet the person does not change when we change the label.

Terrorist and terrorism have been called clichés in search of meanings. Christopher Hitchens (1989) asked if an "act of terrorism" always refers to the kind of action taken or whether its use sometimes depends on who takes the action. He quoted a consultant to the U.S. State Department on terrorism, who is also the executive director of the Institute on Terrorism and Subnational Conflict and coeditor of *Fighting Back: Winning the War against Terrorism,* as having said:

> Can I provide a universally acceptable definition of terrorism? I fear I have to say I cannot. (p. 148)

Hitchens cites two associates of the Center for Strategic and International Studies in Washington, D.C., from their book, *Terrorism as State-Sponsored Warfare,* as saying:

> There is no universal agreement about who is a terrorist because the political and strategic goals affect different states differently. There is no value-free definition. (p. 148)

Hitchens then cites the introduction of a Rand Corporation publication:

> What do we mean by terrorism? The term, unfortunately, has no precise or widely accepted definition. The problem of definition is compounded by the fact that *terrorism* has become a fad word that is applied to all sorts of violence. (p.149) (italics in original)

A "freedom fighter" to one person may be a "terrorist" to another. At the end of World War II, when Great Britain still held a mandate over Palestine, many of Israel's contemporary leaders were conducting guerrilla warfare against the British. Yitzhak Shamir, later to become Israel's prime minister, had been a member of *Irgun* and then became one of the three top commanders of *Lehi* (or LHY, *Lohamei Herut Yisrael,* or Fighters for the Freedom of Israel), also known as the Stern Gang, after its first leader. As one writer points out:

> Under his (Shamir's) leadership, the group undertook a campaign of "personal terror," assassinating top British military and government

officers, often gunning them down in the street. . . . Ironically, it was a guerrilla act by the Lehi's chief rival, the Irgun headed by Menachem Begin, that got Shamir in trouble. In 1946, Irgun guerrillas bombed the King David Hotel; a total of 91 people were killed, including British citizens, Jews and Arabs. . . . Was Yitzhak Shamir a terrorist? "Yes" Johnson (a former member of the Palestine Police) said, "to the British Government. But to the Jews, the Stern Gang were freedom fighters. But that is the same as the P.L.O., who are terrorists to the Israelis and freedom fighters to the Arabs." (Brinkley, 1988, p. 68)

Ezer Weizman, a senior Labor Party member and former Israeli Defense Minister, also was a member of the *Irgun,* which blew up Jerusalem's King David Hotel in 1946 (Brooks, 1988).

Some highly respected members of our society today were once "underground" soldiers or "freedom fighters." To their enemies, as with the former police official quoted above, they were "terrorists."

The noted psychosexual therapist Dr. Ruth Westheimer, in an article arguing for women to be assigned combat duty, wrote (1990):

At the age of 16 I immigrated to Palestine from Europe, where I became a member of the Haganah, the main underground army of the Jews . . . and was trained as a sniper so that I could hit the center of the target time after time. . . . I almost lost both my feet as a result of a bombing attack on Jerusalem. (p. 15)

One veteran Middle-East reporter points out (Haberman, 1992):

Invariably, Palestinians responsible for attacks are referred to as "terrorists" in official Israeli statements and in most news articles. It makes no difference who or what the target was, a schoolgirl or an army outpost. By definition, an angry Palestinian with a knife in his hand is a terrorist. In the same way, he is a "fighter" as far as the other side is concerned. At the very least he is an "activist" and not a "militant," as Israelis often insist on calling him. Should he be killed by Israeli soldiers, even while carrying out an extraordinarily violent act, he becomes "a martyr."

It is different, of course, if he is killed by a fellow Palestinian for helping the Israelis in some way. Then he is a "collaborator," and deserving of death in the opinion of many Palestinians. (p. A1)

Whether a person is called an "underground" soldier or "freedom fighter," or a "terrorist" depends on the viewpoint of the person assigning the label, or the side the person assigning the label supports. Often the *activities* of an "underground" soldier or "freedom fighter" and those of a "terrorist" are *identical*—only the *label* changes.

Sometimes name calling can affect the destinies of nations and millions of people. One notable case probably deserves more than passing attention, since it involves one of the pioneers of the public relations industry.

Examples of Name Calling.   In the early 1950s the United Fruit Company was faced with the expropriation of its vast uncultivated land holdings in Guatemala for redistribution to landless peasants by the new Arbenz government. In his book *An American Company* (1976), the former vice president for corporate public relations of the United Fruit Company, Thomas P. McCann, tells how the company circulated the rumor that the move was Communist-inspired. He tells how press junkets to Guatemala were run for leading U.S. journalists, how "Communist demonstrations" were arranged upon the journalists' arrival, and how public opinion in the United States was turned against the Guatemalan government. This was name calling with a vengeance for the sake of future hundreds-of-millions of dollars of corporate profits. McCann says, "It is difficult to make a convincing case for manipulation of the press when the victims proved so eager for the experience" (p. 47). The compensation offered for the uncultivated land by the Guatemalan government, which was based on the very value placed on the land by the United Fruit Company for purposes of taxation, was rejected as totally inadequate. The U.S. State Department was convinced of the "Communist threat." Secretary of State John Foster Dulles had been a member of the New York law firm Sullivan and Cromwell, which represented United Fruit in Central America. The legitimately elected government of Guatemala was overthrown by a CIA-mounted invasion that used United Fruit Company facilities as a base of operations (Chapter 4). Today Guatemala has the oldest and most violent civil war in Central America, as a result of repression by the extreme rightist oligarchy and the rigid concentration of wealth (Gruson, 1990a). More than 100,000 people have died in the 40-year-old civil war (Greenhouse, 1995). Guatemala is the world's sixth largest producer of opium poppies and has become a major transshipment point for cocaine (Gruson, 1990b; Millett, 1994).

McCann says, "Responsible for putting the best face on corporate strategy was Edward L. Bernays, the 'father of public relations,' the biggest name in the field" (p. 45).

In his 1928 book *Propaganda,* Bernays said:

> The conscious and intelligent manipulation of the organized habits and opinions of the masses is an important element in democratic society. Those who manipulate this unseen mechanism of society constitute an invisible government which is the true ruling power of our country. . . .
>
> It has been found possible so to mold the mind of the masses that they will throw their newly gained strength in the desired direction. . . . But clearly it is the intelligent minorities which need to make use of propaganda continuously and systematically. In the active proselytizing minorities in whom *selfish* interests and public interests coincide lie the progress and development of America. (pp. 9, 19, 31)

Dow Chemical Company engaged in name calling when it spread false "confidential" medical reports claiming that a young woman Greenpeace environmental protester had syphilis. She was one of five protesters arrested during a demonstration against the Midland, Michigan-based chemical giant. The protesters were charged with trespassing when they tried to block Dow from discharging chemicals into the river that flows through Midland. Dow was considered by many to be a major polluter of the river. When the charge that the woman had syphilis was proved false, the company was forced to publish a full-page newspaper ad in apology. The president of Dow U.S.A., Hunter Henry, said, "A serious error in judgment was made by several Michigan division personnel in passing along personal information which reached them about a Greenpeace member" *(Austin American-Statesman,* Oct. 19, 1985, p. A9).

It should be noted that the alleged medical condition of the Greenpeace protester had no connection whatsoever with the reason for the protest (pollution of the river), but was simply an attempt to discredit her. This is a common propaganda method used to *divert attention* from the issue and discredit the credibility of the communicator. (We will return to this topic in later chapters.)

More recently, widely disputed testimony before the Congressional Human Rights Caucus about alleged atrocities by Iraqi soldiers in Kuwait resulted in name calling in the public relations campaign to help steer the United States into the Gulf War. A teen-age girl, Nayirah, testified that she had seen Iraqi soldiers remove hundreds of Kuwaiti babies from incubators and leave them to die on hospital floors (MacArthur, 1992). The chairmen of the congressional group explained that the witness's identity would be kept secret to protect her family in occupied Kuwait. President George Bush cited the incubator story six times in speeches and seven senators cited the story as a reason for voting to give Bush authorization for the Gulf War.

The atrocities of the Iraqis in Kuwait were compared to that of the Nazis.

After the liberation of Kuwait, an ABC-Television reporter interviewed hospital doctors who stayed in Kuwait throughout the Iraqi occupation and indicated that the story was almost certainly false.

Subsequent investigation showed that, unknown to most of the members of the Caucus, the 15-year-old Kuwaiti girl was the daughter of the Kuwaiti ambassador to the United States. As one reporter (MacArthur, 1992) observed, such knowledge might have led to demands of proof of Nayirah's whereabouts when she said she witnessed the atrocities and calls for corroboration of the story.

The congressmen co-chairing the committee, who apparently knew the true identity of the teen-age witness, had close relationships with Hill and Knowlton, the public relations firm hired by Citizens for a Free Kuwait, the group financed by Kuwait which lobbied Congress for U.S. military intervention. A vice president of Hill and Knowlton helped organize the congressional hearings. The same Hill and Knowlton vice president had been previously known for defending the human rights records of Turkey, which has been criticized for jailing people without due process and torturing and killing them. He also lobbied for Hill and

Knowlton in behalf of Indonesia, which has, since 1975, killed more than 100,000 people in East Timor.

A video public relations release of Iraq's invasion of Kuwait was the second most used PR video release in 1990, with 61 million viewers. It was produced by Hill and Knowlton for Citizens for a Free Kuwait (Sonenclar, 1991).

In a letter of rebuttal, the president and CEO of Hill and Knowlton, Thomas E. Eidson, wrote that the firm had not at any time collaborated with anyone to produce knowingly deceptive testimony, that Nayirah was inside Kuwait at the time in question and had volunteered to work under an assumed name at the Al-Adan Hospital, and that the United States Embassy confirms that she was in Kuwait at that time. He also cited testimony to the United Nations by the head of the Kuwaiti Red Crescent (Red Cross) citing firsthand involvement in burying newborn babies taken from their incubators by soldiers (Eidson, 1992).

Syndicated columnist Mary McGrory (1992) commenting on this incident wrote of:

> . . . the incestuous relationship between public relations and public policy and the coziness between Congress and people who are paid vast sums to influence them—and what countries do when they want to go to war. It is overlaid with fine scum. (p. C1)

Glittering Generality

"Glittering generality—associating something with a 'virtue word'—is used to make us accept and approve the thing without examining the evidence" (Lee & Lee, 1939, p. 47).

The use of glittering generalities is so pervasive that we hardly notice it.

Product Names and Promotion. One of the common uses of virtue words is in the very names of products, such as Gold Medal flour, Imperial margarine, Wonder bread, Southern Comfort, Super Shell, and Superior Dairy. Some cereals are given names that will particularly appeal to children—Cheerios, Cap'n Crunch, Froot Loops.

Sometimes the glittering generalities used by advertisers can involve deception to such a degree that legal action is taken. Some shampoo manufacturers were requested by the Federal Trade Commission to document the statement that their products contained "natural ingredients," a claim played up in advertising. The "natural ingredients" turned out to be things like coconut oil and plain water.

Politics and Business. The glittering generality device shows up in areas other than advertising, such as politics. Calling a proposed law a "right to work" law might be an effective way to get the law passed; who would oppose the right to work? In a similar use, the members of Congress who toured the United States to speak against the Panama Canal treaty called themselves a "truth squad."

Franklin D. Roosevelt's decision to call his program the New Deal was an effective choice of a glittering generality; it sounded good, and it suggested that he was correcting a misdeal.

Most people do not usually regard war positively, but politicians have worked hard in recent years to give war a positive "spin," sometimes even extending its duration. General Norman Schwarzkopf, speaking of the Gulf War of 1991, commented on:

> . . . Washington's order to delay the cease-fire for two hours in order to make the ground attack a "hundred-hour war." General Schwarzkopf's wry comment: "They really know how to package an historic event." (Eisenhower, 1992, p. 49)

Presumably, a "hundred-hour war" is more acceptable than a "war."

Economist Daniel Bell (1976) has brought out what a tricky public relations job it was to introduce installment buying in the United States, where the Protestant ethic, with its emphasis on saving and abstinence, prevailed. The key to the campaign was to avoid the word *debt* and emphasize the word *credit*.

The lexicon of the business world is full of glittering generalities. For example, businesses that incur annual losses now show *negative income*. Public relations releases are now sometimes called *directed communications*.

After a nationwide survey of 1,200 persons indicated that people consider *capitalism* to be associated with certain negative aspects of big business, a business research institute recommended that the term *private enterprise* be substituted by candidates for public office. The researchers found the latter term tends to be associated in most people's minds with small businesses, particularly the "mom and pop stores" of which they hold an overwhelmingly favorable impression (Tindol, 1988).

International Relations.   The U.S. government invaded Panama in December 1989 under the name "Operation Just Cause." After General Manuel Antonio Noriega was brought to the United States, several legal scholars said the apprehension was basically a blunt political act with only after-the-fact legal rationale. A senior lawyer at the World Court said the closest parallel may lie in ancient Rome when defeated leaders were taken to the circus and displayed (Lewis, 1990).

While Dow was engaged in the name calling of the Greenpeace demonstrator, it was also mounting a $60 million advertising campaign ("Dow lets you do great things") to improve its corporate image (Bussey, 1987). The campaign was filled with what many would call glittering generalities. The commercials depicted recent college grads, in conversation with friends, families, and fiancées, who had chosen to accept employment with Dow because of its international humanitarian concerns. Those who do not know or remember the recent past history of Dow may wonder why it felt compelled to spend $60 million a year on advertising to improve its corporate image.

Dow, until that time primarily a manufacturer of chemicals for resale to other manufacturers, had a serious public relations problem. It made napalm, the jellied gasoline that kills in an especially painful way, and the defoliant Agent Orange, both widely used in Vietnam; it refused to make public to disabled Vietnam veterans its data on the biological effects of dioxin (a component of Agent Orange); it canceled contributions to a college that had a speaker who attacked its corporate policies; and it refused to allow EPA inspectors to fly over its plants to collect air samples, an issue that Dow fought to the U.S. Supreme Court and lost (Deutsch, 1987). Because of Dow's falling profits from industrial chemicals the company moved heavily into consumer products, an area where Dow's public image was more important. A few months after beginning the advertising and public relations campaign containing many glittering generalities, the company raised positive reaction to its image by 6 points to 29 percent (Bussey, 1987).

Transfer

"Transfer carries the authority, sanction, and prestige of something respected and revered over to something else in order to make the latter more acceptable" (Lee & Lee, 1939, p. 69). Transfer works through a process of association, but instead of guilt by association it's usually something more like "admiration by association." The communicator's goal is to link an idea or product or cause with something that people admire.

Transfer can take place through the use of symbolic objects. Ku Klux Klan rallies feature the burning of a cross, a Christian symbol. A minor presidential candidate from Chicago named Lar Daley used to campaign in an Uncle Sam suit.

Commercial Uses. During the celebration marking the centennial of the Statue of Liberty in 1986, it was common to link the statue with all kinds of products, from plastic knickknacks to boxer shorts and G-strings.

Often the association is designed to be longer-lasting than a fleeting commercial. Sears featured the Statue of Liberty on the cover of its 1986 Fall-Winter Centennial Edition catalog along with the words "Celebrating Sears' New Century." Included with the catalog was a small bronze coin depicting on the face the head of the statue above the word *Liberty* and the words *Contains Authentic Material* (recovered during the restoration of the statue). The reverse of the coin carries the message "Celebrating Sears' New Century."

One report commenting on commercial ties with Lady Liberty observed, "It gives Corporate America a chance to use the festivities to do some image polishing of its own—and maybe to make a little money, too" (Henriques, 1986). Another writer noted, "Lee Iacocca, the head of the fund-raising effort to restore the statue, sold it as a marketing symbol to bring in millions of dollars from big U.S. corporations" (Maclean, 1986).

Music. Sometimes the transfer takes place through the use of music. Music appears in a television commercial for the telephone company. The words are "Hello, America, how are you?" but the tune, written by Steve Goodman and made popular by Arlo Guthrie, is the song "The City of New Orleans," a tribute to a train with that name. This allows the telephone company to associate itself with the nostalgia for the vanishing railroads as well as with youth.

Sometimes the transfer can take place just through two people appearing together. This kind of transfer can reach a large number of people through a news photograph, film clip, or videotape of the event showing the two people together.

Advertising. Many advertisements and commercials are built primarily around the transfer device. The Marlboro cigarette campaign, thought by some experts to be the most successful advertising campaign in 40 years, was designed to transfer the ruggedness and virility of the cowboys in the ads to the cigarette and to the people who smoke Marlboros.

Many liquor ads around Christmas are designed to build strong associations between Christmas and the use of liquor. J&B Scotch has used the song title "Jingle Bells" in ads of this type with the J and the B in the title emphasized in such a way that there appears to be an intimate connection between the old familiar song and their product. The goal seems to be to make you think of "Jingle Bells" and their product together.

Sometimes the transfer is from a prestige personality that is in itself manufactured. Betty Crocker, a figment of General Mills's corporate public relations imagination since 1921, has sold millions of cookbooks and billions of packages of General Mills products. When first introduced, she was just a name and in 1936 she was given a face. With five makeovers, she has gotten progressively younger with age and has gone from a homespun, grandmotherly housewife to a dressed-for-success yuppie, not a day over 35, just in from the office and ready to whip up something for dinner with the food processor and the microwave.

In late 1995 the General Mills imagemakers announced a proposed sixth remake of Betty to reflect ethnic diversity and invited the public to submit photographs in their search for 75 women (for the 75th anniversary of Betty) who most embody the Betty Crocker essence. They are to be "morphed" (a computer-generated composite) into a new image of Betty. Company spokesman Craig Shulstad said General Mills is hoping for ethnic diversity with a goal of giving Betty more politically correct features (Chavarria Chairez, 1995; Quirk, 1995; Wells, 1995).

In the meantime General Mills's television commercials seem to have taken a different tack, announcing, "Betty Crocker knows what guys want . . . and Betty Crocker makes one hot potato" (television commercial broadcast in September and October 1995). Or, perhaps, the commercial foretells things to come of Betty's image makeover.

Testimonial

"Testimonial consists in having some respected or hated person say that a given idea or program or product or person is good or bad" (Lee & Lee, 1939, p. 74). It is a common technique in advertising and political campaigning.

How true are testimonials? Writer Barry Farrell (1975) did some checking on Peter Ustinov's commercials for Gallo wines. Ustinov was praising the company's new line of varietal wines, but Gallo also makes Ripple, Boone's Farm, and Thunderbird—wines unlikely to appear on Peter Ustinov's table. In the commercials, Ustinov speaks of "my friends Ernest and Julio Gallo" and their passion for making fine wines. Farrell found out that Ustinov never knew the Gallos until he was hired to do the commercials.

Plain Folks

"Plain folks is the method by which a speaker attempts to convince his audience that he and his ideas are good because they are 'of the people,' the 'plain folks'" (Lee & Lee, 1939, p. 92).

Advertising. The "plain folks" device used to be more common in politics than it was in advertising, although such campaigns for commercial products have increased in recent years. Bartles and James wine cooler commercials clearly use that approach. So do the Wilfred Brimley television commercials for oatmeal, the Orville Redenbacher popcorn ads, and Charlie Welch playing "Mr. Titus" in Pepperidge Farm television commercials. A model in a television commercial promoting beauty aids says, "Don't hate me because I'm beautiful. First thing in the morning, I look just like you." Commercials for a regional brand of baked goods feature "down-home" scenes and a jingle about a "land of gingham blue," while a series for a regional brand of ice cream depicts cows that think a small town is heaven, and rural individuals give testimonials for the ice cream.

Politics. In late April 1992 political professionals trying to get Bill Clinton elected president found that more than 40 percent of the voters did not like the candidate. He was perceived as a "wishy-washy," fast-talking career politician who did not "talk straight." Hillary Clinton was liked even less for "being in the race for herself," "going for power," and intent on "running the show" (Kelly, 1992). Clinton's polling expert, chief strategist, and media consultant agreed to construct a new image for Mr. and Mrs. Clinton as: "an honest, plain-folks ideal-ist and his warm and loving wife" (Kelly, 1992, p. A1).

On the campaign trail in July 1992, the Clintons and Senator and Mrs. Al Gore were photographed in casual attire, sitting on hay bales while talking with farmers near Utica, Ohio. In the background were a cornfield, a farm equipment shed, and a number of "suits." The *New York Times,* with a large photo, used the headline, "Just Folks" (July 26, 1992, The Week in Review, Sec. 4, p. 1).

One day later, a major news article about the Clintons's finances pointed out that, before Clinton was elected president, the Clintons ranked in the top 1 percent of the United States in household income and in the top 3 percent for household net worth (Anrig and MacDonald, 1992).

Three years later President Clinton reverted to the just plain folks image. One reporter wrote (Nichols, 1995):

A folksy President Clinton in blue jeans, cowboy boots . . . finished a 48-hour courtship Thursday of a region where his political standing has sagged. . . . Clinton . . . used his Rocky Mountain visit as a dress rehearsal for the grueling campaign travel to come . . . this two-day visit to Colorado and Montana was a time for Clinton to hone the "just *plain folks*" image he'll deploy in his reelection bid. (p. 8A) (italics added)

Card Stacking

"Card stacking involves the selection and use of facts or falsehoods, illustrations or distractions, and logical or illogical statements in order to give the best or worst possible case for an idea, program, person, or product" (Lee & Lee, 1939, p. 95).

Card stacking is basically identical to the general semantics technique of slanting (see Chapter 5). It is selecting arguments or evidence that support a position and ignoring those that do not support the position. The arguments that are selected can be true or false. The device probably operates most effectively when the arguments are true, but other equally true arguments are ignored, because then it is hardest to detect.

Some of the clearest examples of card stacking can be found in movie ads that present quotations from movie reviews. These quotations are carefully selected to be only the most favorable. The critics no doubt said the things used in the ads, but they probably said some negative or less positive things also, and these were not brought out.

Closely related to movie ads are the coming attractions shown in theaters, also clear examples of card stacking.

One nationally respected movie reviewer wrote (Maslin, 1992):

Never mind: when it comes to trailers (movie parlance for coming attractions), accuracy is not the issue. Salesmanship is . . . competition forces trailer makers to cram as many big moments as possible into very brief promotional vehicles . . . outrageous claims, misleading images, false promises, seductive little lies—did anyone think these things were now behind us? (p. B1)

The reviewer closes by saying:

Of course, any and all of these trailers may turn out to be seriously misleading. But you'd have to go see the finished film to find that out. And once that happens, the trailer has already done its job. (p. B9)

Television Commercials.   Many television commercials that show interviews with ordinary citizens are also using card stacking. This is the type of commercial in which a television interviewer comes across a woman in a shopping center and asks if she would like a free cup of coffee. After she tastes it, she is asked, "Would you say it tastes as rich as it looks?" The person then says, "It tastes as rich as it looks," or perhaps something even more favorable. These commercials show the people who were interviewed who praised the product, but they don't show or even report the number of interviews in which people did not praise the product. One interviewer for this kind of commercial has said, "The bulk of the answers in those things is indifference. People will say, 'Oh, it's all right'" (Grant, 1978, p. 65).

Historical Cases.   Several historical cases of card stacking with wide-ranging implications have come to light in recent years.

THE LUSITANIA

On May 7, 1915, at a time when the United States was maintaining a strong neutral position under President Woodrow Wilson, the British passenger liner *Lusitania,* which had sailed from New York, was sunk by a German submarine off the Irish coast. It went down with a loss of 1,200 men, women, and children, many of them American. German agents in New York knew that the ship was loading thousands of tons of military materials, including munitions. Prior to the sailing the Germans, in statements published in American newspapers, warned passengers not to take passage on the ship, foretelling the sinking of the liner.

The *Lusitania* was one of several ships that had been built eight years earlier under a secret agreement between the British Admiralty and the Cunard Lines and was, in actuality, an armed auxiliary cruiser of the Royal Navy, a fact that, after the sinking, both England and America vehemently denied. Before the sinking, Winston Churchill, then first lord of the admiralty, commissioned a report to speculate about what would happen if a passenger ship with powerful neutrals aboard were sunk by Germans. World War I naval warfare was conducted according to the internationally recognized "cruiser rules," under which noncombatant ships were boarded and searched for military contraband. If found, passengers were given time to debark before their ship was sunk, so long as that ship posed no direct threat to its attacker. Churchill issued orders to his ships, instructing them to threaten at all times and to ram any submarine that surfaced to send aboard search parties, thereby depriving them of any benefit under the cruiser rules.

The English had broken the German naval code and knew the approximate locations of all German U-boats operating around the British Isles. The Germans had information, which many now believe was planted, that military ships would be in the Irish Sea the first week of May. The British ship assigned to guide the *Lusitania* to safety was suddenly and without explanation recalled. These and many other facts were never revealed—they were kept secret for 50 years. The world raged at the barbarity of the Kaiser and the German people, and the act did much to precipitate the later entrance of the United States into World War I (Simpson, 1972).

GULF OF TONKIN

In 1964 President Lyndon Johnson got the U.S. Congress to pass the Gulf of Tonkin resolution, which set into motion military action against North Vietnam. The claim was made that U.S. destroyers *Maddox* and *Turner Joy*, operating in international waters, had come under unprovoked night attack from North Vietnamese patrol boats on August 2 and 4, and was so portrayed to the American people, who were outraged at the attack. It was not disclosed that in that area at that time, South Vietnamese commandos, trained and supported by the United States, were carrying out seaborne raids against North Vietnamese installations under naval cover supplied by the United States. Also not disclosed at the time of the passage of the Gulf of Tonkin resolution was the fact that there was no evidence that either of the two U.S. ships had ever been fired upon. There were no casualties, neither ship was hit, and there were no reports of fire from the North Vietnamese ships (Stone, 1966, 1968a, 1968b).

THE CHINESE "GREAT PROLETARIAN CULTURAL REVOLUTION"

One writer observes that during the Chinese "great proletarian cultural revolution" usually only one side of an issue was presented. She writes (Chang, 1991):

> It was very hard to get behind the rhetoric, particularly when there was *no alternative viewpoint* from the adult population. In fact, the adults positively colluded in enhancing Mao's cult. (p. 261)

Controlling the News

For decades many governments regularly jammed foreign shortwave radio broadcasts to ensure that their people get only the "official" version of events, while enforcing censorship of outgoing information.

Wartime governments usually try to ensure that only the "correct" version of events is broadcast to the world. During the Russian suppression of the Chechen Republic's independence movement, a television correspondent reported (Manyon, 1994):

> The Russian government is now trying to shut down the satellite television operation in Grozny that is sending pictures of the crisis to the outside world. The Russians are threatening to jam the transmissions.

Band Wagon

"Band wagon has as its theme, 'Everybody—at least all of *us*—is doing it'; with it, the propagandist attempts to convince us that all members of a group to which we belong are accepting his program and that we must therefore follow our crowd and 'jump on the band wagon'" (Lee & Lee, 1939, p. 105).

Advertising.   Many examples of band wagon appeals appear in advertising. A deodorant is described as "the people's choice." A recruitment ad for the U.S. Army shows a group of smiling young people in uniform and says, "Join the people who've joined the Army." A jingle for Sara Lee baked goods states, "Nobody doesn't like Sara Lee." McDonald's brags about the billions of hamburgers sold. A soft drink refers to "the Pepsi generation," suggesting that a whole generation is drinking the product.

Wartime Use.   The band wagon is often used in wartime to convince people that everybody is making sacrifices for the war effort, even to the extent of sacrificing their lives. Nations involved in combat need heroes to build morale. If they do not yet have a hero, they can pick a likely candidate and exaggerate his deeds.

The United States was badly in need of a propaganda shot in the arm in the dark days following Pearl Harbor. It was announced that Army Air Force Captain Colin Kelly had sunk the Japanese battleship *Haruna* when, on December 10, 1941, he gave his own life by dropping a bomb down the ship's smokestack, thereby sinking the ship only three days after Pearl Harbor. He became the first American hero of the war, and a song using his name became a national hit in 1942. In truth, no Japanese warship of the *Haruna*'s size was in that area, and the Haruna survived until it was sunk in Kure Harbor, near Hiroshima, more than three years later (Scott, 1982).

During the Falkland Islands war, 22-year-old Sublieutenant Prince Andrew of Great Britain was depicted as a heroic helicopter pilot, hovering above his ship, HMS *Invincible,* willing to sacrifice himself as a decoy for Exocet missiles fired by Argentine aircraft. According to later press reports, he piloted his helicopter only once, during practice, and "never saw one of the sea-skimming missiles heading straight for him," as was splashed on the front pages, and that "the new nickname for Randy Andy among his mates is Prince BS" (Scott, 1982).

Government Propaganda.   On the home front, governments often need models of production for others to emulate. In China, Chairman Mao touted the Tachai (Dazhai) Production Brigade as a model of self-reliance, saying in 1964, "In agriculture, learn from Tachai." It was then copied on walls across China. The brigade was reputed to have increased its grain yield eightfold from 1949 to 1971, despite its being located in an area of rocky soil, erosion, and poor agriculture. In 1980 the Chinese government claimed that the grain yields of Tachai brigade had been falsified and that the "self-reliant" brigade had accepted millions of yuan in government subsidies and help from army labor battalions (Rogers, 1983, pp. 339–340; Butterfield, 1982, pp. 403–404).

EFFECTIVENESS OF PROPAGANDA DEVICES

The Institute for Propaganda Analysis identified the seven propaganda devices, but it did not research their effectiveness. The Institute seemed to assume that the devices were effective.

Scientific evidence is now available on the effectiveness of some of the propaganda devices. Most of it comes from experiments done by social psychologists investigating how attitudes can be changed. Several of these experiments are essentially tests of the propaganda devices of card stacking, testimonial, and band wagon (Brown, 1958). These experiments are discussed briefly here and in greater detail in later chapters on attitude change and the role of groups in communication (Chapters 9, 10, and 11).

Evidence on the effectiveness of card stacking comes from experiments on the effectiveness of one-sided versus two-sided messages (Hovland, Lumsdaine, & Sheffield, 1949; Lumsdaine & Janis, 1953). The one-sided message is essentially a card-stacking message. Only the arguments on one side of a controversy are presented. In the two-sided message, some of the arguments that can be raised on the other side are mentioned briefly. In general, this research has shown that the one-sided messages work best on some kinds of people (those initially tending to agree with the argument of the message or those lower in education), and two-sided messages work best on other kinds of people (those initially tending to oppose the argument of the message or those higher in education).

Evidence on the effectiveness of testimonials comes from experiments on the effects of the credibility of the source (Hovland & Weiss, 1951). In general, these experiments show that a high-credibility source produces more attitude change than a low-credibility source but that even the high-credibility source typically changes the attitudes of fewer than half the people who receive messages attributed to that source.

Evidence on the effectiveness of band wagon appeals comes from experiments on the effects of group pressure and conformity (Asch, 1958; Sherif, 1958). These experiments demonstrate that in a rather contrived situation, most people can be influenced in their judgment when a group of other people present a different view. This effect is strongest when there is a unanimous majority against the person. If one other person breaks the unanimous majority, the influence is not nearly as strong. And even with a unanimous majority against them, one-third of the people put through these experiments remained independent in their judgments.

This evidence on three of the propaganda devices indicates that, in general, the devices can be effective, but *only on some people.* And whether a device will be effective or not depends on some other factors. These include characteristics of the person getting the message, such as education level and initial attitude toward the topic. They also include characteristics of the setting, such as whether the group holding a view different from a person's is unanimous or not. Psychologist Roger Brown summed up this research by saying that the evidence indicates that the propaganda devices are "contingently rather than invariably effective" (1958, p. 306).

It appears from the scientific evidence that the Institute for Propaganda Analysis exaggerated the effectiveness of these devices. Nevertheless, they can be effective enough to increase the sales of a product by a meaningful amount, and that is why they are so widespread in advertising. The seven propaganda devices are also important because they can be viewed as an early attempt to state a theory of attitude change. Some of the devices that the Institute was only guessing about have turned out to be key variables in later attitude-change experiments.

Effectiveness of Nazi Propaganda

The Institute for Propaganda Analysis and others who were concerned may have overreacted when they began flooding the country with pamphlets presenting the seven propaganda devices. It now appears unlikely that a person using these methods could have successfully introduced Nazism to the United States and become an American Hitler. But if this is the case, how does one explain the apparent success of Nazi propaganda in Germany prior to World War II?

There were important differences in the situations in the United States and Germany before World War II. For one thing, the Nazis in Germany had essentially a communication monopoly (Bramsted, 1965). Dissenting views were not permitted, and that is very different from the situation in the United States. Perhaps the most important difference, however, is that propaganda in Germany was wedded to terror and backed up by force. If your neighbor expressed a dissenting view, he could disappear from his home during the middle of the night, never to be seen again. Joseph Goebbels, the Nazi minister of propaganda, is reported to have said that "a sharp sword must always stand behind propaganda, if it is to be really effective" (Bramsted, 1965, p. 450). A book on Nazi radio propaganda written during World War II expressed a similar thought (Kris & Speier, 1944):

> Political propaganda in Nazi Germany is a form of coercion; while it lacks the bluntness and irrevocability of physical violence, it derives its ultimate efficacy from the power of those who may, at any moment, cease talking and start killing. (p. 3)

The Bullet Theory

The idea that mass communication has great power can be considered one of the first general theories of the effects of mass communication. Sometimes this theory is known as the "bullet theory" (Schramm, 1971), the "hypodermic-needle" theory (Berlo, 1960), or the "stimulus-response" theory (DeFleur & Ball-Rokeach, 1989, pp. 163–165). The theory suggests that people are extremely vulnerable to mass communication messages. It suggests that if the message "hits the target," it will have its desired effect.

We now know that this theory of mass communication is oversimplified. A mass communication message does not have the same effect on everyone. Its effect on anyone is dependent on a number of things, including personality characteristics of the person and various aspects of the situation and the context. Nevertheless, the "bullet theory" is a conceivable theory of mass communication:

it seemed borne out by the apparent effectiveness of propaganda after World War I. This was partly because people were naïve and believed lies. The theory will probably never work as well again, but at the time it was accurate.

The "bullet theory" may not be dead yet, however. It appears in a somewhat revised form in the writings of the French philosopher Jacques Ellul (1973). Ellul argues that propaganda is much more effective than analysis by Americans had shown (pp. 287-294). He particularly rejects the evidence from experiments, stating that propaganda is part of a total environment and cannot be duplicated in a laboratory setting (pp. 250-286). Ellul argues that propaganda is so pervasive in American life that most of us are not even aware of it, yet it is controlling our values (p. 65). The central one of these values is, of course, the "American way of life" (p. 252). This thinking is not completely different from the ideas of some American communication scholars. As we shall see, sociologists Paul Lazarsfeld and Robert Merton have discussed the tendency of mass communication to reinforce the economic and social status quo, and communication theorist Joseph Klapper has suggested that the general effect of mass communication is reinforcement of attitudes.

CONCLUSIONS

The analysis of propaganda after World War I expressed certain thinking about the effects of mass communication that we can regard as one of the first general theories about the effects of mass communication. In essence, this theory was what has come to be known as the "bullet theory," which we discuss further in Chapter 14.

The work of the Institute for Propaganda Analysis led to what we can consider a primitive theory of attitude change. Several of the propaganda devices the institute identified are quite similar to techniques later studied more carefully in scientific research on persuasion. Scientific research shows that these devices have some ability to change attitudes but that they don't work on everyone.

Even though their effectiveness is limited, the seven propaganda devices can still serve their initial purpose of providing a checklist of techniques commonly used in mass communication. In one way or another, all the propaganda devices represent faulty arguments. Knowledge of the devices can make people, including professional communicators, better consumers of information.

DISCUSSION

1. Of the various definitions of propaganda, with which do you most agree, and why?
2. Give current examples of the propaganda devices (name calling, glittering generality, transfer, testimonial, plain folks, card stacking, and band wagon) from politics, advertising, and public relations.
3. What is the difference between education and propaganda?

4. What is the difference between news and propaganda?
5. Does the World Wide Web make propaganda easier or more difficult?

REFERENCES

Anrig, Greg Jr., and Elizabeth M. MacDonald (1992). Managing the Clinton's finances. *Denver Post,* July 27, pp. C1, C8.

Asch, S. E. (1958). Effects of group pressure upon the modification and distortion of judgments. In E. E. Maccoby, T. M. Newcomb, and E. L. Hartley (eds.), *Readings in Social Psychology,* 3rd ed., pp. 174-183. New York: Holt, Rinehart and Winston.

Bell, D. (1976). *The Cultural Contradictions of Capitalism.* New York: Basic Books.

Berlo, D. (1960). *The Process of Communication: An Introduction to Theory and Practice.* San Francisco: Rinehart Press.

Bernays, E. L. (1928). *Propaganda.* New York: Liveright.

Bramsted, E. K. (1965). *Goebbels and National Socialist Propaganda: 1925-1945.* East Lansing: Michigan State University Press.

Brinkley, J. (1988). The stubborn strength of Yitzhak Shamir. *New York Times Magazine,* Aug. 21, pp. 27-29, 68-77.

Brooks, G. (1988). Israelis are divided over the meetings between U.S., PLO. *Wall Street Journal,* Dec. 12, pp. A1, A8.

Brown, R. (1958). *Words and Things.* New York: Free Press.

Bussey, J. (1987). Dow Chemical tries to shed tough image and court the public. *Wall Street Journal,* Nov. 20, pp. 1, 18.

Butterfield, F. (1982). *China: Alive in a Bitter Sea.* New York: Bantam.

Cantril, H. (1965). Foreword. In M. Choukas, *Propaganda Comes of Age.* Washington, D.C.: Public Affairs Press.

Chang, Jung (1991). *Wild Swans: Three Daughters of China.* New York: Simon & Schuster.

Chavarria Chairez, Becky (1995). Can just one Betty Crocker do the job? *Dallas Morning News,* Sept. 25, p. 9A.

DeFleur, M., and S. Ball-Rokeach (1989). *Theories of Mass Communication,* 5th ed., New York: Longman.

Deutsch, C. (1987). Dow Chemical wants to be your friend. *New York Times,* Nov. 22, p. F6.

Dulles, F. R. (1928). Problems of war and peace. *Bookman* 67: 105-107.

Eidson, Thomas E. (1992). P.R. firm had no reason to question Kuwaiti's testimony. *New York Times,* Jan. 17, p. A28.

Eisenhower, John (1992). The Norman Conquest. *New York Times,* Oct. 18, Book Review, Sec. 7, pp. 3, 49.

Ellul, J. (1973). *Propaganda: The Formation of Men's Attitudes.* New York: Vintage.

Farrell, B. (1975). Celebrity market. *Harper's,* Dec., pp. 108-110.

Fleming, L. (1980). Pope considers clearing Galileo of heresy. *Austin American-Statesman,* Oct. 26, p. A10.

Grant, M. N. (1978). I got my swimming pool by choosing Prell over brand X. In R. Atwan, B. Orton, and W. Vesterman (eds.), *American Mass Media: Industries and Issues,* pp. 61-67. New York: Random House.

Greenhouse, S. (1995). U.S., protesting rights abuses, ends military aid to Guatemala. *New York Times,* March 11, p. 3.

Gruson, L. (1990a). Guerrilla war in Guatemala heats up, fueling criticism of civilian rule. *New York Times,* June 3, Sec. 1, p. 4.

——— (1990b). Voting isn't helping in Guatemala. *New York Times,* June 3, Sec. 4, p. 5.

Haberman, Clyde (1992). Words, war and sensibility: linguistic fog in the mideast. *New York Times,* Aug. 29, p. A1.

Henriques, D. (1986). Statue of invitation: Corporate America cashes in on celebrations for Lady Liberty. *Austin American-Statesman,* May 30, pp. 1, F8.

Hitchens, C. (1989). Terrorism: A cliche in search of a meaning. *Et cetera* 45 (Summer): 147-152.

Hovland, C. I., A. A. Lumsdaine, and F. D. Sheffield (1949). *Experiments on Mass Communication.* New York: John Wiley.

Hovland, C. I., and W. Weiss (1951). The influence of source credibility on communication effectiveness. *Public Opinion Quarterly* 15: 635-650.

Kelly, Michael (1992). The making of a first family: A blueprint. *New York Times,* Nov. 14, p. A1.

Kris, E., and H. Speier (1944). *German Radio Propaganda: Report on Home Broadcasts During the War.* London: Oxford University Press.

Lasswell, H. D. (1927). *Propaganda Technique in the World War.* New York: Peter Smith.

——— (1937). Propaganda. In E. R. A. Seligman and A. Johnson (eds.), *Encyclopedia of the Social Sciences,* vol. 12, pp. 521-528. New York: Macmillan.

Lee, A. M., and E. B. Lee (eds.) (1939). *The Fine Art of Propaganda: A Study of Father Coughlin's Speeches.* New York: Harcourt, Brace and Company.

Lewis, N. (1990). Scholars say the arrest of Noriega has little legal justification. *New York Times,* Jan. 10, p. 8.

Lumsdaine, A. A., and I. L. Janis (1953). Resistance to "counterpropaganda" produced by one-sided and two-sided "propaganda" presentations. *Public Opinion* 17: 311-318.

MacArthur, John R. (1992). Remember Nayirah, witness for Kuwait? *New York Times,* Jan. 6, p. A17.

Maclean, J. (1986). Opportunism flickers in Lady Liberty's torch: Statue's history shadowed by personal gain. *Austin American-Statesman,* June 29, pp. 1, 14.

Manyon, Julian (1994). Reporting from the Chechen Republic. *The MacNeil/Lehrer NewsHour,* Dec. 16.

Maslin, Janet (1992). Do movie trailers stretch the truth? That's show biz. *New York Times,* Nov. 6, pp. B1, B9.

McCann, T. (1976). *An American Company: The Tragedy of United Fruit.* New York: Crown.

McGrory, Mary (1992). Capitol Hill & Knowlton. *Washington Post,* Jan. 12, p. C1.

Millett, Richard L. (1994). Central America—An Overview. *Jane's Intelligence Review Year Book.* Dec. 31, Sec: International, p. 152.

Mock, J. R., and C. Larson (1939). *Words That Won the War: The Story of the Committee on Public Information 1917-1919.* Princeton, N.J.: Princeton University Press.

Nichols, Bill (1995). Clinton rides "just plain folks" image in West. *USA Today,* June 2, p. 8A.

Quirk, Barbara (1995). Betty of '90s: Soup on apron? *Capital Times* (Madison, Wis.) Oct. 3, p. 1D.

Read, J. M. (1941). *Atrocity Propaganda, 1914-1919.* New Haven, Conn.: Yale University Press.

Rogers, E. (1983). *Diffusion of Innovations,* 3rd ed. New York: Free Press.

Schramm, W. (1971). The nature of communication between humans. In W. Schramm and D. Roberts (eds.), *The Process and Effects of Mass Communication,* rev. ed., pp. 3–53. Urbana: University of Illinois Press.

Scott, W. (1982). Personality parade. *Parade,* Nov. 14, p. 9.

Sherif, M. (1958). Group influences upon the formation of norms and attitudes. In E. E. Maccoby, T. M. Newcomb, and E. L. Hartley (eds.), *Readings in Social Psychology,* 3rd ed., pp. 219–232. New York: Holt, Rinehart and Winston.

Simpson, C. (1972). *The Lusitania.* Boston: Little, Brown.

Sonenclar, Bob (1991). The VNR top ten. *Columbia Journalism Review,* March/April, p. 14.

Stone, I. F. (1966). The provocations behind the Tonkin Gulf clash two years ago. *I. F. Stone's Weekly,* Sept. 12, p. 3.

—— (1968a). *In a Time of Torment.* New York: Random House, Vintage Books.

—— (1968b). Special 8-page issue documenting the Tonkin Gulf fraud. *I. F. Stone's Weekly,* Mar. 4.

Tindol, R. (1988). Capitalism by any other name. . . . *On Campus* (The University of Texas at Austin), June, p. 22.

Wells, Sheila Taylor (1995). Hey, Betty! It's time to lighten up. *St. Louis Post-Dispatch,* Oct. 5, p. 2.

Westheimer, R. (1990). Women know how to fight. *New York Times,* Feb. 10, p. 15.

chapter 7

The Measurement of Readability

Mass communication, which by definition attempts to reach the largest audience possible, should be committed to writing and other forms of expression that are as easy to understand as possible.

A newspaper editorial might be making the most important statement in the world, but if it is written so that a person needs a college education to understand it, it will go over the head of 80 percent of the population. The same principles apply to a magazine advertisement, a news story, an editorial page column, even the spoken messages on the broadcast media, although the evidence is less clear here.

What factors make writing easy to understand or difficult to understand? Can a method be developed to measure how easy or difficult it is to understand a piece of writing? The area of research that attempts to answer these questions is known as *readability* research.

The study of readability is important for two reasons. First, it may give us a way to measure the readability of written material. Readability refers to "ease of understanding or comprehension due to the style of writing" (Klare, 1963, p. 1). Ideally, one would like to find a simple formula for measuring readability. A useful formula might involve making some simple counts in a book or news story and then doing some simple computations to get some kind of score. Of course, such a formula should be reliable and valid. There should be evidence that different applications of the formula (by different people, for instance) would give the same readability score, and there should be evidence that the score really measures ease or difficulty of understanding.

Second, the search for a formula could provide some information about the most important aspects of style influencing ease of understanding. This could lead to some helpful advice for writers. Then we would be able to say that certain factors make a real difference in understanding, and therefore a writer should pay some attention to them in his or her writing.

THE HISTORY OF READABILITY MEASUREMENT

The term *readability formula* is used here, following Klare (1963), to mean "a method of estimating the probable success a reader will have in reading and understanding a piece of writing" (p. 34).

Although some interest in counting words can be traced back to biblical times, the first attempts to develop a readability formula were made by educators involved in selecting reading material for both children and adults. The first readability formula is usually attributed to Lively and Pressey (1923), although some earlier work by Sherman (1888) and Kitson (1921) dealt with factors that would later be important in formulas. Sherman and Kitson did not take the step of constructing a predictive formula, however.

Sherman published what appears to be the first investigation of sentence length, one of the elements often included in later readability formulas. He pointed out an interesting decline in the average sentence length of authors as one moves through the centuries from Chaucer to Emerson. Sherman did not relate sentence length to difficulty of understanding, however. Kitson's work is significant because he came up with the very same two elements later used by Flesch and others in the modern readability formulas.

The Lively and Pressey study—a frequent choice for the first readability formula—was based on the assumption, common among educators at that time, that vocabulary difficulty was a key factor in determining the difficulty of understanding for written material. They were concerned with the practical problem of selecting junior high school science textbooks. Many of these textbooks were so heavily laden with technical vocabulary that the teaching of the course almost became the teaching of vocabulary. They argued that it would be useful to have a means of measuring this "vocabulary burden." They also suggested that such a technique might be useful in measuring the vocabulary difficulty of supplementary reading, such as novels that might be assigned in addition to texts.

A more comprehensive look at the elements that might influence readability was published in 1935 by Gray and Leary under the title *What Makes a Book Readable*. These authors were particularly interested in the problem that many American adults were not reading widely and apparently found much of the available reading material too difficult. Rather than assume that any one element was an adequate measure of difficulty of understanding of writing, Gray and Leary began their research with an exhaustive search aimed at finding all the possible elements that might influence readability. They began by surveying a number of librarians, publishers, and other persons interested in adult education. These experts were asked what elements they thought contributed to readability for adults of limited education. This produced a list of 289 elements.

Gray and Leary eventually reduced their list to five key elements that they put in a formula: the number of different hard words in a passage of 100 words; the number of first-, second-, and third-person pronouns; the average sentence length in words; the percentage of different words; and the number of prepositional phrases.

The Readability Laboratory of Teachers College, Columbia University, became the scene of the next two important developments in readability measurement. This lab was set up by the American Association for Adult Education and focused on the problem of assessing reading materials for adults. Two of the researchers who worked there were Irving Lorge and Rudolf Flesch. Lorge (1939) paved the way for the modern, streamlined formulas by suggesting that a two-element formula might work. He studied a number of two-element combinations and found a higher multiple correlation with reading comprehension scores for some of them than Gray and Leary had with their five-element formula. Combinations that worked well included number of prepositional phrases and number of different hard words (giving a multiple correlation of .7456), average sentence length and number of different hard words (.7406), and number of prepositional phrases and average sentence length (.6949).

Flesch set forth in his doctoral dissertation to develop a still better formula. He took as his starting point the finding that the Gray and Leary formula failed to indicate clear differences in readability beyond a certain level of difficulty. Flesch kept the sentence length measure that had been used by Gray and Leary and others because it appeared to be a good measure of readability at both the children's and the adult levels. And he included a count of personal words because Lyman Bryson, the director of the Readability Laboratory, said that "appeal" was an important part of readability. Gray and Leary had included a count of personal pronouns in their formula. Flesch decided to disregard all neuter pronouns and count all words referring to people either by names or by words meaning people. He was assuming that human interest was the most important part of appeal and that the types of words he classified as "personal references" would correlate with human interest.

The result of this research was the first Flesch readability formula. It was based on three variables: average sentence length in words, number of affixes within a 100-word sample, and number of personal references within a 100-word sample. The resulting score could be looked up on a chart that would supply either a verbal description of style such as "very easy" or a school grade level of the potential audience.

Flesch showed that his formula produced a multiple correlation coefficient of .7358 with paragraph meaning comprehension test scores, an improvement over the multiple correlation coefficient of .6435 that Gray and Leary obtained with five elements. Flesch went on to popularize and publicize his formula probably more than any other readability researcher. His dissertation, *Marks of a Readable Style,* was published as a book. Flesch himself said that since it was a Ph.D. dissertation it "was not a very readable book." He rewrote it in a simplified version, and the result was published in 1946 as *The Art of Plain Talk.*

THE FLESCH FORMULAS

Flesch came out with a revised formula the following year. The new formula (Flesch, 1948) dropped the count of "personal references" from the readability formula and used it to create a new "human interest" formula. Another change was that the count of affixes in the readability formula had been replaced by a measure of word length, the number of syllables per 100 words. The results were two formulas, the reading ease formula and the human interest formula, both still in use today.

The reading ease formula takes this form:

$$R.E. = 206.835 - .846 \; wl - 1.015 \; sl$$

where R.E. = reading ease score

wl = number of syllables per 100 words

sl = average number of words per sentence

The resulting score should range between 0 and 100 and can be looked up in a chart such as the one presented in Table 7.1.

The human interest formula takes this form:

$$H.I. = 3.635 \; pw + .314 \; ps$$

where H.I. = human interest score

pw = number of personal words per 100 words

ps = number of personal sentences per 100 sentences

The resulting score should fall between 0 and 100 and can be looked up in a chart such as the one in Table 7.2.

TABLE 7.1 Chart for interpreting Flesch reading ease scores

Reading Ease Score	Description of Style	Estimated Reading Grade
90–100	Very easy	5th grade
80–90	Easy	6th grade
70–80	Fairly easy	7th grade
60–70	Standard	8th and 9th grade
50–60	Fairly difficult	10th to 12th grade
30–50	Difficult	college
0–30	Very difficult	college graduate

SOURCE: Table (page 177) from *The Art of Readable Writing* by Rudolf Flesch. Copyright © 1949, 1974 by Rudolf Flesch. Reprinted by permission of HarperCollins Publishers, Inc.

TABLE 7.2 Chart for interpreting Flesch human interest scores

Human Interest Score	Description of Style
0–10	Dull
10–20	Mildly interesting
20–40	Interesting
40–60	Highly interesting
60–100	Dramatic

SOURCE: Table (page 179) from *The Act of Readable Writing* by Rudolf Flesch. Copyright © 1949, 1974 by Rudolf Flesch. Reprinted by permission of HarperCollins Publishers, Inc.

The Flesch reading ease formula has proved to be the most widely used readability formula (Klare, 1963). It was popularized in Flesch's book, *The Art of Readable Writing,* first published in 1949.

The Flesch reading ease formula has produced a number of useful offshoots. The Gunning fog index, developed by Robert Gunning (1952), is based on two elements: average sentence length in words and number of words of three syllables or more per 100 words. These two numbers are added and multiplied by .4, and the resulting number is the approximate grade level at which the material can be read. When Gunning began his consulting work with newspapers, he was using the original Flesch formula that counted affixes (Gunning, 1945), and the formula that he later developed resembles the reading ease formula. At the earlier stage in Gunning's career, the term *fog index* also had a different meaning—it referred to a "measure of uselessly long and complex words" (p. 12). The main advantage of the Gunning fog index over the Flesch reading ease formula is that the former gives a grade level immediately while a reading ease score has to be looked up in a table to produce a grade level.

In another step of simplification, Wayne Danielson and Sam Dunn Bryan (1963) developed a computerized readability formula in which the computer does the counts and the computations and gives a readability score. The formula is based on two elements that are similar to the two in the Flesch reading ease formula except that they are defined in units that the computer can recognize easily. They are: average number of characters per space (essentially a measure of word length) and average number of characters per sentence (essentially a measure of sentence length). The resulting score is very much like a reading ease score and in fact can be looked up on the Flesch reading ease chart.

Also available are tables that eliminate the computation necessary to apply the Flesch reading ease and human interest formulas (Farr & Jenkins, 1949). To determine the reading ease score of a sample, you simply look up the average sentence length at the side of the table and the number of syllables per 100 words across the top of the table. Where the row and the column intersect can be found the reading ease score. A similar table for the human interest score has percentage of personal sentences at the side and percentage of personal words across the top.

USING A FORMULA

An example will help to bring out exactly how the Flesch reading ease formula can be applied to a piece of writing. We will take a sample of writing and make the necessary counts and do the computations to come up with a reading ease score.

Before we begin, we need to present exact definitions of some of the things we will be counting. Flesch defines a word as a letter, number, symbol, or group of letters, numbers, or symbols surrounded by white space. Thus, *1949, C.O.D.,* and *unself-conscious* would all be counted as words. Flesch defines a sentence as a unit of thought that is grammatically independent and is usually marked by a period, question mark, exclamation point, semicolon, colon, or dash. Syllables are counted the way you would pronounce the word. For example, *1916* would count as a four-syllable word. Since you need to find the number of syllables per 100 words, one shortcut that is sometimes useful is to start by writing down 100 and then count only the words of two syllables or more, writing down a 1 for a two-syllable word, a 2 for a three-syllable word, and so forth. Then you simply add all the numbers you have written down, including the 100. This can often save time because many words have only one syllable. Writing down the number of syllables for each word permits you to go back and check your work. Now we are ready to apply the reading ease formula to the following sample—the beginning paragraphs of a news story written by a student.

The Texas Water Rights Commission (TWRC) voted Tuesday to allow the South Texas Nuclear Project the use of Colorado River water despite a warning from Atty. Gen. John Hill that such action could result in state instituted court proceedings against TWRC.

Hill's warning came at the commission's meeting, after he advised it that the Lower Colorado River Authority (LCRA) had no control over the unallocated waters involved in a debate between LCRA and TWRC and should not be paid for the use of them.

The debate stemmed from a dispute between TWRC, which controls all the unallocated water in the state, and LCRA, which has power over all Colorado River water within a 10-county area, over who would profit from sale of the water.

This sample is more than 100 words long, so it is adequate to illustrate the workings of the formula, although you would probably measure the entire story if you were seriously attempting to determine its readability.

First, it is necessary to determine the average sentence length *(sl)*. Remember that *LCRA, TWRC* and *10-county* should count as one word each. The sample contains 3 sentences and 124 words. Dividing 124 by 3 gives an average sentence length of 41.33 words.

Next, it is necessary to determine the number of syllables per 100 words (wl). The easiest way to determine this is to count the syllables in the first 100 words. The 100th word is the word *the* before the word *state* in the third paragraph. The only tricky parts in counting the syllables might be the word *TWRC*, which includes six syllables when it is pronounced, and the words *Atty.* and *Gen.*, which include three syllables each when pronounced in full. The number of syllables in the first 100 words is 189. Next, we substitute these numbers for sl and wl in the reading ease formula, and obtain the following:

$$R.E. = 206.835 - .846(189) - 1.015(41.33)$$

Performing the two multiplications gives the following:

$$R.E. = 206.835 - 159.894 - 41.950$$

And doing the final subtractions gives 4.991, the reading ease score. This is a very low reading ease score. In the reading ease chart in Table 7.1, it falls in the very difficult category, where the estimated reading grade is "college graduate. "This is understandable when we look at the long sentences used, the possibly unfamiliar initials (*LCRA* and *TWRC*), and the use of complicated terms (*unallocated water*). Of course, if the entire story had been analyzed, the reading ease score might have been higher. Newswriters often attempt to pack a great deal of information into the beginning of a news story, and this can make the beginning less readable than the rest of the story. This practice can be questioned, however; if the beginning of the story is not readable, people might not get to the later sections.

THE FRY GRAPH FOR ESTIMATING READABILITY

A slightly different approach to readability is the Fry Graph, developed by Edward B. Fry. The researcher using this method first determines the average number of syllables per 100 words and the average number of sentences per 100 words for the text in question (Fry, 1988). These figures are then looked up on a graph, and the point where the two values intersect gives an approximate grade level at which the material can be read (see Figure 7.1, p. 140). Klare (1988) suggests that the Fry Graph is now the most widely used readability technique.

APPLICATIONS OF READABILITY FORMULAS

Readability measurement has been used in a number of areas, including textbook evaluation, analysis of mass communication, writing for new literates, and improving corporate and government documents. We turn now to some of these applications.

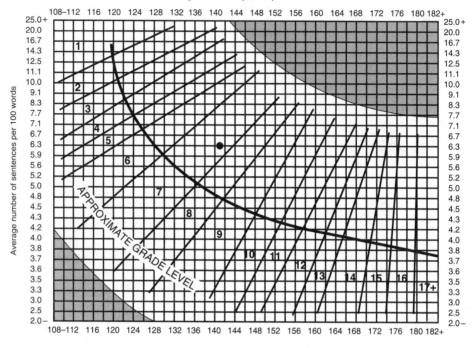

Average number of syllables per 100 words

FIGURE 7.1 Fry Graph for estimating readability

DIRECTIONS: Randomly select 3 one hundred word passages from a book or an article. Plot average number of syllables and average number of sentences per 100 words on graph to determine the grade level of the material. Choose more passages per book if great variability is observed and conclude that the book has uneven readability. Few books will fall in gray area but when they do grade level scores are invalid.

Count proper nouns, numerals and initializations as words. Count a syllable for each symbol. For example, "1945" is 1 word and 4 syllables and "IRA" is 1 word and 3 syllables.

EXAMPLE:	SYLLABLES	SENTENCES
1st Hundred Words	124	6.6
2nd Hundred Words	141	5.5
3rd Hundred Words	158	6.8
AVERAGE	141	6.3

READABILITY 7th GRADE (see dot plotted on graph)

FIGURE 7.1 Fry Graph for estimating readability

SOURCE: From B. L. Zakaluk and S. J. Samuels (eds.), *Readability: Its Past, Present & Future,* p. 95. Newark, Del.: International Reading Association, 1988. Reproduction permitted. No copyright.

Textbook Evaluation

The main reason Lively and Pressey and some of the other pioneers developed their measures of readability was to help in textbook selection. Gray and Leary had a similar purpose—the selection of suitable books for adult readers.

Researchers have used Flesch formulas to study the readability of psychology texts (Gillen, 1973; Cone, 1976), educational psychology texts (Hofmann & Vyhonsky, 1975), and journalism texts (Tankard & Tankard, 1977). The latter study of nine books using the reading ease formula showed that five were in the "difficult range, two were in the "fairly difficult" range, and two were in the "standard" range. The human interest formula placed one journalism text in the "dull" category, three in the "mildly interesting" category, and five in the "interesting" category.

A professor who used the first edition of this book selected 50 random samples of 100 words each and had 50 students apply the Flesch reading ease formula to them. The results, for the total sample, indicated a mean sentence length of 23.73 words, 168.15 syllables per 100 words, and a reading ease score of 40.49. As Table 7.1 indicates, this puts the score in the middle of the college level.

Readability formulas are also being used by a number of college textbook publishers to make sure texts are not being written at too difficult a level. Some of these publishers have recently been criticized for placing too much reliance on readability formulas to make texts easy to understand (Fiske, 1987). Critics say the formulas encourage choppy writing that fails to challenge students. Readability formulas, like any tool, can be misused. It seems clear that the mechanical application of a formula cannot take away the need for human judgment and will never solve all the problems of textbook development.

Newspapers and Wire Services

Soon after Flesch's first formula was published in 1943, Robert Gunning began applying it in consulting work for newspapers (Gunning, 1945). He studied the readability of eight newspapers in 1944 and concluded, "Today's newspapers are offering the public some of the most difficult reading material published" (p. 2).

Several readability experts—including Gunning, Flesch, and Danielson—have served as consultants to the major wire services. Gunning worked with United Press in the 1940s and reported that "within three weeks the reading difficulty of U.P. copy had been cut by five grade levels" (1945, p. 2).

Flesch and Danielson have served at different times as consultants to the Associated Press. Flesch studied the AP news report from 1948 to 1950. In keeping with his formulas, Flesch recommended that AP writers use short sentences, short words, and human interest writing.

Charles Seib, the ombudsman of the *Washington Post,* conducted a non-scholarly but informative study of sentence length, one of the two elements in the popular readability formulas. Seib (1976) found the average sentence length on the front pages of three Sunday newspapers to be as follows: *Washington*

Star, 31 words; *New York Times,* 33 words; *Washington Post,* 38 words. By contrast, he found the average sentence length for several popular books to be as follows: Saul Bellow's *Humbolt's Gift,* just under 12 words; Woody Allen's *Without Feathers,* just over 12 words; Jimmy Breslin's *How the Good Guys Won,* under 11 words. Seib concluded, "News stories can't be judged on the same basis as fiction or even Breslin's free-style journalism. But an average of over 30 words per sentence is too much for comfortable reading. Particularly when the tube is waiting just across the room" (p. B25).

As Seib's analysis points out, readability research can be used to formulate some advice for journalists. That advice would be to use short sentences and short words. Flesch has been even more specific in his advice about sentence length: he has recommended to the AP that newswriters use an average sentence length of 19 words. Several popular magazines are already doing a good job of following his advice—the average sentence length a number of years ago in *Time* and *Reader's Digest* was 17 words or less (Gunning, 1952).

Research has also shown that the readability level of a newspaper article has a definite effect on how much of the article will be read. Swanson (1948) conducted a controlled field experiment to determine the effect of readability on readership. Two versions of the same story were produced—one with a Flesch reading ease score of 49.84 (difficult) and the other with a reading ease score of 84.94 (easy). Then two versions of an experimental campus newspaper were produced—one with the difficult story and one with the easy story. In a "trailer village" where married students lived, one version was delivered to odd-numbered trailers and the other to even-numbered trailers. Interviewers arrived within 30 hours to ask the adult male at each trailer about his readership of every paragraph in the paper. The mean number of paragraphs read was 13 for the "difficult" story and 24 for the "easy" story. The story with the greatest reading ease had nearly twice as many paragraphs read, on the average, as the story with the difficult readability.

Catalano (1990) studied the readability of leads on stories from the Associated Press, United Press, Scripps Howard News Service, the New York Times News Service, the *Washington Post,* and the *Los Angeles Times.* Using Flesch's reading ease formula, he found most of the leads would fall in the "difficult" or "very difficult" reading category.

240 Years of Novels

Danielson and Lasorsa (1989) studied stylistic variables in 240 novels covering a 240-year time span, and found a definite relationship between four stylistic factors and the passage of time. They found a tendency for more recent novels to have fewer words per sentence (Figure 7.2), a smaller percentage of long words, a smaller percentage of rare punctuation, and a greater degree of informality (as measured by the number of contractions using apostrophes). At least two of these factors, average sentence length and average word length, are typically found in readability formulas, and therefore the results suggest that novels are becoming more readable.

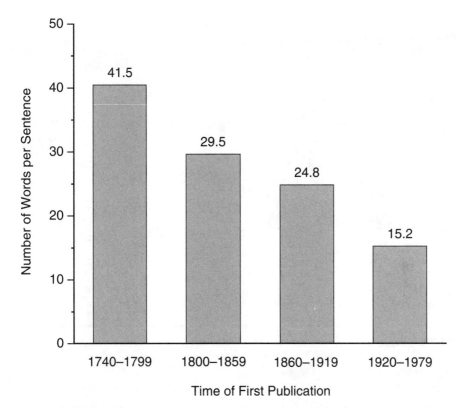

FIGURE 7.2 Average sentence length in novels for four time periods

SOURCE: Adapted from W. A. Danielson and D. L. Lasorsa, "A New Readability Formula Based on the Stylistic Age of Novels," *Journal of Reading* 34 (1989): 194–197.

Danielson and Lasorsa (1989) offer the following speculation as to why this might have occurred:

> Does our faster paced life demand shorter sentences? Has the rise of photography, motion pictures, and television influenced prose styles? Are writers today less capable of producing elaborate, detailed sentences than were their literary forebears? Are today's readers less skilled in decoding extended and involved expressions than were their grand-parents or their great-grandparents? Is modern style a reflection of the democratization of society and the decline of class distinctions in the written word? We tend toward the latter interpretation, but realize the difficulty of establishing anything resembling proof. (p. 197)

Danielson, Lasorsa, & Im (1992) studied the readability of novels and two leading newspapers (the *New York Times* and the *Los Angeles Times*) from 1885 to 1989. They found that the novels tended to become more readable over the

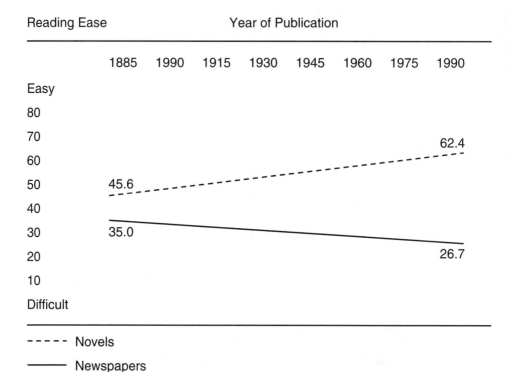

FIGURE 7.3 Readability of newspapers and novels, 1889–1989

SOURCE: From W. A. Danielson, D. L. Lasorsa, and D. S. Im, "Journalists and Novelists: A Study of Diverging Styles," *Journalism Quarterly* 69 (1992): 436–446.

104-year period, while the front pages of the two newspapers tended to become less readable (Figure 7.3). The results indicated that the lower readability of the newspapers was due more to the use of longer words rather than the use of longer sentences.

News Releases

Thomas Haven Miller (1984) used computerized Flesch reading ease and Danielson-Bryan formulas to study the readability of computer industry news releases. The average reading ease score for releases was 25.5 on Flesch's 100-point scale—a score in the "very difficult" range. Releases from computer hardware companies (with a reading ease score of 31.8) were slightly more readable than those from companies making peripherals (27.9), companies making software (27.3), or a category of "other" companies (16.8), which were involved in fiberoptic cable, office equipment, training manuals, copiers, and accounting machines. Miller found no relationship between size of the company and readability of the news release.

Advertising Copy

A study of the readability of advertisements found a relationship between readability score of the ad copy and the number of people who recalled seeing the ad. Wesson (1989) acquired recall measures obtained by Starch-Hooper research for all the advertisements in selected issues of *Sports Illustrated, Woman's Day,* and *Reader's Digest.* He then computed Gunning fog index scores for the copy in the advertisements. Finally, he looked at the relationship between the recall measures and the readability scores. The relationship he found was a curvilinear one in the form of a U-shaped curve, with the greatest recall for low readability scores and high readability scores. Wesson expected to find the greatest recall for low readability scores, but he did not expect that recall would also be high for high readability scores. He speculated that reading the more difficult text required greater cognitive involvement in the form of attention in processing the message.

Broadcast News

Leonard Arthur Stevens (1949) wanted to know whether readability formulas were also applicable to material that was going to be spoken, as in a radio news broadcast. He conducted an investigation of the "hearability" of written prose. Stevens conducted an experiment in which two groups of subjects were each exposed to six news stories. One group read the stories from written pages, while the other group heard recordings of the stories with a competent newscaster doing the reading. Subjects in each situation were then tested for comprehension with a set of multiple-choice test questions that covered the six stories. Overall, Stevens found no significant differences in comprehension between the two modes—reading and hearing. Stevens concluded that these findings indicate that the Flesch reading ease formula can be used to measure "hearability" as well as readability.

Irving E. Fang (1966–67) developed his Easy Listening Formula as a simple formula that could be used by professional media writers as they worked. It was particularly aimed at broadcast newswriting, although Fang also applied it to printed text. The Easy Listening Formula is applied to one sentence at a time. The procedure is simply to count each syllable above one per word. For example, the sentence "The quick brown fox jumped over the lazy dog" gets one count for the second syllable in "over" and one count for the second syllable in "lazy," giving it an ELF score of 2. The scores for a number of sentences can then be averaged to obtain an ELF score for a longer passage.

Fang's research suggested to him that the most highly rated television newswriters use a style that averages an Easy Listening Formula score below 12. He says an ELF score above 12 should be interpreted as a warning sign that a sentence may need rewriting. In a later book (Fang, 1980), he suggested that writers take a second look at any sentence scoring above 20.

The Easy Listening Formula is based on word difficulty (measured by word length) and sentence length, as are many of the other popular formulas. The advantage of the Easy Listening Formula may be its ease of application.

Health, Medicine, and Self-Help

Cardinal and Seidler (1995) studied the readability and comprehensibility of the "Exercise Lite" brochure released in 1993. The purpose of the brochure was to recommend that Americans get 30 minutes of moderate physical activity each day. The brochure was particularly targeted at the 24 percent of the public who are totally sedentary and the 57 percent who engage in little or no physical activity. Readability was measured with commercial readability software, as well as Flesch's and Fry's formulas, and with cloze procedure (see page 147). The readability measures suggested that the brochure was written at a grade level of 17, or a level appropriate to people with some graduate education.

A paragraph from the brochure is reprinted in Figure 7.4. The paragraph scores 7.7 on the Flesch reading ease chart. The cloze procedure analysis suggested that only 30 percent of the test group were fully capable of understanding the brochure, and that comprehension was strongly related to educational level. These results take on added importance since studies have repeatedly shown that lower education is associated with physical inactivity.

A study of the readability of the instructions included with condoms used the Dale-Chall Formula, the Fry Readability Graph, and the SMOG Grading Formula (Richwald, Wamsley, Coulson, & Morisky, 1988). The researchers concluded that 8 of the 14 sets of instructions were written at the reading level of a high school graduate and that none required less than a tenth grade level of reading.

Mills (1989) used the Flesch formula to study the readability of the book *Alcoholics Anonymous,* popularly referred to as the "Big Book." He found a Reading Ease score of 70.60, which puts the book at the boundary between "standard difficulty" and "fairly easy." Mills concludes that the book is probably within the reading ability of most users, but that individuals reading at less than a seventh-grade level may have difficulty.

FIGURE 7.4 The first paragraph of the "Exercise Lite" brochure

SOURCE: From "Exercise Lite," a brochure published by the Amercian College of Sports Medicine and the U.S. Centers for Disease Control and Prevention.

Despite the recognized value of physical activity, few Americans are regularly active. Only 22% of adults engage in leisure time physical activity at the level recommended for health benefits in *Healthy People 2000.* Fully 24% of adult Americans are completely sedentary and are badly in need of more physical activity. The remaining 54% are inadequately active and they, too, would benefit from more physical activity. Participation in regular physical activity appears to have gradually increased during the 1960s, 1970s, and early 1980s, but has plateaued in recent years. Among ethnic minority populations, older persons, and those with lower incomes or levels of education, participation in regular physical activity has remained consistently low.

Reading Ease score = 7.7 (reading level of college graduates)

Readability of Documents

A number of states, including New York, New Jersey, Hawaii, Connecticut, and Minnesota, have passed Plain Language Laws (Fry, 1988). The purpose of these laws is to make sure consumer contracts such as rent agreements, money lending forms, and insurance policies are written in a way that most people can understand. In New York, the state education commissioner requires his 250 highest-ranking officials to take a class on writing (Verhovek, 1991). Emphasis in the class is put on using common words and writing succinctly.

A readability formula played a key role in a lawsuit brought against Medicare (Fry, 1988). A class action suit argued that the notice sent to people appealing their Medicare claim dispositions was not written in an understandable way. Application of the Fry Readability formula found that the notice was written at levels ranging from that appropriate for high school graduates to that suitable for college graduates. A judge found that the notices were "incomprehensible" and requested that appropriate action be taken.

CLOZE PROCEDURE

A very different approach to measuring readability has been introduced by communication scholar Wilson L. Taylor (1953). He noticed that readability formulas had a weakness in that their basic assumptions could be contradicted. Most of the formulas are based on the assumption that a short word is easier to understand than a long word. Yet anyone can think of examples in which that would not be true. The word *erg* is shorter than the word *respectability,* but most people would not know the meaning of *erg* while they would know the meaning of *respectability.* If a sample of writing had a lot of words of this type that violated the assumptions of the formulas, the formulas would give very misleading readability scores.

Taylor invented another procedure for measuring readability that he says measures all the potential elements that influence readability. He called this method "cloze procedure." The name is based on the word *closure,* which stands for the human tendency to complete a familiar but incomplete pattern.

To use cloze procedure, you take the sample of writing you are interested in and "mutilate" it by replacing some of the words with blanks. This can be done in different ways, but a common way is just to replace every fifth word with a blank. Then the mutilated passage is given to a test group of subjects who are asked to fill in the missing words. The cloze score becomes the number or percentage of blanks that are filled in correctly. The simplest scoring procedure is to count only the exact word and not synonyms. Attempting to count synonyms introduces a subjective element into the scoring and slows it down considerably.

The theory behind cloze procedure is, in its most basic form, that the simpler a piece of writing is, the easier it will be for a test reader to replace the missing words. Putting it another way, cloze procedure measures the extent to which a sample of prose is written in the patterns that a reader is naturally anticipating. And these patterns can involve all the different factors that might influence readability—overall organization, sentence structure, appropriateness of vocabulary, simplicity of vocabulary, and so forth.

We can also think of cloze procedure as a measure of *redundancy* (see Chapter 3). The more redundant a piece of writing is, the easier it will be for someone to fill in the blanks. Two communication scholars, in an article about information theory, recently commented that cloze procedure "is also an ingenious method to distinguish highly informative words (those that are difficult to predict) from highly redundant ones (those that are easily guessed)." They added, "Thus, cloze scores have come to be used not only as an indication of the readability of a prose passage relative to a particular audience, but also as an indication of comprehension for individuals within that audience" (Finn & Roberts, 1984, p. 464).

Taylor did not just assume that his method measured readability, but provided some evidence of its validity. First he showed that his procedure ranked passages very similarly to the Flesch reading ease formula and other orthodox formulas when the passages studied were "standard."

Then Taylor devised an "acid test" for cloze procedure: could it give a more trustworthy rating of readability for material that might fool the readability formulas? The kind of material he needed was written prose that might violate a lot of the assumptions basic to the formulas. Taylor decided that this kind of material could be found in two novels recognized by literary critics as being highly experimental—James Joyce's *Finnegan's Wake* and Gertrude Stein's *Geography and Plays.* Taylor set up a test in which both Flesch reading ease scores and cloze procedure scores would be determined for passages from these two experimental novels and six other, more standard books. Taylor predicted that the reading ease scores would indicate that the Joyce and Stein books were easy reading because they contain short words and short sentences, even though critics find both books difficult to read. Cloze procedure, in contrast, was expected to rank the two experimental novels as more difficult than the other six books. In the cloze procedure for this test, Taylor deleted every seventh word in a passage from each book until he had 25 deletions for each book. Each passage was read by 18 subjects, giving a possible total cloze score for each book of 18 times 25, or 450. The results of the test are summarized in Table 7.3.

The Flesch reading ease scores indicate that the Stein passage is the easiest of the eight, and that the Joyce is somewhere in the middle. These scores fall in the "very easy" and "fairly easy" categories. In contrast, the cloze scores rank the Stein and Joyce selections seventh and eighth in difficulty. This supports Taylor's argument that in the case of written material that violates the assumptions of the formulas, cloze procedure would give a truer indication of reading difficulty than the formulas.

Cloze scores are probably easiest to interpret when two or more samples of writing are being compared. Then the several passages can be tested on the same group of subjects, and the passages can be ranked according to difficulty.

TABLE 7.3 Comparisons of Flesch reading ease scores and cloze procedure scores for samples from eight books

Work	Reading Ease Score	Rank by Reading Ease Score	Cloze Score	Rank by Cloze Score
Stein, *Geography and Plays*	96	1	123	7
Boswell, *Life of Johnson*	89	2	186	3
Swift, *Gulliver's Travels*	80	3	170	4
Caldwell, *Georgia Boy*	79	4.5	336	1
Joyce, *Finnegan's Wake*	79	4.5	49	8
Dickens, *Bleak House*	69	6	263	2
Huxley, *Man Stands Alone*	68	7	155	5
James, *The Ambassadors*	47	8	135	6

SOURCE: Adapted from W. L. Taylor, "Cloze Procedure: A New Tool for Measuring Readability," *Journalism Quarterly* 30 (1953): 428. Reprinted by permission.

The passages with the highest average cloze scores are the easiest ones and the passages with the lowest cloze scores are the most difficult. Meaning can also be assigned to individual cloze scores. Rankin and Culhane (1969), extending earlier work by Bormuth (1968), have developed a scale for interpreting cloze scores. Their research indicates that a cloze score of 61 percent or higher shows that the material is at the "independent level" of reading, a score of 41 percent or higher shows that the material is at the "instructional level" of reading, and a score below 41 percent indicates that the material is too difficult to be used with that particular class.

Seth Finn (1985) applied cloze procedure and Shannon's entropy formula to test unpredictability in news articles as a correlate of reader enjoyment. Nine articles (taken from five magazines, three newspapers, and one wire service), all dealing with the Apollo moonwalk of July 20, 1969, were rated by 144 college students. Each student read one article and indicated reader enjoyment on a seven-point scale. Another group of 144 comparable students then filled in blanks in a cloze procedure test of the same articles (with every eighth word deleted). He concluded that reader enjoyment of the articles related to both syntactic and semantic unpredictability (see Table 7.4, p. 150).

NEWER APPROACHES TO READABILITY MEASUREMENT

Much of the early work on readability was not based to a great extent on theory. The theoretical approach was a kind of brute-force empiricism in which all possible variables related to reading difficult were dropped into a hopper and then the statistical technique of multiple regression was used to find the best

TABLE 7.4 Ratings of reader enjoyment and unpredictability scores for nine sample articles

Publication or Source	Reader Enjoyment	Function-Word Unpredictability	Content-Word Unpredictability
Time	5.69	1.08	2.42
Associated Press	5.38	1.05	1.89
New York Times	5.25	.98	2.00
Newsweek	5.19	1.11	2.29
Readers Digest	5.19	1.04	2.12
Life (Edwin Aldrin)	5.13	1.32	2.28
Life (Neil Armstrong)	4.38	1.17	2.00
St. Louis Post-Dispatch	4.25	1.25	1.88
San Francisco Examiner	4.19	1.54	2.31

SOURCE: From Seth Finn, "Unpredictability as a Correlate of Reader Enjoyment of News Articles," *Journalism Quarterly* 62, no. 2 (1985): 334–339, 345. Reprinted with permission.

predictors of comprehension. More recent research on readability has become more theoretical, drawing upon work on human information processing and theoretical approaches to writing.

The newer, more complex picture of reading comprehension is illustrated in Figure 7.5, a diagram of reader performance developed by George Klare.

Newer approaches to measuring readability try to look at reader characteristics as well as characteristics of the style of the text. To a certain extent, the focus has shifted from readability of the text to comprehensibility of the text. These new approaches try to measure some aspects of the information processing being done by the individual reader.

Binkley and Chapman have developed an approach based on cloze procedure (Binkley, 1988). But their method is different from cloze procedure in these ways:

a. Words are not deleted randomly. Certain classes of words are deleted systematically in proportion to their frequency in the text as a whole. These classes reflect five different types of "cohesive ties" that provide structure to the writing: reference (for example, *he, that, there*), substitution (*one, same, do so*), conjunction (*and, or, later*), lexical (*kayak, boat*), and ellipsis.

b. The scoring is not based on whether or not the exact word appears. In the Binkley and Chapman system, responses are scored on a continuum ranging from "inappropriate" to "syntactically correct" to "syntactically and semantically correct."

This approach allows the researcher or teacher to pinpoint the kinds of weaknesses in reading that students have, so that they can be addressed with lessons. For instance, readers may have difficulty filling in the blanks representing substitution ties, and lessons could be developed to address that weakness. The

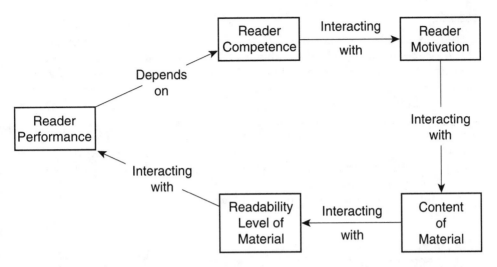

FIGURE 7.5   A model of reader performance

SOURCE: From G. R. Klare, "The Formative Years." In B. L. Zakaluk and S. J. Samuels (eds.)., *Readability: Its Past, & Present, Future,* p. 29. Newark, Del.: International Reading Association, 1988. Reprinted by permission.

approach also allows, with the scoring on a continuum, an assessment of the degree of comprehension for an individual or group.

Zakaluk and Samuels (1988), who have also developed a newer formula, fault the earlier readability formulas for concentrating only on text characteristics and neglecting how cognitive processing factors influence the comprehensibility of text, and for disregarding higher-level text organization.

They argue that another weakness in previous formulas is that they ignore the utility of highlighting important information in the text as a means of facilitating comprehension. They call the various methods for highlighting information *adjunct comprehension aids.* Such aids include questions interspersed throughout a text, lists of instructional objectives at the beginning of a text, and subheads.

The Zakaluk and Samuels approach is based on two "outside the head factors" (text readability level and adjunct comprehension aids) and two "inside the head" factors (word recognition skill and knowledge of the text topic). These four factors are then plotted on a chart or nomograph which yields a predicted level of reading comprehension that ranges on a scale from "low" to "average" to "high."

THE "WRITEABILITY" MOVEMENT

One negative result of the development of readability formulas has been that some people have taken the major elements of the formulas—word difficulty and sentence length—and applied them in a mechanical way to the editing or rewriting of prose. This procedure, if taken too far, can actually lead to bad writing. As Klare (1988) has pointed out, the variables in the formulas are only index variables, standing for other things that are going on in the text. Therefore, rewriting that addresses only word difficulty and sentence length may not address all the problems in a piece of writing that is difficult to understand.

Readability researchers have apparently felt some responsibility for the misapplication of formula variables in efforts to improve writing, and the result has been a new emphasis on writeability (Fry, 1988). Fry has drawn up a checklist for improving writeability, and the list goes beyond word difficulty and sentence length to include recommendations for short paragraphs; lists; subheads; pictures, diagrams, maps, and graphs; high imageable or concrete words; selection of interesting topics; and trials with sample audiences.

READABILITY MEASUREMENT IN OTHER LANGUAGES

The utility of readability measurement has led to readability formulas being developed in other languages (Rabin, 1988). Some of this development work has been done by researchers working in the United States and some by researchers in other parts of the world. The languages for which readability formulas have been developed now include Chinese, Danish, Dutch, French, German, Hebrew, Hindi, Korean, Russian, Spanish, Swedish, and Vietnamese.

CONCLUSIONS

Readability formulas have been applied to a great variety of written materials, including textbooks, wire service news, newspaper articles, insurance contracts, health brochures, and so forth. Readability formulas are useful for measuring the difficulty of comprehension of samples of writing, and they do this quickly and with a fairly high degree of accuracy.

Readability formulas are also useful in providing us with some solid evidence about which elements make writing easy or difficult to understand. The two most important elements, identified through a series of studies building on one another, are vocabulary burden and sentence complexity. We can translate this into advice for writers and editors and recommend that they use short words and short sentences.

Flesch has recommended that newswriters use an average sentence length of 19 words. That does not mean that every sentence has to be exactly that length. Some variety in sentence length is usually more pleasing than having all sentences the same length. But it means that in newswriting, 19 words is a good average length to aim for over a number of sentences.

Newer research on readability has become more theoretically based and has tended to draw upon related research on human information processing. The concept of readability has been enlarged to incorporate more elements. Many researchers now feel that it is insufficient to merely focus on two variables that can be easily measured in text—word difficulty and sentence length—as many formulas do. Newer attempts at developing formulas have acknowledged the information processing that takes place in the reader, and have attempted to incorporate cognitive variables that are measured for each individual reader. Recent formulas have also given more attention to the organization and structure of a piece of writing, as well as to various visual elements or comprehension aids such as lists, subheads, statements of objectives, charts, tables, and diagrams.

As we move more into a world of multimedia communication, the concept of readability may need to be expanded even further, bringing in the various elements of a multimedia message, including font, color, background, the amount of text on a screen, use of scrolling, use of links to other texts, and so forth.

DISCUSSION

1. How can readability formulas be useful to people working in the mass communication field?
2. How can readability formulas be misused?
3. The classic readability formulas focused on sentence length and vocabulary as the two important factors in whether or not prose is understandable. What other factors have been added in more recent formulas?
4. How do we know readability formulas are measuring what they claim to be measuring—the difficulty of a piece of writing?
5. What are the advantages and disadvantages of cloze procedure?
6. What advice for writing has come out of the "writeability" movement?
7. Research by Danielson, Lasorsa, and Im suggests that novels have been getting more readable over the years while newspapers have been getting less readable. How would you explain this discrepancy?
8. Suppose you wanted to measure the readability of a piece of writing for several different audiences that differed in ethnic background, income, and education. What approach to measuring readability would you take?

REFERENCES

Binkley, M. R (1988). New ways of assessing text difficulty. In B. L. Zakaluk and S. J. Samuels (eds.), *Readability: Its Past, Present & Future*, pp. 98-120. Newark, Del.: International Reading Association.

Bormuth, J. R. (1968). Cloze test readability: Criterion reference scores. *Journal of Educational Measurement* 5: 190-196.

Cardinal, B. J., and T. L. Seidler (1995). Readability and comprehensibility of the "Exercise Lite" brochure. *Perceptual and Motor Skills* 80: 399-402.

Catalano, K. (1990). On the wire: How six news services are exceeding readability standards. *Journalism Quarterly* 67: 97-103.

Cone, A. L. (1976). Six luxury models. *Contemporary Psychology* 21: 544-548.

Danielson, W. A., and S. D. Bryan (1963). Computer automation of two readability formulas. *Journalism Quarterly* 40: 201-206.

Danielson, W. A., and D. L. Lasorsa (1989). A new readability formula based on the stylistic age of novels. *Journal of Reading* 33 (no. 3): 194-197.

Danielson, T. A., D. L. Lasorsa, and D. S. Im (1992). Journalists and novelists: A Study of diverging styles. *Journalism Quarterly* 69: 436-446.

Fang, I. E. (1966-67). The "Easy Listening Formula." *Journal of Broadcasting* 11: 63-68.

————. (1980). *Television News, Radio News.* St. Paul, Minn.: Rada Press.

Farr, J. N., and J. J. Jenkins (1949). Tables for use with the Flesch readability formulas. *Journal of Applied Psychology* 33: 275-278.

Finn, S. (1985). Unpredictability as a correlate of reader enjoyment of news articles. *Journalism Quarterly* 62: 334-339, 345.

Finn, S., and D. F. Roberts (1984). Source, destination, and entropy: Reassessing the role of information theory in communication research. *Communication Research* 11: 453-476.

Fiske, E. B. (1987). The push for smarter schoolbooks. *New York Times,* Aug. 2, education supplement, pp. 20-23.

Flesch, R. (1943). *Marks of a Readable Style: A Study in Adult Education.* New York: Teachers College, Columbia University.

———— (1946). *The Art of Plain Talk.* New York: Harper & Row.

———— (1948). A new readability yardstick. *Journal of Applied Psychology* 32: 221-233.

———— (1974). *The Art of Readable Writing,* rev. ed. New York: Harper & Row.

Fry, E. B. (1988). Writeability: The principles of writing for increased comprehension. In B. L. Zakaluk and S. J. Samuels (eds.), *Readability: Its Past, Present & Future,* pp. 77-95. Newark, Del.: International Reading Association.

Gillen, B. (1973). Readability and human interest scores of thirty-four current introductory psychology texts. *American Psychologist* 28: 1010-1011.

Gray, W. S., and B. E. Leary (1935). *What Makes a Book Readable with Special Reference to Adults of Limited Reading Ability: An Initial Study.* Chicago: University of Chicago Press.

Gunning, R. (1945). Gunning finds papers too hard to read. *Editor & Publisher,* May 19, p 12.

———— (1952). *The Technique of Clear Writing.* New York: McGraw-Hill.

Hofmann, R. J., and R. J. Vyhonsky (1975). Readability and human interest scores of thirty-six recently published introductory educational psychology tests. *American Psychologist* 30: 790-792.

Kitson, H. D. (1921). *The Mind of the Buyer: A Psychology of Selling.* New York: Macmillan.

Klare, G. R. (1963). *The Measurement of Readability.* Ames: Iowa State University Press.

————. (1988). The formative years. In B. L. Zakaluk and S. J. Samuels (eds.), *Readability: Its Past, Present & Future,* pp. 14-34. Newark, Del.: International Reading Association.

Lively, B. A., and S. L. Pressey (1923). A method for measuring the "vocabulary burden" of textbooks. *Educational Administration and Supervision* 9: 389-398.

Lorge, I. (1939). Predicting reading difficulty of selections for children. *Elementary English Review* 16: 229-233.

Miller, T. H. (1984). A readability study of computer industry news releases. Unpublished master's thesis, University of Texas at Austin.

Mills, K. R. (1989) Readability of Alcoholics Anonymous: How accessible is the "Big Book"? *Perceptual and Motor Skills* 69: 258.

Rabin, A. T. (1988). Determining difficulty levels of text written in languages other than English. In B. L. Zakaluk and S. J. Samuels (eds.), *Readability: Its Past, Present & Future*, pp. 46-76. Newark, Del.: International Reading Association.

Rankin, E. F., and J. W. Culhane (1969). Comparable cloze and multiple-choice comprehension test scores. *Journal of Reading* 13: 193-198.

Richwald, G. A., M. A. Wamsley, A. H. Coulson, and D. E. Morisky (1988). Are condom instructions readable? Results of a readability study. *Public Health Reports* 103: 355-359.

Seib, C. (1976). Papers need to work on handling the English Language. *Austin American-Statesman,* Feb. 29, p. B25.

Sherman, L. A. (1888). Some observations upon the sentence-length in English prose. *University Studies of the University of Nebraska* 1 (no. 2): 119-130.

Stevens, L. A. (1949). Reliability of readability formulas as applied to listener comprehension of radio newscasts. Unpublished master's thesis, Iowa State University.

Swanson, C. (1948). Readability and readership: A controlled experiment. *Journalism Quarterly* 25: 339-345.

Tankard, J. W., and E. F. Tankard (1977). Comparison of readability of basic reporting texts. *Journalism Quarterly* 54: 794-797.

Taylor, W. L. (1953). "Cloze procedure": A new tool for measuring readability. *Journalism Quarterly* 30: 415-433.

Thorndike, E. L. (1975). *A Teacher's Word Book of the Twenty Thousand Words Found Most Frequently and Widely in General Reading for Children and Young People,* rev. ed. Detroit, Mich.: Gale. (Reprint of 1932 edition)

Verhovek, S. H. (1991). Educating educators in using (not utilizing!) plain English. *New Times,* Oct. 4.

Wesson, D. A. (1989). Readability as a factor in magazine ad copy recall. *Journalism Quarterly* 66: 715-718.

Zakulak, B. L., and S. J. Samuels. (1988). Toward a new approach to predicting text comprehensibility. In B. L. Zakaluk and S. J. Samuels (eds.), *Readability: Its Past, Present & Future*, pp. 121-144. Newark, Del.: International Reading Association.

part IV

The Social-Psychological Approach

Communication is obviously a social act, and we can go only so far in understanding it by approaching it at the individual level, as we did in Part III. In approaching communication as a social act, it is useful to draw upon theories that have been developed and research that has been conducted in the field of social psychology.

A number of theories have been developed around the idea that individuals strive for consistency between their attitudes, beliefs, values, and behaviors. This striving for consistency has a social aspect because it is often the perception of others that puts pressure on people to be consistent, and also because the source of much of our inconsistency comes through communication with others. The various theories of cognitive consistency are discussed in Chapter 8.

One of the primary functions of communication is persuasion, or the influencing of others through the use of symbols. Many researchers have been interested in the process of persuasion, and a number of theories have been proposed to explain persuasion. These theories are discussed in Chapter 9.

A fundamental lesson of social psychology is that people often act and think as members of groups rather than as individuals. This impact of groups on individuals applies to the reception of messages, and to other aspects of communication. Chapter 10 describes the role of groups in the communication process.

The social aspect of communication shows up in another way—it is getting more and more difficult to draw a sharp line between mass communication and interpersonal communication. Mass communication often depends on interpersonal communication to extend its reach, and research on adoption of innovations has shown that people at certain stages of the adoption process are more dependent on interpersonal communication than on mass communication. The relationship between mass communication and interpersonal communication is explored in Chapter 11.

chapter **8**

Cognitive Consistency and Mass Communication

The general notion of consistency underlies all of science. It is the notion that phenomena are ordered (or consistent) that allows predictability. Predictability, in turn, allows the scientist to formulate and test hypotheses, make generalizations from them, build theory, and predict future outcomes. The purpose of the communication researcher and theorist is, to a great measure, to predict the effect or future outcomes of messages.

The concept of consistency in human behavior is an extension of the general notion from the physical world to the area of human behavior. Various theorists contend that humans strive for consistency in a number of ways—between attitudes, between behaviors, between attitudes and behaviors, in our perception of the world, and even in the development of personality. In short, we try to organize our world in ways that seem to us to be meaningful and sensible.

The concepts of human consistency are based on the notion that human beings act in rational ways. However, we also use *rationalization*—the attempt to explain irrational behavior in a rational or consistent way. Rationalization emphasizes that in our desire to appear rational or consistent to ourselves we often employ means that may seem irrational or inconsistent to others.

The notions of consistency assume that inconsistency generates "psychological tension" or discomfort within human beings, which results in internal pressure to eliminate or reduce the inconsistency and, if possible, achieve consistency.

Examples of the consistency principles in everyday affairs are widespread.

A first-ranked football team in an area where football reigns supreme suffered a humiliating defeat at the hands of a long-standing rival. The following day both the media and individual conversations were filled with rationalizations and justifications.

As noted, consistency theories recognize human attempts at rationality, but in achieving it we often display striking irrationality. The concept of rationalization assumes both rationality and irrationality—we often use irrational means to achieve understanding, to justify painful experiences, or to make the world fit our "frame of reference."

Mass communication research is concerned, in part, with how individuals deal with discrepant or inconsistent information, which is often presented with the purpose of bringing about attitude change. This attitude change is one of the many ways in which we can reduce or eliminate the discomfort or psychological pressure of inconsistency.

Although a number of consistency theories are of interest to behavioral scientists (Kiesler, Collins, & Miller, 1969; Abelson et al., 1968), for the purposes of this book only four major ones will be discussed.

HEIDER'S BALANCE THEORY

Most writers usually credit Fritz Heider (1946) with the earliest articulation of a consistency theory, although the informal concept can be traced back to earlier work (see Kiesler et al., 1969, p. 157). As a psychologist, Heider was concerned with the way an individual organizes attitudes toward people and objects in relation to one another within that individual's own cognitive structure. Heider postulated that unbalanced states produce tension and generate forces to restore balance. He says that "the concept of a balanced state designates a situation in which the perceived units and the experienced sentiments co-exist without stress" (1958, p. 176).

Heider's paradigm focused on two individuals, a person (P), the object of the analysis, some other person (O), and a physical object, idea, or event (X). Heider's concern was with how relationships among these three entities are organized in the mind of one individual (P). Heider distinguished two types of relationships among these three entities, liking (L) and unit (U) relations (cause, possession, similarity, etc.). In Heider's paradigm, "a balanced state exists if all three relations are positive in all respects or if two are negative and one is positive" (1946, p. 110). All other combinations are unbalanced.

In Heider's conception, degrees of liking cannot be represented; a relation is either positive or negative (Figure 8.1). It is assumed that a balanced state is stable and resists outside influences. An unbalanced state is assumed to be unstable and is assumed to produce psychological tension within an individual. This tension "becomes relieved only when change within the situation takes place in such a way that a state of balance is achieved" (Heider, 1958, p. 180). This pinpoints the communicator's interest in the theory for it implies a model of attitude change and resistance to attitude change. Unbalanced states, being unstable states, are susceptible to change toward balance. Balanced states, being stable states, resist change. Data supporting Heider's balance theory are discussed in Zajonc (1960), Kiesler et al. (1969), and Abelson et al. (1968).

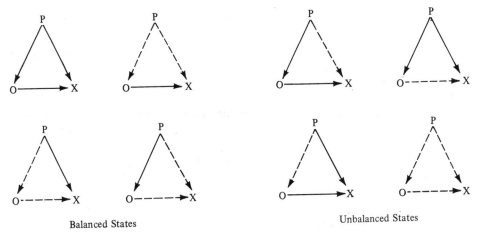

Balanced States   Unbalanced States

FIGURE 8.1 Examples of balanced and unbalanced states according to Heider's definition of balance. Solid lines represent positive, and broken lines negative relations.

SOURCE: From R. B. Zajonc, "The Concepts of Balance, Congruity and Dissonance," *Public Opinion Quarterly* 24 (1960): 280–296. Reprinted with permission of the University of Chicago Press.

NEWCOMB'S SYMMETRY THEORY

Social psychologist Theodore M. Newcomb took Heider's idea of balance out of the head of one person and applied it to communication between people. He uses the term *symmetry* to distinguish it from balance theory and contends that we attempt to influence one another to bring about symmetry (or balance or equilibrium). As discussed in some detail in Chapter 3, Newcomb postulates that attempts to influence another person are a function of the attraction that one person has for another. In this respect Newcomb's theory is more of a theory of interpersonal attraction than one of attitude change. If we fail to achieve symmetry through communication with another person about an object important to both of us, we may then change our attitude toward either the other person or the object in question in order to establish symmetry.

Because Newcomb's model (see Chapter 3) deals with two people and the communication between them, he labels them A and B (rather than Heider's P and O) and retains X to represent the object of their attitudes. As with Heider, he assumes a human need for consistency, which he calls a "persistent strain toward symmetry." If A and B disagree about X, the amount of this strain toward symmetry will depend on the intensity of A's attitude toward X and A's attraction for B. An increase in A's attraction for B and an increase in A's intensity of attitude toward X will result in (1) an increased strain toward symmetry on the part of A toward B about their attitudes toward X, (2) the likelihood that symmetry will be achieved, and (3) the probability of a communication by A to B about X. The last item, of course, is the focus of our concern.

Newcomb says, "The likelihood of a symmetry-directed A to B re X varies as a multiple function of the perceived discrepancy (i.e., inversely with perceived symmetry), with valence toward B and with valence toward X" (Newcomb, 1953, p. 398).

Newcomb, in contrast to Heider, stresses communication. The less the symmetry between A and B about X, the more probable that A will communicate with B regarding X. Symmetry predicts that people associate with or become friends of people with whom they agree. The Greek dramatist Euripides recognized this facet of human behavior more than 2,400 years ago when he said, "Every man is like the company he is wont to keep." (Today we say, "Birds of a feather flock together.")

However, for attitude change to take place, a person must come into contact with information that differs from his or her present attitudes. Newcomb's symmetry model predicts that the more A is attracted to B (a person or a group), the greater the opinion change on the part of A toward the position of B.

OSGOOD'S CONGRUITY THEORY

The congruity model is a special case of Heider's balance theory. Though similar to balance theory, it deals specifically with the attitudes persons hold toward sources of information and the objects of the source's assertions. Congruity theory has several advantages over balance theory, including the ability to make predictions about both the direction and the degree of attitude change. The congruity model assumes that "judgmental frames of reference tend toward maximal simplicity." Because extreme judgments are easier to make than refined ones (see discussion of either-or thinking and two-valued evaluation in Chapter 5), valuations tend to move toward the extremes, or there is "a continuing pressure toward polarization." In addition to this maximization of simplicity, the assumption is also made that identity is less complex than discrimination of fine differences (either-or thinking and categorization). Because of this, related "concepts" are evaluated in a similar manner.

In the congruity paradigm a person (P) receives an assertion from a source (S), toward which he or she has an attitude, about an object (O), toward which he or she also has an attitude. In Osgood's model, how much P likes S and O will determine if a state of congruity or consistency exists (Figure 8.2).

According to congruity theory, when a change occurs, it is always toward greater congruity with prevailing frames of reference. Osgood uses his semantic differential to measure the amount of liking a person may have for a source and the object of an assertion.

In essence, the definitions of balance and congruity are identical. Incongruity exists when the attitudes toward the source and the object are similar and the assertion is negative or when they are dissimilar and the assertion is positive. An unbalanced state has either one or all negative relations.

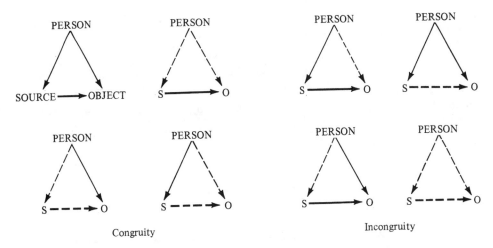

Congruity   Incongruity

FIGURE 8.2 Examples of congruity and incongruity. Heavy lines represent assertions, light lines attitudes. Solid heavy lines represent assertions which imply a positive attitude on the part of the source, and broken heavy lines negative attitudes. Solid light lines represent positive attitudes, and broken light lines negative attitudes.

SOURCE: From R. B. Zajonc, "The Concepts of Balance, Congruity and Dissonance." *Public Opinion Quarterly* 24 (1960): 280–296. Reprinted with permission of the University of Chicago Press.

Percy Tannenbaum had 405 college students evaluate three sources—labor leaders, the *Chicago Tribune,* and Senator Robert Taft—and three objects—gambling, abstract art, and accelerated college programs. Some time later the students were presented with newspaper clippings that contained assertions attributed to the sources about the objects. The entire range of predicted changes was supported by Tannenbaum's data, as summarized in Table 8.1. The direction of change is indicated by either a plus or a minus sign, while the extent of change is indicated by one or two such signs.

Incongruity and the Media

A graphic example of this phenomenon in the media world occurred when Walter Cronkite and CBS covered the Democratic National Convention in Chicago in August 1968. CBS News reported at the time what the Walker Commission later called a "police riot" on the streets of Chicago. Walter Cronkite expressed the opinion on the air that the convention floor seemed to be under the control of a "bunch of thugs" after Dan Rather was "decked" while "on camera" when he attempted to interview delegates from a southern state being removed from the convention floor. CBS News (the source) had made negative assertions about objects (Mayor Richard Daley and the Chicago police) that apparently were held in high esteem by many persons in the television audience. Feedback to CBS

TABLE 8.1 Change of attitude toward the source and the object when positive and negative assertions are made by the source

Original Attitude toward the Source	Positive Assertion about an Object toward Which the Attitude Is		Negative Assertion about an Object toward Which the Attitude Is	
	Positive	*Negative*	*Positive*	*Negative*
Change of Attitude toward the Source				
Positive	+	——	——	+
Negative	++	—	—	++
Change of Attitude toward the Object				
Positive	+	++	——	—
Negative	——	—	+	++

SOURCE: From R. B. Zajonc, "The Concepts of Balance, Congruity and Dissonance." *Public Opinion Quarterly* 24 (1960): 280–296. Reprinted with permission of the University of Chicago Press.

News expressed considerable dissatisfaction on the part of audience members with the news coverage. Presumably their attitude toward the source, Walter Cronkite and CBS News, became more negative. If, in a democracy, we cannot behead the messenger who brings unpleasant news (that does not agree with our "prevailing frame of reference" of reality), as was the case in ancient Persia, congruity theory predicts that we come to dislike the bearer of information that does not agree with our view of the world. We have incorporated this into the folk saying, "Don't confuse me with the facts, I have already made up my mind."

Incongruity does not always produce attitude change. There is some basis for the belief that much material in the media that would produce incongruity in an individual never does so. In the process of selecting what we will pay attention to, we may avoid messages that we suspect will not agree with our concept of the world (selective exposure) or perhaps pay attention to only the parts of a message that agree with our "prevailing frame of reference" (selective attention).

If we do receive a message that causes incongruity, we may misperceive the message (selective perception) to make it fit our view of reality. The French painter and sculptor Degas is reported to have said, "One sees as one wishes to see." When National Public Radio's "Morning Edition" marked its 15th anniversary (October 31, 1994), Susan Stamberg reviewed "where we all were and what we were doing when this daily program began." In her commentary, she said:

> . . . on the how-to list, two books to help our waistlines . . . and the Complete Scarsdale Medical Diet by Herman Tarnower . . . before the Scarsdale doctor had a *run-in* with the headmistress of the Maderia School. (Emphasis added)

Actually the "run-in" resulted in Tarnower's death and the headmistress, Jean Harris, being sentenced to prison for having murdered him. She was parolled in early 1993, after having served 12 years. Most people would probably call murder something more than a *run-in.*

Statements by the chairman of the Federal Reserve Board have over the years, been notorious for varying interpretations by the mass media. The "MacNeil/Lehrer Newshour" recognized such selective perception when Elizabeth Farnsworth said:

> . . . this morning the major newspapers ran very different stories about what the chairman said. While the *Washington Post* reported that Greenspan had signalled a cut in interest rates, the *Wall Street Journal* and *New York Times* reported the opposite. (June 21, 1995)

In the following discussion, Paul Volcker, a former chairman of the Federal Reserve Board, recognizing the selective perception of the media, said:

> . . . You try to give a balanced statement. A reporter can pick out one side or the other of the balance that you made, and frankly, arrive at his own interpretations and there's always an insistence to make a complicated story short and brief. You arrive at some theme for the headline, two different editors arrive at two different themes, and you get contrasting stories. (June 21, 1995)

In mid-October 1995, African-Americans held a "Million Man March" in Washington, D.C. The following evening (October 17, 1995) ABC's *Nightline*, titled, "What Happened Yesterday?," interviewed dozens of people, from many walks of life. Their responses were a good example of selective perception in action. The television anchor, Ted Koppel, introduced the program by saying:

> People see what they want to see. . . . Some heard hate, others heard the need to bring the community back together again. . . . People hear what they expect to hear. . . . What happened? It depends on whom you ask.

On the same day as the "Million Man March," President Clinton spoke at the University of Texas in Austin, with the theme of healing American society. Almost everyone praised the speech, but one honors program senior in American Studies, writing in the student newspaper, said (*Daily Texan,* Oct. 17, 1995):

> To begin a stream of inconsistencies, Clinton warned, "We dare not tolerate the existence of two Americas," and then proceeded to address part of his remarks "to our white audience" and another set of remarks "to our black citizens." After referring to Lincoln's house divided, "Our house" will soon be split into "the house of white America" and the

house of black America. Suddenly the idea of "e pluribus unum" gave way to housing segregation. (p. 3)

Feedback to the student paper indicated that many readers were unable to see any connotation of housing segregation.

News items that refute public opinion, which presumably cause psychological discomfort, are relatively uncommon.

A study found that in 1989 wage earners with incomes between $25,000 and $30,000 gave a larger percentage of their incomes to charity than did those with incomes of $50,000 to $75,000 (Barringer, 1992).

Another article observed (Odendahl, 1990):

> But it's time we recognized that most of the benefits of philanthropy go to the wealthy, not the needy or even the middle class. . . . (a) small group of elite nonprofit institutions—Ivy League universities, museums, symphonies, think-tanks, private hospitals, prep schools and the like—that, by best available estimates, receive more than two-thirds of private charitable giving.
>
> About half of philanthropy is donated by multimillionaires. Most of this money goes to groups that sustain the culture, education, policy positions and status of the well to do. . . . Contrary to popular belief, less than a third of nonprofit organizations serve the needy. In much of their charitable giving, in fact, the wealthy end up funding their own interests.
>
> Even more disturbingly, the philanthropic wealthy also exert control over public funds, and over money contributed in smaller amounts by the less well-off,without the accountability we expect in a government agency or publicly held corporation. (A15)

Two years later the *Chicago Sun-Times*, citing the national Council of Nonprofit Associations in an editorial, wrote (Sept. 28, 1992):

> In 1980, there were 4,300 millionaires in America, whose annual giving averaged $207,089. In 1989, there were 59,954 millionaires, giving an average $83,929. . . . Things aren't much better in the corporate sphere, where the amount donated to nonprofit organizations has declined 39 percent since the tax reform act was passed. (p. 25)

O. J. Simpson, at the end of his murder trial, called the Larry King television talk show and said, in part, that after a day in court he would go back to his cell and watch TV news and wonder if the "experts" on television had been in the same courtroom he had been in (Oct. 4, 1995).

Different people may not only see different things in a message, but they often attend a message for different reasons. Two researchers asked more than 700 adults for their reasons for watching televised sports (Gantz & Wenner,

1991). They found that men watch sports to relax, to see athletic drama, and to have something to talk about. Women, on the other hand, were more likely to watch for companionship with those already gathered around the set.

If we are unable to misperceive the message, we may attack the credibility of the communicator. Credibility is, after all, the most important thing a communicator has. A communicator in the news media who lacks credibility probably also has no audience.

The credibility of the communicator was attacked when the *New York Times Magazine* published a photo essay by Eugene Richards about drug-ridden urban America. One writer commented (Carton, 1994):

> As the bearer of an unpleasant message Richards. . . . has found himself the center of a controversy over political correctness and race: Did he focus too heavily on black cocaine addicts and hustlers? (p. 30)

Immediately after publication of the photo essay black leaders called the *New York Times* insensitive for running the photo essay and demanded an apology or face the threat of a boycott. The *Amsterdam News*, the city's oldest black newspaper, ran a front page editorial denouncing the photos (Taylor, 1993). The photographer replied (*New York Times Magazine*, Jan. 23, 1994):

> Name calling doesn't alter the facts and nature of the drug plague choking our country. (p. 10)

And later, in a reply to a review of his book, *Cocaine True, Cocaine Blue*, he called it (*New York Times*, March 6, 1994, Book Review):

> a continuation of the ancient tradition of trying to kill the bearer of bad news . . . the weapon of choice here is to charge bias . . . (p. 31)

Denial or incredulity is another means of dealing with incongruity.

The New York City health commissioner, speaking of the AIDS epidemic, said, "The way mankind responds to crisis is first disbelief, then denial, then the third stage is mobilization, and we're at that horizon now" (*New York Times*, Feb. 14, 1988, p. 1).

If, indeed, an incongruous message does reach an individual, there is still no guarantee of attitude change. Selective retention may enter the picture, and we may well remember only points that support our "prevailing frame of reference."

In the mid-1990s, at the height of "ethnic cleansing" in Bosnia, author Kenneth Davis (1995) was compelled to write:

> Virtually absent from the discussion is any acknowledgment that when it comes to the sorts of horrors now defining the Balkan conflict, Americans have been there and done that, in a manner of speaking. To put it bluntly: The United States may not have written the book on

ethnic cleansing, but it certainly provided several of its most stunning chapters—particularly in its treatment of the American Indian in the transcontinental drive for territory justified under the quasi-religious notion of "manifest destiny."

Why do we tend to forget? There's no big surprise: Americans, as deTocqueville long ago recognized, are a future-oriented people with a short historical memory. And the accepted, widely taught versions of history are written by the victors, presented in schools as sanitized costume pageantry. This is especially true when the victory is as total as that of America's forefathers over the American Indians, who were nearly "cleansed" from an entire continent—an outcome the likes of which Bosnia's Serbs can only dream. (p. 1)

The Role of Media Gatekeepers

According to many reports, the Japanese are not taught in school about the surprise attack on Pearl Harbor. Some Japanese see in their nation a sort of collective amnesia (Chira, 1985, 1988a, 1988b; Lehner, 1988). When the epic film *The Last Emperor* was shown in Japan, a part showing Japanese soldiers committing atrocities in Nanjing in December 1937 and January 1938—the six-week orgy of murder, rape, and mayhem known as the "Rape of Nanjing"—was cut out (Haberman, 1988). In May 1994 Japan's new justice minister stirred up considerable anger in Asia when he was quoted as saying that the Nanjing massacre never happened (Reuter, May 3, 1994).

It has been pointed out that Americans hold a highly ethnocentric view of Columbus.

One lecturer in psychology wrote (Strong, 1989):

Most school history texts do not tell that Columbus was the first European to bring slavery to the New World. . . . On his second voyage, in December 1494, Columbus captured 1,500 Tainos on the island of Hispaniola and herded them to Isabela, where 550 of the "best males and females" were forced aboard ships bound for the slave markets of Seville.

Under Columbus's leadership, the Spanish attacked the Taino, sparing neither men, women nor children. Warfare, forced labor, starvation and disease reduced Hispaniola's Taino population (estimated at one million to two million in 1492) to extinction within 30 years.

Until the European discovery of America, there was only a relatively small slave trade between Africa and Europe. Needing labor to replace the rapidly declining Taino, the Spanish introduced African slaves to Hispaniola in 1502; by 1510, the trade was important to the Caribbean economy. (p. 14)

College seniors in the United States often claim that little or nothing is said in high school or college about the Vietnam War, the Pentagon Papers, or

Watergate, all having taken place before they were born or during their child-hood and all, apparently, to be collectively forgotten.

A study done in a graduate school of education found that of seven social studies textbooks examined, four contained no coverage of Watergate, two had what was called minimal coverage, and only one was termed adequate. The writer wonders whether the lessons of Watergate have been forgotten for a generation of schoolchildren (Woodward, 1987).

On March 16, 1968, U.S. troops entered the village of My Lai in southern Vietnam and "wasted" more than 450 unarmed civilians, including old men, women, and children with automatic weapons fire. The news was suppressed for 20 months. In a later series of trials the company commander, Capt. Ernest L. Medina, was acquitted; the platoon commander, Lt. William Laws Calley, Jr., the only soldier ever convicted of premeditated murder of "not less than 22 civilians," actually served three days in a military stockade and four and a half months in prison, after legal appeals and a pardon. "A good many of the participants would later offer the explanation that they were obeying orders, a defense explicitly prohibited by the Nuremberg Principles and the United States Army's own rules of war" (O'Brien, 1994, p. 52).

In 1970 General Samuel W. Koster resigned as superintendent of the U.S. Military Academy at West Point following accusations that he and 13 other officers suppressed information. In 1968 he had commanded the U.S. Army division whose men committed the massacre as My Lai. The charge was made that as the accusations of the mass murders moved through the division's chain of command, the number of murders was systematically reduced in number.

One veteran, who served a year in Vietnam, much of it in the My Lai area says (O'Brien, 1994):

> Now, more than 25 years later, the villainy of that Saturday morning in 1968 has been pushed off the margins of memory. In colleges and high schools I sometimes visit, the mention of My Lai brings on null stares, a sort of puzzlement, disbelief mixed with utter ignorance. (p. 52)

He adds:

> I know what occurred here, yes, but I also feel betrayed by a nation that so widely shrugs off barbarity, by a military judicial system that treats murderers and common soldiers as one and the same. . . . In a way, America has declared itself innocent. (p. 53)

One researcher (Ehrenhaus, 1989) points out that for more than a decade the Vietnam War was collectively forgotten. He asks, how does a society com-memorate its failures? When faced with the obligation to commemorate Vietnam and its veterans the United States chose not to remember. The author says:

> The end of war brings with it the obligation to remember. . . . Remem-brance entails reaffirming the legitimacy of purpose for which a community

has issued its call for sacrifice . . . the significance of commemoration lies not in the occurrence of events; it lies in the fact that certain events are remembered while others are not. . . . (pp. 97–98)

Ehrenhaus points out that President Ford urged Americans not to reflect upon the meaning of the past. Ehrenhaus argues that such reflection might challenge the assumptions of the relationships between individuals and the state. He says that "fundamental belief in U.S. righteousness was confronted by revelations of political cowardice and lies at home . . ." (p. 104). For these and other reasons, Ehrenhaus contends the society and its leaders chose to "forget" Vietnam for more than a decade.

And, of the millions of Vietnamese, Cambodian, and Laotian civilian casualties, little or nothing is ever said in the United States, other than a few references to widespread birth defects as the result of the massive spraying of Agent Orange.

FESTINGER'S THEORY OF COGNITIVE DISSONANCE

The most general of all the consistency theories and, as one might expect, the one that has generated the largest body of empirical data is Leon Festinger's theory of cognitive dissonance. It is also a theory that has generated considerable controversy in the field of social psychology.

Dissonance theory holds that two elements of knowledge "are in dissonant relation if, considering these two alone, the obverse of one element would follow from the other" (Festinger, 1957, p. 13). As with other consistency theories, it holds that dissonance, "being psychologically uncomfortable, will motivate the person to try to reduce dissonance and achieve consonance" and "in addition to trying to reduce it the person will actively avoid situations and information which would likely increase the dissonance" (p. 3).

In cognitive dissonance the elements in question may be (1) irrelevant to one another, (2) consistent with one another (in Festinger's terms, consonant), or (3) inconsistent with one another (dissonant in Festinger's terms). Relationships need not be logically related for consistency or inconsistency. A relationship may be logically inconsistent to an observer while psychologically consistent to an individual who holds these obverse beliefs.

Several rather interesting consequences follow from dissonance theory, especially in the areas of decision making and role playing. The focus of this book is on how people use information, and dissonance theory is important in that respect.

Decision Making

Upon making a decision, dissonance is predicted to follow to the extent that the rejected alternative contains features that would have resulted in its acceptance and that the chosen alternative contains features that could have caused its rejection. In other words, the more difficult a decision is to make, the greater the predicted dissonance after the decision (postdecision dissonance). It also follows that postdecision dissonance is greater for more important decisions. A number of studies report evidence to support these hypotheses.

One researcher reports that purchasers of new cars were more apt to notice and read ads about the cars they had just bought than about other cars (Ehrlich, Guttman, Schonbach, & Mills, 1957). Since ads are supposed to stress "benefits" of the products they promote, presumably the new car buyers were seeking reinforcement for their decisions by reading ads for the cars they had just purchased.

Evidence has also been cited for a change in the attractiveness of alternatives once a decision has been made. In other words, after a decision has been made between alternatives ranked as nearly equal in desirability, the chosen alternative is later seen as more desirable than it had been before the decision, and the rejected alternative is ranked as less desirable than it was before the decision was made (Brehm, 1956). The authors of one book on attitude change state, "The postdecision process involves cognitive change not unlike that of attitude change; indeed the effects of this process may legitimately be referred to as attitude change" (Kiesler, Collins, & Miller, 1969, p. 205).

An article about computer owners resolving postdecision dissonance put it this way (Lewis, 1987):

> For some inexplicable reason, people who would not ordinarily think of criticizing your preferences in automobiles, underwear or religion, for example, feel justified in castigating you on a personal level for your choice of computer. Dr. Mark Spiegel, a psychiatrist in Manhattan, was asked to fathom the thinking of such computer zealotry. "Rational human beings don't do that," he said. Granted. So what explains all the irrational behavior of computer owners? "It could be a number of things," he suggested, "but cognitive dissonance is a psychological mechanism in which the individual, finding that his actions don't necessarily coincide with his ideas or psychological precepts, has to find some way to make them correlate, or bring them into assonance. If you spend a lot of money on a computer, you have to justify it," explained Dr. Spiegel. (p 19)

Forced Compliance

An interesting area, even if not directly related to the mass media, is attitude change following forced compliance. Dissonance theory postulates that when an individual is placed in a situation where he or she must behave publicly in a way that is contrary to that individual's privately held beliefs or attitudes, the individual experiences dissonance from knowledge of that fact. Such situations often occur as the result of a promise of a reward or the threat of punishment, but sometimes it may be simply as the result of group pressure to conform to a norm an individual does not privately agree with. Role playing is one such example.

If a person performs a public act inconsistent with his or her beliefs, it is predicted that dissonance will follow. One way of resolving this dissonance is to change the privately held beliefs to conform with the public act. The least amount of pressure necessary (promise of reward or threat of punishment) to induce an individual to act publicly in a way contrary to his or her privately held beliefs will result in the greatest dissonance. The greater the dissonance, the greater the pressure to reduce it, hence the greater the chance for attitude change in the direction of the public act or behavior. In the case of a relatively large promised reward or threatened punishment, the individual can always rationalize the public behavior that was contrary to the privately held beliefs or attitudes (e.g., "I did it for the money" or "Anybody would do the same under such a threat").

One foreign teacher at the Shanghai Institute of Foreign Trade said in an interview that her students were given summer assignments to write essays about the student demonstrations in China in 1989. She reported that their scholarships depended on what they wrote (National Public Radio, Oct. 14, 1989).

Selective Exposure and Selective Attention

Dissonance theory is of greatest interest to us in the areas of information seeking and avoidance, often called *selective exposure* and *selective attention*. Dissonance theory predicts that individuals will avoid dissonance-producing information, and there is considerable evidence indicating that media personnel are acutely aware of this.

In recent years some attention has been given to the effects of Agent Orange on Vietnam veterans, but almost no attention has been given to its effects on the Vietnamese people. One Vietnam combat veteran, now an Emmy and Peabody Award-winning television producer, who recently returned to Vietnam, says (Bird, 1990):

> We saw the lunarlike landscape near the Cambodian border which had been defoliated by Agent Orange. We met disabled veterans, war widows, orphans and deformed children in desperate need. . . . Isn't there a studio in Hollywood today that will buck the system and make a movie about the Vietnamese? . . . We need a movie or movies in which the Vietnamese are in the forefront. We still owe them a peace. (p. 16)

Oliver Stone tried to remedy that omission in 1994 with the last of his Vietnam trilogy, *Heaven & Earth,* a film that attempted to portray the war from the Vietnamese viewpoint.

While the 2,265 Americans missing in the Vietnam War are often mentioned, we forget the missing Vietnamese, more than 300,000, or, in absolute numbers, 132 times as many, and proportionately a far greater number given the disparities in the populations of the two countries.

Some researchers have contended that individuals do not ordinarily select or reject entire messages (selective exposure) because we often cannot judge the message content beforehand. Others have observed that usually we are surrounded by people and media that agree with us on the major issues (McGuire, 1968). Some researchers argue that more typically individuals will pay attention to the parts of a message that are not contrary to their strongly held attitudes, beliefs, or behaviors (selective attention) and not pay attention to the parts of a message that are counter to strongly held positions and might cause psychological discomfort or dissonance. There is some evidence that people will pay attention to material that does not support their position if they believe it will be easy to refute, but they will avoid information that is supportive of their position if it is weak. The latter may cause them to lose confidence in their initial position (Brock & Balloun, 1967; Lowin, 1969; Kleinhesselink & Edwards, 1975).

In a summary of research, several authors concluded that there is little evidence to support the hypothesis that individuals will avoid entire messages (selective exposure) that are contrary to their beliefs (Brehm & Cohen, 1962; Freedman & Sears, 1965; Sears, 1968). Researchers have found that individuals seeking novelty will not necessarily avoid dissonance-producing information. The perceived utility of information (e.g., the learning of "implausible" counter-arguments to one's position cited in Chapter 4) may impel an individual to pay attention to dissonance-producing information. Contradictory information that is new, interesting, salient, personally relevant, or entertaining will probably not be avoided. Contradictory information that is useful in learning a skill or solving a problem will probably be attended to. In other words, if the message contains rewards that exceed the psychological discomfort or dissonance it may generate, the message will probably not be avoided. Individuals are more apt to pay attention to material that is contradictory to their beliefs, behaviors, or choices if they are ones not strongly held. With strongly held beliefs, people who are highly confident of their views will not avoid contradictory material because they believe they can easily refute it. For differing positions on this issue, see Freedman and Sears (1965), who concluded that people do not avoid dissonant information, and Mills (1968), who argued that under some circumstances they do. Both are included in Abelson et al. (1968), which provides an extended, in-depth treatment of consistency theories.

However, Cotton (1985), in an exhaustive review of research dealing with selective exposure, concluded that the earlier studies suffered from a variety of methodological flaws. He believes that earlier studies contained a variety of artifacts that may have affected their findings. Cotton concludes, "Later research on selective exposure, generally more carefully controlled, has produced more positive results. Almost every study found significant selective-exposure effects" (p. 25).

At this point we can say only that the jury is still out on the question of selective exposure and the final verdict is yet to come.

Entertainment Choices

There is some evidence that choices in entertainment are made "on impulse," or spontaneously, rather than with deliberate selective exposure (Zillmann & Bryant, 1986). However, research (Bryant & Zillmann, 1984) has shown that people seem to select entertainment intuitively, depending upon their mood. The researchers say:

> The data revealed that exciting programs attracted bored subjects significantly more than stressed subjects and that relaxing programs attracted stressed subjects significantly more than bored subjects. . . . It was found that almost all subjects had chosen materials that helped them to escape effectively from undesirable excitatory states. In fact almost all subjects overcorrected, that is, bored subjects ended up above base levels and stressed ones below base levels of excitation. (pp. 307–308)

Other studies (Zillmann & Bryant, 1985) suggest that "all people who are down on their luck may be expected to seek, and obtain, mood lifts from comedy" (p. 309). However, "provoked, angry persons were found to refrain from watching hostile comedy and turn to alternative offerings" (Zillmann, Hezel, & Medoff, 1980).

Crime-apprehensive people selected drama that was lower in violent victimization and higher in justice restoration than did nonapprehensive counterparts. Apprehensive persons exhibited a tendency to expose themselves to information capable of reducing their apprehensions. One researcher (Zillmann, 1980) concludes that "the main message of television crime drama—namely, that criminals are being caught and put away, which should make the streets safer— apparently holds great appeal for those who worry about crime" (p. 311).

In recent years there has been considerable discussion concerning the effects of the new communication technologies on viewing behavior. Today, besides the TV set there are VCRs, cable systems, and remote controls. One survey of 583 Florida residents found that, contrary to popular opinion, the new technologies are having little effect on viewing habits (Ferguson, 1992). Cable owners said they watched regularly about six channels, while nonsubscribers reported watching regularly four channels.

Selective Retention

Earlier, several studies were cited in support of the concept of selective retention, that people tend to remember material that agrees with their "prevailing frame of reference" or attitudes, beliefs, and behaviors and forget material that disagrees with them. More recent research tended to cast some doubt on these findings. One study concluded that neither prior attitudes nor prior familiarity was related to learning of material and that novelty enhances learning of propagandistic information (Greenwald & Sakamura, 1967). Another study, which tested the hypotheses of both the Levine and Murphy study and the Jones and Kohler study (cited in Chapter 4), concluded that only under certain conditions does an attitude-memory relationship exist, if at all, and that "the specific nature of these conditions is not as yet understood" (Brigham & Cook, 1969, p. 243).

As with all scientific research, this is an area in which theory is being refined and sharpened. Recent studies are applying more rigid controls and investigating alternative explanations. At this point we can say only that the factors that influence selective retention of information are yet to be determined, and much work remains to be done concerning the selective retention of information.

CONCLUSIONS

As should be obvious by now, consistency theories have many implications for how humans perceive the world, communicate, and use, distort, ignore, or forget the contents of the mass media. In their generality and scope they apply to both media practitioners and media consumers—from the reporter at the scene of the news or the producer of an advertisement to the final destination of the message.

As we have seen, nations can selectively forget unpleasant past events and deny current problems, individuals can selectively perceive objective data, even from highly sophisticated electronic instruments, and presidents can and do selectively misperceive questions and data. People reduce postdecision dissonance with selective retention of facts and nations attempt to change attitudes through forced role playing. The media not only vary in their perceptions of an event, but often also ignore unpleasant facts about their own societies.

DISCUSSION

1. Give an example of how you have tried to achieve consistency between your attitudes; your behaviors; your attitudes and behaviors.
2. Can you remember an example of your rationalizing an inconsistency between your attitudes and/or your behaviors?
3. Was your rationalization caused by your feeling psychologically uncomfortable about your inconsistency?
4. Can you cite examples of selective exposure (avoidance of entire messages)?
   How about examples of selective attention (avoidance of parts of messages)?
5. Give an example of selective perception in the mass media.
6. Have you, or anyone you know, recently attacked the credibility of the communicator of a message you disagreed with, rather than address the contents of the message itself? Can you give an example?
7. When confronted with dissonant information have you reacted with denial or incredulity?
8. Give an example of selective retention on the part of society.
9. Have you ever made a decision of some importance and later questioned your correctness in making the decision? If so, what did you do to reduce your doubt about the correctness of your decision?

10. How do you decide what to watch on television? How many of your decisions are the result of impulse? How many are the result of selective exposure?

REFERENCES

Abelson, R. P., E. Aronson, W. J. McGuire, T. M. Newcomb, M. H. Rosenberg, and P. H. Tannenbaum (eds.) (1968). *Theories of Cognitive Consistency: A Sourcebook.* Skokie, Ill.: Rand-McNally.

Barringer, Felicity (1992). Charity giving by millionaires fell in '80's, federal study finds. New York Times News Service in *Austin American-Statesman*, July 4, p. A28.

Bird, T. (1990). Man and boy confront the images of war. *New York Times*, May 27, Sec. 2, pp. 11, 16.

Brehm, J. W. (1956). Post-decision changes in the desirability of alternatives. *Journal of Abnormal and Social Psychology* 52: 384-389.

Brehm, J. W., and A. R. Cohen (1962). *Explorations in Cognitive Dissonance.* New York: John Wiley.

Brigham, J., and S. Cook (1969). The influence of attitude on the recall of controversial material: A failure to confirm. *Journal of Experimental Social Psychology* 5: 240-243.

Brock, T. C., and J. L. Balloun (1967). Behavioral receptivity to dissonant information. *Journal of Personality and Social Psychology* 6: 413-428.

Bryant, J., and D. Zillmann (1984). Using television to alleviate boredom and stress: Selective exposure as a function of induced excitational states. *Journal of Broadcasting* 28: 1-20.

Carton, Barbara (1994). Photographer accused of shooting with a biased lens; Eugene Richards' pictorial of addicts sparks a furor. *Boston Globe*, March 14, Sec.: Living, p. 30.

Chira, S. (1985). Japanese confront history at Pearl Harbor attack site. *Austin American-Statesman*, Dec. 8, p. A16.

———— (1988a). For Japanese, textbook drops a lesson on war. *New York Times*, Oct. 5, p. 19.

———— (1988b). Despite new efforts, Japan avoids making peace with the war. *New York Times*, Dec. 25, p. E12.

Cotton, J. L. (1985). Cognitive dissonance in selective exposure. In D. Zillmann and J. Bryant (eds.), *Selective Exposure to Communication,* pp. 11-33. Hillsdale, N.J.: Lawrence Erlbaum.

Davis, Kenneth C. (1995). Ethnic cleansing didn't start in Bosnia. *New York Times*, Sept. 3, Week in Review, p. 1.

Ehrenhaus, P. (1989). Commemorating the unwon war: On not remembering Vietnam. *Journal of Communication* 39: 96-107.

Ehrlich, D., I. Guttman, P. Schonbach, and J. Mills (1957). Post-decision to relevant information. *Journal of Abnormal and Social Psychology* 54: 98-102.

Ferguson, Douglas A. (1992). Channel repertoire in the presence of remote control devices, VCRs and cable television. *Journal of Broadcasting & Electronic Media*, 36 (no. 1, Winter): 83-91.

Festinger, L. A. (1957). *A Theory of Cognitive Dissonance.* Stanford, Calif.: Stanford University Press.

Freedman, J. L., and D. Sears (1965). Selective exposure. In L. Berkowitz (ed.), *Advances in Experimental Social Psychology,* pp. 57-97. New York: Academic Press.

Gantz, Walter, and Lawrence A. Wenner (1991). Men, women, and sports: audience experiences and effects. *Journal of Broadcasting and Electronic Media* 35 (no. 2, Spring): 233-243.

Greenwald, A., and J. Sakamura (1967). Attitude and selective learning: Where are the phenomena of yesteryear? *Journal of Personality and Social Psychology* 7: 387-397.

Haberman, C. (1988). Japanese remove sequence from film "Last Emperor." *New York Times*, Jan. 21, p. 8.

Heider, F. (1946). Attitudes and cognitive organization. *Journal of Psychology* 21: 107-112.

——— (1958). *The Psychology of Interpersonal Relations*. New York: John Wiley.

Kiesler, C. A., B. E. Collins, and N. Miller (1969). *Attitude Change*. New York: John Wiley.

Kleinhesselink, R., and R. Edwards (1975). Seeking and avoiding belief-discrepant information as a function of its perceived refutability. *Journal of Personality and Social Psychology* 31: 787-790.

Lehner, U. (1988). More Japanese deny nation was aggressor during World War II. *Wall Street Journal*, Sept. 8, p. 1.

Lewis, P. (1987). I.B.M.? Mac? Feelings may prevent cool look. *New York Times*, Dec. 1, p. 19.

Lowin, A. (1969). Further evidence for an approach-avoidance interpretation of selective exposure. *Journal of Experimental Social Psychology* 5: 265-271.

McGuire, W. J. (1968). Selective exposure: A summing up. In R. Abelson et al. (eds.), *Theories of Cognitive Consistency: A Sourcebook*, pp. 797-800. Skokie, Ill.: Rand-McNally.

Mills, J. (1968). Interest in supporting and discrepant information. In R. Abelson et al. (eds.), *Theories of Cognitive Consistency: A Sourcebook*, pp. 771-776. Skokie, Ill.: Rand-McNally.

Newcomb, T. M. (1953). An approach to the study of communicative acts. *Psychological Review* 60: 393-404.

O'Brien, Tim (1994). The Vietnam in me. *New York Times Magazine*, Oct. 2, pp. 48-57.

Odendahl, Theresa (1990). A thousand pointless lights? *New York Times*, July 21, p. A15.

Sears, D. O. (1968). The paradox of de facto selective exposure without preferences for supportive information. In R. Abelson et al. (eds.), *Theories of Cognitive Consistency: A Sourcebook*, pp. 777-787. Skokie, Ill.: Rand-McNally.

Strong, B. (1989). Slavery and colonialism make up the true legacy of Columbus. *New York Times*, Nov. 4, p. 14.

Taylor, Curtis L. (1993). Blacks hit *N.Y. Times* mag shots. *Newsday*, Dec. 10, p. 39.

Woodward, A. (1987). In search of Watergate in the textbooks. *New York Times*, Mar. 11, p. 26.

Zajonc, R. B. (1960). The concepts of balance, congruity and dissonance. *Public Opinion Quarterly* 24: 280-296.

Zillmann, D. (1980). Anatomy of suspense. In P. H. Tannenbaum (ed.), *The Entertainment Functions of Television*, pp. 133-163. Hillsdale, N.J.: Lawrence Erlbaum.

Zillmann, R. T. Hezel, and N. J. Medoff (1980). The effect of affective states on selective exposure to televised entertainment fare. *Journal of Applied Social Psychology* 10: 323-339.

Zillmann, and J. Bryant (1985). Affect, mood, and emotion as determinants of selective exposure. In D. Zillmann and J. Bryant (eds.), *Selective Exposure to Communication*, pp. 157-190. Hillsdale, N.J.: Lawrence Erlbaum.

——— (1986). "Exploring the entertainment experience." In J. Bryant and D. Zillmann (eds.), *Perspectives on Media Effects*, pp. 303-324. Hillsdale, N.J.: Lawrence Erlbaum.

chapter 9

Theories of Persuasion

Persuasion is only one type of mass communication, but it is a type in which many people are interested. The advertiser using mass communication to sell soft drinks, headache remedies, or automobiles is engaged in persuasion. So is the nuclear power industry when it hires public relations experts to help it convince the public that nuclear power is safe. So are the political candidates who buys newspaper ads, the public health organization that prepares radio spots to encourage people to stop smoking, and the religious organization that puts evangelical messages on television. All of these people are attempting to use mass communication messages to produce some kind of change in other people.

Persuasion has been defined as "attitude change resulting from exposure to information from others" (Olson & Zanna, 1993, p. 135). Persuasion has probably always been a part of human life. It seems inevitable that people will try to influence other people, even their closest friends and family members. As Eagly and Chaiken (1993) have noted, persuasion is particularly likely to make up part of life in a democracy, where attitudinal influence is the form of control that is most relied on.

For centuries people must have operated on the basis of intuition and common sense in their attempts to persuade. Aristotle was one of the first to try to analyze and write about persuasion, in his classic works on rhetoric. Years later, particularly when mass communication became more widespread, people began to study persuasion even more systematically. The Institute for Propaganda Analysis, with its identification of seven techniques of propaganda, was doing some of this early work.

Part of the motive for the Institute's careful study of persuasion was obviously fear—the war-inspired fear that propaganda could win the hearts and minds of people. The Institute was operating in that panicky period just before

World War II. A few years later, the same war was to produce the first careful scientific studies of persuasion, or attitude change, as it became known. This work was done by psychologist Carl Hovland and his associates, all of whom were working for the Research Branch of the U.S. Army's Information and Education Division. This work was so original and influential that it has been called "the most important fountainhead of contemporary research on attitude change" (Insko, 1967, p. 1). The Hovland work was based on controlled experiments in which variables were carefully manipulated in order to observe their effects.

Some earlier work on attitude change was done before Hovland, but rather poorly. A study sometimes cited as the first attitude change study was an investigation by Rice and Willey of the effects of William Jennings Bryan's address on evolution at Dartmouth College in 1923 (described in Chen, 1933). A group of 175 students indicated their acceptance or rejection of evolution on a five-point scale. The students were asked to give their attitudes after hearing the speech, and, from retrospection, their attitudes before hearing the speech. They found that more than one-quarter of the students showed substantial change in attitude, but the use of the retrospective report makes the finding highly questionable.

THE CONCEPT OF ATTITUDE

The concept of attitude has been described by psychologist Gordon Allport (1954) as "probably the most distinctive and indispensable in contemporary American social psychology" (p. 43). Allport points out that the term came to replace in psychology such vague terms as *instinct*, *custom*, *social force*, and *sentiment*.

Some recent definitions of attitude include the following:

> Attitude is primarily a way of being "set" toward or against certain things. (Murphy, Murphy, & Newcomb, 1937, p. 889)

> A mental and neural state of readiness, organized through experience, exerting a directive or dynamic influence upon the individual's responses to all objects and situations with which it is related. (Allport, 1954, p. 45)

> An enduring, learned predisposition to behave in a consistent way toward a given class of objects. (English & English, 1958, p. 50)

> An enduring system of positive or negative evaluations, emotional feelings and pro or con action tendencies with respect to a social object. (Krech, Crutchfield, & Ballachey, 1962, p. 177)

HOVLAND'S ARMY RESEARCH

Hovland's approach to attitude change was essentially a learning theory or reinforcement theory approach. He believed that attitudes were learned, and that they were changed through the same processes that occurred when learning took place. Hovland had studied and worked at Yale with Clark Hull, whose theory was probably the most influential theory of learning between 1930 and 1950 (Hilgard & Bower, 1966).

During World War II, the U.S. Army began using films and other forms of mass communication on an unprecedented scale. Most of this material was used in the training and motivation of U.S. soldiers. The Experimental Section of the Research Branch of the War Department's Information and Education Division was given the task of evaluating the effectiveness of these materials. Much of the research of the Experimental Section is reported in the volume *Experiments on Mass Communication,* first published in 1949 (Hovland, Lumsdaine, & Sheffield, 1965). The section did two basic types of research: evaluation studies of existing films and experimental studies in which two different versions of the same film (or message) were compared. The section had to do much of the first type of research because it suited the practical purposes of the Army. The researchers felt, however, that the second type of research was really more useful because it could lead to general principles of attitude change. These experimental studies, in which certain variables were manipulated, really constituted the beginning of attitude change research. But, the evaluation studies of existing films also made some useful contributions to communication theory.

One of the first tasks the section took on was to evaluate the first four films of a series of films called *Why We Fight.* This series was produced by Frank Capra, the famous Hollywood filmmaker who would later direct *It's a Wonderful Life*. The *Why We Fight* films were designed as motivational films to be used in the training and orientation of American soldiers. They were based on the assumptions that many draftees did not know the national and international events that led to America's entrance into World War II and that a knowledge of these events would lead men to accept more easily the transition from civilian life to that of a soldier.

One of the films studied in great detail was *The Battle of Britain*, a 50-minute film with the purpose of instilling greater confidence in America's British allies. Hovland and his associates designed research to determine the film's impact in three main areas: specific factual knowledge gained from the film, specific opinions concerning the Battle of Britain, and acceptance of the military role and willingness to fight. The research procedure was simply to have an experimental group that saw the film and a control group that did not, and then one week later to give both groups a questionnaire that appeared unrelated but measured knowledge and opinions on subjects related to the film. These Army studies were conducted with military units and therefore ended up with large sample sizes—the *Battle of Britain* study involved 2,100 people.

The results showed that the film was quite effective in conveying factual information about the air war over Britain in 1940, that it was somewhat effective in changing specific opinions about the conduct of the air war, and that it had essentially no effect at all on motivation to serve or in building increased resentment of the enemy. Thus the film failed in its ultimate objective, increasing soldiers' motivations. Similar results showed up for the other *Why We Fight* films studied.

This research on the *Why We Fight* series became part of the growing body of evidence indicating that a single mass communication message is unlikely to change strongly held attitudes. Similar evidence comes from other studies as different as the Cooper and Jahoda investigation of antiprejudice cartoons (Chapter 4) and research by Lazarsfeld and his associates on political campaigns (Chapter 11).

ONE-SIDED AND TWO-SIDED MESSAGES

Hovland and his associates turned to the second type of research—the same message is produced in two versions that differ in only one variable—in an experiment on the effectiveness of one-sided and two-sided messages. On many issues there are arguments on both sides. Which is the better strategy—to mention only the arguments on the side you are pushing or to mention the arguments on both sides but focus on the ones on the side you are pushing? This is essentially the old question of the effectiveness of card stacking, one of the propaganda devices identified by the Institute for Propaganda Analysis.

Hovland and his associates were trying to answer this question because they faced a real communication dilemma. After the defeat of Germany in 1945, many soldiers apparently felt the war was almost over. The Army wanted to get across the idea that there was still a tough job ahead in defeating the Japanese.

The researchers realized that there were arguments for each strategy. A one-sided presentation can be defended on the basis that a two-sided presentation raises doubts in the minds of people unfamiliar with the opposing arguments. A two-sided presentation can be defended on the basis that it is more fair and that it will help prevent people who are opposed to a message from rehearsing counterarguments while being exposed to the message. A specific purpose of the study was to measure the effectiveness of the two kinds of message presentation on two kinds of audience members—those initially opposed to the message and those initially sympathetic to the message.

Two versions of a radio message were prepared. Both presented the general argument that the war would take at least two more years. The one-sided message was 15 minutes long and brought out arguments such as the size of the Japanese army and the determination of the Japanese people. The two-sided message was 19 minutes long and brought out arguments on the other side, such as the advantage of fighting only one enemy, but it focused mostly on the arguments that the war would be a long one.

One week before the presentation of the radio message, subjects were given a preliminary questionnaire on which they expressed their estimates of how long the war in the Pacific would take. Then one group made up of eight platoons heard the one-sided message, a second group of eight platoons heard the two-sided message, and a third group heard neither message and served as the control group. Then all three groups received another questionnaire differing from the first one in its form and its announced purpose, but again asking for an estimate

TABLE 9.1 Soldiers who estimated a war of more than $1\frac{1}{2}$ years after hearing one-sided and two-sided messages

	Group 1 (8 platoons)	Group 2 (8 platoons)	Control Group (8 platoons)
Preliminary survey	37%	38%	36%
Exposure to message	one-sided	two-sided	none
Follow-up survey	59%	59%	34%

SOURCE: Adapted from C. I. Hovland, A. A. Lumsdaine, and F. D. Sheffield, *Experiments on Mass Communication* (New York: Wiley, 1965), Vol. III, Studies in Social Psychology in World War II, p. 210. Copyright 1949, © renewed 1977 by Princeton University Press. Reprinted by permission of Princeton University Press.

of how long the war in the Pacific would take. All questionnaires were anonymous, but the before and after questionnaires for the same person could be matched on the basis of the answers to questions about date of birth, schooling, and so forth.

Looked at in general for all groups, the results (Table 9.1) indicated that both kinds of presentations produced clear opinion change in comparison with the control group, but that neither presentation was more effective than the other.

The researchers had anticipated that the two-sided presentation might work better with an audience initially opposed to the message, so they proceeded to check out this possibility. They did this by dividing each test group into subjects initially opposed to the message and subjects initially favorable to the message. The men who had given initial estimates that the war would take $1\frac{1}{2}$ years or less were considered to be initially opposed to the message, while those who gave initial estimates of more than $1\frac{1}{2}$ years were considered to be initially favorable to the message. Results of this analysis are shown in Table 9.2. Results are presented in terms of *net effect*, or the percentage in a group who increased their estimate minus the percentage in that group who decreased their estimate.

TABLE 9.2 Effects on one-sided and two-sided messages on men who were initially either opposed or favorable to the message

	Initially Opposed (%)	Initially Favorable (%)
One-sided	36	52
Two-sided	48	23

Note: The number in the table is the *net effect,* or the percentage in a group who increased their estimate minus the percentage in that group who decreased their estimate.
SOURCE: Adapted from C. I. Hovland, A. A. Lumsdaine, and F. D. Sheffield, *Experiments on Mass Communication* (New York: Wiley, 1965), Vol. III, Studies in Social Psychology in World War II, p. 213. Copyright 1949, © renewed 1977 by Princeton University Press. Reprinted by permission of Princeton University Press.

TABLE 9.3 Effects of the one-sided and two-sided messages on men who graduated from high school and men who did not

	Didn't Graduate (%)	Did Graduate (%)
One-sided	46	35
Two-sided	31	49

Note: The number in the table is the *net effect,* or the percentage in a group who increased their estimate minus the percentage in that group who decreased their estimate.
SOURCE: Adapted from C. I. Hovland, A. A. Lumsdaine, and F. D. Sheffield, *Experiments on Mass Communication* (New York: Wiley, 1965), Vol. III, Studies in Social Psychology in World War II, p. 214. Copyright 1949, © renewed 1977 by Princeton University Press. Reprinted by permission of Princeton University Press.

This examination of results according to initial attitude shows the one-sided message is most effective with persons initially favorable to the message and the two-sided message is most effective with persons initially opposed to the message. This is what the researchers had predicted.

Hovland and his associates also found that a one-sided message is most effective with people of less education and the two-sided message is most effective with people of greater education (see Table 9.3).

Both additional analyses—the one by initial opinion and the one by education level—show that the kind of presentation that is most effective depends on the characteristics of the audience. These results brought out the complexity of attitude change—that variables in the message sometimes interact with other variables, such as personal characteristics of the audience. This is part of the evidence that led psychologist Roger Brown (1958), in his analysis of propaganda, to conclude that the propaganda devices are "contingently effective rather than invariably effective" (p. 306).

THE YALE COMMUNICATION RESEARCH PROGRAM

After the war, Hovland returned to Yale University, where he had been a faculty member, and continued his research on attitude change. This program had the purpose of "developing scientific propositions which specify the conditions under which the effectiveness of one or another type of persuasive communication is increased or decreased" (Hovland, Janis, & Kelley, 1953, p. v). The project had three characteristics: (1) it was primarily concerned with theoretical issues and basic research; (2) it drew upon theoretical developments from diverse sources, both within psychology and related fields; and (3) it emphasized testing propositions by controlled experiment (Hovland, Janis, & Kelley, 1953).

The first book from the Yale program, *Communication and Persuasion* (Hovland, Janis, & Kelley, 1953), dealt with a number of topics that would later receive entire volumes or else become topics investigated extensively by later researchers. Two of these topics—source credibility and fear appeals—are particularly important because they led to many later studies. The book also reported some further research on one-sided and two-sided messages.

SOURCE CREDIBILITY

One of the variables in a communication situation over which communicator typically has some control is the choice of the source. And, judging from many day-to-day examples of communication campaigns, there appears to be a widespread belief that having the right source can increase the effectiveness of your message.

In the presidential election of 1992, President Bush was endorsed by such popular country music stars as Ricky Skaggs, the Judds, Marty Stuart, Lee Greenwood, and Tanya Tucker. Rock musicians such as Frank Zappa, Natalie Merchant, and Madonna gave their support to rival candidate Bill Clinton. In another illustration of a deliberately chosen message source, Nickelodeon, the television network for children, centered a program on AIDS prevention around Magic Johnson, the basketball superstar who had announced that he was HIV-positive. The program, titled "Special Edition: A Conversation with Magic," was hosted by journalist Linda Ellerbee.

The selection of an effective source to speak for your idea or product is essentially the propaganda device of the testimonial. But the effectiveness of this technique was not really investigated by the Institute for Propaganda Analysis. Hovland and Weiss (1951) designed an experiment to test the effectiveness of source credibility. They apparently became interested in the possible impact of source credibility after learning of a phenomenally successful radio program involving entertainer Kate Smith. In an 18-hour program during World War II, Kate Smith received pledges for an astounding $39 million for war bonds. Researchers who studied the Kate Smith broadcast concluded that key elements in her success were her perceived *sincerity* and *trustworthiness*.

Hovland and Weiss designed an experiment in which the same messages would be presented to some people as coming from a high-credibility source and to other people as coming from a low-credibility source. This would allow them to determine the effect of the source variable alone. The experiment was done with four messages on four different topics. Each subject received a booklet containing four articles. Each article was on a different topic. The subjects' opinions on the four topics were measured with questionnaires before getting the communication, immediately after getting it, and four weeks after getting it. Each article was presented with a high-credibility source for half the subjects and a low-credibility source for the other half. The four topics were controversial ones at the time and revolved around the following opinion questions:

1. "Should antihistamine drugs continue to be sold without a doctor's prescription?" The high-credibility source on this issue was the *New England*

Journal of Biology and Medicine. The low-credibility source was identified in the research report as "a mass circulation monthly pictorial magazine."

2. "Can a practicable atomic-powered submarine be built at the present time?" The high-credibility source was J. Robert Oppenheimer, the head of the team of scientists that developed the atomic bomb. (This was before Oppenheimer's security clearance investigation, which undoubtedly damaged his credibility.) The low-credibility source was *Pravda,* the Russian newspaper.

3. "Is the steel industry to blame for the current shortage of steel?" The high-credibility source was the *Bulletin of National Resources Planning Board.* The low-credibility source was identified as an "anti-labor, anti-New Deal, 'rightist' newspaper columnist."

4. "As a result of TV, will there be a decrease in the number of movie theaters in operation by 1955?" The high-credibility source was *Fortune* magazine. The low-credibility source was identified as "a woman movie-gossip columnist."

The design was counterbalanced so that every source argued both pro and con on his or her topic, although each subject would see only the pro or the con message.

The results for the immediate aftertest (see Table 9.4) show that the high-credibility source did produce more opinion change on three of the four topics. The exception was the topic of the future of movies, where the results show slightly more opinion change for the low-credibility source.

The retest of opinion after four weeks produced a striking finding. Results for this retest are presented in Figure 9.1 for all four topics combined.

The figure shows that when the subjects were retested after four weeks, the amount of opinion change retained was approximately equal for the high-credibility and low-credibility sources. But for the low-credibility source, there appeared to be *greater* opinion change after four weeks than there was immediately after receiving the communication. This was the second occurrence of what

TABLE 9.4 Subjects who changed their opinion in direction of communication for high- and low-credibility sources

	High-Credibility Source (%)	Low-Credibility Source (%)
Antihistamines	23	13
Atomic submarines	36	0
Steel shortage	23	−4
Future of movies	13	17

Note: The number in the table is the net percentage of subjects who changed their opinions in the direction of the communication, or the percentage who changed in the direction of the communication minus the percentage who changed in the opposite direction.
SOURCE: Adapted from C. I. Hovland, I. L. Janis, and H. H. Kelley, *Communication and Persuasion* (New Haven, Conn.: Yale University Press, 1953), p. 30. Copyright © 1953 by Yale University Press. Reprinted by permission.

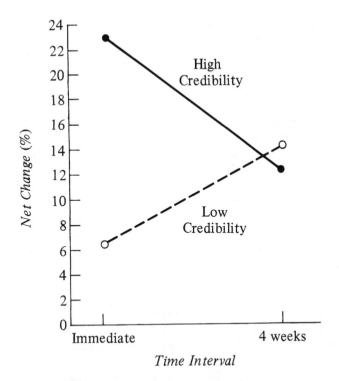

FIGURE 9.1 Changes in extent of agreement with high-credibility and low-credibility
sources after four weeks

SOURCE: From C. I. Hovland and W. Weiss, "The Influence of Source Credibility on Communication Effectiveness," *Public Opinion Quarterly* 15 (1951): 646.
Copyright 1951 by Princeton University Press. Reprinted
by permission of the University of Chicago Press.

Hovland, Lumsdaine, and Sheffield earlier had called a "sleeper" effect. Hovland
and Weiss did some further research and found that this was not due to the
forgetting of the source, suggested in the earlier study, but to a tendency after
the passage of time to dissociate the source and the opinion.

Much research since the Hovland and Weiss experiment has gone into
attempting to find the dimensions of source credibility. Hovland and Weiss had
suggested that the dimensions of expertness and trustworthiness might be
important. Many of these studies used factor analysis of rating scales applied to
speakers to try to find the common dimensions used in the ratings. In one of
the more comprehensive of these studies, Whitehead had subjects rate two
speakers on 65 semantic differential scales solely on the basis of tape-recorded
introductions (Whitehead, 1968). Whitehead found four dominant factors:
trustworthiness, professionalism or competence, dynamism, and objectivity. The

trustworthiness factor was based on the scales *right-wrong, honest-dishonest, trustworthy-untrustworthy*, and *just-unjust.* The professionalism or competence factor was based on the scales *experienced-inexperienced* and *has professional manner-lacks professional manner.* The dynamism factor was based on the scales *aggressive-meek* and *active-passive.* The objectivity factor was based on the scales *open minded-closed minded* and *objective-subjective.*

Whitehead's results are similar to the suggestions of Hovland and Weiss in that they showed trustworthiness to be an important dimension. The professionalism or competence dimension is also similar to Hovland and Weiss's dimension of expertness, although it differs in dealing more with *manner* of presentation than with the actual knowledge that a person might possess. Whitehead's research suggests that source credibility is more complicated than that, however, with dynamism and objectivity being important components.

If a high-credibility source is effective in producing attitude change, does that source lose or gain effectiveness if it becomes associated with a number of messages? This problem can come up in the field of advertising, where celebrities may be hired to endorse a number of different products. For instance, basketball superstar Michael Jordan was at one time endorsing products for 14 companies. An experiment by Tripp, Jensen, and Carlson (1994) exposed viewers to advertisements that involved endorsements of Visa credit cards, Kodak film, Colgate toothpaste, and Certs breath mints by Dustin Hoffmann and Matthew Broderick. When one of these celebrities endorsed four products, he was perceived as less trustworthy and less of an expert than when he endorsed one or two. The attitude toward the ad also became more negative with four products than with one or two. So there is evidence that making multiple endorsements can reduce the effectiveness of a high-credibililty source.

Still other research has been done on source credibility since the original Hovland and Weiss study. Some researchers have challenged the existence of a sleeper effect. Gillig and Greenwald (1974) were unable to produce a sleeper effect—that is, a statistically significant increase in opinion change for a group exposed to a low-credibility source—in seven replications of an experiment designed to show this effect. Furthermore, their review of the literature indicated no previous study had really shown that kind of sleeper effect. What the earlier studies, including that of Hovland and Weiss, had shown was a significant difference in the effects of high- and low-credibility sources over time, but that is not the same as a significant increase in opinion change for a group exposed to a low-credibility source.

Other research has shown additional support for a sleeper effect, however. Cook and Flay (1978) used the term *absolute sleeper effect* to refer to the kind of change mentioned above—a statistically significant increase in attitude change over time for a group exposed to a low-credibility source. They report that "*demonstrably* strong tests of the absolute sleeper effect have recently been conducted, and they repeatedly result in absolute sleeper effects" (p. 19).

In applying source credibility research, one should remember that the same source will not have high credibility for all audience members. In an effort to get newly eligible (teen-age) voters to vote, the Rock the Vote campaign enlisted Madonna and Rapper Ice-T for their television public service announcements. The same sources probably would not work with older audience members.

FEAR APPEALS

Another common tactic in mass communication is to threaten or arouse some fear in the audience. Films shown to teenagers to promote safe driving sometimes show terrible traffic accidents and what they do to people. A television commercial for an insurance company arouses fear by saying, "You need something to help keep these promises, even if you're not there."

The book *Communication and Persuasion* (Hovland et al., 1953) describes a classic experiment by Janis and Feshbach aimed at investigating the effectiveness of fear appeals in producing attitude change. On the basis of learning theory, a key element in the Hovland approach, it can be predicted that a strong fear appeal would lead to increased attitude change because it would increase arousal and bring about greater attention and comprehension. Motivation to accept the recommendations of the communication would also be increased. In reinforcement theory terms, learning and practicing the recommended procedure should become associated with the reinforcement of reduced fear and anxiety. On the other hand, the researchers realized that a high degree of emotional tension could lead to spontaneous defensive reactions and the possibility of the audience distorting the meaning of what is being said. Part of their research purpose was to investigate this potentially adverse effect of a strong fear appeal.

Janis and Feshbach designed an experiment that was based on three different messages with three different levels of fear appeal. They selected dental hygiene as their topic. The subjects were the entire freshman class of a large Connecticut high school. The class was randomly divided into four groups, three of which were to get the different fear messages and one of which was to be a control group. The basic message, common to all three fear levels, was a standard lecture on dental hygiene. The level of fear was varied primarily through changing the material used to illustrate the lecture. In the minimal fear appeal message, the illustrative material used x-rays and drawings to represent cavities, and any photographs used were of completely healthy teeth. In the moderate fear appeal version, photographs of mild cases of tooth decay and oral diseases were used. In the strong fear appeal version, the slides used to illustrate the lecture included very realistic photographs of advanced tooth decay and gum diseases. The strong fear condition also contained some personalized threats, such as the statement, "This can happen to you." The control group received a lecture on the structure and function of the human eye.

Subjects were given a questionnaire asking specific questions about their dental hygiene practices one week before the lecture and one week after. Comparison of these questionnaires would show whether subjects changed their dental hygiene behavior after being exposed to the various types of messages.

TABLE 9.5 Conformity to dental hygiene recommendations in subjects who received messages with different levels of fear

	Strong Fear Appeal (%)	Moderate Fear Appeal (%)	Minimal Fear Appeal (%)	Control Group (%)
Increased conformity	28	44	50	22
Decreased conformity	20	22	14	22
No change	52	34	36	56

SOURCE: Adapted from C. I. Hovland, I. L. Janis, and H. H. Kelley, *Communication and Persuasion* (New Haven, Conn.: Yale University Press, 1953), p. 80. Copyright © 1953 by Yale University Press. Reprinted by permission.

The results in Table 9.5 show that the minimal fear appeal was the most effective in getting the students to follow the dental hygiene recommendations in the lecture. The strong fear appeal was the least effective. This was definite evidence that a fear appeal can be too strong and can evoke some form of interference that reduces the effectiveness of the communication.

This experiment had several strengths that have not always been present in later attitude change studies. One is that the message was shown to have an effect on reported behavior, and not just on a paper-and-pencil measure of a hypothetical attitude. The field of attitude change research was involved in a controversy a few years later in which many studies were criticized for producing slight changes in unimportant attitudes. Second, the study showed that the persuasive messages used by Janis and Feshbach produced long-term attitude change. Another criticism of some later attitude change studies is that they dealt only with short-term attitude change, often measured immediately after the message. Janis and Feshbach went back to their subjects a year later and still found the differences in attitude change between their experimental groups.

The Janis and Feshbach study was the first of a number of studies on fear appeals. Not all these studies have agreed with the finding that strong fear produces less attitude change. One possible explanation for the findings of Janis and Feshbach is that the recommendation of brushing your teeth properly was not seen as a believable recommendation for preventing the kinds of horrible consequences presented in the strong fear appeal message. Other studies have shed some light on this possibility. Leventhal and Niles (1964) presented a message to audiences at a New York City health exposition recommending that they get a chest x-ray and that they stop smoking. The message was presented to different groups with differing levels of fear: high fear (featuring a color movie of removal of a lung), medium fear (featuring the same color movie but without the graphic scene of a lung removal), and low fear (with no movie). They found that the amount of reported fear in audience members was correlated with stated intentions to stop smoking and to get a chest x-ray. These results suggest that fear facilitates attitude change—the opposite of the Janis and Feshbach finding. What could account for this difference? Possibly the difference was due to the degree to which the recommendations appeared to be effective. Toothbrushing may not have seemed adequate to prevent the rotted teeth and bloody gums seen in the Janis and Feshbach experiment. In contrast, stopping smoking may appear to be a believable recommendation for preventing lung cancer.

On the basis of the Janis and Feshbach experiment and other research, Janis (1967) formulated a model suggesting that the relationship between fear appeal and attitude change is curvilinear. This model specifies that low and high levels of fear in a message will lead to small amounts of attitude change and that moderate levels of fear will lead to the greatest amount of attitude change. This inverted U-shaped curve was the dominant view of the relationship between fear and attitude change for many years.

A different approach to the role of fear in persuasion, protection motivation theory, was developed by Rogers (1975) as an alternative to Janis's curvilinear theory. Advocates claim that "the PM model is superior to the curvilinear approach because it provides a clearer prescription for how to develop messages that can influence adaptive behavior" (Tanner, Hunt, & Eppright, 1991, p. 37).

Building on the Leventhal and Niles research as well as on some other research of his own, Rogers (1975) developed a model that summarizes three key elements in the operation of a fear appeal: (1) the magnitude of noxiousness of a depicted event, (2) the probability of that event's occurrence, and (3) the efficacy of a recommended response. Each component brings about a process of cognitive appraisal, and these cognitive appraisal processes then determine the amount of attitude change (see Figure 9.2). That is, when audience members receive a fear appeal, they weigh it in their minds. If the portrayed noxiousness or horribleness of the event is not believed, or the event is thought to be unlikely, or the recommended actions are not believed to be adequate to deal with the threat, then attitude change is not likely. Rogers calls his model a protection motivation theory of fear appeals and attitude change. Attitude change is said to be a function of the amount of protection motivation aroused by the cognitive appraisal that the audience member goes through.

Reardon (1989) discussed how fear appeals might best be used in a communication about AIDS that is addressed to teenagers (who typically perceive the threat of death as remote). She suggested that mass media messages aimed at adolescents emphasize the more immediate consequences of the disease, including mental problems, skin rashes and sores, and the negative effect on a teenager's social life. She suggested, furthermore, that the media campaigns be combined with interpersonal question-and-answer sessions, in which discussion can bring out information regarding methods for avoiding the problems described or depicted in the media messages.

The effectiveness of fear appeals in condom advertisements that stress the prevention of AIDS was studied by Hill (1988). He found that subjects had more positive attitudes toward a moderate fear appeal commercial (stating that sex can be a risky business) than either a nonfear appeal (stressing the sensitivity

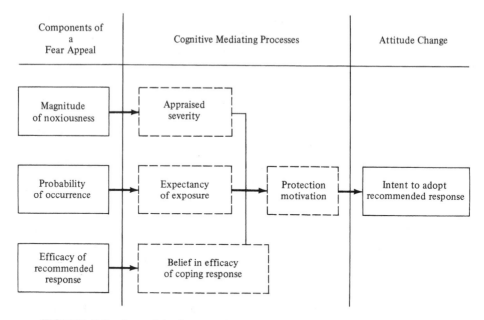

FIGURE 9.2   A model of protection motivation theory

SOURCE: From R. W. Rogers, "A Protection Motivation Theory of Fear Appeals and Attitude Change," *Journal of Psychology* 91 (1975): 99. Reprinted with permission of the Helen Dwight Reid Educational Foundation. Published by Heldref Publications, 4000 Albemarle St., N.W., Washington, D.C. 20016. Copyright © 1975.

of the condom and saying nothing about AIDS) or high fear appeal (mentioning the possibility of death). Hill speculated that a nonfear appeal may appear inappropriate in an AIDS environment, but that a high fear appeal may be viewed as too threatening when it is combined with the individual's existing level of AIDS-related anxiety.

Fear appeals are attempting to bring about changes in people's motivations, a tricky enterprise at best. As Ross (1985) noted, "Audience motivation through symbolic interaction is terribly complex; we should be wary of 'infallible' motive appeals" (p. 48).

RESISTANCE TO COUNTERPROPAGANDA

With so much energy being devoted to changing attitudes, it might be extremely useful to discover some methods of making attitudes resistant to change. Lumsdaine and Janis report a study in *Communication and Persuasion* (Hovland et al., 1953) that deals with building resistance of an attitude to change. Their experiment follows up on the earlier work on one-sided and two-sided messages by Hovland, Lumsdaine, and Sheffield.

Lumsdaine and Janis produced one-sided and two-sided messages arguing that Russia would be unable to produce large numbers of atomic bombs for at least five years. This was a realistic issue for differences of opinion in the early 1950s. The one-sided message argued that the Russians lacked some crucial secrets, that their espionage was not effective, and that Russia was lacking in industry. The two-sided message added brief mentions of the arguments that Russia had uranium mines in Siberia, that it had many top scientists, and that its industry had grown since the war. Several weeks before the messages were presented, all subjects were given a questionnaire to determine their initial opinions. One group received the one-sided message and another received the two-sided message. A week later, half of each group was exposed to an opposing communication from a different communicator arguing that Russia had probably already developed the atomic bomb. This counterpropaganda brought out some new arguments not included in the two-sided message. Both the initial messages and the counterpropaganda were presented in the form of recorded radio programs. Finally, all subjects were given another questionnaire.

The key question, asked in both the initial and final questionnaires, was this: "About how long from now do you think it will be before the Russians are really producing large numbers of atomic bombs?"

The net opinion change from initial to final questionnaire for those who received counterpropaganda and those who did not in both the one-sided and two-sided conditions is presented in Figure 9.3. The results show that for those receiving no counterpropaganda, the one-sided and two-sided messages were about equally effective. This replicates the finding of the earlier study by Hovland,

FIGURE 9.3 Comparison of the effectiveness of Programs I and II: Changes in opinions concerning the length of time before Russia produces large numbers of atomic bombs

SOURCE: From A. Lumsdaine and I. Janis, "Resistance to 'Counterpropaganda' Produced by One-Sided and Two-Sided 'Propagnda' Presentations," *Public Opinion Quarterly* 17 (1953): 316. Copyright © 1953 by Princeton University. Reprinted by permission of the University of Chicago Press.

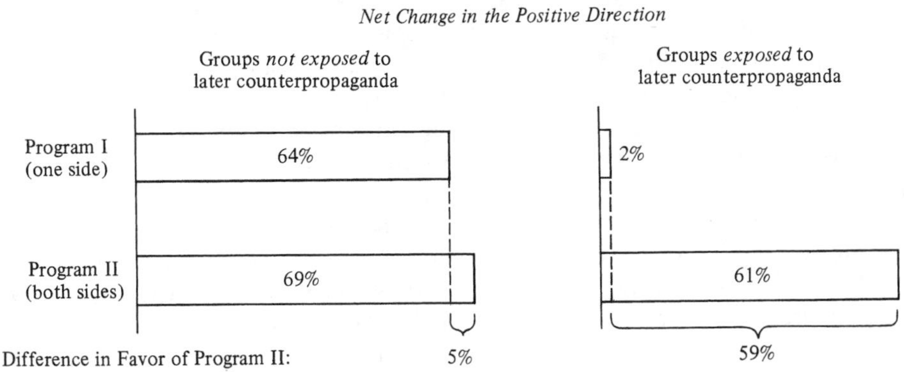

Net Change in the Positive Direction

	Groups *not exposed* to later counterpropaganda	Groups *exposed* to later counterpropaganda
Program I (one side)	64%	2%
Program II (both sides)	69%	61%
Difference in Favor of Program II:	5%	59%

Lumsdaine, and Sheffield. The results show a striking difference for those receiving counterpropaganda, however. Those receiving a one-sided message showed almost no remaining attitude change after they were exposed to counter-propaganda. In contrast, those receiving a two-sided message showed almost as much attitude change remaining after counterpropaganda as they did when they weren't exposed to counterpropaganda.

One of the advantages of the two-sided message over the one-sided message, then, is that it is more effective in building resistance to later persuasive efforts.

Lumsdaine and Janis speak of the recipient of the two-sided message as becoming "inoculated." This is a medical analogy that William McGuire and Demetrios Papageorgis drew upon later in developing their "inoculation theory."

INOCULATION THEORY

McGuire and Papageorgis's theory rests on the medical analogy that is suggested by its name. They point out that most people have many unchallenged beliefs, and that these beliefs can often be easily swayed once they are attacked because the person is not used to defending them. The situation is similar to that in the medical field when a person is brought up in a germ-free environment and is suddenly exposed to germs. That person's body is vulnerable to infection because it has not developed any resistance. Such a person can be given resistance either by supportive treatment—good diet, exercise, rest, and so forth—or by inocu-lation, a deliberate exposure to a weakened form of the germ that stimulates the development of defenses. In the medical area the inoculation approach has been more effective than supportive treatment in producing resistance. The word *immunization* can be applied to either of these methods of building immunity—the supportive approach or the inoculation approach.

McGuire and Papageorgis have conducted a number of experiments to test this theory. One of the first (McGuire & Papageorgis, 1961) tested the basic prediction that the supportive approach of preexposing a person to arguments supporting basic beliefs would have less immunizing effectiveness than the inoculation approach of preexposing the person to weakened, defense-stimulating forms of arguments attacking the beliefs. It also tested a second hypothesis that active participation during exposure to a defense should be less effective than passive participation in producing immunity to later persuasion. The researchers made this prediction because they theorized that subjects would not be accus-tomed to active participation in defending their basic beliefs and so would not do it very well. Furthermore, they thought that active participation might interfere with the reception of any defensive material presented. (There was also a complicated third hypothesis that need not concern us here.)

McGuire and Papageorgis selected for their study some beliefs that were hardly ever attacked in our culture, which they called "cultural truisms." The four beliefs were these: "Everyone should get a chest x-ray each year in order to detect any possible tuberculosis symptoms at an early stage." "The effects of penicillin have been, almost without exception, of great benefit to mankind." "Most forms of mental illness are not contagious." "Everyone should brush his teeth after every meal if at all possible." These cultural truisms were so widely believed that control groups of subjects rated them at an average level of 13.26 on a scale ranging from 1 for "definitely false" to 15 for "definitely true."

Subjects took part in two one-hour experimental sessions held two days apart. The first exposed subjects to the two types of immunizing material designed to make the basic beliefs ("cultural truisms") more resistant to change; the second exposed subjects to strong counterarguments attacking the basic beliefs. Questionnaires were administered at the end of each session to measure strength of acceptance of beliefs.

The two major types of immunizing material presented to subjects were "supportive" and "refutational." The supportive material was made up of arguments supporting the cultural truisms. The refutational material consisted of possible counterarguments against the cultural truisms together with refutations of these counterarguments. The amount of participation in the defense was varied primarily by having subjects write in a high-participation condition and read in a low-participation condition. Each subject was tested on one cultural truism for which he or she received no immunization but did receive the later counterarguments. The average scale position for these beliefs after they were attacked was 6.64, compared with the average level of 13.26 prior to attack. This result shows that the cultural truisms were highly vulnerable to attack if no immunization was given.

McGuire and Papageorgis found, as they had predicted, that the refutational defenses were more effective in making the cultural truisms resistant to change than were the supportive defenses. After the supportive defenses, the counterarguments were able to reduce the belief in the cultural truisms to an average rating of 7.39, only slightly better than the 6.64 level achieved when there was no prior preparation at all. After the inoculation defenses the counterarguments were able to reduce the beliefs in the cultural truisms only to an average scale rating of 10.33. The authors also found support for their second hypothesis: the passive (reading) conditions had a greater effect in making beliefs resistant to persuasion than did the active (writing) conditions.

The McGuire and Papageorgis experiment was limited in one respect that needed further investigation. The attacks on the cultural truisms that were presented and then refuted in the inoculation were the same attacks that were presented in the next session when the cultural truisms were assailed. It was not clear whether presenting and refuting one set of attacks would also provide later immunity to a different set of attacks. This question was investigated in another experiment by Papageorgis and McGuire (1961).

Papageorgis and McGuire predicted that a kind of generalized immunity would develop when people were exposed to attacks on basic beliefs and refutations of those attacks. That is, they predicted that this procedure would develop a general resistance that would make the basic belief unlikely to change even when it was exposed to attacks that were not the same. They expected this result for two reasons: (1) The experience of seeing the first attacks refuted could lower the credibility of the later attacks. (2) Preexposure to attacks may make a person more aware that his or her beliefs are indeed vulnerable and motivate the person to develop additional supporting arguments. Their results showed that inoculation led to an immunity to differing counterarguments that was almost as strong as the immunity to the same counterarguments. In fact, the final attitude positions in these two conditions were not significantly different. This, of course, increases the potency of an inoculation—the developers of the inoculation program do not have to anticipate all the attacks on a belief to which a person might later be exposed.

KATZ'S FUNCTIONAL APPROACH

The two major theoretical approaches to attitude change—the learning theory approach, primarily associated with Hovland, and the consistency theory approach, primarily associated with Festinger, Newcomb, Heider, and Osgood and Tannenbaum—existed side by side with little apparent relation to one another for some time. But eventually researchers became interested in reconciling these rather different ways of dealing with attitude change. Daniel Katz and his colleagues, Irving Sarnoff and Charles McClintock, tackled this problem, and it led them to develop the functional approach to attitude change.

These authors were trying to bring together two different models of human behavior that have been presented over the years—the rational model and the irrational model. The irrational model suggests that human beings are nonthinking creatures whose beliefs are easily influenced by people around them and who even can have their perception of reality influenced by their own desires. The rational model suggests that human beings are intelligent and critical thinkers who can make wise decisions when given ample information. How can both of these models be true? Katz and his associates suggest that the answer to this dilemma is that human beings are both rational and irrational, depending on the situation, the motivations operating at the time, and so forth. And they argue that this tendency for people to operate with different ways of thinking has important implications for understanding attitude change.

Katz argues that both attitude formation and change must be understood in terms of the functions that attitudes serve for the personality. As these functions differ, so will the conditions and techniques of attitude change. Katz points out that much of the earlier research on mass communication dealt with factors that are not really psychological variables, such as exposure to a motion picture. Since being exposed to a motion picture can serve different functions for different individuals, Katz argues that the researcher dealing only with exposure to a film is not really able to understand or predict attitude change. Katz makes the key point that the same attitude can have a different motivational basis in different people. He suggests that "unless we know the psychological need which is met by the holding of an attitude we are in a poor position to predict when and how it will change" (Katz, 1960, p. 170).

Katz identifies the following four major functions that attitudes can serve for the personality:

1. *The instrumental, adjustive, or utilitarian function.* Some attitudes are held because people are striving to maximize the rewards in their external environments and minimize the penalties. For instance, a voter who thinks taxes are too high might favor a political candidate because that candidate promises to reduce taxes.

2. *The ego-defensive function.* Some attitudes are held because people are protecting their egos from their own unacceptable impulses or from knowledge of threatening forces without. Feelings of inferiority are often projected onto a minority group as a means of bolstering the ego. This would be an example of an attitude of prejudice serving the ego-defensive function.

3. *The value-expressive function.* Some attitudes are held because they allow a person to give positive expression to central values and to the kind of person one feels he or she is. For instance, a teenager who likes a particular rock and roll group is expressing his or her individuality through this attitude.

4. *The knowledge function.* Some attitudes are held because they satisfy a desire for knowledge or provide structure and meaning in what would otherwise be a chaotic world. Many religious beliefs serve this function, as do other attitudes such as the shared norms of a culture.

Katz presented a table (see Table 9.6, p. 198) summarizing the origin and dynamics, the arousal conditions, and the change conditions for attitudes serving each of the four functions.

Katz warns that an attempt to change an attitude may backfire if it is not based on an understanding of the functions the attitude is serving. For instance, an attempt to change attitudes of prejudice by presenting factual information on the accomplishments of minority group members would be an attempt to change the attitudes as if they were serving the knowledge function. It is not likely to succeed if the attitudes of prejudice are held for ego-defense reasons.

ATTITUDES AND BEHAVIOR

Despite all the research on attitude change, researchers for a long time neglected an important question. In its more general form, the question is whether attitudes as they are measured by social science methods have any real relation to behavior. In its more specific form, the question is whether attitude change produced by persuasive messages is accompanied by any meaningful change in behavior.

One early study had indicated that attitudes might not bear much of a relationship to behavior. A social scientist, Richard LaPiere, traveled in the early 1930s around the United States with a young Chinese couple. They made 251

TABLE 9.6 Determinants of attitude formation, arousal, and chance in relation to type of function

Function	Origin and Dynamics	Arousal Conditions	Change Conditions
Adjustment	Utility of attitudinal object in need satisfaction. Maximizing external rewards and minimizing punishments	1. Activation of needs 2. Salience of cues associated with need satisfaction	1. Need deprivation 2. Creation of new needs and new levels of aspiration 3. Shifting rewards and punishments 4. Emphasis on new and better paths for need satisfaction
Ego defense	Protecting against internal conflicts and external dangers	1. Posing of threats 2. Appeals to hatred and repressed impulses 3. Rise in frustrations 4. Use of authoritarian suggestions	1. Removal of threats 2. Catharsis 3. Development of self-insight
Value expression	Maintaining self-identity; enhancing favorable self-image; self-expression and self-determination	1. Salience of cues associated with values 2. Appeals to individual to reassert self-image 3. Ambiguities which threaten self-concept	1. Some degree of dissatisfaction with self 2. Greater appropriateness of new attitude for the self 3. Control of all environmental supports to undermine old values
Knowledge	Need for understanding, for meaningful cognitive organization, for consistency and clarity	1. Reinstatement of cues associated with old problem or of old problem itself	1. Ambiguity created by new information or change in environment 2. More meaningful information about problems

SOURCE: From D. Katz, "The Functional Approach to the Study of Attitudes," *Public Opinion Quarterly* 24 (1960): 192. Copyright 1960 by Princeton University. Reprinted by permission of the University of Chicago Press.

visits to hotels and restaurants, and in only one case were they refused service. Six months later, LaPiere sent a questionnaire to each establishment asking: "Will you accept members of the Chinese race as guests in your establishment?" He received replies from 128 of these businesses. The responses from 92 percent of the restaurants and 91 percent of the hotels were *no*. Only one person gave a definite *yes* (LaPiere, 1934). This classic study, then, provided some evidence that people's verbal reports of their attitudes might not be very good predictors of their actual behavior.

In an address in 1963, Leon Festinger, the psychologist who developed the theory of cognitive dissonance, raised some basic questions about attitude change experiments and subsequent behavior. Festinger (1964) said he had been reading a manuscript by Arthur R. Cohen when he came across the statement that very little work on attitude change had dealt explicitly with the behavior that may follow a change in attitude. Festinger was intrigued by this notion and attempted to find as many studies as he could that showed an effect of attitude change on subsequent behavior change. He found only three. One of these was the Janis and Feshbach study of fear appeals. Their study did not investigate actual behavior change, but it did look at verbal reports of toothbrushing behavior and other dental hygiene behavior. Festinger was willing to accept this verbal report since it did purportedly deal with actual behavior. In all three of the studies that Festinger found, there seemed to be a slight inverse relationship between attitude change and behavior change. For instance, in the Janis and Feshbach study, the individuals who indicated the most concern about their teeth after receiving the persuasive messages showed the least change in their reported behavior. Festinger argued that this inverse relationship indicates that the relationship between attitude change and behavior is not a simple one.

One reason attitude change might not be automatically followed by behavior change, Festinger (1964) suggested, is that the environmental factors that had produced an original attitude would usually still be operating after that attitude was changed. Thus there would be a tendency for an attitude to revert to its original position after exposure to a persuasive message.

Festinger was suggesting to attitude change theorists the disturbing possibility that they had conducted hundreds of experiments on variables that make very little difference in terms of human behavior.

Realizing that the prediction of a specific behavior depends on a number of factors in addition to some kind of measure of attitude, Martin Fishbein attempted to develop a model that would include all the important factors. The model (see Ajzen & Fishbein, 1970) takes the form of the following equation:

$$B \sim BI = [A_{act}]w_0 + [NB(M_c)]w_1$$

Although the model looks complicated, it becomes easier to understand when it is put into words. The letters in the equation can be translated as follows:

B	=	overt behavior
BI	=	the behavioral intention to perform that behavior
A_{act}	=	attitude toward performing a given behavior in a given act situation
NB	=	normative beliefs, or beliefs that significant others think one should or should not perform the behavior
M_c	=	motivation to comply with the norm C
w_0 and w_1	=	regression weights to be determined empirically

The equation can be rephrased in the following English sentence: A person's intention to perform a given behavior is a function of (1) the person's attitude toward performing that behavior and (2) the person's perception of the norms governing that behavior and the individual's motivation to comply with those norms.

This model brings in some of the key situational factors, particularly the beliefs that other people have about the behavior and the individual's motivation to conform to those beliefs. If precise measurements could be made of all the variable quantities in the model, it should be possible to make rather exact predictions of behavioral intention and then of actual behavior. Fishbein (1973) reports that a number of experiments using the model to predict behavioral intention have produced multiple correlations of about .80, which are quite high. These experiments also found correlations between behavioral intention and overt behavior of .70, so all the key parts have been supported. In a continuation of the Fishbein research, Ajzen (1971) has used the Fishbein model to demonstrate behavioral change as the result of persuasive communication, the phenomenon that Festinger had difficulty finding in 1963.

One significant development in attitude change research is that many researchers are now including behavioral measures in their studies. For instance, many fear appeal studies now include behavioral measures such as the "disclosing wafer" test of how well teeth are actually cleaned (Evans, Rozelle, Lasater, Dembroski, & Allen, 1970) or the actual act of going to get a shot or vaccination (Krisher, Darley, & Darley, 1973). Similarly, the Stanford project aimed at reducing heart disease through communication used such behavioral measures as blood pressure, cholesterol level, weight, and number of cigarettes smoked (Maccoby & Farquhar, 1975).

CLASSICAL CONDITIONING OF ATTITUDES

Some other researchers besides Hovland have also attempted to apply learning theory to attitude change. In particular, Staats and Staats have applied classical conditioning to the learning of attitudes (Staats, 1968).

Staats and Staats begin by demonstrating the application of classical conditioning to the learning of the emotional meaning of language. They point out that in our everyday experience certain words are systematically paired with certain emotional experiences. For instance, words like *joy, happy, play, dinner, pretty,* and *good* are typically paired with positive emotions, while words like *angry, hurt, dirty, awful, sick, sad,* and *ugly* are typically paired with negative emotions. In the terms of classical conditioning, the emotional stimuli can be considered the unconditioned stimuli that elicit emotional responses. When a word stimulus is systematically paired with such an unconditioned stimulus, the word should become a conditioned stimulus and also elicit the emotional responses.

In an experiment to test this possibility, researchers exposed two groups of subjects to a list of spoken words (Staats, Staats, & Crawford, 1962). For the experimental group, 9 of the 14 times a subject was presented with the word *large,* it was followed by a negative stimulus—either a loud noise delivered by earphone or a shock to the right forearm. Both noise and shock were set at a level where they were "uncomfortable" but not "painful." Members of the control group also received the negative stimuli 9 times, but they were paired with different "filler" words other than *large.* Results showed that those subjects who experienced the word *large* being paired with the aversive stimulus came to display an emotional reaction, as measured by the galvanic skin response (GSR), when presented with this word. This was not true for the control group. Furthermore, measurements with semantic differential scales showed that *large* had acquired a negative rating on the evaluative scale for the experimental group that it did not have for the control group.

Staats and Staats (1957) went on to hypothesize that this conditioning of meaning should work from word to word as well as from a physical stimulus to a word. In another experiment, nonsense syllables such as *yof, laj, xeh, wuh, giw,* and *qug* were presented visually on a screen while words were presented aurally. For one group of subjects, two of the nonsense syllables were always paired with words that had high loadings on evaluative meaning, such as *beauty, win, gift, sweet,* and *honest.* A different high evaluation word was used in every pairing, so that subjects would not associate particular pairs of words. The other four nonsense syllables were paired with words that had no systematic meaning. For another group of subjects, the procedures were identical except that the two nonsense syllables were always paired with words with negative emotional meaning, such as *thief, bitter, ugly, sad,* and *worthless.* Subjects were later given semantic differential scales to measure their evaluative meanings for the nonsense syllables, and those scales showed positive ratings in general for the group receiving positive stimulus words and negative ratings in general for the group receiving negative stimulus words.

Staats and Staats argue that attitude is nothing more than this kind of emotional meaning for a word that has been established by classical conditioning. In another experiment (Staats & Staats, 1958), names of nations and familiar masculine names were used as the conditioned stimulus rather than nonsense syllables. The national names were *Dutch* or *Swedish,* and the masculine names were *Tom* and *Bill.* For all four of these, subjects would be expected to have existing attitudes on the basis of prior experience. Thus, the experiment was really a study of attitude change. The experiment showed that pairing any of the four words with either positive or negative words could condition the subjects' attitudes in either a positive or a negative direction. The Staats and Staats research provides a theoretical explanation for some of the propaganda devices, such as "glittering generality," which attempts to link a person or idea to a virtue word, or "name calling," which attempts to associate a person or idea with a bad label.

This conditioning of attitudes also seems to be related to much of what goes on in advertising. Many product names, such as Ipana or Qantas, are essentially nonsense syllables to the public when they are first introduced. A major goal of advertising is to associate them with positive words or experiences, which, through conditioning, might give them a positive meaning. A slogan such as "Coke is the real thing" is attempting to transfer positive associations to Coke. In the cases of some other products, such as Fab or Sprite, the product name might be chosen because of positive associations that it already has.

TECHNIQUES OF PERSUASION

We now turn to four important techniques commonly used in persuasion: use of pictures, appeals to humor, appeals to sex, and extensive repetition of an advertising message. Audiences and communicators need to understand their applications—and their potential misuse.

Use of Pictures

A common technique in communication, particularly in advertising, is to use pictures to accompany a textual verbal message.

Pictures can add to the persuasiveness of a message in the following ways (Miniard, Bhatla, Lord, Dickson, & Unnava, 1991):

1. They can help attract attention to the message.
2. They can enhance learning of the message's content.
3. A positive emotional response to the picture might transfer to other aspects of the message.

The use of pictures with persuasive messages is probably more complicated than that, however. We probably need to look in greater detail at some characteristics of the picture and at the cognitive state of the individual receiving the message. One important aspect of the picture is whether or not it is relevant to the persuasive message. One important aspect of the cognitive state of the individual is the level of involvement in processing the message.

Miniard et al. (1991) looked at the effects of receiver involvement and picture relevance in advertisements on attitudes toward the product and purchase intentions. The two variables interacted, with irrelevant pictures having their greatest impact on attitude change when receiver involvement was low and relevant pictures having their greatest impact when receiver involvement was high.

Appeals to Humor

The use of humor is a popular technique in communication. Many public speakers obviously believe in the importance of beginning their talks with a humorous story. Studies have suggested that 15 to 20 percent of television commercials contain some element of humor (Kelly & Solomon, 1975; Duncan & Nelson, 1985).

Humor could also be used to help create a positive mood when attempting to communicate about a serious topic, such as AIDS. One company has used a humorous approach to selling condoms with its "Rubber Ducky condoms" campaign (Frankenberger & Sukhdial, 1994). In a similar approach, a film strip trying to promote AIDS preventive behavior featured a character called "Captain Condom" (Frankenberger & Sukhdial, 1994).

In the typical study of the effects of humor on attitude change or other variables in the hierarchy of effects, different groups are exposed to different versions of the same message—one with humor and one without. For instance, Brooker (1981) examined the effects of humor in two commercials—one for a toothpaste and one for a flu vaccine. Examples of the humorous appeals used in his study appear in Table 9.7.

When attitude change or persuasion is the dependent variable of interest, most studies have not found a significant effect due to humor (Gruner, 1965, 1967, 1970, 1972; Brooker, 1981). Other studies of the effectiveness of humor indicate that it has more of an effect on lower-order communication effects (responses lower in the response hierarchy) than on higher-order communication

TABLE 9.7   Humor appeals used in Brooker's experiment

Pun

Toothbrush: Here's an idea with some "teeth" in it.
Vaccine: Song of the spring camper: "We're tenting tonight on the old damp ground."

Limerick

Toothbrush: If your lady friend turns aside her nose
              Whenever you begin to propose
              The halitosis demon
              Might be what sends her screamin'
              And your toothbrush could help to solve your woes.
Vaccine: There was an old lade of Crewe
              Who was horribly frightened of flu.
              She spoilt her complexion
              Through fear of infection
              Having fixed on her gas mask with glue.

Joke

Toothbrush: Detecting decay in the tooth of a beautiful young woman, the dentist said, "What's a place like this doing in a girl like you?"
Vaccine: A little boy was found watching a movie by the manager in the morning. "Why aren't you in school?" he asked the boy. "It's O.K., mister, I'm just getting over the flu."

One-liner

Toothbrush: Oscar Levant once said, "The first thing I do in the morning is brush my teeth and sharpen my tongue."
Vaccine: Many flu sufferers have said, "I hope I'm really sick. I'd hate to feel like this if I'm well."

SOURCE: G. W. Brooker, "A Comparison of the Persuasive Effects of Mild Humor and Mild Fear Appeals," *Journal of Advertising* 10, no. 4 (1981): 32. Used by permission.

effects (Gelb & Pickett, 1983; Duncan & Nelson, 1985). That is, humor is more effective in attracting attention, generating liking for the communicator, and so forth, than it is in producing attitude change or changes in behavior.

Not all studies agree, however, that humor is even effective in generating liking for the communicator. One study showed that a woman speaker was liked less when she used humor than when she did not (Taylor, 1974). The author suggests that the speaker was perceived as "trying too hard to curry favor." Similarly, another study showed that college teachers who use humor are perceived with "suspicion and hostility" because they are acting contrary to student expectations that a teacher's behavior will be controlling and evaluative (Darling & Civikly, 1984).

The research on the effectiveness of humor that has been conducted so far should be interpreted in light of its limitations, however. One limitation is that the settings of the studies have often been classrooms or laboratories, which might not be representative of the settings where humor is expected. Another limitation is that the research has tended to be nontheoretical, with little discussion of why humor might or might not be effective in achieving various effects. Markiewicz (1974) has suggested that learning theory and distraction theory are two promising theories for understanding the relationship of humor to persuasion. A learning theory approach might suggest that humor would provide reinforcement and thus lead to greater attitude change. A distraction theory approach might make the prediction that humor would be distracting. This distraction, in turn, might lead to greater attitude change by preventing counterarguing (Festinger & Maccoby, 1964). Or distraction might lead to less attitude change by interfering with attentiveness to the message.

It has also been suggested that the use of humor needs to be studied in relation to other variables (Kelly & Solomon, 1975). For instance, in advertising, is the humor more effective when it relates to the topic or when it does not? In a commercial, should the humor come at the beginning, at the end, or throughout the commercial?

Appeals to Sex

The use of sexy models and other sexual appeals is a common technique in advertising. One study indicated that more than one-fourth of magazine ads contain "obviously alluring" female models (Sexton & Haberman, 1974). Furthermore, these kinds of ads are on the increase. The same study showed that ads with "obviously alluring" models increased from 10 percent in 1951 to 27 percent in 1971. Many advertisers apparently believe that "sex sells." But does it?

Theoretically, the use of sex in a message could have an impact on persuasion in at least three ways (Gould, 1994):

1. The sexual material could increase attention to the message, a necessary condition for attitude change.

2. The sexual material could lead to arousal, and the pleasantness of the arousal condition could transfer to the product or recommendations of the message, leading to attitude change.
3. The product, institution, or recommendations in the message could become sexualized, or pick up a sexual charge, through their association with the sexual stimulus. This sexual charge could then make the product, institution, or recommendations more acceptable.

At least one study suggests that a sexy model can affect the perception or image of a product, even if there is very little logical connection between the model and the product. Smith and Engel (1968) prepared a print ad for an automobile in two versions. In one version, a female model clad in black lace panties and a simple sleeveless sweater stood in front of the car. She held a spear—on the assumption that the spear might be regarded as a phallic symbol and might lead the model to be seen as more aggressively seductive. In the other version, there was no model. When the car was pictured with the woman, subjects rated it as more appealing, more youthful, more lively, and better designed. Even objective characteristics were affected. When the car appeared with the woman, it was rated as higher in horsepower, less safe, more expensive by $340, and able to move an average 7.3 miles per hour faster. In general, male and female subjects responded the same way to the ads.

In contrast to the Smith and Engel study, however, a number of studies investigating the effects of sexy models on brand recall have shown either no effect or less recall with the sexy model (Chestnut, LaChance, & Lubitz, 1977; Alexander & Judd, 1978). It appears that the sexy models distract the viewers' attention away from the portion of the ad presenting the product or company name.

One study suggests that for certain products, an attractive female might not be as effective in stimulating sales as an attractive male (Caballero & Solomon, 1984). This study changed the displays for a brand of beer and a brand of tissue that appeared at the end of an aisle in a Tom Thumb supermarket. They found that overall, the male models tended to stimulate more beer sales among both male and female customers than either the female stimulus or the control (no model) treatment. There are also some clear-cut age differences in responses to sex appeals in advertising, with more approval from younger people than from older people (Wise, King, & Merenski, 1974).

Even though sex in advertising is common, it appears that there are some risks in using it. Appeals to sex might be disapproved of by some audience members, might be misperceived or missed by others, and might distract still others from the real purpose of the ad. Few, if any, studies exist that show a positive effect of sex in advertising on brand recall or product sales. While the Smith and Engel study shows a sexy model having the effect of increasing the favorable evaluation of an automobile in an ad, it did not test for brand recall after seeing the ad. It is possible that the subjects did not recall the brand name of the automobile any better with the sexy model than without, and this would defeat the purpose of the ad.

Jib Fowles, author of an article "Advertising's Fifteen Basic Appeals," draws this conclusion about appeals to the need for sex: "As a rule, though, advertisers have found sex to be a tricky appeal, to be used sparingly. Less controversial and equally fetching are the appeals to our need for affectionate human contact" (1982, p. 278).

Effects of Repetition

Many mass communication messages, particularly advertisements—whether commercial or political—are repeated extensively. There are a number of reasons why this might be a good idea. Not all audience members will be watching at the same time, or, in the print media, not all readers will see a single printing of an advertisement. Another advantage of repetition is that it might remind the audience of a source for a message from a high-credibility source, and thus prevent the drop-off in attitude change from a high-credibility source found over time by Hovland and Weiss. Repeating a message might help the learning of attitudes and emotional meanings for words discussed by Staats and Staats, since a repeated association of the two stimuli is part of the process of conditioning. Repetition might help the audience remember the message itself. Zielske (1959) showed that advertising is quickly forgotten if not continuously exposed.

Krugman (1972) presents the intriguing argument that three exposures might be all that are needed for a television advertisement to have its desired effect. But he adds the important qualification that it might take 23 exposures to get the three that produce the particular responses that are needed. Krugman suggests that the first exposure to an ad is dominated by a cognitive "What is it?" response. The second exposure is dominated by an evaluative "What of it?" response. And the third exposure is a reminder, but also the beginning of disengagement. Krugman points out a fundamental difficulty, however, in that people can screen out television ads by stopping at the "What is it?" response without further involvement. Then, on perhaps the 23rd exposure, they might, or might not, move on to the "What of it?" response. Thus, Krugman's analysis is stating that three exposures to an advertisement might be enough under ideal circumstances, but that it might take a number of repetitions to achieve those three.

Too much repetition can also have some undesirable effects, however. In one study, three groups of subjects were presented with one, three, or five repetitions of a persuasive message (Cacioppo & Petty, 1979). The researchers found that the message repetition led at first to increasing agreement with the advocated position, but that after a certain point it led to decreasing agreement with the advocated position. They found repetition led to decreasing, then increasing, counterarguing against the message by the recipient of the message. And they found that any amount of repetition led to increasing topic-irrelevant thinking. This kind of curvilinear relationship between repetition and communication effects was also found in a study of political advertising. Becker and Doolittle (1975) found that both liking for a candidate and seeking of information about a candidate were highest with a moderate amount of repetition but declined with high repetition. Another study found that humor ratings declined steadily with repetition of ads (Gelb & Zinkham, 1985). A change in the creative execution of the ad was found to boost the humor ratings back up.

THE NEWER PROCESS MODELS OF PERSUASION

One of the newer developments in the field of persuasion has been the creation of models of persuasion that emphasize persuasion as a process. Three major process models of persuasion are McGuire's information processing theory, Anderson's information integration theory, and Petty and Cacioppi's elaboration likelihood model.

These models share the following characteristics:

1. They present attitude change or persuasion as a process that takes place through several steps and over time.
2. They involve an emphasis on cognition or information-processing.
3. They give a more active role to the receiver as an information-processing agent than earlier conceptions of persuasion or attitude change.

McGuire's Information-Processing Theory

McGuire's theory suggests that attitude change involves six steps, with each step being a necessary precedent for the next (McGuire, 1968). The steps are as follows:

1. The persuasive message must be communicated.
2. The receiver will attend to the message.
3. The receiver will comprehend the message.
4. The receiver yields to and is convinced by the arguments presented.
5. The newly adopted position is retained.
6. The desired behavior takes place.

McGuire notes that any independent variable in the communication situation can have an effect on any one or more of the six steps. A variable such as intelligence, for instance, might lead to less yielding, because the more intelligent person is better able to detect flaws in an argument and is more willing to maintain an opinion not held by others. But it might lead to more attention because the more intelligent person has a greater interest in the outside world.

McGuire also points out that it is typical for independent variables to affect one step in a positive way and another step in a negative way. A fear appeal, for instance, might increase attention to the message but interfere with yielding.

In a later article, McGuire (1976) presented eight steps in the information-processing theory: exposure, perception, comprehension, agreement, retention, retrieval, decision making, and action. It is obvious that this list of steps is built upon the earlier six-step sequence, but with some of the earlier steps reconceptualized and some additional steps added.

In a still later article, McGuire (1989) presented twelve steps in the output or dependent variable side of the persuasion process: 1. exposure to communication; 2. attending to it; 3. liking or becoming interested in it; 4. comprehending it (learning what); 5. skill acquisition (learning how); 6. yielding to it (attitude change); 7. memory storage of content and/or agreement; 8. information search and retrieval; 9. deciding on basis of retrieval; 10. behaving in accord with decision; 11. reinforcement of desired acts; and 12. post-behavioral consolidating.

As initially presented, McGuire's theory tended to deal almost exclusively with the dependent variables in the persuasion process, splitting them into more and more categories until there were 12. In other works, such as his 1989 chapter, McGuire also discusses the roles of independent variables.

McGuire's information-processing theory gives us a good overview of the attitude change process, reminding us that it involves a number of components. Few previous theories have addressed all of these components, and few, if any, attitude change studies looked at the effects of independent variables on all of these steps. In fact, as McGuire pointed out, most of the extensive attitude change literature has probably focused on the step of yielding or agreement.

Finally, McGuire's theory reminds us of the difficulty of attitude change. The theory suggests that many independent variables tend to cancel themselves out in their overall effects by having a positive effect on one step in the process of attitude change but a negative effect on other steps in the process of attitude change. Furthermore, we must face the fact that successful attitude change attempts need to accomplish the desired effects specified by each of the various steps.

Anderson's Information Integration Theory

Information integration theory is a general theory developed by Norman Anderson to explain how human beings bring together different pieces of information (Anderson, 1981). Anderson suggests that the process involves a kind of "cognitive algebra" and can be represented mathematically. The theory was originally developed to explain how people can integrate a few basic personality traits to arrive at an overall impression of a person. But it was found to be applicable to many areas of psychology, including attitude change.

Information integration theory describes attitude change as a process of integrating new information with old information (Anderson, 1971). The old information consists of the present attitude, and the new information consists of the persuasive message. Each piece of information comes with two attributes—a scale value (represented by s) and a weight (represented by w). The scale refers to the favorability rating assigned by the receiver to the piece of information. The weight refers to the importance or relevance of the piece of information.

The ratings (scale values and weights) for the various pieces of information can be combined by the individual processing the information in several ways. Anderson suggested that processing involves averaging the scale values and weights. Another researcher, Martin Fishbein, proposed a similar model but suggested that processing involves summing or adding the scale values and weights (Fishbein, 1967). In practice, these procedures can lead to some rather different outcomes.

As an example, let us take a presidential election campaign. The campaign staff is interested in changing the attitudes of the voters in a direction that is favorable to their candidate. Imagine the following scale values are held by a receiver about various positions taken by the presidential candidate. To simplify the discussion, assume that all weights are equal.

	Scale
Candidate favors increased welfare	+2
Candidate opposes capital punishment	+3
Candidate favors equal rights for women	+3

The candidate's campaign is considering putting out a message that the candidate is in favor of increased gun control.

Assume that for our hypothetical receiver, this piece of information would have this scale value:

Candidate favors increased gun control	+2

Using the addition rule for information integration, the attitude would be +8 before the new piece of information and +10 after.

Using the averaging rule for information integration, the attitude would be 8/3 or +2.67 befor the new piece of information and 10/4 or +2.5 after.

This example suggests that in the practical application of persuasion, it will make a difference which rule for information integration is correct. There are situations where the addition rule would suggest that attitude change would take place in a positive direction and the averaging rule would suggest that attitude change would take place in a negative direction. Although the issue is not completely resolved, the research evidence at this point provides more support for the averaging rule (McGuire, 1976).

The Elaboration Likelihood Model

Most people living in contemporary society are bombarded by mass media messages, many of them attempting to persuade them of something. It is obviously impossible for a receiver to deal with all these messages at great length. Typically, we select some messages for detailed examination and deal with others in a more peremptory fashion, if at all. A model of persuasion that acknowledges these two different means of processing messages is Petty and Cacioppo's elaboration likelihood model (Petty & Cacioppo, 1986).

The elaboration likelihood model suggests that there are are two routes to attitude change—the central route and the peripheral route. The central route is involved when the receiver actively processes the information and is persuaded by the rationality of the arguments. The peripheral route is involved when the receiver does not expend the cognitive energy to evaluate the arguments and process the information in the message, and is guided more by peripheral cues. These cues can include source credibility, the style and format of the message, the mood of the receiver, and so forth.

When the central route to persuasion is active, the receiver is said to be involved in high elaboration. When the peripheral route to persuasion is active, the receiver is said to be involved in low elaboration. Elaboration refers to cognitive work involved in processing a persuasive message. Petty and Cacioppo (1986, p. 7) state that elaboration refers to "the extent to which a person carefully thinks about issue-relevant information." Elaboration involves attending carefully to the appeal, attempting to access relevant information (from memory or external sources), scrutinizing and making inferences about the arguments, drawing conclusions about the merits of the arguments, and reaching an overall evaluation of the recommended position.

Persuasion can take place under either a high degree of elaboration or a low degree of elaboration, or at any point in between, but the model suggests that the process of attitude change will be very different at different degrees of elaboration. When persuasion occurs through the central route, it is usually because high-quality arguments are being strongly presented. With the central route, persuasion is most likely to occur when the receiver is led to have predominantly favorable thoughts about the advocated position. So a key question becomes, what factors lead the receiver to have either favorable or unfavorable thoughts about the recommended position? Two factors seem to be important. The first is the agreement between the receiver's initial position and the recommended position. If an advocated position is one toward which a receiver is already inclined, presumably the receiver will be favorably disposed to the message. The second factor is the strength of the argument. The stronger or more carefully defined the argument, the more likely it is that the receiver will be favorably disposed to the message.

Under the peripheral route, persuasion will not depend on thoughtful consideration of the message but on the receiver's use of simple decision rules, or heuristics. These principles are activated by cues in the persuasion situation. The three major heuristics are credibility, liking, and consensus (O'Keefe, 1990, pp. 186–187). The credibility heuristic refers to the tendency for people to believe sources that have credibility. The liking heuristic refers to the tendency for people to agree with people they like. The consensus heuristic refers to the tendency for people to agree with positions that a lot of other people support.

An example of persuasion through the peripheral route might involve someone who wants to vote in a local or state election but doesn't want to take the time to gather information about all the candidates and come to an original decision. Such a person might take the endorsements of candidates from an editorial in the local newspaper and just vote straight down the list. Or a person might choose a straight party ticket, voting for all the Democrats or all the

Republicans. In these cases, the decision rule being used is "Vote the way this trusted source recommends."

What kinds of factors determine which route will be taken, central or peripheral? Two main factors influence the degree of elaboration by a receiver: the receiver's motivation to engage in elaboration and his or her ability to engage in elaboration (O'Keefe, 1990). Overall, the elaboration likelihood model helps to account for a variety of attitude change studies by bringing them together in the same model. We begin to see that rational models of persuasion, such as information processing theory, and less rational models, such as the source credibility model, can both be true. The model also helps us to reconcile conflicting results of studies of the same factor in persuasion. It may be the case that a high-credibility source will lead to attitude change in one situation but not in another if attitude change is taking place through the peripheral route in one situation and the central route in the other.

The elaboration likelihood model also gives a more active role in attitude change to the receiver than we have seen in some earlier models of persuasion. Under the elaboration likelihood model, the receiver—to some degree, at least—decides whether to take the central route or the peripheral route. And certainly if the central route is taken, the receiver becomes active in analyzing the message.

One problem with the elaboration likelihood model centers around the concept of the quality of arguments. This concept is basic to the process of persuasion through the central route—higher-quality arguments should lead to more attitude change. To some extent, the theory defines strong or high quality arguments as those that are persuasive. If researchers then conduct experiments that show that strong arguments produce more attitude change than weak arguments, we are not really finding out anything new. There seems to be some circularity in the presentation of the theory at this point.

CONCLUSIONS

The field of attitude change research has expanded greatly since the early days when the learning theory approach and the consistency theory approach were dominant. Katz's functional approach was developed specifically to reconcile these two divergent views and fit them both into a larger picture. The Katz approach has drawn particular attention to the problem of changing attitudes serving the ego-defensive function—not an easy kind of attitude to change.

McGuire and Papageorgis's inoculation theory provides a nice kind of balance to the many studies of attitude change. While others have been trying to discover the best means of persuading people, McGuire and Papageorgis have been investigating the best means of making people resistant to persuasion.

Festinger raised the important issue of whether attitude change produced by persuasive messages was accompanied by any real behavior change. About the same time, researchers began a serious study of whether attitudes in general as they were measured by researchers were useful in predicting behavior. One of the beneficial results of all this questioning is that many attitude change studies now incorporate behavioral measures as well as attitude measures.

Staats and Staats's theory that attitudes are learned through classical conditioning suggests a strategy for use in advertising and other persuasive efforts. Under this theory, the goal of a persuasive message is to cause the learning of a positive or negative response to a word.

We also discussed four techniques that are common in persuasive communication—pictures, humor, sex, and repetition. The research on humor and sex suggests that they should be used carefully, because they can be misunderstood or can distract from the message, and there is little evidence that they actually bring about attitude change. Repetition has its pros and cons and should also be used carefully. It increases the chances of penetrating through audience indifference or resistance, and it can lead to greater learning—of a message, of a relationship between a product name and positive associations, or of the connection between a credible source and particular message. But it can also lead to increased counterarguing and increased thinking about other irrelevant topics.

Finally, we discussed three newer models of persuasion that emphasize persuasion as a process and the active role of the receiver. These models are McGuire's information processing theory, Anderson's information integration theory, and Petty and Cacioppi's elaboration likelihood model. These models remind us that persuasion is a complex endeavor. They also offer promise of bringing together some of the diverse findings of research on attitude change into more unified theories.

DISCUSSION

1. Much of the early attitude change research was based on the notion that attitudes are learned responses. What are some other ways to think of attitudes?
2. Research has shown that attempts to persuade that are based on fear appeals can backfire. What are some alternatives to the use of fear appeals in messages?
3. Evaluate Rogers's protection motivation theory. What are its advantages over the notion of a curvilinear relationship between fear and attitude change proposed by Janis?
4. What are the advantages of the new process models of persuasion over the older Hovland approach to attitude change theory?
5. What are the disadvantages of the new process models of persuasion?
6. Newspaper reporters can be thought of in terms of low-credibility or high-credibility sources. Why do you think the public has low confidence in newspaper reporters, as public opinion poll results sometimes suggest?

7. What are some of the likely consequences of the low confidence ratings that the public assigns to newspaper reporters?
8. Pick a worthwhile social issue, such as prevention of AIDS. Drawing upon your knowledge of persuasion theory, design a communication campaign to deal with the issue.

REFERENCES

Ajzen, I. (1971). Attitudinal vs. normative messages: An investigation of the differential effects of persuasive communications on behavior. *Sociometry* 34: 263–280.

Ajzen, I., and M. Fishbein (1970). The prediction of behavior from attitudinal and normative variables. *Journal of Experimental Social Psychology* 6: 466–487.

Alexander, M. W., and B. Judd (1978). Do nudes in ads enhance brand recall? *Journal of Advertising Research* 18 (no. 1): 47–50.

Allport, G. W. (1954). The historical background of modern social psychology. In G. Lindzey (ed.), *Handbook of Social Psychology*, vol. 1, pp. 3–56. Reading, Mass.: Addison-Wesley.

Anderson, N. H. (1971). Integration theory and attitude change. *Psychological Review* 78: 171–206.

Anderson, N. H. (1981). Integration theory applied to cognitive responses and attitudes. In R. E. Petty, T. M. Ostrom, and T. C. Brock (eds.), *Cognitive Responses in Persuasion*, pp. 361–397. Hillsdale, N.J.: Lawrence Erlbaum.

Becker, L. B., and J. C. Doolittle (1975). How repetition affects evaluations of and information seeking about candidates. *Journalism Quarterly* 52: 611–617.

Brooker, G. W. (1981). A comparison of the persuasive effects of mild humor and mild fear appeals. *Journal of Advertising* 10 (no. 4): 29–40.

Brown, R. (1958). *Words and Things*. New York: Free Press.

Caballero, M. J., and P. J. Solomon (1984). Effects of model attractiveness on sales response. *Journal of Advertising* 13 (no. 1): 17–23.

Cacioppo, J. T., and R. E. Petty (1979). Effects of message repetition and position on cognitive responses, recall, and persuasion. *Journal of Personality and Social Psychology* 37: 97–109.

Chen, W. (1933). The influence of oral propaganda material upon students' attitudes. *Archives of Psychology* 150: 1–43.

Chestnut, R. W., C. C. LaChance, and A. Lubitz (1977). The "decorative" female model: Sexual stimuli and the recognition of advertisements. *Journal of Advertising* 6 (no. 4): 11–14.

Cook, T. D., and B. R. Flay (1978). The persistence of experimentally induced attitude change. In L. Berkowitz (ed.), *Advances in Experimental Social Psychology*, vol. 11, pp. 2–57. New York: Academic Press.

Darling, A. L., and J. M. Civikly (1984). The effect of teacher humor on classroom climate. *Proceedings of the Tenth International Conference on Improving University Teaching*, pp. 798–806.

Duncan, C. P., and J. E. Nelson (1985). Effects of humor in a radio advertising experiment. *Journal of Advertising* 14 (no. 2): 33–40, 64.

Eagly, A. H., and Chaiken, S. (1993). *The Psychology of Attitudes*. Fort Worth, Tex.: Harcourt Brace Jovanovich.

English, H. B., and A. C. English (1958). *A Comprehensive Dictionary of Psychological and Psychoanalytical Terms: A Guide to Usage*. New York: Longmans, Green.

Evans, R. I., R. R. Rozelle, T. M. Lasater, T. M. Dembroski, and B. P. Allen (1970). Fear arousal, persuasion and actual versus implied behavioral change: New perspective utilizing a real-life dental hygiene program. *Journal of Personality and Social Psychology* 16: 220-227.

Festinger, L. (1964). Behavioral support for opinion change. *Public Opinion Quarterly* 28: 404-417.

Festinger, L., and N. Maccoby (1964). On resistance to persuasive communications. *Journal of Abnormal and Social Psychology* 68: 359-366.

Fishbein, M. (1967). A behavior theory approach to the relations between beliefs about an object and the attitude toward the object. In M. Fishbein (ed.), *Readings in Attitude Theory and Measurement*, pp. 389-400. New York: Wiley.

Fishbein, M. (1973). Introduction: The prediction of behaviors from attitudinal variables. In C. D. Mortensen and K. K. Sereno (eds.), *Advances in Communication Research*, pp. 3-31. New York: Harper & Row.

Fowles, J. (1982). Advertising's fifteen basic appeals. *ETC.* 39: 273-290.

Frankenberger, K. D., and A. S. Sukhdial. (1994). Segmenting teens for AIDS preventive behaviors with implications for marketing communications. *Journal of Public Policy & Marketing* 13: 133-150.

Gelb, B. D., and C. M. Pickett (1983). Attitude toward the ad: Links to humor and to advertising effectiveness. *Journal of Advertising* 12 (no. 2): 34-42.

Gelb, B. D., and G. M. Zinkham (1985). The effect of repetition on humor in a radio advertising study. *Journal of Advertising* 14 (no. 4): 13-20, 68.

Gillig, P. M., and A. G. Greenwald (1974). Is it time to lay the sleeper effect to rest? *Journal of Personality and Social Psychology* 29: 132-139.

Gould, S. J. (1994). Sexuality and ethics in advertising: A research agenda and policy guideline perspective. *Journal of Advertising* 23 (no. 3): 73-80.

Gruner, C. R. (1965). An experimental study of satire as persuasion. *Speech Monographs* 32: 149-153.

Gruner, C. R. (1967). Effect of humor on speaker ethos and audience information gain. *Journal of Communication* 17 (no. 3): 228-233.

Gruner, C. R. (1970). The effect of humor in dull and interesting informative speeches. *Central States Speech Journal* 21: 160-166.

Gruner, C. R. (1972). Effects of including humorous material in a persuasive sermon. *Southern Speech Communication Journal* 38: 188-196.

Hilgard, E. R., and G. H. Bower (1966). *Theories of Learning*. New York: Appleton-Century-Crofts.

Hill, R. P. (1988). An exploration of the relationship between AIDS related anxiety and the evaluation of condom advertisements. *Journal of Advertising* 17: 35-42.

Hovland, C. I., I. L. Janis, and H. H. Kelley (1953). *Communication and Persuasion*. New Haven, Conn.: Yale University Press.

Hovland, C. I., A. A. Lumsdaine, and F. D. Sheffield (1965). *Experiments on Mass Communication*. New York: Wiley.

Hovland, C. I., and W. Weiss (1951). The influence of source credibility on communication effectiveness. *Public Opinion Quarterly* 15: 633-650.

Insko, C. A. (1967). *Theories of Attitude Change*. New York: Appleton-Century-Crofts.

Janis, I. (1967). Effects of fear arousal on attitude change: Recent developments in theory and experimental research. In L. Berkowitz (ed.), *Advances in Experimental Social Psychology*, vol. 3, pp. 166-224. New York: Academic Press.

Katz, D. (1960). The functional approach to the study of attitudes. *Public Opinion Quarterly* 24: 163-204.

Kelly, J. P., and P. J. Solomon (1975). Humor in television advertising. *Journal of Advertising* 4 (no. 3): 31-35.

Krech, D., R. S. Crutchfield, and E. L. Ballachey (1962). *Individual in Society: A Textbook of Social Psychology*. New York: McGraw-Hill.

Krisher, H. P. III, S. A. Darley, and J. M. Darley (1973). Fear-provoking recommendations, intentions to take preventive actions, and actual preventive actions. *Journal of Personality and Social Psychology* 26: 301-308.

Krugman, H. E. (1972). Why three exposures may be enough. *Journal of Advertising Research* 12 (no. 6): 11-14.

LaPiere, R. T. (1934). Attitudes vs. actions. *Social Forces* 13: 230-237.

Leventhal, H., and P. Niles (1964). A field experiment on fear arousal with data on the validity of questionnaire measures. *Journal of Personality* 32: 459-479.

Lumsdaine, A., and I. Janis. (1953). Resistance to "counterpropaganda" produced by one-sided and two-sided "propaganda" presentations. *Public Opinion Quarterly* 17: 316.

Maccoby, N., and J. W. Farquhar (1975). Communicating for health: Unselling heart disease. *Journal of Communication* 25 (no. 3): 114-126.

Markiewicz, D. (1974). Effects of humor on persuasion. *Sociometry* 37: 407-422.

McGuire, W. J. (1968). Personality and attitude change: An information-processing theory. In A.C. Greenwald, T. C. Brock, and T. M. Ostrom (eds.), *Psychological Foundations of Attitudes*, pp. 171-196. San Diego, Calif.: Academic Press.

McGuire, W. J. (1976). Some internal psychological factors influencing consumer choice. *Journal of Consumer Research* 2: 302-319.

McGuire, W. J. (1989). Theoretical foundations of campaigns. In R.E. Rice and C. K. Atkin (eds.), *Public Communication Campaigns*, 2nd ed., pp. 43-65. Newbury Park, Calif.: Sage.

McGuire, W., and D. Papageorgis (1961). The relative efficacy of various types of prior belief-defense in producing immunity against persuasion. *Journal of Abnormal and Social Psychology* 62: 327-337.

Miniard, P. W., S. Bhatla, K. R. Lord, P. R. Dickson, and H. R. Unnava (1991). Picture-based persuasion processes and the mediating role of involvement. *Journal of Consumer Research* 18: 92-107.

Murphy, G., L. B. Murphy, and T. M. Newcomb (1937). *Experimental Social Psychology: An Interpretation of Research upon the Socialization of the Individual*, rev. ed. New York: Harper and Brothers.

O'Keefe, D. J. (1990). *Persuasion: Theory and Research*. Newbury Park, Calif.: Sage.

Olson, J. M., and M. P. Zanna (1993). Attitudes and attitude change. *Annual Review of Psychology* 44: 117-154.

Papageorgis, D., and W. McGuire (1961). The generality of immunity to persuasion produced by pre-exposure to weakened counterarguments. *Journal of Abnormal and Social Psychology* 62: 475-481.

Petty, R. E., and J. T. Cacioppo (1986). *Communication and Persuasion: Central and Peripheral Routes to Attitude Change*. New York: Springer-Verlag.

Reardon, K. K. (1989). The potential role of persuasion in adolescent AIDS prevention. In R. E. Rice and C. K. Atkin (eds.), *Public Communication Campaigns*, 2nd ed., pp. 273-289. Newbury Park, Calif.: Sage.

Rogers, R. W. (1975). A protection motivation theory of fear appeals and attitude change. *Journal of Psychology* 91: 93-114.

Ross, R. S. (1985). *Understanding Persuasion: Foundations and Practices,* 2nd ed. Englewood Cliffs, N.J.: Prentice-Hall.

Sexton, D. E., and P. Haberman (1974). Women in magazine advertisements. *Journal of Advertising Research* 14 (no. 4): 41–46.

Sherif, M., and C. I. Hovland (1961). Social Judg*ment: Assimilation and Contrast Effects in Communication and Attitude Change.* New Haven, Conn.: Yale University Press.

Smith, G. H., and R. Engel (1968). Influence of a female model on perceived characteristics of an automobile. *Proceedings of the 76th Annual Convention of the American Psychological Association* 3: 68–682.

Staats, A. W. (1968). *Learning, Language, and Cognition.* New York: Holt, Rinehart, and Winston.

Staats, C. K., and A. W. Staats (1957). Meaning established by classical conditioning. *Journal of Experimental Psychology* 54: 74–80.

Staats, A. W., and C. K. Staats (1958). Attitudes established by classical conditioning. *Journal of Abnormal and Social Psychology* 57: 37–40.

Staats, A. W., C. K. Staats, and H. L. Crawford (1962). First-order conditioning of meaning and the parallel conditioning of a GSR. *Journal of General Psychology* 67: 159–167.

Tanner, J. F., J. B. Hunt, and D. R. Eppright (1991). The protection motivation model: a normative model of fear appeals. *Journal of Marketing* 55: 36–45.

Taylor, P. M. (1974). An experimental study of humor and ethos. *Southern Speech Communication Journal* 39: 359–366.

Tripp, C., T. D. Jensen, and L. Carlson. (1994). The effects of multiple product endorsements by celebrities on consumers' attitudes and intentions. *Journal of Consumer Research* 20: 535–547.

Whitehead, J. L. (1968). Factors of source credibility. *Quarterly Journal of Speech* 54: 59–63.

Wise, G. L., A. L. King, and J. P. Merenski (1974). Reactions to sexy ads vary with age. *Journal of Advertising Research* 14 (no. 4): 11–16.

Zielske, H. A. (1959). The remembering and forgetting of advertising. *Journal of Marketing* 23 (no. 3): 239–243.

chapter 10

Groups and Communiction

The Dutch philosopher Baruch Spinoza pointed out 300 years ago that human beings are social animals. His statement has been strongly reinforced by modern psychology, which has shown that other people have a great influence on our attitudes, our behavior, and even our perceptions.

The other people that influence us are in the groups that we belong to, large or small, formal or informal. These groups can have a great effect on the way we receive a mass communication message. This was hinted at in Chapter 4, where we reported Cooper and Jahoda's suggestion that group membership can make attitudes of prejudice hard to change. Groups influence people's communication behavior in other ways, as we shall see.

The scientific study of the influence of groups on human behavior began in the 1930s, primarily with the work of social psychologist Muzafer Sherif. Solomon Asch, another social psychologist, did some noteworthy work on group pressures and conformity. Another important name in the study of groups was Kurt Lewin, the founder of the field known as *group dynamics*. The importance of groups in the formation of political attitudes and the making of voting decisions was brought out in some classic election studies conducted in the 1940s by sociologist Paul Lazarsfeld and his associates.

The following are three of the most important types of groups. A *primary group* is a group (two or more persons) involving longstanding, intimate, face-to-face association. Examples are a family, a work group, a team, a fraternity, or a military unit. A *reference group* is a group identified with and used as a standard of reference, but not necessarily belonged to. For instance, a student wishing to belong to a certain fraternity might begin to dress like members and adopt their attitudes even though he is not a member. A *casual group* is a one-time group of people who didn't know each other before they were brought

217

together. Examples are people riding in an elevator, people riding a bus, or strangers sitting together at a football game.

SHERIF'S RESEARCH ON GROUP NORMS

Groups often share certain rules or standards, and these can be referred to as *norms*. Norms operate in almost every area of human behavior. Some everyday examples of areas for the operation of norms are hair style, skirt length, taste in popular music, courtship behavior (such as whether or not to kiss on the first date), style of greeting, and form of handshake. Some norms are shared by an entire society. Many people may not realize that the norms of their society are basically arbitrary until they see that different norms operate in a different culture. In some countries, the evening meal is served much later than it is in the United States. In some countries, it is customary to take a midday siesta— not an American habit. Many other differences in food preferences and habits, sexual mores, conversational styles, gestures, clothing choices, and even values show up between cultures. All can be thought of as norms.

Sherif (1936, 1937) wanted to study the process of the formation of norms. He found a laboratory situation that was ideal for this purpose. Sherif built his research around a phenomenon known as the *autokinetic light effect*. When a person is seated in a completely darkened room and a tiny stationary point of light is made to appear, the person usually sees the light begin to move. The light appears to move because the nervous system is overcompensating for the dim light, and in doing so it sends the same type of impulses to the brain that are normally sent when the eye is following a moving object (McBurney & Collings, 1977). This gave Sherif a situation that was high in ambiguity and would therefore work well for the study of norms. Almost everyone sees the light move, but since it really isn't moving, no one can really know how far it moves.

Sherif set up an experimental situation in which a subject was placed in a darkened room with a telegraph key in a convenient place. Five meters away was a device for presenting a point of light. The person was given these instructions: "When the room is completely dark, I shall give you the signal *ready,* and then show you a point of light. After a short time the light will start to move. As soon as you see it move, press the key. A few seconds later the light will disappear. Then tell me the distance it moved. Try to make your estimates as accurate as possible." When the subject pressed the key, a timer began ticking off. It ticked for two seconds, and then the light went off.

Sherif first ran this experiment with an individual alone in the room. After repeated trials, a person usually settles on a personal standard. The estimates might range between 4 and 6 inches but would generally be around 5 inches. Other people would settle on very different personal ranges, however. One person might have a personal standard of 1/2 inch and another might have a standard of 2 feet.

In the next stage of the experiment, Sherif took several people who had been in the room alone and had established their own standards and put them in the room together. They went through the experiment together and could hear one another giving their estimates. The usual finding in this situation was that as trials were repeated, the different estimates became closer and closer together. Eventually the group adopted a norm of its own, which often would be somewhere around the average of the separate standards of the individuals.

In the third stage of the experiment, Sherif took individuals who had been in the group situation and put them back in the room alone for further trials. In this situation, the individual usually stayed with the norm that he or she had formed in the group.

Sherif's experiment shows that in a situation of uncertainty, people are dependent on other people for guidance. It also shows that the influence of the group can extend to situations in which the group is not present. Many norms in society must develop through the process that Sherif has isolated. After all, many situations in life are full of uncertainty. In some of the most important areas of human concern—politics, religion, morality—there is little that is certain. On the basis of Sherif's work, we might expect to find that groups have a great deal of influence on attitudes in these and other ambiguous areas.

ASCH'S RESEARCH ON GROUP PRESSURE

Sherif's research dealt with groups in a situation with high ambiguity. Asch (1955, 1956) investigated similar forces at work in a situation with little ambiguity. Asch wanted to investigate group pressure and the tendency for people to either conform to the pressure or be independent of it.

Asch set up an experimental situation that appeared to be an investigation of a subject's ability to judge the length of some drawn lines. Subjects were shown two cards. One card had a single line. The other had three lines of different lengths labeled 1, 2, and 3. The task for the subject was to call out the number for the one of the three that was the same length as the single line. There were 12 different sets of cards. This is a relatively easy perceptual task that people can do quite well in the absence of group pressure. A control group of 37 included 35 people who made no errors, one who made one error, and one who made two errors.

Asch was really interested in what happens when group pressure is introduced into the situation. In this phase of the experiment, he had subjects participating in the line-judging task in groups of eight. Actually only one of these eight was a true subject, and the others were allies of the experimenter who were instructed to begin giving wrong answers after a couple of trials with correct answers. They all would give the same incorrect answer, so the subject would hear everyone else appear to agree on a single answer, but one that his or her senses indicated was the wrong one. What would a person do in this situation?

TABLE 10.1   Error rates on 12 trials for 123 subjects in the Asch experiment

Error Rate	Number of Subjects	Percentage of Subjects
0 errors	29	24
1–7 errors	59	49
8–12 errors	35	27
	123	100

The results for 123 subjects (Table 10.1) showed 76 percent of them yielding to the group pressure and giving the wrong answer at least once. In the total number of answers given, the subjects were influenced by group pressure to give the wrong answer in 36.8 percent of their answers.

Asch modified his experiment in several ways and came up with additional findings of interest. The size of the group giving the incorrect judgment was varied from 1 to 15. The striking finding here was that a group of 3 giving a unanimous opinion was essentially as effective in producing conformity to wrong answers as were larger groups.

Asch also investigated the effect of having one other person give the correct answer in addition to the subject. He found that having one lone supporting partner of this type eliminates much of the power of group pressure. Subjects answered incorrectly only one-fourth as often as they did when confronted with a unanimous majority.

Asch also attempted to make the physical difference in the length of lines so great that no one would still be susceptible to group pressure. He was not able to do this. Even with a difference of 7 inches between the correct and incorrect lines, some people still gave in to the group response.

Asch's research gives a striking demonstration that some people will go along with the group even when it means contradicting information derived from their own senses. The Sherif and Asch studies also show that even casual groups, people who had never seen each other before, exert a strong influence. It seems likely that the power of groups would be even greater when we are dealing with primary groups such as families or work groups.

HOW NORMS ARE DEVELOPED

Sherif's research showed the dramatic power of norms, but it did not show in detail how norms are actually formed. Some years later, Bettenhausen and Murnighan (1985) focused on the interaction among group members as the key to understanding how norms form. They described the process of norm formation as involving the following process. In new groups, members are uncertain about appropriate behavior. They look to similar, previously experienced situations for scripts to serve as guidelines. If group members do not adopt common interpretations of the novel situation, they must develop a group-based under-standing of the situation. As group members interact, their shared experiences form the basis for expectations about future interactions. Challenges to evolving norms may lead nonchallengers to revise their interpretations of the experience or lead them to attempt to persuade the group to accept their interpretations. Once a norm has formed, any further attempts to alter the behavior controlled by the norm will be met with sanctions.

LEWIN'S FOOD HABITS STUDIES

Kurt Lewin made a number of contributions that are important in the study of communication, including the idea of the gatekeeper, the statement that "there is nothing so practical as a good theory," and the founding of the group dynamics movement. Lewin was a brilliant scholar and teacher whose students, including Leon Festinger, Alex Bavelas, Ron Lippitt, and Dorwin Cartwright, went on to make additional major contributions to psychology.

During World War II, Lewin participated in a program designed to use communication to get people to change some of their food habits. He became involved in this work through his friendship with anthropologist Margaret Mead. Mead was helping M. L. Wilson, director of extension in the U.S. Department of Agriculture, to apply social science to problems of social change. He appointed Mead secretary for the Committee on Food Habits of the National Research Council (Marrow, 1977).

In one group of experiments, Lewin (1958) and his associates were attempt-ing to get housewives, as part of the war effort, to increase their use of beef hearts, sweetbreads, and kidneys—cuts of meat not frequently served. Assisted by Bavelas, Lewin set up two experimental conditions—a lecture condition and a group decision condition. In the three groups in the lecture condition, oral presentations were given describing the nutrition, economics, and methods of preparation of the unpopular cuts of meat, and mimeographed recipes were handed out. In the three groups in the group decision conditions, people were given some initial information but then a discussion was begun on the problems "housewives like themselves" would face in serving these cuts of meat. Tech-niques and recipes were offered, but only after the groups became sufficiently involved to want to know whether some of the problems could be solved.

At the end of the meeting, the women were asked to indicate by a show of hands who was willing to try one of the cuts of meat in the next week. A follow-up showed that only 3 percent of the women who heard the lectures served one of the meats they hadn't served before, while 32 percent of the women in the group decision condition served one of them.

A number of factors were at work in this experiment, including group discussion, public commitment, coming to a decision on future action, and perception of group consensus. A subsequent experiment by Edith Bennett Pelz (1958) indicates that the first two factors did not have much of an impact and that the latter two alone were sufficient to cause differences as large as those found by Lewin and his associates.

GROUPS AND POLITICAL ATTITUDES

In the 1940s, researchers carried out some of the first careful studies of how people decide whom to vote for in an election. These studies were conducted by Paul Lazarsfeld and his associates at the Bureau of Applied Social Research at Columbia University. They studied voters in Erie County, Ohio, during the 1940 election between Roosevelt and Willkie (Lazarsfeld, Berelson, & Gaudet, 1968), and voters in Elmira, New York, during the 1948 election between Truman and Dewey (Berelson, Lazarsfeld, & McPhee, 1954). Both studies were sample surveys of the panel type, in which the same respondents are interviewed several times.

Both studies made a point of looking at the mass media as important factors in the election decision-making process. Both studies came up with the surprising finding that the mass media played a weak role in election decisions compared with personal influence, or the influence of other people. In fact, it is sometimes said that these studies rediscovered personal influence, a factor communication researchers had tended to overlook as they began to think along the lines of the "bullet theory."

These studies showed a strong tendency for people to vote the same way as the members of their primary groups. The family is one of the most important of these primary groups. The influence of the family is indicated by the fact that 75 percent of the first voters in the Elmira study voted the same way their fathers did. People also tend to vote like their friends and coworkers.

Table 10.2 reports data from the Elmira study that show a strong tendency for people to vote like their three best friends, particularly when the three best friends are unanimous.

Table 10.3 reports additional data from the Elmira study that show a strong tendency for people to vote like their three closest coworkers. Berelson,

TABLE 10.2 Respondents who intended to vote Republican and the vote intentions of their three closest friends

	Vote Intentions of Their Three Closest Friends			
	Republican Republican Republican	Republican Republican Democrat	Republican Democrat Democrat	Democrat Democrat Democrat
Respondents who intended to vote Republican (%)	88	74	48	15

SOURCE: Adapted from B. R. Berelson, P. F. Lazarsfeld, and W. N. McPhee, *Voting: A Study of Opinion Formation in a Presidential Campaign* (Chicago: University of Chicago Press, 1954).

TABLE 10.3 Respondents who intended to vote Republican and the vote intentions of their three closest coworkers

	Vote Intentions of Their Three Closest Coworkers			
	Republican **Republican** **Republican**	**Republican** **Republican** **Democrat**	**Republican** **Democrat** **Democrat**	**Democrat** **Democrat** **Democrat**
Respondents who intended to vote Republican (%)	86	75	53	19

SOURCE: Adapted from B. R. Berelson, P. F. Lazarsfeld, and W. N. McPhee, *Voting: A Study of Opinion Formation in a Presidential Campaign* (Chicago: University of Chicago Press, 1954).

Lazarsfeld, and McPhee refer to this strong consistency as the "political homogeneity of the primary group" (1954, p. 88). The findings are strikingly parallel to the Asch research on group pressure, which showed that a unanimous majority of three was sufficient to influence many people's judgments.

This homogeneity of opinion in the political area could be explained by two different processes. One is that the group exerts pressure on and influences the individual's judgment, just as it did in the Asch experiments. The other is that people might select friends whose political attitudes agree with their own. Both are probably true to some extent. But the second explanation would not be sufficient alone. People have a great deal of choice in selecting their friends. But they have less choice in selecting their coworkers, and often no choice in selecting their families.

People also belong to certain larger groups due to their sex, age, race, occupation, religious preference, and other serendipitous criteria. People in these types of very broad groups also tend to vote alike. This similarity in voting is shown in Table 10.4, based on data from the Elmira study. Knowledge of just two factors—religion and socioeconomic status—makes a person's vote predictable with a fairly high degree of accuracy. Using several more factors—say five or six—makes a person's vote even more predictable. This tendency of people

TABLE 10.4 Respondents who voted Republican, tabulated by religious affiliation and socioeconomic status

	High Status		Middle Status		Low Status	
	Protestant	**Catholic**	**Protestant**	**Catholic**	**Protestant**	**Catholic**
Respondents who voted Republican (%)	98	50	83	31	66	31

SOURCE: Adapted from B. R. Berelson, P. F. Lazarsfeld, and W. N. McPhee, *Voting: A Study of Opinion Formation in a Presidential Campaign* (Chicago: University of Chicago Press, 1954).

in certain broad categories to vote alike is also the basis of the election night projections that the television networks use to announce the winners of elections on the basis of as little as 5 percent of the vote (Skedgell, 1966).

THE SOCIAL IDENTIFICATION MODEL

The recognition that people are influenced by their membership in broad categories has led to a refinement of thinking about the psychology of groups. Several researchers, including particularly psychologists John C. Turner and Henri Tajfel, have developed what they call the *social identification model* of group influence. This model proposes that a social group be defined as two or more individuals who share a common social identification or perceive themselves to be members of the same social category (Turner, 1982). Under this view, group members do not have to relate to each other face to face, nor does the group require a structure. Group membership is seen primarily as a cognitive process, often resulting from attempts of the person to answer the question, "Who am I?" This question can be answered in terms of the groups that a person belongs to or identifies with. Thus, a person gets a sense of *social identity* from the groups that are admired and identified with. Furthermore, this sense of social identity does not appear to be operating all the time but seems to be switched on and off by certain situations. Once it is switched on, the individual attempts to behave in accordance with the norms of the social categories that he or she belongs to and that are relevant to the situation.

The social identification model alters our thinking about groups in some significant ways. First, it suggests that an important kind of group membership is based on cognitive responses ("Who am I?") rather than on emotional responses ("Do I like these people?"). Second, it suggests that the social categories to which people assign themselves are not just weak associations but are an important kind of group membership in themselves. Third, it suggests that this process of identification with social categories might have important consequences. Individuals take these category memberships seriously because they are related to their concept of who they are.

Communication scholar Vincent Price suggested that the social identification model is useful for helping us understand the formation of public opinion and the role the mass media play in that process. Price (1988) argues that the mass media play an important role in bringing social identification processes to bear on the formation of public opinion. First, the mass media depict which groups are at odds over a particular issue, therefore signaling which group identities are relevant to that issue. Second, by depicting how the groups are responding to the issue, the media can indicate the opinions that are being held by each group and thus the norms that should be followed by people identifying with that group. Third, the opinion norms of the group are likely to become perceptually exaggerated in the minds of audience members. Fourth, people impute their group's perceived opinion norm to themselves and become more likely to express this exaggerated norm. It is at this point that public opinion on various issues might appear to solidify or crystallize.

GROUPS AS INSTRUMENTS OF CHANGE

Because of the power of social influence, groups can sometimes be used as agents or instruments of change. Group structure and group dynamics are very much a part of the process at work in organizations such as Alcoholics Anonymous, Weight Watchers, and some groups that help people to stop smoking. The principles of group norms and group pressure can often be seen at work in these kinds of efforts. Alcoholics Anonymous, for instance, has a group norm that permits and encourages people to talk about their problems with alcohol (Alcoholics Anonymous, 1967). This is a reversal of the norm in the culture at large, which discourages talking about an individual's alcohol problem and almost makes such discussion a taboo. AA members also share other norms, such as the willingness to be available to talk to another member at any time of night or day. Similar forces are at work in stop-smoking groups, whose members often are encouraged to select a "Quit Day" and publicly announce it to the group. This then generates group pressure for the individual actually to quit on that day and then stick by the decision.

Reference groups may be particularly important in communicating with teenagers about AIDS. Frankenberger and Sukhdial (1994) suggest that group norms are important predictors of adoption of AIDS preventive behaviors. They state that teenagers who see AIDS preventive behaviors as consistent with reference group norms are more likely to disseminate helpful prevention information and are more likely to practice these behaviors themselves. They argue that AIDS campaigns aimed at teenagers should be based on a thorough understanding of existing norms, should use appropriate sources to convey the message, and should provide a consistent message over time.

GROUPS AND MASS COMMUNICATION

The importance of group influence has been well understood by many people involved in mass communication. Father Coughlin, the "radio priest" who was such a skillful user of propaganda, would ask his audience to listen to him in groups. He also began his broadcasts with music and told audience members to take that time to call a friend and ask the person to listen to the program. Many advertisements and commercials attempt to incorporate some form of group influence. For instance, a television commercial for a dye for gray hair makes the statement, "I bet a lot of your friends are using it and you don't even know it." Basically, this type of commercial is using the old propaganda device of band wagon. Another promising idea is to use mass communication channels to attempt to stimulate interpersonal discussion. For instance, one California grocery chain's campaign theme was "Tell a Friend" (Solomon, 1989, p. 100).

The state of Massachusetts started an aggressive anti-smoking campaign supported by a 25-cent per pack cigarette tax. The campaign uses advertising but goes beyond ads to take advantage of promotions with the Celtics basketball and Red Sox baseball teams. Young people are also encouraged to organize petition drives aimed at banning cigarette machines or eliminating smoking in public places. Greg Connolly, the director of the program, said, "I don't think any TV ad is going to make anybody quit." But he added that an ad campaign tied to grass-roots efforts "can result in hundreds of thousands of people quitting" (Birch, 1995, p. 1A).

Researchers working in the field of health communication have found an approach based on group influence to be an effective one. One example of this work is the Stanford Heart Disease Prevention Program, a joint effort by Stanford's Department of Communication and School of Medicine (Maccoby & Farquhar, 1975, 1976). The purposes of the program were to apply communication theory to the development of a health communication campaign and to use evaluation research to measure change due to the campaign. The campaign was intended to change people's habits relating to the three leading risk factors in heart disease—diet, smoking, and lack of exercise. The researchers picked three California towns that were as alike as possible to test their approaches. The first was given an eight-month media campaign involving local TV and radio spots, a newspaper tabloid, billboards, and direct mail. The second town was given the same media campaign but selected groups of high-risk people were also given intensive group instruction in reducing risks. The third town served as a control group and received no campaign or instruction.

The results showed some effect of the media-only campaign in changing attitudes and behavior related to heart disease risk, but much greater effect with the people receiving the media campaign plus the intensive group instruction. Cholesterol level was down 1 percent in the media-only town, down 5 percent in the media-plus-group-instruction town, and up 2 percent in the town receiving no campaign. The Stanford Heart Disease Prevention Program also found that using mass mailings to send nutrition tip sheets and refrigerator magnets to hold them was effective in stimulating some discussion of nutrition issues (Solomon, 1989, p. 100).

A follow-up study of the Stanford Heart Disease Prevention Program (Roser et al., 1990) found that age was the strongest predictor of learning from the campaign, with younger audience members learning more than older audience members. In a way, this does not make sense, since younger adults are at less risk of having heart disease than older adults. The researchers explain the results by suggesting that younger adults were more interested in the campaign because of a group norm. The group norm was the shared belief in the youth culture that physical fitness is important and that there is a connection between fitness and beauty.

Flay (1987), in a summary of research on mass media programs designed to help people stop smoking, found that television self-help clinics that included social support in the form of group discussion were particularly effective. The studies examined by Flay suggested that making written materials available to accompany a television program will double its effectiveness, and that adding group discussions can triple it. Flay estimates that television self-help clinics are able to help 5–15 percent of participating smokers to quit permanently. Although this may sound like a small effect, if such a clinic were conducted once nationally, it could help between 2.5 million and 7.5 million of the nation's 50 million smokers to quit. It has been suggested that the same kind of television self-help clinic might be useful in getting people to modify other health-related behaviors such as alcohol and drug abuse, or sexual practices increasing the risk of AIDS and other sexually transmitted diseases (McAlister, Ramirez, Galavotti, & Gallion, 1989).

AUDIENCE SEGMENTATION

Another means for applying groups to mass communication is through audience segmentation. This technique was originally developed by advertisers, who referred to it as *market segmentation.* By segmenting the market, or dividing it into groups, advertisers could plan different communication strategies for each group. The groups targeted by advertisers are often groups identified by life-style. Television programming decisions are also often influenced by notions of audience segmentation. If a televison program is not attracting a viewing audience with the right demographics—and this usually means an audience with the income and desire to buy the program sponsors' products—the program is not likely to survive.

Audience segmentation has also become a useful technique in public relations. One approach recommended by Vogel (1994) involves using survey research to identify several different audience components:

1. *Active opponents.* Those who think the topic is important but disagree with your message.
2. *Active supporters.* Those who agree with you.
3. *Disinterested opponents.* Those who have little interest in the subject and disagree with your position.
4. *Disinterested supporters.* Those who don't have enough interest to be in the market for your message.
5. *Potential converts.* Those who have high interest in the subject but no firm opinion about it.
6. *The uninvolved.* Those who have no firm opinion and little interest.

Vogel argues that only two groups—active supporters and potential converts—are good candidates for messages. Different communication strategies should be used for the two target audiences. Active supporters need to receive reinforcing messages so that their support does not waver. Potential converts need to receive carefully designed persuasive messages, and they need to receive them more frequently than active supporters. Vogel also recommends addressing active supporters with short, snappy "sound bites" in the hope that they will pass them on to potential converts. This technique would be a deliberate effort to take advantage of the two-step flow of communication. This kind of analysis can help public relations clients to concentrate their efforts where their messages are likely to have the greatest effect.

Audience segmentation has also become an important technique in social marketing, or the use of communication techniques to help accomplish desirable social goals. For instance, audience segmentation has been recommended as a technique for addressing the problem of AIDS prevention in teenagers (Frankenberger & Sukhdial, 1994). Teenagers in general are at risk of acquiring the HIV, but subgroups of poor, racial, and ethnic minorities are at even greater risk.

The researchers recommend targeting each group with specific messages that are appropriate to that group. For example, if a group has perceptions of invulnerability, messages should provide information about teen AIDS cases. Media should also be chosen that are most appropriate for each group. For example, if African American teenagers receive most of their information from radio, then messages should be distributed through radio spots. Also, some of these groups are at much greater risk of acquiring AIDS than others, and probably should be the object of more intensive campaigns.

CONCLUSIONS

Groups have impact on mass communication in a number of ways:

1. Groups serve to anchor attitudes and make them hard to change. This was suggested by the Cooper and Jahoda study of the Mr. Biggott cartoons and also documented in the area of politics by the election studies of Lazarsfeld and his associates.

2. Knowledge of the groups that a person belongs to or identifies with can often help us predict the person's behavior. This is particularly true in the area of political preferences, where knowledge of five or six broad group categorizations about a person will often give a high degree of accuracy in predicting an election vote.

3. Effective programs of communication often involve a combination of mass communication and interpersonal communication. This is true of many of the well-organized charity fund drives and many election campaigns. Programs aimed at reducing the risk of heart disease or helping people to stop smoking suggest that a combination of mass media and interpersonal communication is also an effective approach in the health area.

4. Sometimes ways can be found to obtain some of the advantages of interpersonal communication through mass communication. Television programs in which a candidate answers questions telephoned in by viewers would be an example. So would presidential "citizens press conferences," in which the president answered questions phoned in by citizens during a national radio broadcast. Some of the same advantages can be obtained by having a panel of typical citizens in the studio to question a political candidate in a kind of "town meeting" format.

DISCUSSION

1. Asch's research reveals a strong tendency for people to conform to group pressure. But not everyone in the Asch experiments goes along with the group. What might be some characteristics of people who do not give in to group pressure?
2. What are some examples of behaviors that are the norm in one culture but not in other cultures?
3. Think of an example from your own life in which social norms exerted some control over your behavior.
4. What is the process by which norms are formed?
5. How does the social identification model change our thinking about the influence of groups?
6. What are some examples of advertisements that appeal to group norms or feelings of group membership?
7. The combination of mass communication and interpersonal communication seems to be particularly effective. What is an example of a communication campaign that has combined mass communication and interpersonal communication?
8. How is the idea of audience segmentation useful in a communication campaign in which you are trying to change people's attitudes?

REFERENCES

Alcoholics Anonymous World Services, Inc. (1967). *The A. A. Way of Life: A Reader by Bill*. New York: Author.

Asch, S. E. (1955). Opinions and social pressure. *Scientific American*, Nov., pp. 31-35.

Asch, S. E. (1956). Studies of independence and conformity. I. A minority of one against a unanimous majority. *Psychological Monographs* 70 (no. 9): 1-70.

Berelson, B. R., P. F. Lazarsfeld, and W. N. McPhee (1954). *Voting: A Study of Opinion Formation in a Presidential Campaign*. Chicago: University of Chicago Press.

Bettenhausen, K., and J. K. Murnighan (1985). The emergence of norms in competitive decision-making groups. *Administrative Science Quarterly* 30: 350-372.

Birch, D. (1995). Anti-smoking ads can work, experts say. *The Baltimore Sun*, Aug. 12, p. 1A.

Flay, B. R. (1987). *Selling the Smokeless Society: Fifty-Six Evaluated Mass Media Programs and Campaigns Worldwide*. Washington, D.C.: American Public Health Association.

Frankenberger, K. D., and A. S. Sukhdial (1994). Segmenting teens for AIDS preventive behaviors with implications for marketing communications. *Journal of Public Policy & Marketing* 13: 133-150.

Lazarsfeld, P. F., B. Berelson, and H. Gaudet (1968). *The People's Choice: How the Voter Makes Up His Mind in a Presidential Campaign,* 3rd ed. New York: Columbia University Press.

Lewin, K. (1958). Group decision and social change. In E. E. Maccoby, T. M. Newcomb, and E. L. Hartley (eds.), *Readings in Social Psychology,* 3rd ed., pp. 197-211. New York: Holt, Rinehart and Winston.

McAlister, A., A. G. Ramirez, C. Galavotti, and K. J. Gallion (1989). Antismoking campaigns: Progress in the application of social learning theory. In R. E. Rice and C. K. Atkin (eds.), *Public Communication Campaigns,* 2nd ed., pp. 291-307. Newbury Park, Calif.: Sage.

McBurney, D. H., and V. B. Collings (1977). *Introduction to Sensation/Perception.* Englewood Cliffs, N.J.: Prentice-Hall.

Maccoby, N., and J. W. Farquhar (1975). Communicating for health: Unselling heart disease. *Journal of Communication* 25 (no. 3): 114-126.

Maccoby, N., and J. W. Farquhar (1976). Bringing the California health report up to date. *Journal of Communication* 26 (no. 1): 56-57.

Marrow, A. J. (1977). *The Practical Theorist: The Life and Work of Kurt Lewin.* New York: Teachers College Press.

Pelz, E. B. (1958). Some factors in "group decision." In E. E. Maccoby, T. M. Newcomb, and E. L. Hartley (eds.), *Readings in Social Psychology,* 3rd ed., pp. 212-219. New York: Holt, Rinehart and Winston.

Price, V. (1988). On the public aspects of opinion: Linking levels of analysis in public opinion research. *Communication Research* 15 (no. 6): 659-679.

Roser, C., J. A. Flora, S. H. Chaffee, and J. W. Farquhar. (1990). Using research to predict learning from a PR campaign. *Public Relations Review* 16 (no. 2): 61-77.

Sherif, M. (1936). *The Psychology of Social Norms.* New York: Harper & Brothers.

Sherif, M. (1937). An experimental approach to the study of attitudes. *Sociometry* 1: 90-98.

Skedgell, R. A. (1966). How computers pick an election winner. *Transaction* 4 (no. 1): 42-46.

Solomon, D. S. (1989). A social marketing perspective on communication campaigns. In R. E. Rice and C. K. Atkin (eds.), *Public Communication Campaigns*, 2nd ed., pp. 87-104. Newbury Park, Calif.: Sage.

Turner, J. C. (1982). Towards a cognitive redefinition of the social group. In H. Tajfel (ed.), *Social Identity and Intergroup Relations*, pp. 15-40. Cambridge, Eng.: Cambridge University Press.

Vogel, A. (1994). Model aids in cost-effective communications. *Public Relations Journal* 50 (no. 2): 8-11.

chapter **11**

Mass Media and Interpersonal Communication

The decades between the two world wars saw an increasing concern with and a fear of the all-powerful nature of the mass media. During the decade of the 1920s many people became aware of how widespread and effective had been the use of propaganda during the First World War. After the war the use of advertising increased dramatically. The decade of the 1930s saw the rising use of radio to address huge audiences on both sides of the Atlantic. In the United States President Franklin Roosevelt overcame both a hostile press and a hostile Congress by going over their heads directly to the American people with his "fireside chats" on the radio. The impact of radio on the general public can be illustrated by the effect of a 1938 Halloween radio broadcast, Orson Welles's "War of the Worlds," which caused panic in some communities. In Europe radio was put to far different and more sustained and dangerous uses by Adolf Hitler in his attempt to conquer the world.

Under these conditions it is no surprise that the prevalent image of the mass media was that of a hypodermic needle or a bullet. This was a concept of the media with direct, immediate, and powerful effects on any individual they reached. It was parallel to the stimulus-response principle that characterized much of psychological research in the 1930s and 1940s.

The decade of the 1940s began with both Europe and Asia at war. Japanese armies were deep in China. Hitler's blitzkrieg had overrun Poland in a few weeks, then turned west, invaded Denmark and Norway, defeated France in six weeks, and forced the British to evacuate the remains of their army from the beaches of Dunkirk to defend their home islands. Under these circumstances President Roosevelt announced that he would run for a third term—a move unprecedented in American history.

At Columbia University a group of social scientists at the Bureau of Applied Social Research became concerned about the apparently all-pervasive direct effects of the media on individuals and what this might imply for the give and take of the democratic process.

THE MASS MEDIA AND VOTING BEHAVIOR

To investigate the effects of the mass media on political behavior, the researchers from the Columbia Bureau of Applied Social Research selected four groups of registered voters from Erie County, Ohio. This was a typical county in that it had voted in every presidential election as the nation had voted up to that time. These voters were then interviewed at intervals throughout the campaign to determine what factors had the greatest influence in their decision making regarding the election.

The design used three control groups to check on any effects of the seven monthly interviews of the main panel. All four groups (with 600 registered voters in each) were interviewed in May. The panel was interviewed every month after the May interview up to the November election and then immediately after it. Each of the three control groups was interviewed once after the initial interview—one in July, one in August, and one in October (Lazarsfeld, Berelson, & Gaudet, 1948).

Because the hypodermic model of the effects of mass media prevailed among communication researchers at the time, the 1940 Erie County study was designed to demonstrate the power of the mass media in affecting voting decisions. Two researchers said, "This study went to great lengths to determine how the mass media brought about such changes" (Lazarsfeld & Menzel, 1963, p. 96).

What the researchers found was that "personal contacts appear to have been both more frequent and more effective than the mass media in influencing voting decision" (Katz, 1957, p. 63). However, only 8 percent of the respondents actually switched from one candidate to another between the first interview in May and the last one in November. The researchers proposed that messages from the media first reach opinion leaders, who then pass on what they read or hear to associates or followers who look to them as influentials. This process was named the *two-step* flow of communication.

Because the design of the study did not anticipate the importance of interpersonal relations, the two-step flow concept was the one least well documented by the data. As a result, a number of other studies were later done to verify and refine the concept.

Among the conclusions of the 1940 voting study were the following (Katz, 1957):

1. Voters who decided late in the campaign or changed their minds during the campaign were more likely than others to cite personal influence as having figured in their decisions.

2. Opinion leaders were found at every social level and were presumed to be very much like the people they influenced.
3. Opinion leaders were found to be more exposed to the mass media than people who were not designated opinion leaders. (p. 63)

In the 1940 voting study, a panel of voters was drawn at random. Respondents were asked if they had tried to convince anyone of their political ideas or if anyone had asked their advice on political matters. Besides the question of the validity of designating opinion leaders by this method, there is also another problem. The data result in only two subgroups, those who report themselves to be opinion leaders and those who do not. There is no way to compare individual opinion leaders with the specific individuals who look to them for advice.

As the 1940 voting study was being completed, another study in Rovere, a small New Jersey town, was begun. A sample of 86 persons was asked to name the people from whom they sought information and advice. Individuals named four or more times were considered opinion leaders and were interviewed in depth. In Rovere there was certainly greater validity in designating individuals as opinion leaders than in the Erie County study, and they were no doubt influential with a greater number of people. In the Rovere study the original sample was used only to identify the opinion leaders. After that all of the attention was focused on the attributes of the opinion leaders.

When the war ended, the researchers were able to resume their work on opinion leadership with a study in Decatur, Illinois. Here the research was able to compare the leader with the person who named the leader or, more technically, to examine the adviser-advisee dyad. Do the adviser and advisee tend to be of the same social class, age, and sex? Is the leader more exposed to the mass media than the follower? Is the leader more interested in the topic of influence than the follower?

It was during the Decatur research that the investigators saw the need to examine chains of influence longer than a dyad. Opinion leaders were reporting that they had been influenced by other opinion leaders. Also, opinion leaders were found to be influential only at certain times and only on certain issues. Opinion leaders are influential not only because of who they are (social status, age, sex, etc.) but also because of the structure and values of the groups they are members of.

THE ROLE OF THE COMMUNITY
IN DECISION MAKING

It also became clear that although the earlier research had allowed for the study of individual decisions, it did not permit study of decision making on a community level. The next study introduced the notion of diffusion, or widening communication of a new idea, over time through the social structure of a community (Katz, 1957).The diffusion study examined how medical doctors make decisions to adopt new drugs. All doctors in several specialties in four midwestern cities were interviewed. Besides the usual demographic data (age, medical school attended, etc.) and data about attitudes, prescription of drugs, exposure to information sources and influence, and other details, the doctors were asked to name the three colleagues they were most apt to talk with about cases, the three they were most apt to seek information and advice from, and the three they were most likely to socialize with.

These questions regarding a doctor's interactions with colleagues allowed the researchers to "map" the interpersonal relations in the medical communities. The study also allowed focus on a specific item (a new drug) as it gained acceptance, and a record over time (through prescriptions on file at pharmacies).

In the drug study, an objective record of decision making (the prescriptions) was available as an additional source of information (along with the self-report of the doctor). Also inferences could be drawn about the different influences on the making of a decision. For example, early adopters were more likely to attend out-of-town medical meetings in their specialties. The mapping of inter-personal relations made possible inferences regarding the effect of social relations in decision making.

Findings about Opinion Leadership

The following conclusions were reached from the series of studies after the 1940 voting study:

1. Personal influence was both more frequent and more effective than any of the mass media, not only in politics but also in marketing, fashion decisions, and movie attendance (these last three were investigated in the Decatur study). In the case of the drug diffusion study, the doctors most integrated in the medical community were the ones most likely to be early adopters of the innovation. The doctors most frequently named as discussion partners were most apt to be innovators. Extent of integration proved more important than the doctor's age, medical school, income of patients, readership of medical journals, or any other factor examined. The researchers attributed the innovativeness of doctors who are integrated in their respective medical communities to their being in touch and up to date with medical developments. They also noted that these were the doctors who could count on social support from their colleagues when facing the risks of innovation in medicine.

2. Interpersonal influence in primary groups is effective in maintaining a high degree of homogeneity of opinions and actions within a group. In the voting studies, voters who changed their minds reported initially that they had intended to vote differently from their families or friends. Medical doctors tended to prescribe the same drugs as their closest colleagues, especially when treating the more puzzling diseases.

3. In the decision-making process, different media play different roles. Some media inform about or announce the existence of an item, while others legitimate or make acceptable a given course of action.

Who will lead and who will follow is determined, to a large extent, by the subject matter under consideration. In the area of marketing, opinion leadership was concentrated among older women with larger families. In the Rovere study, some individuals were opinion leaders in "local" affairs while others were influential in "cosmopolitan" affairs. In the areas of fashion and movie attendance the young unmarried woman was most often the opinion leader. The researchers found that an opinion leader in one area is unlikely to be an opinion leader in another, unrelated area.

But people talk most often to others like themselves. In marketing, fashions, movie attendance, and public affairs, opinion leaders were found at every socioeconomic and occupational level.

If opinion leaders are found at all levels, what distinguishes the leaders from their followers?

The researchers concluded that the following factors differentiate leaders from their followers:

1. Personification of values (who one is)
2. Competence (what one knows)
3. Strategic social location (whom one knows)

Strategic social location actually involves two sets of contacts: whom one knows within the group in which opinion leadership is exercised and whom one knows outside of the group for information on topics salient to the group.

Personification of values is another way of saying that the influential person is someone that followers wish to emulate. The "influencee" admires the influential and wishes to become as similar as possible. However, the opinion leader must also be regarded as knowledgeable or competent in the area in which leadership is sought. We seldom pay attention to the opinions of people who don't seem to know what they are talking about.

Even if one is both the type of person others want to emulate and is competent, one must also be accessible to the people who are interested in the area in which leadership is sought. To be a leader one must have followers. As mentioned, an individual is also most apt to be an opinion leader if he or she maintains contacts outside the group, who in turn provide information and opinions of interest to the group members. This was found to be true in many diverse areas of opinion leadership (politics, medicine, and farming, among others).

Opinion leaders were found to be more exposed to media appropriate to their sphere of influence than their followers. The Rovere study found that opinion leaders on "cosmopolitan" matters were more likely to read national news magazines than people who were influential on "local" matters. In the drug study the influential medical doctors were more likely to read a large number of professional journals and value them more highly than their less influential colleagues. They also attended more out-of-town meetings and had more out-of-town contacts as well. One researcher observed, "the greater exposure of the opinion leader to the mass media may only be a special case of the more general proposition that opinion leaders serve to relate their groups to relevant parts of the environment through whatever media happen to be appropriate" (Katz, 1957, p. 76).

The Interpersonal Environment

Opinion leaders and their followers are very similar and usually belong to the same groups. It is highly unlikely that the opinion leader will be very far ahead of followers in level of interest in a given topic. Interpersonal relations are not only networks of communication but also sources of social pressure to conform to the group's norms and sources of social support for the values and opinions an individual holds.

Two other authors, in discussing this interaction of media, social, and psychological variables in the communication process, have written (De Fleur & Larsen, 1958):

> In more recent times it has been realized that mass media information is received, passed on, distorted, assimilated, rejected, or acted upon in ways which are in part determined by the operation of various social and social-psychological systems at various points of transmission and reception as the flow of information takes place. Therefore, for the student of mass communication the operation of primary groups, role structures, voluntary associations, personality variables, and vast complexes of other variables related to the operation of "diffusion networks" have become a new research domain. The developing model of the operation of the mass media couples the mass communication process to the social networks of family, work, play, school and community. (p. xiii)

As pointed out at the beginning of this chapter, most media researchers during the 1930s and even the 1940s employed the hypodermic needle model of communication in their thinking of media effects—direct, immediate, and powerful. As more sophisticated methods were employed by media researchers, the hypodermic model was recognized as far too simplistic. Throughout the 1940s and 1950s communication researchers began to recognize many psychological and sociological variables that intervene between the media and the mind of the receiver (selective exposure, attention, perception, and retention; group memberships, norms, and salience; opinion leadership, etc.).

Two of the researchers involved in the series of studies done at Columbia concluded, "The whole moral . . . is that knowledge of an individual's interpersonal environment is basic to an understanding of his exposure and reactions to the mass media" (Katz & Lazarsfeld, 1955, p. 133).

CRITICISMS OF THE TWO-STEP FLOW

Numerous criticisms have been made of the two-step flow model. Here is a review of some of them.

1. Many studies indicate that major news stories are spread directly by the mass media to a far greater extent than by personal sources. Westley (1971, p. 726) cites several studies supporting this and discusses them briefly.

2. Findings show that opinions on public affairs are reciprocal or that often there is "opinion sharing rather than opinion giving." Troldahl and Van Dam (1965, p. 633) say that opinion givers "were not significantly different [from seekers] in their exposure to relevant media content, their information level on national news, their occupational prestige, and four of five attributes of gregariousness."

3. Related to point 2 is the observation by Lin (1971, p. 203) that "the definition of the opinion leader versus non-opinion leader dichotomy is also unclear and the problem is further confounded by varying operationalizing methods." He adds that opinion leadership has been determined by both self-designation and nomination and has been applied to both specific topics and general activities.

4. Empirical definitions of mass media vary. In some instances specialized media (special bulletins, medical journals, farm journals) have been used; in other instances they have not been part of the definition of the mass media (Lin, 1971, p. 204).

5. Other investigators (Rogers & Shoemaker, 1971, p. 206) have pointed out that opinion leaders can be either active or passive whereas the two-step flow model implies a dichotomy between active information-seeking opinion leaders and a mass audience of passive individuals who then rely on the opinion leaders for guidance.

6. The original model is limited to two steps, whereas the process may involve more or even fewer. As already mentioned, however, the Columbia group saw the need to investigate longer chains of influence during the Decatur study and followed this line of study in the drug diffusion research.

7. It is implied that opinion leaders rely on mass media channels only. Sometimes, especially in developing countries without extensive networks of mass media, personal trips and conversations with change agents assume the information role that mass media might normally play.

8. Early knowers and late knowers of the same information behave differently. It was found that early knowers of information more often rely on media sources and late knowers more on interpersonal sources (Rogers & Shoemaker, 1971, pp. 259, 348).

9. In the diffusion of an innovation it was found that mass media serve primarily to inform whereas interpersonal channels are most important at persuading. Rogers and Shoemaker (1971, p. 208) contended that these differences applied to both opinion leaders and followers.

The criticisms of the two-step flow model are mainly that it originally did not explain enough. As we shall see, subsequent work has considerably expanded and refined the model—as one would expect in the case of any cumulative research.

DIFFUSION OF INNOVATIONS

The two-step flow model has evolved gradually into a multistep flow model that is often used in diffusion research, the study of the social process of how innovations (new ideas, practices, objects, etc.) become known and are spread throughout a social system. The two-step flow model is mainly concerned with how an individual receives information and passes it along to others; the diffusion process concentrates on the final stage of the adoption or rejection of an innovation.

Probably the best-known and most widely respected researcher in diffusion research today is Everett Rogers. In his book, *Diffusion of Innovations* (third edition published in 1983), he examines more than 2,000 empirical diffusion research reports and 3,000 publications to revise earlier theory about the innovation decision process, a result of the vast increase in diffusion research in recent years. Rogers defines an innovation as "an idea, practice, or object that is perceived as new by an individual or another unit of adoption" (pp. xviii, 11).

One of the most influential diffusion studies of all time dealt with the diffusion of hybrid seed corn among Iowa farmers (Ryan & Gross, 1943). The innovation, released to Iowa farmers in 1928, resulted in agricultural innovations for more than 20 years and a revolution in farm productivity. The Ryan and Gross study formed the classical diffusion paradigm. The investigation included each of the four main elements of diffusion: (1) an innovation, (2) communicated through certain channels, (3) over time, and (4) among the members of a social system. The following steps were taken:

1. Some 259 farmers were interviewed to ascertain when and how they adopted hybrid seed corn and to obtain information about them and their farm operations.
2. The rate of adoption was plotted over time (resulting in the familiar S curve).
3. Farmers were assigned to adopter categories based on time of adoption of the new seed corn.
4. Various communication channels were identified as playing different roles in the innovation decision process. (See Rogers, 1983, pp. 32–34; 54–56.)

In his third edition, Rogers shifts emphasis from a unidirectional communication activity to information exchange among participants in a communication process. As a theoretical framework Rogers uses the concepts of uncertainty and information of Shannon and Weaver. An innovation generates a kind of uncertainty in that it provides an alternative to present methods or ideas.

Rogers categorizes the characteristics of an innovation that affect their rate of adoption as follows (1983):

1. *Relative advantage*—the degree to which an innovation is perceived as better than the idea it supersedes
2. *Compatibility*—the degree to which an innovation is perceived as being consistent with the existing values, past experiences, and needs of potential adopters
3. *Complexity*—the degree to which an innovation is perceived as difficult to understand and use
4. *Trialability*—the degree to which an innovation may be experimented with on a limited basis
5. *Observability*—the degree to which the results of an innovation are visible to others (pp. 15-16, ch. 6)

Rogers adds that "in general, innovations that are perceived by receivers as having greater relative advantage, compatibility, trialability, observability, and less complexity will be adopted more rapidly than other innovations" (1983, p. 16).

In a major article dealing with the adoption of technology, Rosenberg (1995) lists and discusses constraints on an innovator's ability to foresee the impact of an innovation. They include: its initial primitive form; its potential specialized uses; complementary and competitive relationships among technologies; and the economic value of the innovation.

Two other researchers, Rosen and Weil (1995), look at the demographic and psychological characteristics which might explain technological avoidance. They conclude that across 32 types of technology certain "discriminators" predict which *adults* will use or not use business and consumer technology. These characteristics, in order of importance, include: age; technophobia; computer training; and income.

For *teenagers* the factors rank somewhat differently: family income level; ethnic background; and, in some cases, technophobia. Their data demonstrate, as might be expected, that as family income increases teenagers are more likely to have used a personal computer, and significantly more black and Hispanic teenagers have never used a personal computer. Additionally, those who never used a personal computer had substantially more technophobia.

Heterophily and Homophily

Diffusion is defined as a special type of communication concerned with the spread of innovations. In the discussion of the two-step flow model we have seen that opinion leaders and their followers are remarkably similar in many attributes. Diffusion research calls this similarity *homophily,* or the degree to which pairs of individuals who interact are similar in certain attributes such as beliefs, values, education, or social status. However, in the diffusion of an innovation, heterophily is most often present. *Heterophily* is the degree to which pairs of individuals who interact are different in certain attributes (the mirror opposite of homophily). A high degree of source-receiver heterophily, often present in the diffusion of innovations since new ideas often come from people who are quite different from the receiver, creates unique problems in obtaining effective communication.

The Innovation Decision Process

The innovation decision process is a mental process through which an individual or other unit making decisions passes. The process consists of five stages:

1. *Knowledge*—exposure to an innovation and some understanding of how it functions
2. *Persuasion*—formation of an attitude toward the innovation
3. *Decision*—activity resulting in a choice to adopt or reject the innovation
4. *Implementation*—putting the innovation into use
5. *Confirmation*—reinforcement or reversal of the innovation decision made (see Rogers, 1983, ch. 5)

Rogers specifies five adapter categories, classifying individuals or other decision-making units in their rate of adoption of an innovation:

1. *Innovators*—venturesome; eager to try new ideas, more cosmopolite relationships than their peers
2. *Early adopters*—respectable localities, usually highest degree of opinion leadership within social system
3. *Early majority*—deliberate, interact frequently with their peers but seldom hold leadership positions
4. *Late majority*—skeptical; often adopt an innovation because of economic necessity or increasing network pressure
5. *Laggards*—traditionals; most localite; many are near-isolates; point of reference is the past (see Rogers, 1983, ch. 7)

Consequences are the changes that occur to an individual or to a social system as a result of the adoption or rejection of an innovation (Rogers, 1983, p. 31). Rogers lists three classifications of consequences:

1. *Desirable* versus *undesirable* consequences, depending on whether the effects of an innovation in a social system are functional or dysfunctional
2. *Direct* versus *indirect* consequences, depending on whether the changes to an individual or to a social system occur in immediate response to an innovation or as a second-order result of the direct consequences of an innovation

3. *Anticipated* versus *unanticipated* consequences, depending on whether or not the changes are recognized and intended by the members of a social system (see Rogers, 1983, pp. 31–32, ch. 11)

As Rogers points out, not all innovations, however well intended, have desirable consequences. The effects of an innovation on a social system may well be dysfunctional.

An undesirable consequence of the introduction of television in many developing countries has been to raise expectations above levels which a society is able to meet. One reporter (Weinraub, 1991, p. 2), in an article about India, wrote:

What is significant, however, is that at least one television set has now entered even many of the most primitive villages. The pictures of refrigerators and toilets, running water, clean clothes and other facets of middle-class life raise expectations, and India has witnessed an unprecedented level of restlessness and rage among the poor. . . . Gangs of the poor and so-called untouchables are increasingly murdering and hacking landlords and upper-caste Indians, out of sheer rage at their plight.

Millions of farmers in Asia were taught to grow rice the modern way, using lots of insecticides. International researchers now say that according to the latest studies, using insecticides actually hurts rice farmers because they disrupt the ecological balance. They make insect problems worse and make farmers sick. Now the researchers have to go back to those millions of farmers and teach them to stop using the insecticides they once insisted were necessary. Today the U.N. Food and Agriculture Organization is using "shade tree" farm schools in Indonesia, Vietnam, Thailand, and the Philippines to train small groups of farmers to use less chemicals. They are also developing new ways to teach illiterate people how to change their behavior. (Zwerdling, 1994)

Communication channels may either be interpersonal or mass media in nature or may originate from either localite or cosmopolite sources (Rogers, 1983, p. 198). Cosmopolite communication channels are those from outside the social system being investigated; localite channels are from inside the social system being investigated (p. 200). Research shows that these channels play different roles in the diffusion process. Mass media channels reach large audiences rapidly, spread information, and change weakly held attitudes. Interpersonal channels provide a two-way exchange of information and are more effective than the mass media in dealing with resistance or apathy on the part of the receiver. An interpersonal source can add information or clarify points and perhaps surmount psychological and social barriers (selective exposure, attention, perception, retention; group norms, values, etc.). In the process of diffusion of an innovation, the mass media channels and the cosmopolite channels are relatively more important at the knowledge stage, whereas the interpersonal channels and local channels are more effective at the persuasion stage. Mass media channels and cosmopolite channels are relatively more important than interpersonal channels and localite channels for earlier adopters than for late adopters (Rogers, 1983, pp. 197–201).

Change Agents

In the diffusion of innovation, change agents play key roles in the evaluation and trial stages. A *change agent* is a professional person who attempts to influence adoption decisions in a direction that he or she feels desirable. Often a change agent will use local opinion leaders to assist in diffusing an innovation or to prevent the adoption of what may be seen as a harmful innovation. Change agents usually have more education and status than the individuals they are trying to influence, making them heterophilous from their clients. To overcome this they frequently use aides, often recruited from the local population, who are usually more homophilous with the people they are trying to reach. Change agents can be salespeople and dealers in new products (e.g., hybrid seed corn), representatives of pharmaceutical companies promoting new drugs to medical doctors, technical assistance workers in developing nations, and many others who serve to link individual social systems together. The role of change agents in the evaluation and trial of innovations is especially important to advertising and public relations (see Rogers, ch. 9).

One author points out that (Lerbinger, 1972):

> when a gatekeeper is a commercial change agent, his integrity is questioned by the people he seeks to change. His vulnerability is best understood by seeing him in a conflict situation: he is responsible to the bureaucracy that pays him, but he must simultaneously satisfy the need of the so-called client system—the people he seeks to influence. His credibility is impaired if he appears to execute the demands of the bureaucracy while disregarding the expectations of the client system. This happens to a commercial change agent when people feel that he promotes the over-adoption of new ideas to secure higher sales. These findings suggest that a public communicator's credibility will be low when he is seen as ignoring the interests of a public in favor of his employer's interests. (p. 197)

In an earlier edition Rogers and Shoemaker (1971) contended that a "combination of mass media and interpersonal communication is the most effective way of reaching people with new ideas and persuading them to utilize these innovations" (p. 260). They cite and discuss the use of media forums (organized small groups of individuals who meet regularly to receive a mass media program, broadcast or print, and then discuss its content) in Canada, India, Africa, China, Latin America, and Italy. Father Coughlin apparently used media forums in the United States in the 1930s. We have also seen the use of discussion groups in Kurt Lewin's efforts to change housewives' attitudes toward less desirable cuts of meat during World War II.

Diffusion of News

One of the subcategories within diffusion research is news diffusion. Melvin L. De Fleur (1988) summarized four decades of research about the flow of news from media sources through a population.

He concluded that the 1960s were the most active period for news diffusion research.

From more than two dozen studies of the diffusion of information conducted since the Erie County study of 1944, De Fleur makes the following generalizations:

1. Changing media technologies in the United States have led to changes in the way people receive their first information about important news events. Television has become the most frequently cited source, followed by radio. Newspapers have become, for the most part, suppliers of greater detail at a later time. Word of mouth remains important in some cases.

2. Most people get most of their news directly from a medium, rather than from other people. The two-step flow model does not describe the pattern by which most of the daily news reaches the public. The majority have firsthand contact with television or radio, and, on some occasions, with a newspaper for their first exposure to a story.

3. News events of deep concern to large numbers of people will move faster and farther within a population, whatever the first source, than stories of less emotional nature. This generalization refers to the so called news value of a story. It remains a poorly defined, if intuitively understood, concept. The uses and gratifications provided by news stories of high versus low news values are largely unknown.

De Fleur adds that word of mouth may still be the most significant source of learning about an event for stories of very high news value. But even then, truly urgent news travels between all kinds of people, rather than only from opinion leaders as described by the two-step flow.

Patterns of first exposure to sources of news and later diffusion vary depending on the time of day. Different sources (media and interpersonal) are used at different times of the day.

Individual differences and social categories shape people's interest in a news item and the social networks from which they get information. Different types of people use different ways to learn about a particular event (1988, p. 81).

De Fleur concludes with the statement:

The news industry may have a special responsibility to support research on the diffusion of news. The industry often claims that it enjoys a privileged status within our society, protected and guaranteed by constitutional law. Traditionally, the press has justified those claims by maintaining that it serves the needs of citizens in a democracy, by providing them with accurate information about what is really going on. This is supposed to provide the basis for intelligent decision making, which leads to better government, and so forth. But there appear to be real questions as to whether these claims have a solid foundation in fact. Does the present system that our society uses to disseminate the news actually keep citizens informed, thereby achieving those cherished democratic ideals? From the research evidence already accumulated, even with all of its warts, there are grounds to suspect that the system does not work all that well. (p. 81)

De Fleur concludes with a series of unanswered questions about the diffusion of information in our society. He raises questions about who is informed by which medium, with what completeness, and with how much distortion. He also asks what media people rely on for confirmation and interpretation, how this information shapes their view of reality, and whether these views differ from the actual events reported in the media. De Fleur wonders how the system can be redesigned to improve its quality and thoroughness and ends by asking if the press is "forever beyond accountability in assessments of its performance" (p. 81).

CONCLUSIONS

The available evidence indicates that the greatest effect is achieved when media messages advocating innovation or attitude change are coupled with small group discussion. Among the reasons given are social expectations and the pressures applied by the group on individuals to attend and participate and the effects of group pressures on attitude change. As Rogers and Shoemaker pointed out, "Media forums serve to heighten the impact of change-oriented messages by reducing the possibility of selective exposure and selective perception" (1971. p. 264).

As the De Fleur review of research about diffusion of information demonstrated, we have much to learn about how various types of news are diffused and what can be done to improve the diffusion of information. These are important questions for our form of government.

DISCUSSION

1. What is meant by the bullet or hypodermic image of the mass media?
2. Give examples of significant media campaigns before 1945.
3. What was the Erie County study? What did it conclude?
4. What is an opinion leader? What are his or her traits?
5. What factors differentiate opinion leaders from followers?
6. What are some of the criticisms of the two-step flow?
7. Define "innovation."

8. What characteristics of an innovation affect its adoption?
9. What characteristics of adults predict who will use new technologies? What characteristics of teenagers predict who will use new technologies?
10. What are "heterophily" and "homophily"?
11. Name and discuss the steps in the decision process.
12. What are Rogers's five adopter categories? How are they defined?

REFERENCES

De Fleur, M. L. (1988). Diffusing information. *Society* 25: 72–81.

De Fleur. M. L., and O. Larsen (1958). *The Flow of Information.* New York: Harper.

Katz, E. (1957). The two-step flow of communication: An up-to-date report of an hypothesis. *Public Opinion Quarterly* 21: 61–78. Also in W. Schramm (ed.) (1960), *Mass Communications.* Urbana: University of Illinois Press.

Katz. E., and P. F. Lazarsfeld (1955). *Personal Influence: The Part Played by People in the Flow of Mass Communications.* Glencoe, Ill.: Free Press.

Lazarsfeld, P F., B. R. Berelson, and H. Gaudet (1948). *The People's Choice.* New York: Columbia University Press.

Lazarsfeld, P. F., and H. Menzel (1963). Mass media and personal influence. In W Schramm (ed.), *The Science of Human Communication.* New York: Basic Books.

Lerbinger. O. (1972) *Designs for Persuasive Communication.* Englewood Cliffs, N.J.: Prentice-Hall.

Lin. N. (1971). *The Study of Human Communication.* Indianapolis, Ind.: Bobbs-Merrill.

Rogers, E. (1983) *Diffusion of Innovations.* 3rd ed. New York: Free Press.

Rogers, E., and F. Shoemaker (1971). *Communication of Innovations.* New York: Free Press.

Rosen, Larry D., and Michelle M. Weil (1995). Adult and teenage use of consumer, business, and entertainment technology: potholes on the information superhighway? *Journal of Consumer Affairs* 29 (no. 1, June 22): 55.

Rosenberg, Nathan (1995). Why technology forecasts often fail. *The Futurist* 29 (no. 4, July): 16.

Ryan, B., and N. Gross (1943). The diffusion of hybrid seed corn in two Iowa communities. *Rural Sociology* 8: 15–24.

Troldahl, V., and R. Van Dam (1965). Face-to-face communication about major topics in the news. *Public Opinion Quarterly* 29: 626–634.

Weinraub, Bernard (1991). India peers at its future with a sense of gloom. *New York Times,* July 14, p. E2.

Westley, B. (1971). Communication and social change. *American Behavioral Scientist* 14: 719–742.

Zwerdling, Daniel (1994). Philippines farmers learning to return to green. *National Public Radio, All Things Considered,* Aug. 7, Transcript #1567-5 (Available in Lexis/Nexis news data bank.)

part V

Mass Media Effects and Uses

A major concern of communication theory for years—and probably rightfully so—has been to investigate the effects of mass communication. The mass media have become a major force in society, and it is reasonable to wonder about the effects that this force is producing. Are the effects of mass communication large or small? Are they malevolent or benign? Are they obvious or subtle? Communication theorists have tried to answer these and other questions about the effects of mass communication.

One of the effects of mass communication seems to be to direct our attention to certain problems or issues. This effect is called the agenda-setting function of the mass media, and it is described in Chapter 12.

Information is sometimes thought of as the cure for many problems, and there is undoubtedly some truth in that idea. But if information is thought of as a method of reducing the social inequality gap between the rich and the poor in society, the cure may not work the way it is expected to. Recent research has indicated that an increased flow of information can lead to the widening of a knowledge gap between the well-off and the not-so-well-off. Chapter 13 takes an in-depth look at this knowledge gap hypothesis.

There are a number of other possible effects of mass communication besides the agenda-setting function and the knowledge gap. These range from Marshall McLuhan's visionary thinking about the effects of new communication technology on our very thought processes to

Elisabeth Noelle-Neumann's spiral of silence, a theory of the formation of public opinion that draws heavily on earlier research on the power of social groups. Chapter 14 is devoted to these and a number of other theories of the effects of mass communication.

Focusing on the effects of mass communication can have its drawbacks, however. This approach to theory can cause us to view the audience as a passive target that is vulnerable and inactive in the communication process. It can cause theorists—and those of us reading their theories—to overlook the active role of the communication receiver. The active role of the communication receiver is a basic premise of the uses and gratifications approach to the study of mass communication, an approach that is described in Chapter 15.

chapter 12

Agenda Setting

From 1986 to 1989, public opinion polls show a public becoming more and more concerned about the drug problem in the United States (see Figure 12.1, p. 250). During the same time period, the percentage of people reporting illegal drug use steadily dropped. What could cause this apparent misperception by the public (Bare, 1990)?

During this period, the Bush administration declared its "war on drugs." The number of newspaper stories dealing with the drug war increased dramatically at this time, particularly toward the end (see Figure 12.2, p. 251).

One explanation for the public's increasing tendency to perceive drugs as the nation's most important problem lies in the concept of agenda setting. The agenda-setting function of the media refers to the media's capability, through repeated news coverage, of raising the importance of an issue in the public's mind.

This example of the "war on drugs" has a clear lesson for the working journalist—look beyond the rhetoric of official statements. The "war on drugs" episode suggests that reporters should look for data that can indicate what is really going on.

Another example of agenda setting comes from the muckraking period of American journalism. Lincoln Steffens describes it in a chapter of his autobiography titled "I Make a Crime Wave." Steffens was working for a New York newspaper, the *Evening Post*. He says that there were always a lot of crime stories being told in the basement of the police station that were not reported in the newspapers. One day he decided to report one of these stories because it involved a well-known family. When the story came out, Jake Riis, the police reporter for the *Evening Sun*, was asked by his newspaper why he didn't have the story. Riis had to find another crime story to make up for it. Soon, all the New York papers were working to find crimes of their own to keep up with

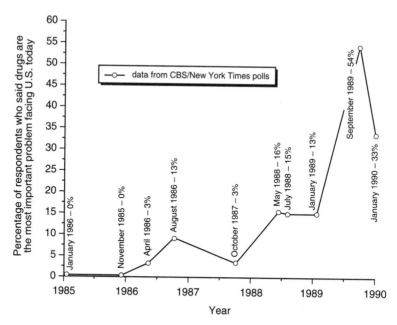

FIGURE 12.1 Percentage of respondents who said drugs are the most important problem facing the country today

SOURCE: From J. Bare, "The War on Drugs: A Case Study in Opinion Formation," *The Public Perspective,* November/December, 1990, p. 31. © *The Public Perspective,* a publication of the Roper Center for Public Opinion Research, University of Connecticut, Storrs. Reprinted by permission.

the others. They would even rewrite each other's, adding still more. The result was a sudden increase in crimes reported in the newspaper, which was perceived as a "crime wave." Teddy Roosevelt, who was police commissioner, personally looked into the "crime wave," and also took credit for stopping it once he found out it was really caused by Steffens and Riis (Steffens, 1931).

In the Steffens example, the public, as well as public officials, came to see crime as an important issue simply because crime stories were getting more play in the newspapers. That is agenda setting at work. In both these examples, we see the possible action of agenda setting—mass media attention to an issue causing that issue to be elevated in importance to the public.

THE CHAPEL HILL STUDY

The first systematic study of the agenda-setting hypothesis was reported in 1972 by McCombs and Shaw (1972). They studied agenda setting in the presidential campaign of 1968 and hypothesized that the mass media set the agenda for each

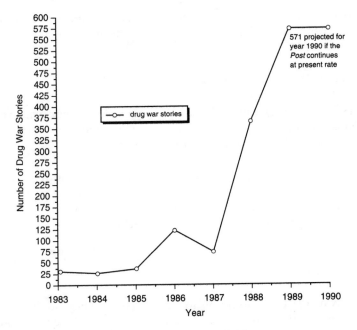

FIGURE 12.2 Drug war stories in the
Washington Post

SOURCE: From J. Bare, "The War on Drugs: A Case Study in
Opinion Formation." *The Public Perspective,* November/December,
1990, p. 31. © *The Public Perspective,* a publication of the
Roper Center for Public Opinion Research, University of
Connecticut, Storrs. Reprinted by permission.

political campaign, influencing the salience of attitudes toward the political
issues. They conducted their study by focusing on undecided voters in Chapel
Hill, North Carolina, because "undecideds" should be most susceptible to agenda-
setting effects. The researchers interviewed a sample of 100 respondents and
simultaneously conducted a content analysis of the mass media serving these
voters—five newspapers, two newsmagazines, and two television network
evening news broadcasts. Respondents were asked to cite the major problems
in the country, as they saw them. These responses were coded into 15 categories
representing the major issues, as well as other types of campaign news. The
news media content dealing with the election was also sorted into these
15 categories, by amount. News media content was also divided into "major"
and "minor" categories.

The findings supported an agenda-setting effect. For major items, the
correlation between emphasis in the media on an issue and voter perception of
that issue as important was .967. For minor items, the correlation was .979. As
the authors point out, these data suggest a very strong relationship between the

emphasis placed on different campaign issues by the media and the judgments of voters as to the salience and importance of various campaign topics.

PRECURSORS OF THE HYPOTHESIS

Researchers before McCombs and Shaw had some ideas that were very similar to the agenda-setting hypothesis. A rather direct statement of the agenda-setting idea appears in a 1958 article by Norton Long (1958):

> In a sense, the newspaper is the prime mover in setting the territorial agenda. It has a great part in determining what most people will be talking about, what most people will think the facts are, and what most people will regard as the way problems are to be dealt with. (p. 260)

Kurt Lang and Gladys Engel Lang (1959) also came up with an early statement on the agenda-setting idea:

> The mass media force attention to certain issues. They build up public images of political figures. They are constantly presenting objects suggesting what individuals in the mass should think about, know about, have feelings about. (p. 232)

Another statement of the agenda-setting idea that is repeated in almost every book or article on the topic is this statement by Bernard Cohen (1963) about the power of the press:

> It may not be successful much of the time in telling people what to think, but it is stunningly successful in telling its readers what to think about. (p. 13)

A CHANGE IN THINKING

The agenda-setting hypothesis came about when researchers became dissatisfied with the dominant theoretical position in mass communication research during the 1950s and 1960s—the limited effects model. Joseph Klapper stated this model well in his book *The Effects of Mass Communication* (1960) when he wrote, "Mass communication ordinarily does not serve as a necessary and sufficient cause of audience effects, but rather functions among and through a nexus of mediating factors and influences" (p. 8).

To some people, the idea that the mass media ordinarily did not have any effects just did not seem very reasonable. Researchers also began to consider the possibility that they might have been looking for effects in the wrong places. For many years, the approach used in communication research was to look for attitude change and most of the research had found that the mass media have little effect in this area. But perhaps researchers were looking at the wrong target. Maybe the mass media had their effects on people's perceptions—their views of the world—rather than on their attitudes.

This change in thinking by communication researchers might also have been reinforced by a change taking place at the same time in the field of psychology. The 1950s marked the emergence of cognitive psychology as a rival to the then-dominant approach, behaviorism. Behaviorism stressed the importance of reinforcement, rewards and punishments, and conditioning in shaping behavior, and attempted to use these concepts to explain even human thought and language (Skinner, 1957). Cognitive psychology, in contrast, saw men and women as active seekers of knowledge who function in the world on the basis of this knowledge (Neisser, 1967). In this view, people are seen as "problem solvers" rather than as objects of conditioning or manipulation. Cognitive psychology is concerned with the "representations" of the world people build in their heads and how they go about building them. The agenda-setting hypothesis, by investigating the salience or importance that people assign to certain issues and how these saliences are arrived at, is very compatible with cognitive psychology.

THE MEDIA AGENDA AND REALITY

Researcher G. Ray Funkhouser was interested in the relationship between news coverage and public perception of the importance of issues. Funkhouser also brought in another aspect, however—the actual prominence of the specific issues in reality. He focused his study on the 1960s, an active decade in which many issues were prominent. To get his measure of public opinion about which issues were important, Funkhouser used Gallup polls in which people were asked about "the most important problem facing America." He obtained his measures of media content by counting the number of articles on each issue appearing in the three weekly newsmagazines (*Time, Newsweek,* and *U.S. News and World Report*) for each year in the decade. The measure of the importance of an issue in reality was based on statistics taken from *Statistical Abstracts of the United States* and other sources.

Funkhouser then looked at the relationship between public opinion and media content, and the relationship between media content and reality. The first relationship—the relationship between public rating of the importance of issues and media content—is shown in Table 12.1. The table shows a strong correspondence between public ranking of an issue as important and the amount of coverage given the issue by the media. The issues to which the public gave a high ranking were also the issues to which the mass media (or, at least, the three newsmagazines) were giving a lot of coverage.

In the second part of his study, Funkhouser looked at the relationship between media coverage and reality. This analysis is not one that can be summarized easily in a table. The pattern that Funkhouser found, however, seemed to

TABLE 12.1 Amount of coverage given by national news magazines to various issues during the 1960s, and rank scores of the issues as "Most important problem facing America" during that period.

Issue	Number of Articles	Coverage Rank	Importance Rank
Vietnam War	861	1	1
Race relations (and urban riots)	687	2	2
Campus unrest	267	3	4
Inflation	234	4	5
Television and mass media	218	5	12*
Crime	203	6	3
Drugs	173	7	9
Environment and pollution	109	8	6
Smoking	99	9	12*
Poverty	74	10	7
Sex (declining morality)	62	11	8
Women's rights	47	12	12*
Science and society	37	13	12*
Population	36	14	12*

Rank-order correlation between coverage and importance = .78 (p = .001).
* These items were never noted as "the most important problem" in the Gallup findings, so they are ranked equally below the items that did.
SOURCE: From G. R. Funkhouser, "The Issues of the Sixties: An Exploratory Study in the Dynamics of Public Opinion," *Public Opinion Quarterly* 37 (1973): 66. Copyright 1973 by Columbia University Press. Reprinted by permission of the University of Chicago Press.

be that media coverage did not correspond very well to the realities of the issues. For instance, media coverage of the Vietnam War, campus unrest, and urban riots peaked a year or two before these happenings reached their climaxes in reality. Coverage of drugs and inflation was somewhat in line with reality, but coverage of race relations, crime, poverty, and pollution bore little, if any, relation to actuality.

Funkhouser's study suggests that the news media did not give a very accurate picture of what was going on in the nation during the 1960s. Funkhouser concludes, "The news media are believed by many people (including many policymakers) to be reliable information sources, but the data presented here indicate that this is not necessarily the case" (1973a, p. 75).

THE CHARLOTTE STUDY

An important question left open by the original McCombs and Shaw study of agenda setting is the question of causal order. The original Chapel Hill study found strong correlations between the media agenda and the public agenda during the 1968 election campaign, but it could not show which was influencing which. It is possible that the media agenda was influencing the public agenda, as the hypothesis suggests, but it is also plausible that the public agenda may have been influencing the media agenda.

As their next step in exploring agenda setting, McCombs and Shaw planned an additional study focusing on the 1972 presidential election campaign (Shaw & McCombs, 1977). This study was set in Charlotte, North Carolina. It used a larger sample than the Chapel Hill study, and it was a panel design, with respondents being interviewed at several points throughout the campaign. One of the specific purposes of this study was to obtain evidence concerning the causal direction of agenda setting. The use of a panel design, with several measures repeated through time, would allow some investigation of the causal sequence.

In the Charlotte survey, the same random sample of voters was interviewed during June prior to the national political conventions, again in October during the height of the campaign, and finally in November when the election returns were in. In order to investigate the causal direction of agenda setting, the authors focused on the two time periods of June and October. For each time period, they also had a measure of the media agenda, based on content analysis of the Charlotte newspaper and the evening newscasts of two television networks (CBS and NBC). These data for the two time periods were looked at with a technique known as cross-lagged correlation. The results—for newspapers only—are presented in Figure 12.3.

FIGURE 12.3. Cross-lagged correlation comparison of Charlotte voters and the contents of the *Charlotte Observer* in June and October 1972

SOURCE: Reprinted by permission from page 91 of *The Emergence of American Political Issues: The Agenda Setting Function of the Press* by D. L. Shaw and M.E. McCombs (eds.), Copyright © 1977 by West Publishing Company. All rights reserved.

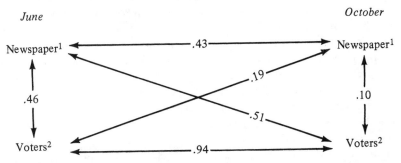

[1]Correlations are based on the "official" newspaper agenda.

[2]Analysis is based on panel members who read *only* the *Charlotte Observer*
$(N = 178)$.

The key correlations to look at in the diagram are those on the two diagonals. Comparing these correlations gives us an indication of the causal sequence. Which correlation is larger, the correlation between newspaper agenda at time 1 and the voters' agenda at time 2, or the correlation between newspaper agenda at time 2 and the voters' agenda at time 1? If the first correlation—the correlation between newspaper agenda at time 1 and the voters' agenda at time 2—is larger, that would provide support for agenda setting. And that is indeed what the figure shows.

The results are not as clear-cut as we might wish. For instance, the high correlation of .94 between the voters' agenda at time 1 and the voters' agenda at time 2 is troublesome, as researcher Bruce Westley pointed out (Westley, 1978). How can there be an agenda-setting effect when the public's agenda essentially remains unchanged? Furthermore, the cross-lagged correlation analysis for television does not show the support for agenda setting that Figure 12.3 does for newspapers. Nevertheless, the results of the Charlotte study do provide some evidence for causal direction—that it is likely that the media (or newspapers, at least) do have a causal effect in shaping the public's agenda, rather than vice versa.

EXPERIMENTAL EVIDENCE

How could investigators obtain more powerful evidence regarding causality? We pointed out in Chapter 2 that the most effective method for showing a causal relationship is the experiment. Is it possible that an experiment could be conducted to investigate the effects of agenda setting?

Researcher Shanto Iyengar of Yale University and two colleagues conducted several experiments just for this purpose (Iyengar, Peters, & Kinder, 1982). In general, their approach was to take videotapes of television network newscasts and alter them by editing out some stories and replacing them with others. This allowed them to manipulate the content of the news media in such a way that certain issues were played up and others were played down. Subjects in various experimental conditions were then exposed to these altered newscasts and were later questioned about their rankings of the importance of various issues, including those manipulated in the newscasts.

Table 12.2 comes from an experiment in which newscasts were doctored to play up inflation for one group, while the control group saw no defense stories. The table shows an increase in the rating of importance of defense for those subjects exposed to the high defense condition, but a decrease in the rating of importance for the control group.

Table 12.3 depicts results from an experiment in which one group saw newscasts playing up pollution, a second group saw newscasts playing up inflation, and a third group saw newscasts playing up defense. The group seeing the newscasts emphasizing pollution increased its rating of importance of pollution as an issue. The group seeing the newscasts emphasizing defense

TABLE 12.2 Adjusted change scores for problem importance in Experiment 1

Problem	Condition	
	Defense	Control
Defense*	.90	−.79
Inflation	−.49	.23
Energy	−.40	.22
Drug addiction	−.19	−.48
Corruption	−.67	.05
Pollution	−.58	.60
Unemployment	.28	.54
Civil rights	−.27	−.27

* $p < .05$, one-tailed test.
SOURCE: From S. Iyengar, M.D. Peters, and D. R. Kinder, "Experimental Demonstrations of the 'Not-So-Minimal' Consequences of Television News Programs," *American Political Science Review* 76 (1982): 852. Reprinted by permission.

TABLE 12.3 Adjusted change scores for problem importance in Experiment 2

Problem	Pollution	Inflation	Defense
Pollution	1.53**	−.71	−.23
Inflation	−.11	.11	−.06
Defense	−.44	−.34	.76*

* $p < .05$.
** $p < .01$.
SOURCE: From S. Iyengar, M. D. Peters, and D. R. Kinder, "Experimental Demonstrations of the 'Not-So-Minimal' Consequences of Television News Programs," *American Political Science Review* 76 (1982): 852. Reprinted by permission.

similarly increased its rating of importance of defense as an issue. The expected effect did not show up for the group viewing newscasts emphasizing inflation, but the researchers speculate that subjects were already so concerned about inflation that it was not really possible to increase this importance rating.

In a later book, Iyengar and Kinder (1987) reported a series of additional experiments that provided further evidence for agenda setting. In some of these experiments, viewers' perceptions of whether a problem was one of the country's most important were significantly affected by exposure to a single television news story.

PRIMING

Iyengar and his associates also discovered a special way that television newscasts might be having an impact on presidential elections. By setting the agenda for an election campaign, the media also determine the criteria by which presidential candidates will be evaluated. Iyengar and his associates call this process *priming*. Priming is the process in which the media attend to some issues and not others and thereby alter the standards by which people evaluate election candidates.

The researchers found some evidence of priming in their experiments. Subjects in the experiments, in addition to the measures we have already discussed, also rated President Carter on his performance in the three specific problem areas—defense, pollution, and inflation. They also gave general ratings of Carter's overall performance, competence, and integrity. As predicted by the concept of priming, the correlation between the overall rating and the rating in a specific problem area was greater for respondents who saw coverage emphasizing that problem area than it was for respondents who saw coverage neglecting that problem area. For example, when respondents saw coverage emphasizing inflation, the correlation between Carter's performance rating on inflation and his overall performance rating was .63. But when respondents saw coverage neglecting inflation, the correlation between Carter's performance rating on inflation and his overall performance rating was .39.

In other words, respondents were evaluating President Carter in terms of topics they had seen emphasized in the news recently. This is a rather subtle but powerful way that agenda setting could be influencing our most important elections.

Iyengar and Simon (1993) investigated priming in news coverage of the Persian Gulf crisis in 1990-91. First, they found a basic agenda-setting effect. As the Gulf crisis began to dominate news coverage, it also emerged in public opinion polls as the most important national problem. But they also found that the increased coverage of this issue carried over to influence overall evaluation of President Bush. During the Gulf crisis, opinions of Bush's foreign policy performance were more strongly related to overall evaluation of Bush than were opinions of Bush's economic performance. Before the Gulf crisis, the opinions of his economic performance had carried more weight than the opinions of foreign policy performance.

PRESIDENTIAL AGENDAS

One question of interest to researchers has been: Who sets the agenda for the media? This might be a particularly important question if, as Funkhouser's study suggested, the media agenda differs somewhat from reality.

One very likely choice for an influence on the media agenda is the president of the United States. He is the number one newsmaker in the country, and has access to mass communication not available to many others. One of the places where the president presents a fairly explicit agenda of issues, as he sees it, is in the State of the Union address. If the president has the capability to influence the media agenda, one of the instances where this influence might show up clearly is in this annual address. Although ostensibly for the benefit of Congress, the address is also broadcast on radio and television to the nation as a whole.

To investigate the possible influence of the State of the Union address on the media agenda, Gilberg, Eyal, McCombs, and Nicholas (1980) conducted a study of President Carter's second State of the Union address. They performed a content analysis of the address to identify the issues mentioned and then ranked the eight issues on the basis of the length of time the address spent dealing with each one. They then looked at press coverage in two major newspapers and the three television networks for four weeks prior to the State of the Union address and for four weeks after. Four weeks before was included as a control—it could help in interpreting the correlations between the president's agenda and the subsequent press agenda.

Contrary to their hypothesis, the correlations between the president's agenda and the subsequent media agenda were weaker than the correlations between the president's agenda and the prior media agenda. That is, the evidence from the study suggested not that President Carter was setting the press's agenda, but that the press was setting President Carter's agenda. In order to better understand this surprising outcome, McCombs, Gilbert, and Eyal (1982) attempted to replicate the study with Richard Nixon's 1970 State of the Union address. This study dealth with a president with a different style and an earlier period in history when the issues were different. In both cases, the studies examined a president's second State of the Union address.

Content analysis of Nixon's address produced a list of 15 issues, compared with 8 from Carter's address. As in the first study, the authors then examined press coverage in two major newspapers and the three television networks for the four weeks prior to the address and the four weeks after.

The results showed stronger support for the original hypothesis of presidential agenda setting than for the revised hypothesis that the press influences the presidential agenda. In all five comparisons (for the two newspapers and the three networks), the correlations between the presidential agenda and the postspeech media agenda were stronger than the correlations between the presidential agenda and the prespeech media agenda. McCombs and his colleagues also found that correlations between the prespeech media agenda and the postspeech media agenda were even stronger than either of the correlations between the presidential agenda and prespeech or postspeech media agendas. This suggests a kind of stability or consistency of news coverage—probably due to news routines, news values used by journalists, and other factors in journalism itself.

The different outcome of these two studies of presidential State of the Union addresses suggests that situational factors need to be taken into account when trying to understand agenda setting. In this particular area, presidential influence on an agenda, factors such as difference in presidential leadership style and the number and nature of the issues being dealt with played a role in determining the direction of an agenda-setting effect.

In an additional study of the role of the president as agenda setter, Wanta and Miller (1995) surveyed 577 respondents after President Clinton's 1994 State of the Union address. They performed a content analysis of the president's speech to determine which issues were emphasized, and another content analysis of media in two communities for a period after the speech to see what issues were being emphasized. Respondents to the survey were asked whether or not they had seen the broadcast of the president's speech, some questions about their media exposure, and their levels of concern about 12 issues—some mentioned in the president's speech and some not, and some emphasized in the media and some not.

Wanta and Miller found that viewing the president's speech and being exposed to the media both increased the agenda-setting effect, but that being exposed to the media actually increased it more. They speculate that the president actually needs the media to further highlight and explain the issues that he deems important. The State of the Union address is only one exposure of his message, and coverage and analysis in the news media gives it a chance to be repeated.

Beinhoff (1995) looked at the question of whether the president of the United States can elevate a single issue into prominent coverage just by emphasizing it. She picked the issue of the "information superhighway," arguing that it was essentially an example of "staged" or "artificial" news that would not be as important if the president did not mention it. Her study examined the *Weekly Compilation of Presidential Documents* to obtain a measure of how often President Clinton was talking about the information highway. She then examined newspapers, popular magazines, and specialized computer magazines to get her measures of media coverage. The study covered the period of January 18, 1993 (the first date for which the *Weekly Compilation* dealt with Clinton documents) to September 25, 1994. Beinhoff's results suggest that the president does not have all the power when a single issue begins to rise on the public agenda. She found several stages in which the public's attention to the information superhighway began to develop. The researcher suggests that Lang and Lang's (1983) concept of agenda building, in which the media, the president, and the public all interact, seemed to apply to the information highway issue.

THE OBTRUSIVENESS OF ISSUES

Several of the later agenda-setting studies that attempted to show causal direction by using panel studies at two points in time have shown only weak agenda-setting effects. This is true of the Charlotte study by McCombs and others, which found evidence of the proper time sequence for newspapers but not for television, and of a study by Tipton, Haney, and Baseheart (1975). Harold Gene Zucker hypothesized that the reason for this could be that these earlier studies were based on an incorrect assumption—that the agenda-setting effect would take place for all issues (Zucker, 1978).

Zucker went on to suggest that the obtrusiveness of the issue may be an important factor in whether or not agenda setting takes place. Zucker argued that the less direct experience the public has with a given issue area, the more it will have to depend on the news media for information about that area. Issues that the public experiences directly, like unemployment, are obtrusive issues. Issues that the public may not experience as directly, like pollution, are unobtrusive issues.

Zucker conducted a study comparing three obtrusive issues—the cost of living, unemployment, and crime—with three issues that were unobtrusive at the time—pollution, drug abuse, and the energy crisis. The amount of coverage of the six issues over an eight-year period was taken from the *Television News Index,* a monthly publication. The measure of public opinion on the importance of the six issues was taken from a number of Gallup polls that asked, "What is the most important problem facing the country today?"

Zucker found that for the three unobtrusive issues, heavy news media coverage preceded the rise of importance of an issue in the public opinion polls. For the three obtrusive issues, however, heavy news media coverage did not precede the rise of importance to the public. Rather, the two seemed to increase together.

Zucker's research demonstrates that agenda setting may take place for unobtrusive issues but not for obtrusive issues and suggests that the obtrusiveness of issues is an important concept that should be added to the agenda-setting hypothesis.

Zucker makes another interesting suggestion. He argues that agenda-setting effects should show up for both users and nonusers of the news media. If agenda setting takes place mostly on unobtrusive issues, then the only ways people can find out about them are through the media or through talking to other people who have been exposed to the media. That is, agenda setting and the two-step flow of communication may combine in having an effect.

ABSTRACT AND CONCRETE ISSUES

Yagade and Dozier (1990) attempted to determine whether agenda setting effects occurred more readily for concrete issues than abstract issues. They speculated that audience members find it difficult to visualize abstract issues, such as the federal budget deficit, and that this may reduce the likelihood of agenda setting taking place.

Issue abstractness is a concept that is distinct from issue obtrusiveness. Yagade and Dozier conceptualize abstractness as the degree to which an issue is difficult to conceptualize, or to be made sensible. Yagade and Dozier first tested four issues to see how abstract respondents perceived them to be. Respondents were asked how easily they could visualize each issue, whether the issue was real for them, whether the issue was easy to understand, and so forth. The issues were two the researchers thought would be abstract—the federal budget deficit and the nuclear arms race—and two the researchers thought would be concrete—drug abuse and energy. Analysis of responses showed that the first two were perceived as more abstract than the last two.

The researchers then picked one abstract issue—nuclear arms—and one concrete issue—energy—and investigated the occurrence of agenda setting effects for each. Basically, they conducted a content analysis of *Time* magazine to determine media importance for each issue over a period of weeks, and they used the Gallup poll "most important problem" question to determine importance to the public. They found a significant relationship between the media and public agendas for the concrete issue, energy, but not for the abstract issue, the nuclear arms race. The study suggests that the media may not set the public agenda for abstract issues. This may be a noteworthy consideration in thinking about the effects of the mass media, because public issues that are quite important can also be rather abstract.

BIAS BY AGENDA

Conservatives have sometimes claimed that the evening television newscasts have a liberal bias. Senator Jesse Helms of North Carolina has made that accusation about CBS News. Furthermore, Fairness in Media, a group with which he is affiliated, indicated that it was attempting to buy controlling stock in CBS. One of the charges the conservatives sometimes make is that the networks do not so much say liberal things as imply them by covering topics that either make conservatives look bad (such as inefficiency in the Pentagon) or make liberal causes look good (such as the plight of migrant workers). This notion is really a kind of "bias by agenda," with the issues that are being played up by the media being the ones that reflect favorably or unfavorably on a particular ideology.

Some support for bias by agenda was found in a massive study of television network news by Michael J. Robinson and his colleagues at George Washington University (Robinson, 1985; Fischman, 1985). The results showed some liberal bias by agenda for CBS and NBC but some conservative bias by agenda for ABC (see Table 12.4).

TABLE 12.4 Percentage of network news time devoted to "liberal" or "conservative" issues

	CBS	NBC	ABC
Liberal	37	21	13
Neither	40	72	56
Conservative	23	7	31

SOURCE: Adapted from J. F. Fischman, "Views of Network News," *Psychology Today*, July 1985, p. 16.

THE QUESTION OF TIME LAG

Agenda setting, as we have noted, is a causal hypothesis suggesting that media content has an influence on the public perception of the importance of issues. If this hypothesis is correct, an important question concerns the time lag. How long does it take for media content to have an effect on the public's subjective rankings?

Researchers Gerald Stone and Maxwell McCombs (1981) conducted a study aimed at investigating the time lag for agenda setting. Their basic technique was to obtain data on the public's agenda from some studies done previously and then conduct an additional analysis of media content over a long period of time prior to the time the public's agenda was measured. They then looked at the correlation between the public's agenda and the media agenda (actually based on *Time* and *Newsweek*), with the media agenda entered into the analysis for a number of different time points prior to the interviews with the public. Stone and McCombs did this analysis for three different sets of survey data—the June interviews from the Charlotte survey, the October interviews from the Charlotte survey, and an additional survey of male sophomores at Syracuse University. The different data sets agreed in showing that a period ranging from two months to six months seemed to be necessary for an item to move from the media agenda to the public agenda.

In a different study, Winter and Eyal (1980) investigated time span by focusing on a single issue, civil rights. They looked at coverage in the *New York Times* of the civil rights issue from 1954 to 1976 and compared it with Gallup poll data on the public perception of the importance of civil rights. The public agenda was based on the percentage of respondents who replied to the question "What is the most important issue facing the American public today?" with a response categorized as "civil rights." This percentage ranged from 0 to 52 percent over the 22 years.

Winter and Eyal found that the strongest correlations between the media agenda and the public agenda on the civil rights issue were for a four- to six-week span. They call this period—which might be different for other issues—the "optimal effect span." The Winter and Eyal figure is rather different from the one obtained by Stone and McCombs, but the difference could be due to some variations in the studies. One variation is that Winter and Eyal looked at only one issue. It seems quite likely that different issues will take different amounts of time to arouse a sufficient clamor to attract the public's attention. As Eyal, Winter, and DeGeorge (1981) point out, an oil embargo may suddenly thrust the issue of energy shortage onto the public agenda, while it may take years for the "honesty in government" issue to rise in public awareness.

Shoemaker, Wanta, and Leggett (1989) attempted to resolve the issue of the time span needed for agenda setting in their study of public concern about the drug problem. They found evidence that both the Stone and McCombs and the Eyal, Winter, and DeGeorge time intervals were correct. Their study revealed two time periods in which media coverage of drug issues correlates with later public concern about drugs—one to two months and four to five months.

Wanta and Roy (1995) also looked at some of the time-related issues in agenda setting. These researchers were interested in how long it takes for an agenda-setting effect to develop in an audience, and how long it will last before it disappears due to memory decay. To look at these questions, they measured the public agenda in a specific U.S. community by conducting a telephone survey. They then examined the *Vanderbilt Television News Abstracts* for six months prior to the survey, looked at local television station logs for a period of 50 days prior to the survey, and conducted a content analysis of the front page of the local newspaper for six months prior to the survey. These procedures allowed the researchers to determine the agenda each day in a period prior to the survey for ABC News, local television, and the local newspaper. The researchers then computed correlation coefficients between the public agenda and the media agenda for every day prior to the survey, and they did this separately for all three news media.

The analysis for ABC News revealed that international problems received a great deal of coverage, but ranked low on the public agenda. The researchers dropped international problems from the analysis, and then found agenda-setting effects appeared after four days. Agenda-setting effects showed up for local television news after six days and for the local newspaper after eight days. The agenda-setting effect for ABC News disappeared after six days. The effect for local TV newscast disappeared after 11 days. The agenda-setting effect for newspapers lasted longer, only disappearing after 85 days. As the authors point out, these results support an earlier argument by Shaw and McCombs (1977) that television news has a strong short-term effect, but newspapers have a longer-lasting effect. They also suggest that memory plays a role in agenda-setting effects, and that agenda-setting effects can diminish over a period of time because of memory decay. The results showed that ABC News had its strongest agenda setting effects four or five days after a newscast

The question of time span is important for media practitioners. Public relations professionals and other information campaign workers can plan their campaigns better if they know how long it takes to elevate an issue into public consciousness. The findings concerning time span also tell us something about how agenda setting works. It does not take place overnight, but it does not take years, either.

THE ROLE OF EXPOSURE

Although the agenda-setting hypothesis assumes that audience members are being exposed to mass media messages that emphasize certain issues, surprisingly few agenda-setting studies have actually measured exposure. Part of the reason for this is that few studies have actually examined agenda setting at the level of the individual audience member. More typically, agenda-setting studies have gathered an aggregate measure of the importance of issues for a sample of the public as a whole, and then compared this ranking of issues with an aggregate measure of the importance of issues for the media as a whole.

Several recent studies of agenda setting have included a direct examination of media exposure as part of the process. Wanta and Wu (1992) tested the hypothesis that the more individuals are exposed to the news media, the higher the level of issue salience for media issues. They conducted a survey in which 341 respondents were asked how often in the last week they read a newspaper, watched a national news broadcast, or watched a local news broadcast. They were also asked to rate the importance of a number of issues, half of which had received heavy media coverage and half of which had received scant media coverage. Analysis showed that the more exposure individuals had to the news media, the more they tended to be concerned about the five issues receiving heavy media coverage.

AGENDA BUILDING

Researchers Gladys Engel Lang and Kurt Lang (1983) studied the relationship between the press and public opinion during the Watergate crisis, and found that the original notion of agenda setting needed to be expanded in order to explain this complicated chapter of American history. They suggested that the concept of agenda setting be expanded into the concept of agenda building, which they break down into six steps:

1. The press highlights some events or activities and makes them stand out.

2. Different kinds of issues require different kinds and amounts of news coverage to gain attention. Watergate was a high-threshold (or unobtrusive) issue, and therefore it took extensive coverage to bring it to the public's attention.

3. The events and activities in the focus of attention must be "framed," or given a field of meanings within which they can be understood. Watergate was originally framed as a partisan issue in an election campaign, and this made it difficult for it to be perceived in a different frame—as a symptom of widespread political corruption.

4. The language used by the media can affect perception of the importance of an issue. The initial references to the Watergate break-in as a "caper," which persisted for months, tended to belittle it. The later switch to the term *scandal* gave more importance to the issue.

5. The media link the activities or events that have become the focus of attention to secondary symbols whose location on the political landscape is easily recognized. People need to have a basis for taking sides on an issue. In the case of Watergate, they were aided in doing this when the issue became linked to such secondary symbols as "the need to get the facts out" and "confidence in government."

6. Agenda building is accelerated when well-known and credible individuals begin to speak out on an issue. For instance, when Judge John Sirica said the

public was not being told the truth about Watergate, it had a dramatic impact on the public as well as on other prominent persons, including some Republicans, who were then more willing to speak out.

The Langs's concept of agenda building is more complicated than the original agenda-setting hypothesis. It suggests that the process of putting an issue on the public's agenda takes time and goes through several stages. It suggests that the way the media frame an issue and the code words they use to describe it can have an impact and that the role of well-known individuals commenting on the issue can be an important one.

THE NEED FOR ORIENTATION

Agenda setting might not take place to the same extent and in the same way for all individuals. McCombs and Weaver have suggested that individuals differ in their need for orientation and that this may determine whether or not agenda setting takes place (Weaver, 1977). Need for orientation, as they conceived of it, is based on two factors: the relevance of the information (to the individual) and the degree of uncertainty concerning the subject of the message. The greater the relevance of the information and the greater the uncertainty concerning the subject, the greater the need for orientation. They hypothesized that the higher the need for orientation, the more susceptible the individual is to mass media agenda-setting effects. They found evidence in the Charlotte study that the hypothesis is true, although the evidence was stronger for newspapers than for television.

WHO SETS THE MEDIA AGENDA?

Many studies have been done showing the media agenda and its possible effect on the public's agenda, but until recently researchers have tended to ignore an important question: Who sets the media agenda? Or, as Bruce Westley asked concerning the media agenda, "What makes it change?" (Westley, 1976).

Part of the answer lies in events occurring in reality. To some extent, the media are simply passing on issues and events that are occurring in society. This works in only a rough way, however—the Funkhouser and Zucker studies showed that news media coverage often does not correspond well to events in reality. Many other studies have suggested this same conclusion. If that is so, what does determine the media agenda? Westley has provided part of the answer himself. He suggested that in some cases pressure groups or special interest groups are able to boost an issue onto the media agenda. Examples of this would be the Student Nonviolent Coordinating Committee (SNCC) playing a part in putting racial discrimination on the public agenda in the 1960s and the National Organization for Women (NOW) and other women's groups putting women's issues on the public agenda in the 1970s.

Funkhouser (1973b) has suggested a list of five mechanisms in addition to the flow of actual events that operate to influence the amount of media attention an issue might receive:

1. *Adaptation of the media to a stream of events.* As the same pattern of events persists, it may be perceived as "just more of the same" and cease to be considered news.

2. *Overreporting of significant but unusual events.* Some events, such as the Santa Barbara oil spill, are important but receive exaggerated coverage because of their unusualness or sensationalism.

3. *Selective reporting of the newsworthy aspects of otherwise nonnewsworthy situations.* For instance, one well-known study has shown that television coverage of a parade honoring General Douglas MacArthur, by selecting certain details, made the event seem more exciting than it was (Lang & Lang, 1972).

4. *Pseudoevents, or the manufacturing of newsworthy events.* Protest marches, demonstrations, sit-ins, and publicity stunts are examples of pseudoevents that might help to move issues onto the press agenda.

5. *Event summaries, or situations that portray nonnewsworthy events in a newsworthy way.* An example is the release in 1964 of the surgeon general's report showing a relationship between smoking and lung cancer.

The question of who sets the media agenda really becomes the larger question of what are the influences on media content, and there are obviously many. This larger question involves the approach sometimes known as *media sociology,* and it has been the subject of much recent research and theorizing (Shoemaker & Reese, 1991).

One of the important influences on the media agenda suggested by recent research is the content of other media. In particular, it appears that the elite media, such as the *New York Times,* can set the agenda for other media. Danielian and Reese (1989) refer to this process as *intermedia agenda setting.* They found evidence that the prominence of the drug issue in the media in 1985 and 1986 was more a result of intermedia agenda setting than any increase in the drug problem in society. In fact, actual drug use did not rise dramatically in 1985 and 1986, although mass media coverage of the issue did. They found that "a general intermedia agenda setting influence was noted from the *New York Times* to the other media" (p. 48). In general, they found that the print media lead the television networks rather than vice versa (Reese & Danielian, 1989). The process of intermedia agenda setting is also documented in Timothy Crouse's *The Boys on the Bus* (1973), which reports on press coverage of the 1972 presidential campaign. Crouse tells of reporters from other media looking over the shoulder of R. W. (Johnny) Apple, Jr., of the *New York Times* to see the lead of his news story so they would know what to play up in their own stories.

Other evidence suggests that newsmakers are becoming particularly savvy about placing items on the media agenda. When California Governor Pete Wilson announced his candidacy for president in 1995, he did so with the Statue of Liberty in the background. The purpose was to identify Wilson with the issue of immigration. Wilson's position was that there was a right way and a wrong way to come into the United States, and that illegal immigration was the wrong way. Wilson was a backer of California's Proposition 187, which denied state services to illegal immigrants.

Sometimes a politician's attempt to set up a photo opportunity doesn't go exactly the way it was intended. For instance, Speaker of the House Newt Gingrich took a walk in the New Hampshire woods with journalists in 1995, ostensibly to look for moose. Gingrich attempted to chat with two fishermen wading in a nearby stream. One of them turned out to be a history teacher from Vermont, and he blasted Gingrich with, "Your politics are some of the meanest politics I have ever heard. You make Calvin Coolidge look like a liberal."

Shoemaker and Reese (1991), drawing upon work by Herbert Gans and Todd Gitlin, have proposed the following five major categories of influences on media content:

1. *Influences from individual media workers.* Among these influences are communication workers' characteristics, personal and professional backgrounds, personal attitudes, and professional roles.

2. *Influences of media routines.* What gets into the mass media is influenced by the day-to-day practices of communicators, including deadlines and other time constraints, space requirements in a publication, the inverted pyramid structure for writing a news story, news values, the standard of objectivity, and the reliance of reporters on official sources.

3. *Organizational influences on content.* Media organizations have goals, with making money being one of the most widely shared. These goals of the media organization can have an impact on content in numerous ways.

4. *Influences on content from outside of media organizations.* These influences include interest groups lobbying for (or against) certain kinds of content, people creating pseudoevents in order to get media coverage, and government, which regulates content directly through libel and obscenity laws.

5. *The influence of ideology.* Ideology represents a society-level phenomenon. Fundamental to ideology in the United States is "a belief in the value of the capitalist economic system, private ownership, pursuit of profit by self-interested entrepreneurs, and free markets" (Shoemaker & Reese, 1991, p. 184). This all-encompassing ideology probably influences the content of the mass media in many ways.

These five categories range from the influence of individual media workers, representing the most "micro" level, to the influence of ideology, representing the most "macro" level. They make up what Shoemaker and Reese call a "hierarchy of influences," with ideology sitting at the top of the hierarchy and filtering down through all the other levels.

NEW AREAS OF AGENDA SETTING

Some researchers have extended agenda setting to other realms besides that of political issues. Burns (1995), for instance, suggested that music radio stations, by playing songs in rotations which give heavier emphasis to some than others, could influence the popularity of those songs with audiences. Although Burns did not test his notion of an agenda-setting influence in radio music listening, it could be tested with a survey of listeners to a radio station and a content analysis of the songs played by that station during a certain period.

NEW DEVELOPMENTS IN AGENDA SETTING

Recently, agenda setting has been expanded beyond the original notion that the salience of issues in the news media has an effect on the salience of issues for the public. The theory has been extended to deal not only with *which* issues are emphasized in the media, but also *how* these issues are presented. The theory has also been modified to include other effects on audience members besides the increasing salience of issues. These additional effects include attitudinal and behavioral effects.

McCombs (1992) recently argued that every agenda basically consists of a set of objects, and that each of these objects has a set of attributes. These attributes include the aspects that people think about when they think about the issue. These attributes, or perspectives on a topic, can also show agenda-setting effects. As McCombs and Shaw (1993) put it, "Agenda setting is a process that can affect both what to think about and how to think about it" (p. 63).

At this point, the idea of agenda setting begins to link up with the notion of media framing. This second dimension of agenda setting—the set of attributes that represent how an event or issue is presented in the news media—is very similar to the notion of media framing.

HOW DOES AGENDA SETTING WORK?

Despite all the research on agenda setting, one of the things we still don't understand very well is how agenda setting works (McCombs, 1981). That is, we still don't have a very good understanding of the process of agenda setting. What takes place when issue saliences are transferred from the media to the minds of individuals? Are some cues (headline size, front-page play, position in a news broadcast, use of photographs or visuals) more important in suggesting salience than others? Or is the important factor the accumulation of cues over time, no matter what their particular form? How does the mind store the information that it is accumulating on an issue? Is there some kind of mental score sheet or tally sheet involved? To what extent is agenda setting a conscious process in the human mind? Does it achieve some of its effectiveness by being an unconscious process? What is the role of interpersonal communication in agenda setting? Does it augment it, as Zucker suggests? Or does it serve as an anchor, as group influence often does, and thus help people resist the effects of the media?

Many of these questions focus on the processing of information by the individual. It may be that we need more studies focused at this level in order to develop a full understanding of the process of agenda setting.

A study by Wanta and Miller (1995) of the response to President Clinton's 1994 State of the Union address tells us something about the information processing that takes place in an individual when agenda setting occurs. These researchers hypothesized that agenda setting is more likely to take place when respondents think the media are credible. Further, they hypothesized that agenda setting was more likely to take place if respondents believed President Clinton was doing a good job as president. Both these hypotheses were supported. These findings suggest that agenda setting is not a mechanical or automatic process, but that it involves information processing by individual audience members. People evaluate the information they get from the media, and this evaluation may result in agenda-setting effects for some individuals but not for others. To some extent, the processes of selective perception and retention described in Chapter 4 come into play to influence the agenda-setting process.

APPLIED AGENDA SETTING

Some researchers are moving beyond the study of the formation of agendas by the press to consider how ideas of agenda setting might be applied in ways to make society work better.

Gurevitch and Blumler (1990) suggested that democracy requires that the mass media engage in "meaningful agenda setting, identifying the key issues of the day, including the forces that have formed and may resolve them" (p. 270). Carter, Stamm, and Heintz-Knowles (1992) argued, "The study of agenda setting needs to advance beyond furnishing better measures of the media's current effects. We need to understand agenda setting well enough to suggest what the media might do that would improve the public's capability to think together about its common problems" (p. 870).

Shaw and Martin (1992) have suggested that the media, through agenda setting, function to provide just enough agreement on public issues to permit a dialogue between groups with conflicting views. In this sense, agenda setting serves as a consensus-building device that permits democracy to work. Political campaigns seem to be increasingly run by handlers and spin doctors—professionals hired to set the media's agenda (Sumpter and Tankard, 1994). In addition, press coverage of election campaigns has come to focus on the "horse race" aspects to the exclusion of issues and to emphasize the negative.

These deficiencies and others in journalism have led to the notion of public journalism or civic journalism, a kind of journalism that emphasizes serving the community better by identifying the important problems and issues and focusing on them (Shepard, 1994). Part of the notion of public journalism or civic journalism can be seen as a practical application of agenda-setting theory. Jay Rosen, one of the leaders of the public journalism movement, has said about journalists, "Not only must they acknowledge an agenda; they must be able to persuade others—media owners, politicans, critics, the public—that their agenda is a proper one" (Rosen, 1992, p. 8). The agenda that Rosen is recommending for the press is not one made up of particular issues, but a commitment to discussion and debate as a vital part of the political process.

Rosen also endorses *Washington Post* columnist David Broder's ideas for reforming campaign coverage. Broder (1990) recommended five ways to put sanity back into elections, with one of the five being what he called "the preemption strategy." Broder says journalists need to "challenge the operating assumption of the candidates and consultants that the campaign agenda is theirs to determine" (p. B1). Broder says the voters should be determining the agenda for the campaign, and that journalists can determine that voter agenda not only through polls but also through "shoe leather reporting"—walking neighborhoods, talking to people in living rooms, and so forth.

Some newspapers have been changing their election coverage along the lines recommended by Broder. The *Wichita Eagle* selected 10 issues it deemed most important in a 1990 state election and focused continuing coverage on them (Rosen, 1993). The intention was to engage reader interest and force candidates to address the issues. In a similar effort, the *Charlotte Observer* used interviews with readers to identify a "voter's agenda" for the 1992 election (Rosen, 1993). The newspaper then used surveys and meetings with citizens to keep the focus on the public's concerns.

CONCLUSIONS

The agenda-setting hypothesis has been one of the dominant concepts in communication theory since the early 1970s. The hypothesis is important because it suggests a way that the mass media can have an impact on society that is an alternative to attitude change. Furthermore, there are indications that the impact could be a significant one. There is evidence that the media are shaping people's views of the major problems facing society and that the problems emphasized in the media may not be the ones that are dominant in reality.

Recent work on agenda setting suggests that agenda setting works not only at the level of issues, but also at the level of attributes of issues, or subissues. This new direction in agenda setting suggests that the old statement that "the news media may not tell us what to think, but they tell us what to think about" needs to be revised. The newer version says that "the news not only tells us what to think; it also tells us how to think about it" (McCombs, 1992, p. 820).

For the practicing journalist, the concept of agenda setting raises important questions of responsibility. The labels that journalists apply to events can have an important influence on whether the public pays attention to the issues connected with the event, as the analysis of Watergate suggests. In an election campaign, the issues that the media play up can have the effect of favoring one candidate over another through the process of priming. The media can also help to create a certain image for a candidate by playing up some personal characteristics and ignoring others.

For the enterprising reporter, the findings of agenda-setting research also suggest opportunities. If the press typically does not cover significant happenings in proportion to their importance—as the Funkhouser and Zucker studies suggest—this means there are probably crucial news stories waiting to be covered.

For the public relations worker, agenda setting suggests the importance of framing an event in the right way in order to catch the public's attention.

Much of the research on agenda setting suggests that the press is not a mirror that reflects the realities of society as they are (Shoemaker & Mayfield, 1984). As Walter Lippmann (1922/1965, p. 229) suggested many years ago, it is more like a searchlight, and where the searchlight is shining can be affected by groups with special interests in an issue, by pseudoevents created to get attention, and by certain habits and rituals of journalists.

DISCUSSION

1. What were some of the earliest statements of the agenda-setting idea?
2. What is the relationship between the agenda-setting hypothesis and the limited effects model?
3. What is the evidence supporting the agenda-setting hypothesis?
4. This chapter contains a number of different statements of the agenda-setting hypothesis. Find three of them.
5. Some studies of agenda setting are ambiguous about the causal direction—it could be that the media agenda influences the public agenda or it could be that the public agenda influences the media agenda. What evidence do we have that it is the media agenda that influences the public agenda?
6. What is priming? Why is it important?
7. What are obtrusive and unobtrusive issues? Why is the distinction important?
8. The media agenda must come from somewhere. Who or what sets the agenda for the media?
9. How is knowledge of agenda setting useful for the working journalist?

REFERENCES

Bare, J. (1990). The war on drugs: A case study in opinion formation. *The Public Perspective*, Nov./Dec.: 29–31.

Beinhoff, L. A. (1995). The influence of presidental agenda-setting on the mass media's coverage of the "information superhighway." Paper presented at the annual meeting of the Association for Education in Journalism and Mass Communication, Washington, D.C.

Broder, D. S. (1990). Five ways to put some sanity back in elections. *The Washington Post*, Outlook sec., January 14, p. B1.

Burns, J. E. (1995). Agenda setting reconsidered: The process at work in music radio. Paper presented at the annual meeting of the Association for Education in Journalism and Mass Communication, Washington, D.C.

Carter, R. F., K. R. Stamm, and K. Heintz-Knowles (1992). Agenda setting and consequentiality. *Journalism Quarterly* 69: 868–877.

Cohen, B. C. (1963). *The Press and Foreign Policy.* Princeton, N.J.: Princeton University Press.

Crouse, T. (1973). *The Boys on the Bus.* New York: Random House.

Danielian, L. H., and S. D. Reese (1989). A closer look at intermedia influences on agenda setting: The cocaine issue of 1986. In P. J. Shoemaker (ed.), *Communication Campaigns about Drugs: Government, Media and the Public*, pp. 47–66. Hillsdale, N.J.: Lawrence Erlbaum.

Eyal, C. H., J. P. Winter, and W. F. DeGeorge (1981). The concept of time frame in agenda-setting. In G. C. Wilhoit and H. de Bock (eds.), *Mass Communication Review Yearbook*, vol. 2, pp. 212–218. Beverly Hills, Calif.: Sage.

Fischman, J. F. (1985). Views of network news. *Psychology Today*, July, pp. 16–17.

Funkhouser, G. R. (1973a). The issues of the sixties: An exploratory study in the dynamics of public opinion. *Public Opinion Quarterly* 37: 62–75.

Funkhouser, G. R. (1973b). Trends in media coverage of the issues of the '60s. *Journalism Quarterly* 50: 533–538.

Gilberg, S., C. Eyal, M. McCombs, and D. Nicholas (1980). The State of the Union address and the press agenda. *Journalism Quarterly* 57: 584–588.

Gurevitch, M., and J. G. Blumler. (1990). Political communication systems and democratic values. In J. Lichtenberg (ed.), *Democracy and the Mass Media*, pp. 269–289. Cambridge, Eng.: Cambridge University Press.

Iyengar, S., and D. R. Kinder (1987). *News That Matters: Television and American Opinion.* Chicago: The University of Chicago Press.

Iyengar, S., M. D. Peters, and D. R. Kinder (1982). Experimental demonstrations of the "not-so-minimal" consequences of television news programs. *American Political Science Review* 76: 848–858.

Iyengar, S., and A. Simon. (1993). News coverage of the Gulf crisis and public opinion: A study of agenda-setting, priming and framing. *Communication Research* 20: 365–383

Klapper, J. T. (1960). *The Effects of Mass Communication.* New York: Free Press.

Lang, G. E., and K. Lang (1983). *The Battle for Public Opinion: The President, the Press, and the Polls during Watergate.* New York: Columbia University Press.

Lang, K., and G. E. Lang (1959). The mass media and voting. In E. Burdick and A. J. Brodbeck (eds.), *American Voting Behavior*, pp. 217–235. Glencoe, Ill.: Free Press.

Lang, K., and G. E. Lang (1972). The unique perspective of television and its effect: A pilot study. In W. Schramm (ed.), *Mass Communications*, 2nd ed., pp. 544-560. Urbana: University of Illinois Press.

Lippmann, W. (1922, reprinted 1965). *Public Opinion*. New York: Free Press.

Long, N. E. (1958). The local community as an ecology of games. *American Journal of Sociology* 64: 251-261.

McCombs, M. E. (1981). Setting the agenda for agenda-setting research: An assessment of the priority ideas and problems. In G. C. Wilhoit and H. de Bock (eds.), *Mass Communication Review Yearbook*, vol. 2, pp. 209-211. Beverly Hills, Calif.: Sage.

McCombs, M. E. (1992). Explorers and surveyors: Expanding strategies for agenda-setting research. *Journalism Quarterly* 69: 813-824.

McCombs, M., S. Gilbert, and C. Eyal (1982). The State of the Union address and the press agenda: A replication. Paper presented at the annual meeting of the International Communication Association, Boston.

McCombs, M. E., and D. L. Shaw (1972). The agenda-setting function of mass media. *Public Opinion Quarterly* 36: 176-187.

McCombs, M. E., and D. L. Shaw (1993). The evolution of agenda-setting research: Twenty-five years in the marketplace of ideas. *Journal of Communication* 43 (no. 2): 58-67.

Neisser, U. (1967). *Cognitive Psychology*. New York: Appleton-Century-Crofts.

Reese, S. D., and L. J. Danielian (1989). Intermedia influence and the drug issue: Converging on cocaine. In P. J. Shoemaker (ed.), *Communication Campaigns about Drugs: Government, Media and the Public*, pp. 29-45. Hillsdale, N.J.: Lawrence Erlbaum.

Robinson, M. J. (1985). Jesse Helms, take stock. *Washington Journalism Review* 7 (no. 4): 14-17.

Rosen, J. (1992). Politics, vision, and the press: Toward a public agenda for journalism. In J. Rosen and P. Taylor, *The New News v. the Old News: The Press and Politics in the 1990s*, pp.1-33. New York: The Twentieth Century Fund.

Rosen, J. (1993). *Community Connectedness: Passwords for Public Journalism*. St. Petersburg, Fla.: The Poynter Institute for Media Studies.

Shaw, D. L., and S. E. Martin (1992). The function of mass media agenda setting. *Journalism Quarterly* 69: 902-920.

Shaw, D. L., and M. E. McCombs (eds.) (1977). *The Emergence of American Political Issues: The Agenda Setting Function of the Press*. St. Paul, Minn.: West.

Shepard, A. C. (1994). The gospel of public journalism. *American Journalism Review* 16: 28-35.

Shoemaker, P. J., and E. K. Mayfield (1984). Mass media content as a dependent variable: Five media sociology theories. Paper presented at the annual meeting of the Communication Theory and Methodology Division, Association for Education in Journalism and Mass Communication, Gainesville, Fla., August.

Shoemaker, P. J., and Reese, S. D. (1991). *Mediating the Message: Theories of Influences on Mass Media Content*. New York: Longman.

Shoemaker, P. J., W. Wanta, and D. Leggett (1989). Drug coverage and public opinion, 1972-1986. In P. J. Shoemaker (ed.), *Communication Campaigns about Drugs: Government, Media and the Public*, pp. 67-80. Hillsdale, N.J.: Lawrence Erlbaum.

Skinner, B. F. (1957). *Verbal Behavior*. New York: Appleton-Century-Crofts.

Steffens, L. (1931). *The Autobiography of Lincoln Steffens*. New York: Harcourt, Brace and Company.

Stone, G. C., and M. E. McCombs (1981). Tracing the time lag in agenda-setting. *Journalism Quarterly* 58: 51-55.

Sumpter, R., and J. W. Tankard, Jr. (1994). The spin doctor: An alternative model of public relations. *Public Relations Review* 20: 19-27.

Tipton, L., R. D. Haney, and J. R. Baseheart (1975). Media agenda-setting in city and state election campaigns. *Journalism Quarterly* 52: 15-22.

Wanta, W., and R. E. Miller (1995). Sources of the public agenda: The president-press-public relationship. Paper presented at the annual meeting of the International Communication Association, Albuquerque, N.M.

Wanta, W., and M. J. Roy (1995). Memory decay and the agenda-setting effect: An examination of three news media. Paper presented at the annual meeting of the Association for Education in Journalism and Mass Communication, Washington, D.C.

Wanta, W., and Y. C. Wu (1992). Interpersonal communication and the agenda-setting process. *Journalism Quarterly* 69: 847-855.

Weaver, D. H. (1977). Political issues and voter need for orientation. In D. L. Shaw and M. E. McCombs (eds.), *The Emergence of American Political Issues: The Agenda Setting Function of the Press*, pp. 107-119. St. Paul, Minn.: West.

Westley, B. H. (1976). What makes it change? *Journal of Communication* 26 (no. 2): 43-47.

Westley, B. H. (1978). Review of "The emergence of American political issues: The agenda setting function of the press." *Journalism Quarterly* 55: 172-173.

Winter, J. P., and C. H. Eyal (1980). An agenda-setting time-frame for the civil rights issue. Paper presented at the annual meeting of the International Communication Association, Acapulco, Mexico.

Yagade, A., and D. M. Dozier (1990). The media agenda-setting effect of concrete versus abstract issues. *Journalism Quarterly* 67: 3-10.

Zucker, H. G. (1978). The variable nature of news media influence. In B. D. Ruben (ed.), *Communication Yearbook*, vol. 2, pp. 225-240. New Brunswick, N.J.: Transaction.

chapter 13

The Knowledge-Gap Hypothesis

Information is a resource. It has value, and it lets people do things that they could not do otherwise. An old aphorism states that knowledge is power, and this means simply that knowledge gives people the capability to do things, and to take advantage of opportunities.

It is apparent, however, that knowledge, like other kinds of wealth, is not distributed equally throughout our society. People who are struggling with financial poverty are also often information-poor. There are haves and have-nots with regard to information just as there are haves and have-nots with regard to material wealth. The book *The Information-Poor in America* suggests the following list of items as typical information needs of the disadvantaged adult in the United States (Childers & Post, 1975, p. 56):

How do I get my baby into a day-care center?

Whom do I talk to to get rid of rats?

My husband walked out on me three weeks ago. What do I do?

How do I know if I have lead-based paint on the walls?

Where can I get $10 to last till my welfare check comes in?

I need enough food to get us through the weekend.

How do I get an abandoned car removed from in front of my house?

There's a gang of kids terrorizing the neighborhood. Where do I turn?

My daughter has been acting funny lately. Can anyone help?

Childers and Post also suggest the following as a "portrait of the disadvantaged American in his or her native information habitat." The prototypal disadvantaged American, more than his or her average counterpart:

Does not know which formal channels to tap in order to solve his problems, or what specific programs exist to respond to his needs.

Watches many hours of television daily, seldom reads newspapers or magazines and never reads books.

Does not see his problems as information needs.

Is not a very active information seeker, even when he does undertake a search.

May lean heavily on formal channels of information if it becomes apparent that the informal channels are inadequate and if his need is strongly felt.

Is locked into an informal information network that is deficient in the information that is ordinarily available to the rest of society. (p. 42)

Information is important in our society because a democracy depends on well-informed citizens. People elect public officials to run the government, and citizens vote on specific issues such as whether or not a city should participate in a nuclear power plant project. One must be well informed to vote intelligently on such matters.

It appears certain that information will be even more important in the future, as we move into an increasingly technological age. Many contemporary problems, including environmental pollution, nuclear power, the dangers from various food additives, and the risk of nuclear war, will require information, and an informed public, for their solution. One of the great promises of mass communication is that it might be able to help alleviate many of these problems by providing people with the information they need. Mass communication has the potential of reaching people who haven't been reached by other means, including the poor in big cities and rural areas of America and people leading difficult lives in many underdeveloped countries in the world.

THE ROLE OF THE MASS MEDIA

One example of an attempt to use mass communication to provide information to the disadvantaged is the educational television program "Sesame Street." This program, which was first broadcast in 1969, was an attempt to achieve some of the goals of the government Head Start programs for disadvantaged preschoolers through the mass medium of television. "Sesame Street" was a result of extensive research. It attempted a bold, new mission—to reach a large audience of children and hold their interest by combining information and entertainment in a new format.

Other mass communication efforts, it has been suggested, might also have the advantage of getting information to people not usually reached. For instance, televised presidential debates might take the presidential election campaign to people who would not normally be exposed to the campaign, and thus help our democracy to work more effectively.

The attempt to improve people's lives or make democracy work better by increased quantities of information from the mass media might not always work the way the planners would hope, however. An unexpected and undesired possibility is that mass communication might actually have the effect of increasing the difference or gap in knowledge between members of different social classes. This phenomenon, called the "knowledge-gap hypothesis," was first proposed in 1970 in an article titled "Mass Media Flow and Differential Growth in Knowledge" by Tichenor, Donohue, and Olien.

The authors state the knowledge-gap hypothesis this way:

As the infusion of mass media information into a social system increases, segments of the population with higher socioeconomic status tend to acquire this information at a faster rate than the lower status segments, so that the gap in knowledge between these segments tends to increase rather than decrease. (pp. 159–160)

A general picture of the knowledge-gap hypothesis is presented in Figure 13.1. The dimension from the left to the right in the figure represents the passage of time and the infusion of additional information. The hypothesis predicts that people of both low and high socioeconomic status will gain in knowledge because of the additional information but that persons of higher socioeconomic status will gain more. This would mean that the relative gap in knowledge between the well-to-do and the less-well-off would increase. Tichenor, Donohue, and Olien suggest that a knowledge gap is particularly likely to occur in such areas of general interest as public affairs and science news. It is less likely to occur in more specific areas that are related to people's particular interests—areas like sports or lawn and garden care.

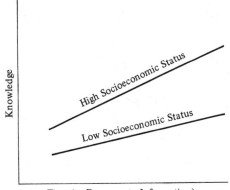

FIGURE 13.1 The knowledge gap hypothesis

OPERATIONAL FORMS OF THE HYPOTHESIS

For purposes of testing, Tichenor, Donohue, and Olien (1970) say the knowledge-gap hypothesis can be stated in the following two ways:

1. Over time, acquisition of knowledge of a heavily publicized topic will proceed at a faster rate among better-educated persons than among those with less education.
2. At a given time, there should be a higher correlation between acquisition of knowledge and education for topics highly publicized in the media than for topics less highly publicized.

Tichenor and his associates present evidence supporting both of the operational forms of the hypothesis. First, they present some time trend data. Figure 13.2 summarizes some data gathered by the American Institute of Public Opinion at several times. In four different polls, respondents were asked whether they believed man would reach the moon in the foreseeable future. The increasing gap between educational levels is readily apparent, with acceptance of the belief going up much more rapidly for college-educated respondents than for persons with less education.

The researchers also present data supporting the second form of the knowledge-gap hypothesis. This operational test suggests that, at a given time, there should be a higher correlation between acquisition of knowledge and education for highly publicized topics than for less publicized topics. Table 13.1 presents some data from a field experiment that is relevant to this test. Respondents were handed two science articles to read and then were asked to recall what the articles said. The general pattern of correlations in the table is consistent with the knowledge-gap hypothesis. That is, in each case the correlation between education and understanding of the article is higher for the more publicized topic than for the less publicized topic. An example may help to make

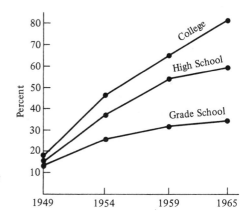

FIGURE 13.2 Respondents in national surveys stating belief that man will reach the Moon, by education and year

SOURCE: From P. J. Tichenor, G. A. Donohue, and C. N. Olien, "Mass Media Flow and Differential Growth in Knowledge," *Public Opinion Quarterly* 34 (1970): 166. Copyright 1970 by Columbia University Press. Reprinted by permission of the University of Chicago Press.

TABLE 13.1 Correlations between education and understanding of science articles for high- and low-publicity topics in two general areas

| | First Article Read | | Second Article Read | |
Area	More Publicized Topics	Less Publicized Topics	More Publicized Topics	Less Publicized Topics
Medicine and biology	$r = .109$ $(N = 84)$ n.s.	$r = 0.32$ $(N = 111)$ n.s.	$r = .264$ $(N = 90)$ $p < .02$	$r = .165$ $(N = 108)$ n.s.
Social sciences	$r = .278$ $(N = 104)$ $p < .01$	$r = .228$ $(N = 93)$ $p < .05$	$r = .282$ $(N = 91)$ $p < .01$	$r = .117$ $(N = 97)$ n.s.

SOURCE: P. J. Tichenor, G. A. Donohue, and C. N. Olien, "Mass Media Flow and Differential Growth in Knowledge," *Public Opinion Quarterly* 34 (1970): 169. Copyright 1970 by Columbia University Press. Reprinted by permission of the University of Chicago Press.

this clear. One of the four comparisons of interest is for the first article read when the area is medicine and biology. In this comparison, the correlation for the more publicized topic is .109. This is larger than the correlation for the less publicized topic of .032, and this is what the operational form of the knowledge-gap hypothesis predicts.

POSSIBLE REASONS FOR A KNOWLEDGE GAP

Why should the knowledge-gap hypothesis be expected to be true? Tichenor, Donohue, and Olien (1970) present five reasons:

1. There is a difference in communication skills between those high and low in socioeconomic status. There is usually a difference in education, and education prepares one for such basic information-processing tasks as reading, comprehending, and remembering.

2. There is a difference in the amount of stored information, or previously acquired background knowledge. Those of higher socioeconomic status might already know of a topic through education, or they might know more about it through previous media exposure.

3. People of higher socioeconomic status might have more relevant social contact. That is, they might associate with people who are also exposed to public affairs and science news and might enter into discussions of such topics with them.

4. The mechanisms of selective exposure, acceptance, and retention might be operating. Persons of lower socioeconomic status might not find information concerning public affairs or science news compatible with their values or attitudes, or they just might not be interested in such information.

5. The nature of the mass media system itself is that it is geared toward persons of higher socioeconomic status. Much of the news of public affairs and science appears in print media and print media are oriented toward the interests and tastes of higher status persons.

THE KNOWLEDGE GAP IN PUBLIC AFFAIRS

The knowledge-gap hypothesis is also supported by a number of other types of evidence gathered by researchers. One prediction from the knowledge-gap hypothesis is that people of higher socioeconomic status are more likely to be exposed to certain types of information (particularly, that dealing with public affairs and science) than people of lower socioeconomic status.

Figure 13.3 shows a breakdown by socioeconomic status of an audience for a major address by President Roosevelt. The bar graph shows the audience declining regularly as socioeconomic status declines. This graph alone provides some evidence for a knowledge gap. Persons of lower socioeconomic status were less likely to listen to the speech, and therefore would be less likely to know the information that was contained in the speech.

Presidential debates, such as those in 1992 between presidential contenders George Bush and Bill Clinton or vice presidential candidates Dan Quayle and Al Gore, are often among the high points of a presidential election campaign. Because of their drama, excitement, and uniqueness, the debates offer the possibility of overcoming the barriers of selective exposure and apathy that keep many citizens from participating in a campaign.

The debates might have many effects, but one of the simplest would be to increase viewers' knowledge of the positions of the candidates on various issues. Research on the 1976 presidential debates, however, suggests that the people most likely to watch the debates are those more politically involved in the first place, and that, furthermore, those people tend to be the ones of higher education (Bishop, Oldendick, & Tuchfarber, 1978). The findings suggest that the

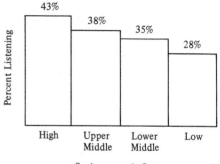

FIGURE 13.3 Radio audience for a speech by President Roosevelt, by socioeconomic status

SOURCE: Adapted from P. F. Lazarsfeld, *Radio and the Printed Page* (New York: Duell, Sloan and Pearce, 1940), p. 28.

result of the debates was that the knowledge-rich got richer and the knowledge-poor got poorer. In other words, the results suggested a widening of the knowledge gap.

Evidence of a knowledge gap on the energy issue showed up in a panel study in West Allis, Wisconsin, conducted by R. J. Griffin (1987). This researcher found that knowledge of energy was related to reading of newspaper energy stories by the more educated, but to viewing televised energy commercials among the less educated. This finding suggests that the planners of information campaigns dealing with energy or similar complex issues might need to choose different media to reach different audience sectors.

"SESAME STREET"

The first-year report on "Sesame Street" states that the prime target of the program was the disadvantaged inner-city child (Ball & Bogatz, 1970, p. 209). The first-year report also states that "Sesame Street" "helped to close the gap between advantaged and disadvantaged children" (Ball & Bogatz, p. 358). Other researchers who examined the test results on "Sesame Street" viewers have challenged that conclusion, however.

Perhaps the major challenge to the conclusion came in a book called *"Sesame Street" Revisited* (Cook et al., 1975). Researcher Thomas Cook and his colleagues based their challenge on extensive reanalysis of the evaluation data gathered by the producers of "Sesame Street." One set of data dealt simply with how much "Sesame Street" was watched in households in which the heads of the households had varying amounts of education. Figure 13.4 shows some 1971 data concerning the percentage of households where "Sesame Street" was viewed at least once a week in the last three months, according to education of head of household. The figure shows a regular pattern: the higher the level of education of the head of household, the more likely it was that "Sesame Street" would be watched. On the basis of these and other data, Cook and his associates concluded, "The implication of these data is that Sesame Street will have great difficulty in narrowing any achievement gaps between groups of different income or education levels" (pp. 308–309).

The data in Figures 13.4 deal only with exposure, and do not actually show a difference in the effects of viewing. Another researcher, however, reexamined some different data that were also gathered by the program producers and had to do more directly with effects (Katzman, 1974). Table 13.2 presents a comparison of achievement score results for disadvantaged and advantaged children viewing "Sesame Street." It shows a number of interesting results, but the most relevant for the present discussion comes from looking at the row for gain scores for disadvantaged and advantaged children. For the first three quartiles of viewing, this comparison shows the advantaged children in each quartile making a greater gain in achievement scores than the disadvantaged children. In other words, even when viewing is the same, the advantaged children are getting more

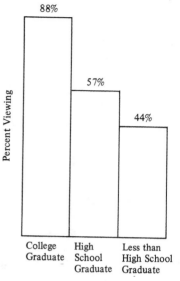

FIGURE 13.4 Households with children under six where "Sesame Street" was viewed at least once in the preceding three months, by education of head and household (1971)

SOURCE: Adapted from T. D. Cook, H. Appleton, R. F. Conner, A. Shaffer, G. Tamkin, and S. J. Weber, *"Sesame Street" Revisited: A Case Study in Evaluation Research* (New York: Russell Sage Foundation, 1975), p. 293.

TABLE 13.2 Pretest and gain scores on battery of achievement tests by amount of "Sesame Street" viewing and background

	Quartile (least to most)			
	Q1	*Q2*	*Q3*	*Q4*
Background				
Total				
Pretest	76	86	94	101
Gain	19	31	39	48
Disadvantaged				
Pretest	76	84	87	97
Gain	19	29	37	47
Advantaged				
Pretest	95	102	113	110
Gain	27	38	40	45

SOURCE: From N. Katzman, "The Impact of Communication Technology: Promises and Prospects," *Journal of Communication* 24, no. 4 (1974): 55. Reprinted by permission.

out of "Sesame Street" than the disadvantaged children. This pattern is not observed in the fourth quartile, however. This holds out the possibility that for the heaviest viewers, the knowledge gap might be narrowed rather than widened. For the first three quartiles, however, the knowledge gap is widened by viewing the program.

In response to the criticisms of Cook and others, the creators of "Sesame Street" have said the program was not intended to reduce the gap between advantaged and disadvantaged children (Lesser, 1974, p. 186). Rather, the goal was to bring all children up to a basic level of preparation for doing well in school. "Sesame Street" has continued to be successful, of course, with 11 million U.S. households watching it every week and with 83 countries now having their own version of the show.

REFINEMENT OF THE HYPOTHESIS

In a later study, Donohue, Tichenor, and Olien (1975) began to explore some of the conditions under which a knowledge gap might be reduced or eliminated. Based on analysis of surveys dealing with the relationships between knowledge and other variables from 15 Minnesota communities, the researchers suggested the following modifications of the hypothesis:

1. When there is perceived conflict over a local issue, the knowledge gap is likely to decline.
2. Widening knowledge gaps are more likely to occur in pluralistic communities, with numerous sources of information, than in homogeneous communities, with informal but common communication channels.
3. When an issue has immediate and strong local impact, the knowledge gap is likely to decline.

In general, this study suggested that an important variable is the extent to which an issue arouses basic social concerns. When it does, the knowledge gap is likely to be reduced or eliminated.

Additional evidence for the narrowing of a knowledge gap comes from the data on "Sesame Street" analyzed by Katzman that we have already noted. It is worth taking another look at these data in another form. Figure 13.5 shows a graph of the posttest scores (pretest scores plus gains) for disadvantaged and advantaged children at four levels of viewing. The closing of the gap for heavy viewers becomes readily apparent. In fact, the heavy viewers in the disadvantaged group have reached achievement scores higher than the two lightest viewing groups for the advantaged.

Many factors might contribute to the widening or closing of a knowledge gap. Perhaps a knowledge gap could be overcome if an infusion of information into a population was massive enough. Or perhaps a well-known celebrity involved in the dissemination of information could help achieve wider visibility for and acceptance of the information.

Researchers Wayne Wanta and William Elliott had conducted a survey of public knowlege of information regarding AIDS in March of 1991. They were thus in a good position to carry out a follow-up survey after Magic Johnson, a star of the Los Angeles Lakers basketball team, announced in November of 1991 that

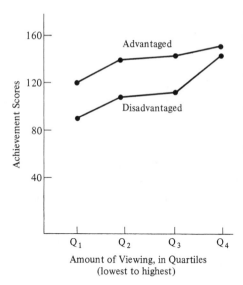

FIGURE 13.5 Posttest achievement scores for advantaged and disadvantaged children at four levels of viewing "Sesame Street"

SOURCE: Adapted from N. Katzman, "The Impact of Communication Technology: Promises and Prospects," *Journal of Communication* 24, no. 4 (1974): 55.

he had tested positive for HIV. Wanta and Elliott (1995) suggested that three factors were at work following the Johnson announcement: the high utility of information about AIDS for individuals, the extensive publicity given to the Johnson announcement, and the drama of having a well-known sports figure involved in the announcement. Because of these three factors, they predicted that the knowledge gap regarding AIDS between highly educated members and less-educated members of the public might narrow rather than increase. Their results showed similar gains in knowledge of AIDS for almost all educational levels following the Johnson announcement. In fact, the proportion of increase was larger for individuals in the lower education group, showing some catching up by individuals of less education.

What these results—and the results of some other studies—suggest is that the knowledge gap is widened under certain circumstances and closed under other circumstances. Television may have a special power to close knowledge gaps, or, if not to close them, at least to keep them from widening. One of the new applications of cable television in a number of communities has been to give live coverage of city council meetings and other government activities, in keeping with the idea that the activities of government should be public and open. It has also been suggested that such television coverage provides a new avenue for the viewer for participating as a citizen. A study of viewers of televised city council meetings in Wichita, Kansas, attempted to see just who the viewers were—and whether a knowledge gap might be developing (Sharp, 1984). The author found that less-educated, lower-income, and minority individuals were just as likely to watch as their better-off counterparts—in other words, that a widening of the knowledge gap did not occur. Sharp found that viewers of the telecast tended to be persons who "had a stake in the community" and that those people were just as likely to be found in the lower socioeconomic status levels as the higher. Having a stake in the community was indicated by things like living in the community a long time, belonging to a community organization, and being able to name a community problem.

The Sharp study, then, suggests that individual motivation is an important factor in information seeking, and that knowledge gaps might narrow rather than widen when motivation to seek information is strong.

THE GENERALITY OF THE HYPOTHESIS

Since the initial formulation of the knowledge-gap hypothesis, several researchers have suggested that it needs to be restated more generally. Rogers (1976) stated that the gap should apply to attitudinal and overt behavioral effects and not just to effects on knowledge. He stated further that the hypothesis should not be limited to mass media efforts alone, but should include also the effects of interpersonal communication and the combination of mass and interpersonal communication. Finally, he suggested that the gap need not occur between only two groups of receivers (those of high and low socioeconomic status, for instance) and that socioeconomic status and its related variables were not the only receiver variables that could be related to a knowledge gap.

Genova and Greenberg (1981) also found evidence that knowledge gaps are more strongly related to audience interest than to socioeconomic status or education. They focused on two kinds of interest—self-interest, or perceived usefulness of news information for one's self; and social interest, or the perceived usefulness of the information to the individual's social milieu or interpersonal networks. They conducted a panel study to examine knowledge of two news events, an ongoing National Football League strike and the Nixon impeachment proceedings. The findings indicated a combined measure of the two types of interest was a stronger predictor of knowledge levels in respondents than education. Furthermore, of the two types of interest, social interest bore the strongest relationship to knowledge acquisition. The authors conclude that "this is a more optimistic proposition than the original knowledge gap hypothesis; it offers an alternative route by which public knowledge could be expanded" (p. 504).

THE KNOWLEDGE GAP AND
THE NEW TECHNOLOGY

Communication technology is changing so rapidly that many people speak of a "communication revolution" or an "information explosion." Some of the new technologies in the process of being developed or presently existing are video-tape recorders, videocassettes, cable television, online newspapers, access of computer information services by home computers, the Internet and the World

Wide Web, and CD-ROMs. Many of these technologies have the dramatic effect of giving the user much more control over the communication process and the information received.

Theoretically, these new technologies can be used to the benefit of people throughout society. As Parker and Dunn (1972) have noted:

> The greatest single potential of an information utility might be the opportunity to reduce the unit cost of education to the point where our society could afford to provide open and equal access to learning opportunities for all members throughout their lives. (p. 1392)

In actual practice, however, it is not yet clear what the effects of these new technologies will be on levels of information held by the public, particularly by different segments of the public. Many of these new technologies are expensive. Because of the cost, these technologies may be more available to the well-to-do than to the less-well-off. For this and other reasons, an unfortunate effect of the technological revolution in communication could be a further widening of the knowledge gap (Lepper, 1985). As Parker and Dunn noted further:

> If access to these information services is not universally available throughout the society, then those already "information-rich" may reap the benefits while the "information-poor" get relatively poorer. A widening of this "information gap" may lead to increased social tension. (p. 1396)

The home computer can provide access to much of the information being provided through new technologies, including the Internet, the World Wide Web, and CD-ROMs. Data on the ownership of home computers provides some evidence on who will have access to the new technology and who will not. Computers are present in 62 per cent of the richest 25 percent of U.S. households, but they are present in only 6.8 percent of the poorest 25 percent of U.S households (Powell, 1995). Figure 13.6 shows ownership of home computers for various ethnic or racial groups. The percentage of homes with computers ranges from 36 percent for Asians and Pacific Islanders to 9.5 percent for African Americans.

Ownership of videocassette recorders shows a similar relationship to income and education (Scherer, 1989). Only 9 percent of those with an income of less than $10,000 own a VCR, while 79 percent of those with an income greater than $40,000 own one. Similarly, 37 percent of those who have not graduated from high school own a VCR, while 73 percent of college graduates own one. Scherer (1989, p. 102) concludes that the VCR is "one in a growing arsenal of media resources that benefit the information-rich more than the information-poor."

Theoretically, the new technology can be used to facilitate grassroots democracy by giving the power of these new devices to political groups and organizations outside the mainstream. In contrast to this hopeful prediction,

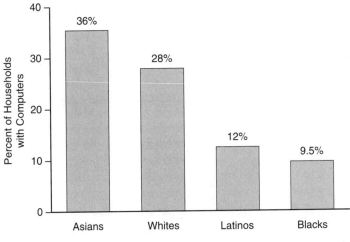

FIGURE 13.6 Households owning computers, by race

SOURCE: Data from Adam Clayton Powell III, "Diversity in Cyber-space," paper presented to the Association for Education in Journalism and Mass Communication, August, 1995, Washington, D.C.

however, Rubinyi (1989) found evidence that differences between the well-off and the not-so-well-off in their abilities to take advantage of new technology extended even to organized groups. He studied 72 small nonprofit organizations and found that resource-poor groups that adopt computer technology do not benefit in the same way from that technology as more affluent groups.

On the other side of the coin, however, Downing (1989) points out some ways in which the new technology can be used to make grassroots democracy work better. As examples, he cites PeaceNet II, an international computer network devoted to peace, and EcoNet, an environmentalist computer network. A different example is Public Data Access, a group devoted to making government data accessible to those sectors of the public most in need of it. One of the products of Public Data Access was *Toxic Wastes and Race in the United States*, a report that showed a correlation between the location of toxic waste dump sites and the location of minority neighborhoods.

NEW DEVELOPMENTS IN KNOWLEDGE-GAP RESEARCH

Pan and McLeod (1991) call for better theoretical development of the knowledge gap thesis. They argue that knowledge gap research has progressed at two different levels—a micro or individual level where the focus has been on individuals' knowledge acquisition, and a macro or social level where the focus has been on information control and its relationship to community structure and power hierarchy. These researchers call for expansion of the theory by formulating linkages between variables at the individual and social levels. For instance, research at the social level suggests that community conflict restricts an editor's choices regarding news coverage of controversial issues. But this research could be expanded by examining individual editors' cognitive processes, including the influence of internalized professional codes and values.

Recent research on the knowledge gap has attempted to clarify the relationships between the most frequently cited causes of knowledge gaps—particularly education, socioeconomic status, and interest (or motivation)—and knowledge gain.

Weir (1995) attempted to add to our understanding of the role of motivation in the processes leading to knowledge gaps. Several studies, including that of Genova and Greenberg (1981), have found that interest (a concept similar to motivation) is a stronger predictor than education of knowledge gained. But other studies did not find a gain in knowledge for people the researchers viewed as motivated. For instance, Griffin (1990) found in his study of energy information that people who were less well-off, older, and living in older homes showed an information deficit. But these people should be motivated to obtain information regarding energy consumption. Also, in a study of information regarding the relationship between cancer and diet, Viswanath, Kahn, Finnegan, Hertog, and Potter (1993), did not find that motivation was a better predictor of knowledge gained than education, but that motivation and education act together with several other variables to affect knowledge level.

Weir asked why it is that people who are expected to be interested or motivated do not always engage in increased information-seeking behavior. He attempted to analyze people's information needs in a manner similar to the way Abraham Maslow analyzed people's needs in general with his "hierarchy of needs." Maslow's hierarchy starts with the most basic needs, physiological needs, and moves up through safety needs, love and belongingness needs, and esteem needs to reach the summit in self-actualization needs. Based on Maslow's work, Weir developed a "hierarchy of information seeking-behavior" (see Figure 13.7, p. 291). Weir argues that a person's information-seeking behavior is determined by his or her place in the hierarchy, and that only after information needs on one level are satisfied can the individual focus on securing information from higher levels. Knowledge gaps occur when information is directed at people who find it unimportant based on their relative position in the hierarchy.

CRITICISM OF THE HYPOTHESIS

Dervin (1980) criticized the knowledge-gap hypothesis for being based on the traditional source-sending-messages-to-receiver paradigm of communication. She argued that this paradigm has been pervasive in U.S. communication research, but that it hides certain assumptions. Basically, this view emphasizes attaining source goals and trying to manipulate receivers to those ends. Dervin said this

The Hierarchy of
Information-Seeking Behavior

A person's information-seeking behavior is dictated by his or her relative place in
a Hierarchy of Information Needs. Only after information needs on one level are
deemed satisfied can he or she focus effort on securing information from higher
levels. Individuals can jump between levels for short periods of time only if lower
needs are seen as being temporarily satisfied.

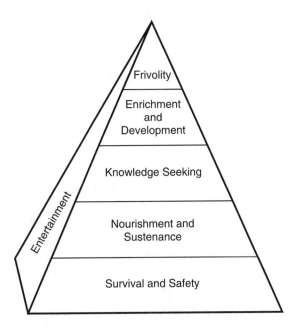

Thus, knowledge gaps occur when information is
directed at people who find it irrevelent based on
their relative position in the hierarchy.

FIGURE 13.7   The hierarchy of information-seeking
behavior

SOURCE: From Tom Weir, "The Continuing Question of Motivation in
the Knowledge Gap Hypothesis," paper presented to the Association
for Education in Journalism and Mass Communication, August, 1995,
Washington, D.C. Reprinted by permission.

approach leads to a "blaming-the-victim" syndrome. She recommended that
communication campaigns (and communication research) be more user-based.
She issued a call for user-constructed information and user-defined information.
This approach emphasizes the user's need for sense making and attempts to
determine the questions people are seeking answers to when they are in certain
situations, such as seeing a doctor about a health problem.

OVERCOMING KNOWLEDGE GAPS

Communicators interested in helping to bridge knowledge gaps can take several steps. Viswanath et al. (1993) suggest that strategies to involve people in groups may help to overcome knowledge gaps. Another useful technique is to identify the target audiences for a particular communication campaign, and then design messages to reach each audience. For instance, Frankenberger and Sukhdial (1994) recommend segmenting a teenage audience for AIDS communication into various groups depending on race and risk factors. They recommend targeting each group with messages and media that are appropriate to that group. McLeod and Perse (1994) suggest that journalists interested in reducing the knowledge gap should highlight the utility of information they present. Zandpour and Fellow (1992) point out that simply putting important messages in both Spanish and English can sometimes help to reduce knowledge gaps.

CONCLUSIONS

The original knowledge-gap hypothesis suggested that as the infusion of mass media information into a social system increases, segments of the population with higher socioeconomic status tend to acquire this information at a faster rate than lower-status segments.

The knowledge-gap hypothesis has been refined and broadened in several ways since its original formulation. First of all, it has become clear that information sometimes causes knowledge gaps to widen and sometimes causes them to narrow. One of the crucial variables in this process identified by several studies is interest or motivation. If there is sufficient interest, and particularly if it is evenly distributed throughout a community, then information can help to close a knowledge gap. Second, the gaps that can occur because of communication are not limited to knowledge. They can also involve attitudes and behavior. For this reason, one researcher (Rogers) suggested that the phenomenon be reconceptualized as a communication effects gap rather than a knowledge gap. Finally, the gaps do not have to be limited to those between people of high and low socioeconomic status (usually measured by education). Significant gaps also occur between people of high and low interest in politics and between the old and the young.

Of course, just because the media can work to narrow a knowledge gap in certain situations does not mean that we should not be concerned about other cases in which the media widen knowledge gaps. The several studies that have found knowledge gaps to narrow have generally shown that motivation to seek knowledge is the key variable leading to a narrowing. But it is not enough to have motivation to seek information—one must also have access to the information. Television may help to serve as a knowledge leveler because it is so universally available. Thus we found a narrowing of the achievement gap for the heaviest viewers of "Sesame Street." In these viewers, we find the combination that is needed—access to the information plus motivation to acquire the information.

If access is a key variable, then there is still plenty of reason to be concerned about knowledge gaps. Some media are much more accessible than others. A full selection of the cable television services available in many cities can cost hundreds of dollars a year. The computer equipment needed to access computer information services is not cheap, and neither are the access fees for the services themselves. Society as a whole may need to take steps to assure that access to information is available to all, or we may indeed expect to see ever-increasing knowledge gaps. Furthermore, knowledge-gap research indicates that on complex issues like energy, the well-to-do get their information from one medium (newspapers) while the less-well-to-do get their information from another medium (television advertisements). These findings suggest that planners of information campaigns need to conduct audience research, and that they will often benefit from choosing different media to reach different segments of the audience. Finally, as Dervin reminds us, information campaigns should probably begin with the needs of the potential user of the information.

DISCUSSION

1. What is the knowledge gap hypothesis? What are the reasons that it might be expected to be true?
2. What are some information needs of the poor?
3. On what topics could television be used to help close knowledge gaps?
4. Are new technological developments such as computers and the Internet likely to help overcome the knowledge gap? Why, or why not?
5. What are the most important factors influencing whether a person will acquire knowledge from the mass media?
6. How does the concept of motivation or interest relate to knowledge gaps?
7. What are some criticisms of the knowledge gap hypothesis made by other scholars?
8. What steps can be taken by professional communicators to help reduce knowledge gaps?

REFERENCES

Ball, S., and G. A. Bogatz (1970). *The First Year of "Sesame Street": An Evaluation.* Princeton, N.J.: Educational Testing Service.

Bishop, G. F., R. W. Oldendick, and A. J. Tuchfarber (1978). Debate watching and the acquisition of political knowledge. *Journal of Communication* 28 (no. 4): 99–113.

Childers, T., and J. Post (1975). *The Information-Poor in America.* Metuchen, N.J.: Scarecrow Press.

Cook, T. D., H. Appleton, R. F. Conner, A. Shaffer, G. Tamkin, and S. J. Weber (1975). *"Sesame Street" Revisited: A Case Study in Evaluation Research.* New York: Russell Sage Foundation.

Dervin, B. (1980). Communication gaps and inequities: Moving toward a reconceptualization. In B. Dervin and M. J. Voight (eds.), *Progress in Communication Sciences,* vol. 2, pp. 73-112. Norwood, N.J.: Ablex.

Donohue, G. A., P. J. Tichenor, and C. N. Olien (1975). Mass media and the knowledge gap: A hypothesis reconsidered. *Communication Research* 2: 3-23.

Downing, J. D. H. (1989). Computers for political change: PeaceNet and Public Data Access. *Journal of Communication* 39 (no. 3): 154-162.

Frankenberger, K. D. and A. S. Sukhdial. (1994). Segmenting teens for AIDS preventive behaviors with implications for marketing communications. *Journal of Public Policy & Marketing* 13: 133-150.

Genova, B. K. L., and B. S. Greenberg (1981). Interests in news and the knowledge gap. In G. C. Wilhoit and H. de Bock (eds.), *Mass Communication Review Yearbook,* vol. 2, pp. 494-506. Beverly Hills, Calif.: Sage.

Griffin, R. J. (1987). Energy, education, and media use: A panel study of the knowledge gap. Paper presented at the annual meeting of the Communication Theory and Methodology Division, Association for Education in Journalism and Mass Communication, San Antonio, Texas, August.

Griffin, R. J. (1990). Energy in the eighties: Education, communication, and the knowledge gap. *Journalism Quarterly* 67: 554-566.

Katzman, N. (1974). The impact of communication technology: Promises and prospects. *Journal of Communication* 24 (no. 4): 47-58.

Lazarsfeld, P. F. (1940). *Radio and the Printed Page.* New York: Duell, Sloan and Pearce.

Lepper, M. R. (1985). Microcomputers in education: Motivational and social issues. *American Psychologist* 40 (no. 1): 1-18.

Lesser, G. S. (1974). *Children and Television.* New York: Random House (Vintage Books).

McLeod, D. M., and E. M. Perse (1994). Direct and indirect effects of socioeconomic status on public affairs knowledge. *Journalism Quarterly* 71: 433-442.

Pan, Z., and J. M. McLeod (1991). Multilevel analysis in mass communication research. *Communication Research* 18: 140-173.

Parker, E. B., and D. A. Dunn (1972). Information technology: Its social potential. *Science* 176: 1392-1398.

Powell, A. C. (1995). Diversity in cyberspace. Address presented to the Association for Education in Journalism and Mass Communication, Washington, D.C.

Rogers, E. M. (1976). Communication and development: The passing of the dominant paradigm. *Communication Research* 3: 213-240.

Rubinyi, R. M. (1989). Computers and community: The organizational impact. *Communication Research* 39 (no. 3): 110-123.

Scherer, C. W. (1989). The videocassette recorder and information inequity. *Journal of Communication* 39 (no. 3): 94-109.

Sharp, E. B. (1984). Consequences of local government under the klieg lights. *Communication Research* 11: 497-517.

Tichenor, P., G. Donohue, and C. Olien (1970). Mass media flow and differential growth in knowledge. *Public Opinion Quarterly* 34: 159-170.

Viswanath, K., E. Kahn, J. R. Finnegan, J. Hertog, and J. D. Potter (1993). Motivation and the knowledge gap: Effects of a campaign to reduce diet-related cancer risk. *Communication Research* 20: 546-563.

Wanta, W., and W. R. Elliott. (1995). Did the "Magic" work? Knowledge of HIV/AIDS and the knowledge gap hypothesis. *Journalism Quarterly* 72: 312–321.

Weir, T. (1995). The continuing question of motivation in the knowledge gap hypothesis. Paper presented at the annual meeting of the Communication Theory and Methodology Division, Association for Education in Journalism and Mass Communication, Washington, D.C., August.

Zandpour, F., and A. R. Fellow (1992). Knowledge gap effects: Audience and media factors in alcohol-related communications. *Mass Comm Review* 19 (no. 3): 34–41.

chapter 14

Effects of Mass Communication

In the early stages of the campaign for the 1996 presidential election, Senate Majority Leader Bob Dole delivered a speech accusing the mass media (music, movies, television, and advertising) of regularly pushing "the limits of decency, bombarding our children with destructive messages of casual violence and even more casual sex" (Dole, 1995). Dole suggested that mass media messages shape children's "view of the 'real world'." He went on to say that "a numbing exposure to graphic violence and immorality does steal away innocence, smothering our instinct for outrage." Dole cited as specific examples the movies *Natural Born Killers* and *True Romance* and the music of such groups as Cannibal Corpse, Geto Boys, and 2 Live Crew.

The heart of Dole's speech was a charge that mass media messages are having certain effects, particularly on children. His speech is only one example of citizens or politicians expressing concerns about potential effects of mass communication. Questions about possible effects of mass media messages are not easy to answer. This chapter discusses a number of theories that have been proposed to help us understand the effects of mass communication. (Two areas of research—agenda setting and the knowledge gap—are so important that they have been dealt with in individual chapters [Chapters 12 and 13].) The present chapter also discusses a topic area where there has been extensive research on effects— and one that Senator Dole expressed concern about—the area of television violence.

THE BULLET THEORY

The "bullet theory" is the name given by later researchers to one of the first conceptions of the effects of mass communication. Also referred to as the "hypodermic needle theory" or the "transmission belt theory" (DeFleur &

Ball-Rokeach, 1982), this essentially naïve and simplistic view predicts strong and more or less universal effects of mass communication messages on all audience members who happen to be exposed to them. The name "bullet theory" was apparently not used by any of the early thinkers about mass communication effects (Chaffee & Hochheimer, 1985). Nevertheless, the phrase is a good description of a view that apparently was widely held. This view was influenced by the power that propaganda appeared to have in World War I, as we have described in Chapter 6. It was a popular view in the years prior to World War II, when many people shared a fear that a Hitler-style demagogue could rise to power in the United States through the force of mass communication. The Institute for Propaganda Analysis was created in response to this fear, and it began a massive campaign of educating the American people on the techniques of propaganda.

THE LIMITED-EFFECTS MODEL

Research on the effects of mass communication, almost from the beginning, did not provide much support for the bullet theory. Rather the evidence supported what came to be called the limited-effects model. Some of the key research leading to this view of mass communication as having small effects included Hovland's Army studies showing that orientation films were effective in transmitting information but not in changing attitudes; Cooper and Jahoda's research on the Mr. Biggott cartoons, indicating that selective perception could reduce the effectiveness of a message; and the election studies of Lazarsfeld and his associates, which showed that few people were influenced by mass communication in election campaigns.

The limited-effects model has been well stated in Joseph Klapper's book *The Effects of Mass Communication* (1960). Klapper presented five generalizations about the effects of mass communication; the first two are the following:

1. Mass communication ordinarily does not serve as a necessary and sufficient cause of audience effects, but rather functions among and through a nexus of mediating factors and influences.
2. These mediating factors are such that they typically render mass communication a contributory agent, but not the sole cause, in a process of reinforcing the existing conditions. . . . (p. 8)

The mediating factors that Klapper was referring to include the selective processes (selective perception, selective exposure, and selective retention), group processes and group norms, and opinion leadership.

This position, that the effects of mass communication are limited, is also sometimes referred to as "the law of minimal consequences." This phrase does not appear in Klapper's book, but was coined by his wife, Hope Lunin Klapper, a faculty member at New York University (Lang & Lang, 1968, p. 273).

CULTIVATION THEORY

When Senator Dole delivered his criticism of mass media messages for debasing U.S. culture, he used an interesting phrase. He addressed part of his criticism at "those who cultivate moral confusion" (Dole, 1995). One wonders if he was aware when he used that phrase that there was an area of communication research called *cultivation theory* that was very relevant to some of the charges he was making.

The area of communication study known as cultivation theory was developed by researcher George Gerbner and his colleagues at the Annenberg School of Communication at the University of Pennsylvania in what has probably been the longest-running and most extensive program of research on the effects of television ever to take place. Gerbner and his colleagues start with the argument that television has become the central cultural arm of American society. "The television set has become a key member of the family, the one who tells most of the stories most of the time," wrote Gerbner and his associates (Gerbner, Gross, Morgan, & Signorielli, 1980, p. 14).

The average viewer watches television four hours a day. The heavy viewer watches even more. The Gerbner team argues that for heavy viewers, television virtually monopolizes and subsumes other sources of information, ideas, and consciousness. The effect of all this exposure to the same messages produces what these researchers call *cultivation,* or the teaching of a common worldview, common roles, and common values.

If cultivation theory is correct, then television could be having important but unnoticeable effects on society. For instance, cultivation theory suggests that heavy television watching makes people feel that the world is an unsafe place. Fearful people might welcome repression if it helps to reduce their anxieties (Signorielli, 1990).

The original research supporting cultivation theory is based on comparisons of heavy and light television viewers. The Gerbner team analyzed answers to questions posed in surveys and found that heavy and light television viewers typically give different answers. Furthermore, the heavy television viewers often give answers that are closer to the way the world is portrayed on television. For instance, surveys have asked what percentage of the world's population lives in the United States (Gerbner & Gross, 1976b). The correct answer is 6 percent. Heavy television viewers tend to overestimate this figure much more than light television viewers. Of course, the leading characters in television entertainment programs are almost always Americans.

Other surveys have asked what percentage of Americans who have jobs work in law enforcement. The correct answer is 1 percent. Heavy television viewers give much higher figures, and they are more likely to do this than light television viewers. On television, about 20 percent of the characters are involved in law enforcement. Still another question asked of heavy and light television viewers is this: "During any given week, what are your chances of being involved in some type of violence?" The correct or real-world answer is 1 percent or less. The answer presented by television is about 10 percent. Heavy television viewers are more likely than light television viewers to give a larger percentage. In response to a question like "Can people be trusted?" the heavy television viewers are more likely than the light viewers to check a response such as "Can't be too careful." The responses to such questions suggest that heavy television viewers are getting a heightened sense of risk and insecurity from television. Television may be leading heavy viewers to perceive a "mean world." The Gerbner team suggests that this may be one of the primary, and widely shared, cultivation effects due to television.

Cultivation researchers have shown that the differences between heavy and light television viewers show up even across a number of other important variables, including age, education, news reading, and gender (Gerbner & Gross, 1976a). That is, these researchers realized that the relationship between television viewing and different views of the world could be actually caused by other variables, and they attempted to control for those variables.

These procedures have not satisfied all other researchers, however. The Gerbner team's research has been criticized by Paul Hirsch for not doing an adequate job of controlling for other variables. Hirsch's (1980) further analysis indicated that if one controls for a number of different variables all at the same time, the effect that is left that can be attributed to television becomes very small.

In response to the criticisms from Hirsch and others, Gerbner and his associates revised cultivation theory (Gerbner et al., 1980). They added two additional concepts—mainstreaming and resonance. These concepts take account of the fact that heavy television viewing has different outcomes for different social groups. *Mainstreaming* is said to occur when heavy viewing leads to a convergence of outlooks across groups. For instance, heavy viewers in both low-income and high-income categories share the view that fear of crime is a very serious personal problem. Light viewers in the two categories, however, do not share the same view. The light viewers who are low in income tend to agree with the heavy viewers in both categories that fear of crime is a problem, while the light viewers who are high in income tend not to agree that fear of crime is a problem. *Resonance* occurs when the cultivation effect is boosted for a certain group of the population. For instance, heavy viewers among both males and females are more likely than light viewers to agree that fear of crime is a serious problem. But the group that agrees the most strongly is females who are heavy viewers, because their particular vulnerability to crime is said to "resonate" with the portrait of a high-crime world presented on television.

The addition of mainstreaming and resonance to cultivation theory is a substantial modification of the theory. The theory no longer claims uniform, across-the-board effects of television on all heavy viewers. It now claims that television interacts with other variables in ways such that television viewing will have strong effects on some subgroups of persons and not on others. The Gerbner team is also admitting that Hirsch was right on one important point— when one controls for other variables simultaneously, the remaining effect attributable to television is rather small. Nevertheless, in light of the cumulative effects over time of the substantial exposure to television that most people (in the United States, at least) are experiencing, the effects might not be negligible.

Rubin, Perse, and Taylor (1988) cast further doubt on cultivation as a general, across-the-board effect due to heavy, ritualistic television viewing. In their survey of viewers, they found effects of television viewing on perceptions of social reality, but the effects were program-specific. That is, viewers of daytime serials tended to score lower in perception of altruism and trust in others, viewers of evening dramas (which often deal with control of others by powerful characters) tended to have lower feelings of political efficacy, and viewers of action and adventure shows expressed more feelings of concern about their own safety. They also found that age, gender, socioeconomic status, viewing intention (planning to watch television), and perceived realism (of television content) were better predictors of faith in others than television exposure. These results provide some evidence that viewers actively and differentially evaluate television content, or, to put it another way, that the television audience is an active one.

NEW DEVELOPMENTS IN CULTIVATION THEORY

One recent refinement of cultivation theory has been to divide possible cultivation effects into effects on two types or variables: first-order beliefs and second-order beliefs (Gerbner et al., 1986; Hawkins & Pingree, 1990). First-order beliefs refer to beliefs concerning various facts about the real world, such as the percentage of people who are victims of violent crime in a year. Second-order beliefs refer to extrapolation from these facts to general expectations or orientations, such as the belief that the world is a safe or a dangerous place. The two kinds of beliefs could be related in that second-order beliefs might be derived by inference from first-order beliefs. But some research has shown that first- and second-order beliefs are not always strongly correlated (Hawkins & Pingree, 1990).

There is some evidence that television viewing affects first-order beliefs, but that second-order beliefs are influenced by television viewing along with other factors, such as the kind of neighborhood a person lives in (Gerbner et al., 1986). Saito (1995) pointed out that both first-order and second-order beliefs can be held at the personal level or the societal level, creating a fourfold typology of possible effects of cultivation.

Many of the critics of cultivation theory have made the point that it is not reasonable to expect overall television viewing to have cultivation effects (Saito, 1995). Several researchers have suggested that cultivation theory might not hold up for all television content in general, but that it might for specific types or genres of television programming (Potter, 1993). McLeod and his associates (1995) have called this hypothesis the *extended cultivation hypothesis*. Gerbner, Gross, Morgan, and Signorielli (1994) have basically rejected the extended cultivation hypothesis, arguing that testing cultivation on the basis of program preferences does not address fundamental assumptions of the theory.

McLeod and associates (1995) tested both the original cultivation hypothesis and the revised cultivation hypothesis in a study of media influences on perceptions of crime. They attempted to explain the tendency for the public to misperceive the presence of crime in society. Many surveys have shown that the public believes crime is on the rise while crime statistics show decreases in crime rates for almost all categories of crime. The McLeod team looked at three media-effects hypotheses that might explain the distortion in crime perception by the public: the original cultivation hypothesis (which would suggest that overall television viewing would correlate with perceptions of crime rates), the revised cultivation hypothesis (which would suggest that viewing of fictional crime programs or other specific genres of television content would correlate with perceptions of crime rates), and the "news refraction hypothesis." The news refraction hypothesis suggests that exposure to local news content might have a strong influence on perceptions of issues such as crime because of the high perceived reality of the message (particularly on television) and the "closeness to home" of the content. The study found support for the news refraction hypothesis, but not for either the original cultivation hypothesis or the revised cultivation hypothesis. The authors conclude that overall, the use of crime-saturated local television news was most strongly implicated in promoting the synthetic crime crisis.

A promising topic for additional research on cultivation is examining the uniformity of television programming and the sources of that uniformity. The original form of cultivation theory assumed that television programming is quite uniform, and later versions of the theory have restated that assumption. The Gerbner research team (1994) suggested that the uniformity of television content comes from the centralized production of television programs and the economic motivations for large audiences. As they put it:

> Given the tight links among the various industries involved in the production and distribution of electronic media content, and the fact that most of them are trying to attract the largest and most heterogeneous audience, the most popular program materials present consistent and complementary messages, often reproducing what has already proven to be profitable (p. 19).

Shapiro (1995) called this the cultural-institutional model of cultivation theory, and argued that little research has been done on this aspect of cultivation theory.

Researchers have also begun to consider the effects of new communication technology on the cultivation process. Some scholars have suggested that new technology, such as cable television and VCRs, will serve mostly to break up the massive exposure of audiences to the same television content that is the basis of cultivation theory (Potter, 1993; Perse, Ferguson, & McLeod, 1994). But Dobrow (1990) found that heavy viewers used their VCRs to watch more of the same type of programming that they already enjoyed, while light viewers used their VCRs to diversify the kind of content to which they were exposed. She concluded that VCRs can enhance cultivation processes rather than reduce them. Gerbner, Gross, Morgan, and Signorielli (1994) argue that using VCRs for time shifting might actually end up decreasing the diversity of what is being watched.

Cultivation theory was originally designed to apply to television viewing, but it is reasonable to explore whether similar processes might take place with other media. As Morgan and Signorielli (1990) put it, "How and what do other media cultivate?" (p. 28)

One interesting extension of cultivation theory has applied it to research on the possible effects of pornography. Feminist scholars argued that pornography is an agent of enculturation, having widespread effects on cultural beliefs about women and sex roles. Preston (1990) argued that the typical laboratory experiment, with its short-term focus, is likely to miss these important effects of pornography on cultural beliefs. Preston used a cultivation theory perspective to examine the effects of exposure to pornography over a longer time period. The exposure to pornography included reading soft-core pornographic magazines and watching X-rated movies on VCRs. The effects on cultural beliefs were examined in terms of four variables: sex-role stereotypes, sex traits, sexuality stereotypes, and rape myths. Results showed that men high in exposure to pornography tended to show greater stereotyping about sex roles, sex traits, and sexuality than men low in exposure to pornography. For women, there was no relationship between exposure to pornography and stereotyping about sex roles. For stereotyping about sex traits and sexuality, women actually showed a reverse effect, with amount of exposure to pornography associated with less acceptance of stereotypes. Exposure to pornography was not related to acceptance of rape myths—for instance, that women can't be raped against their will—for either sex.

McLUHAN'S MEDIA DETERMINISM

Marshall McLuhan startled the entire world in 1964 with his statement that "the medium is the message" (1965, p. 7). McLuhan's writings and speeches were filled with puns and aphorisms to the point of being cryptic, but his classic *Understanding Media* is really fairly clear about what he meant by "the medium is the message." He wrote: "The effects of technology do not occur at the level of opinions or concepts, but alter sense ratios or patterns of perception steadily and without resistance" (p. 18). McLuhan is saying that the most important effect of communication media is that they affect our habits of perception and thinking. The concept of "sense ratios" refers to the balance of our senses. Primitive people emphasized all five senses—smell, touch, hearing, sight, taste—but technology, and especially the communication media, have caused people to emphasize one sense over others. Print, McLuhan says, emphasized vision. In turn, it influenced our thinking, making it linear, sequential, regular, repeated, and logical. It allowed human beings to separate thought from feeling. It led to specialization, and technology, but it also led to a sense of alienation and individualism. On the societal level, print led to the possibility of nations and the rise of nationalism.

Television, in contrast to print, emphasized more of the senses. McLuhan described television as a visual, aural, and tactile medium. It is more involving and participatory than print. McLuhan proposed that television would restore the balance of the sense ratios that print destroyed. On a grander scale, McLuhan said, television is going to retribalize us. We will move away from individual nation states and become a "global village." One of the things that bothered many communication theorists and people working in mass communication is that McLuhan was saying that the content of mass communication doesn't matter. McLuhan put it this way: "The 'content' of the medium is like the juicy piece of meat carried by the burglar to distract the watchdog of the mind" (1965, p. 18). That is, the important effects of the medium come from its form, not its content.

McLuhan said that the television generation is the first postliterate generation. He suggested that parents today are watching their children becoming "Third World," and that due to television and other new media, children do not think the same way that their parents did. "If Homer was wiped out by literacy, literacy can be wiped out by rock," McLuhan said on a public television program dealing with his life and work.

Researchers have attempted to test some of McLuhan's ideas, but one of the problems is that his notions involve such far-reaching and pervasive effects that it is difficult to test them. Some of the studies were flawed in that they dealt with extremely short-term effects, when McLuhan was obviously talking about effects that would take a long time to show up.

Some of McLuhan's ideas are being taken more seriously now than they were when they were first proposed. For instance, the National Assessment of Educational Progress, attempting to explain why the writing skills of young Americans were deteriorating, cited the role of television watching by young people and stated that "the culture is increasingly less print-oriented" (NAEP, 1975, p. 44). One researcher argued that relying on television for political information causes a decline in the ability to perform sophisticated intellectual operations on such information and thus is threatening to our democracy (Manheim, 1976).

McLuhan's notion of two different styles of thinking also seems to have anticipated the discussion of the different roles of the right and left hemispheres of the brain, much of which has occurred since the publication of *Understanding Media* in 1964. This work suggests that the two sides of the brain are specialized, the left side being logical, rational, and language-oriented, while the right side is intuitive, irrational, and picture-oriented. McLuhan later related his own work directly to the work on the hemispheres of the brain (1978).

Joshua Meyrowitz (1985) picked up the baton of McLuhanesque thinking and carried it a bit further. Meyrowitz shares with McLuhan a concern with the social consequences of new electronic media, particularly television. But Meyrowitz felt that the McLuhan notion of sense ratios and sensory balance did not provide a sufficient explanation of how television was affecting people.

Meyrowitz attempted to combine the thinking of McLuhan with that of sociologist Erving Goffman. Goffman wrote about how the "definition of the situation" affects behavior, but he focused on face-to-face interaction and ignored the media. Meyrowitz's main argument is that by bringing many different types of people to the same "place," electronic media have brought about the blurring of many formerly distinct roles. Some of the results have been the merging of masculinity and femininity, the blurring of childhood and adulthood, and the lowering of the political leader to the level of everyone else.

THE SPIRAL OF SILENCE

A theory that gives the mass media more power than many other theories is the "spiral of silence," developed by Elisabeth Noelle-Neumann (1973, 1980). Noelle-Neumann argues that the mass media do have powerful effects on public opinion but that these effects have been underestimated or undetected in the past because of the limitations of research. Noelle-Neumann argues that three characteristics of mass communication—its cumulation, ubiquity, and consonance—combine to produce powerful effects on public opinion. Consonance refers to the unified picture of an event or issue that can develop and is often shared by different newspapers, magazines, television networks, and other media. The effect of consonance is to overcome selective exposure, since people cannot select any other message, and to present the impression that most people look at the issue in the way that the mass media are presenting it.

Another factor that comes into play in the formation of public opinion is what Noelle-Neumann has called the "spiral of silence" (see Figure 14.1). On a controversial issue, people form impressions about the distribution of public opinion. They try to determine whether they are in the majority, and then they try to determine whether public opinion is changing to agree with them. If they feel they are in the minority, they tend to remain silent on the issue. If they think public opinion is changing away from them, they tend to remain silent on the issue. The more they remain silent, the more other people feel that the particular point of view is not represented, and the more they remain silent. The spiral of silence theory postulates that individuals have a quasi-statistical sense organ by which they determine "which opinions and modes of behavior are approved or disapproved of in their environment, and which opinions and forms of behavior are gaining or losing strength" (Noelle-Neumann, 1993, p. 202).

The mass media play an important part in the spiral of silence because they are the source to which people look to find the distribution of public opinion. The mass media can affect the spiral of silence in three ways: (1) they shape impressions about which opinions are dominantl; (2) they shape impressions about which opinions are on the increase; and (3) they shape impressions about which opinions one can utter in public without becoming isolated (Noelle-Neumann, 1973, p. 108).

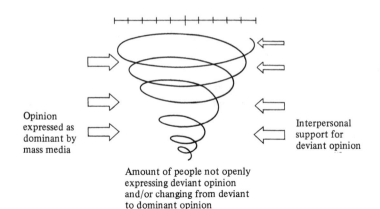

Opinion
expressed as
dominant by
mass media

Interpersonal
support for
deviant opinion

Amount of people not openly
expressing deviant opinion
and/or changing from deviant
to dominant opinion

FIGURE 14.1   The spiral of silence. The mass media's expressing a dominant opinion, combined with an increasing lack of interpersonal support for deviant views, brings about a spiral of silence, with an increasing number of individuals either expressing the dominant opinion or failing to express deviant ones.

SOURCE: From D. McQuail and S. Windahl, *Communication Models for the Study of Mass Communication* (London: Longman, 1981), p. 68.

Noelle-Neumann argues that willingness to speak out on issues is influenced largely by perception of the climate of opinion—if the climate of opinion goes against a person, that person will remain silent. The motivating force for this silence is said to be fear of isolation. Lasorsa (1991) questioned whether the fear of a hostile climate of opinion is really that strong, and undertook a study to investigate the question. He conducted a survey in which he tested whether political outspokenness is affected not only by one's perception of the climate of opinion, as suggested by Noelle-Neumann, but also by other variables such as age, education, income, interest in politics, level of self-efficacy, the personal relevance of the issue, one's news media use, and one's certitude in the correctness of one's position. The results of a regression analysis showed outspokenness being affected by the block of demographic variables (age, education, and income), level of self-efficacy, attention to political information in the news media, and certitude in one's position, but not by personal relevance of the issue or news media use in general. Lasorsa says his results show that people are not quite as helpless in the face of public opinion as Noelle-Neumann's theory suggests and that there are conditions under which it is possible to fight the spiral of silence.

Noelle-Neumann suggests that the mass media play an important role when people are attempting to determine what the majority opinion is. Rimmer and Howard (1990) attempted to test the key hypothesis of the spiral of silence that the mass media are used to assess majority opinion. They conducted a survey dealing with public opinion regarding PCBs (polychlorinated biphenyls), a toxic waste substance believed to cause cancer. They measured respondents' use of several types of mass media, and they also measured how accurately respondents perceived the majority opinion with regard to PCBs (the majority held the opinion that the test community should wait for further testing before taking action regarding PCBs). They found no relationship between media use and the ability to accurately estimate the majority position with regard to PCBs. Thus, these results do not support the idea of the mass media playing a major role in the spiral of silence.

Salwen, Lin, and Matera (1994) studied the willingness of citizens in three communities to express their opinion on the issue of "Official English." They found that a general tendency for willingness to speak out is related to perception of national opinion and perception of national media coverage more than perception of local opinion or local media coverage on the issue. These results provide mixed support for the spiral of silence theory.

THE THIRD-PERSON EFFECT

People sometimes react to mass communication messages as if the messages cannot have an effect on them, but that they might have an effect on other people. The third-person effect hypothesis, as suggested by W. Phillips Davison (1983), proposes that people will tend to overestimate the influence that mass communication messages have on the attitudes and behavior of others. The basic idea of the third-person effect is that certain messages "have little effect on people like you and me, but the ordinary reader is likely to be influenced quite a lot" (Davison, 1983, p. 2).

Gunther (1991) investigated the third-person effect by producing a news story that libeled a police chief. The police chief was known to be an outspoken supporter of handgun control, but the news story said he had contradicted that position in several out-of-town speeches. A control group was not shown the news story but was asked its opinion of the chief on a 19-point scale ranging from negative to positive. Other groups were asked to read the story and then their opinions toward the chief were measured with the same scale. The ones who read the article were then asked to indicate on a similar scale how much opinion change they thought the article would bring about in themselves, other students in the class, other University of Minnesota students, and Minnesota residents in general. Actual change in opinion for those reading the article was determined by comparing their scores with the scores for the control group. On the average, readers of the article expected greater opinion change in others than they actually demonstrated themselves.

The third-person effect hypothesis can be separated into two components. One has to do with perceptions. The hypothesis suggests that people will perceive that a mass communication message will have greater effects on others than on themselves. The other component has to do with effects. Because of this perception, people may take various actions. These actions would constitute an effect—although a less direct one—of the original message. Davison gives the example of the initial announcements in 1975 of the harmful effects of aerosol sprays. Manufacturers responded rather quickly to change to spray and squeeze containers. One explanation could be that they thought that the general public would be influenced by the news messages to stop buying the product or to boycott the companies.

Another application of the third-person effect may be in understanding certain kinds of censorship, or attempts to control or limit information. People who want to limit the kind of information that others will be exposed to sometimes seem to be in the position of saying "It won't have any effect on me, but I am worried about the effects on others." For example, advocates of censorship of pornography sometimes seem to be more worried about the effects on others than on themselves. Gunther (1995) asked a sample of respondents about their perceptions of the effects of pornography on themselves and on others, and also about their support for regulation of pornography. He found evidence for a third-person effect, with people tending to perceive greater effects of pornography on others than on themselves. Furthermore, he found that those who showed the third-person effect the most were most supportive of restrictions on pornographic material.

One interesting interpretation of the third-person effect is that people may be more influenced by the mass media than they think they are. The third-person effect hypothesis suggests that people see others as more influenced by the mass media than they themselves are. But it is of course possible than in some cases they are misperceiving (and underestimating) the effect that the messages are having on them (Davison, 1983).

MEDIA HEGEMONY

Another view that attributes wide (if not powerful) influence to the mass media is the concept of media hegemony. The idea of hegemony, as stated by Gramsci, is that "the routine, taken-for-granted structures of everyday thinking contribute to a structure of dominance" (Gamson, Croteau, Hoynes, & Sasson, 1992, p. 381). The concept of hegemony suggests that the ideas of the ruling class in society become the ruling ideas throughout society. The mass media are seen as controlled by the dominant class in society and as aiding in exerting the control of that class over the rest of society (Sallach, 1974). Media hegemony argues that news and other media content in the United States are shaped to the requirements of capitalist, or corporate, ideology.

The idea of media hegemony is a difficult one to test with research. Although suggesting a powerful influence, it is somewhat vague in its actual implications. If it is true, it is describing such a pervasive phenomenon that it becomes difficult to study because it is nearly impossible to set up a control group that is not subject to the effect being researched. Nevertheless, an attempt to evaluate the idea of media hegemony—at least with regard to news coverage—has been made by one researcher (Altheide, 1984). Altheide says that if you look at the writings on media hegemony, they seem to involve at least three assumptions that could be tested with evidence:

1. The socialization of journalists involves guidelines, work routines, and orientations replete with the dominant ideology.
2. Journalists tend to cover topics and present news reports that are conservative and supportive of the status quo.
3. Journalists tend to present pro-American and negative coverage of foreign countries, especially Third World nations.

Altheide argues that evidence can be found to cast doubt on each of these propositions. In connection with proposition 1, Altheide cites studies showing that foreign affairs reporters take very different approaches to covering détente, depending on their individual backgrounds. In addition, other studies of journalists' backgrounds and attitudes show considerable diversity rather than homogeneity.

In connection with proposition 2, Altheide cites numerous examples, including but not limited to Watergate, in which the reporting done by journalists did not support the status quo.

As for proposition 3, Altheide cites surveys of journalists that indicate they tend to agree with the Third World position on many issues. Furthermore, research on television coverage of Nicaragua during the Sandinista revolt showed that television presented the rebel case repeatedly and in some detail—not exactly the kind of content that supports the status quo.

Two researchers who attempted to find studies testing the media hegemony idea found only three (Shoemaker & Mayfield, 1984). Two supported the media hegemony idea, while one did not. It also seems to be the case, in the United States at least, that the elites have to spend a considerable amount of time defending their ideas against attacks from critics (Gamson, Croteau, Hoynes, & Sasson, 1992). It is difficult to see dominance of everyday thinking taking place in this kind of situation.

EFFECTS OF TELEVISION VIOLENCE

Throughout much of the history of television, a major concern has been the possible effects of television violence. Content analysis shows that a massive diet of violent content is served up on television. One set of figures indicates that by age 12, the average child will have watched 101,000 violent episodes on television, including 13,400 deaths (Steinfeld, 1973).

A number of different hypotheses have been suggested concerning the possible effects of television violence on human behavior. One is the catharsis hypothesis, which suggests that viewing television violence causes a reduction of aggressive drive through a vicarious expression of aggression. Several stimulation hypotheses predict that watching television violence leads to an increase in actual aggressive behavior. One of these is the imitation or modeling hypothesis, which suggests that people learn aggressive behaviors from television and then go out and reproduce them. A slightly different hypothesis is the disinhibition hypothesis, which suggests that television lowers people's inhibitions about behaving aggressively toward other people. If this hypothesis is correct, television violence might be teaching a general norm that violence is an acceptable way to relate to other people.

In all the hundreds of studies investigating the effects of television violence, only a handful support the catharsis hypothesis. Many more studies support the two stimulation hypotheses—imitation and disinhibition. One of the clearest of these studies is the Walters and Llewellyn-Thomas (1963) experiment (see Figure 14.2), which indicated that subjects who saw a violent film segment (a knife fight scene) were more likely to increase the levels of shock they would give another person than subjects who saw a nonviolent film segment (adolescents involved in crafts). This finding supports the disinhibition hypothesis, since the type of aggression engaged in was not the same as that portrayed in the film. A study conducted for the special committee appointed by the surgeon general to look into the effects of television violence reported a similar result.

FIGURE 14.2 Changes in shock level administered after watching violent or nonviolent television

SOURCE: Data from R. H. Walters and E. Llewellyn-Thomas, "Enhancement of Punitiveness by Visual and Audiovisual Displays," *Canadian Journal of Psychology* 17 (1963): 244–255.

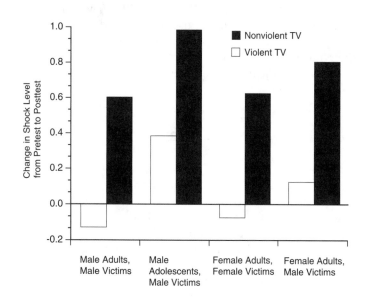

This was the Liebert and Baron (1972) study, which dealt with young children and a violent sequence from the television program "The Untouchables." It is possible to criticize these experiments for dealing only with short-term effects of televised violence and for being somewhat artificial in that they take place in laboratory settings. It could be, for instance, that people are more willing to behave aggressively in the laboratory because they do not have to worry about reprisals, which they would almost always have to do in real life.

Some research dealing with long-term effects of televised violence was also reported by the surgeon general's committee. This was a panel study conducted over a 10-year period. Lefkowitz, Eron, Walder, and Huesmann (1972) had started a study of aggression in young people in 1959 and 1960. When the surgeon general's study came along in 1969, Lefkowitz and his colleagues were able to take advantage of their earlier research to do a follow-up study. Their cross-lagged correlation data for boys showed in real life the same relationship that most of the experiments had shown in the laboratory: that watching television violence leads to an increase in aggressive behavior (see Figure 14.3). In fact, the study's best predictor of aggressive behavior at age 19 was violent television watching while in the third grade. The home environment is often thought to have an effect on whether or not a person becomes violent. The study by Lefkowitz and his associates looked at several aspects of the home environment that might have been related to later aggression: the amount of disharmony between the parents,

FIGURE 14.3 Cross-lagged correlations over a 10-year period for television viewing and aggression scores of 211 males

SOURCE: From M. M. Lefkowitz, L. D. Eron, L. O. Walder, and L. R. Huesmann, "Television Violence and Child Aggression: A Followup Study," in G. A. Comstock and E. A. Rubinstein (eds.), *Television and Social Behavior,* vol. 3 (Washington, D.C.: U.S. Government Printing Office, 1972), p. 49.

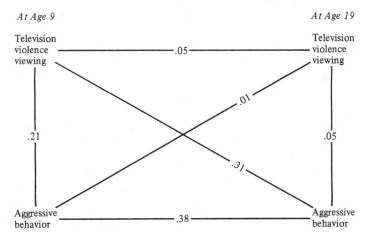

the tendency of the parents to punish the children, and the regularity of church attendance of the parents. None of these measures taken while boys were in the third grade predicted aggressive behavior at age 19 as well as did viewing television violence in the third grade.

These two types of studies—the experiments in the laboratories and the correlation studies from surveys outside the laboratories—agreed in their general finding, that viewing television violence leads to an increase in aggressive behavior. And that was the conclusion of the report of the surgeon general's advisory committee in 1972, although the committee stated it in a rather qualified manner:

> The two sets of findings converge in three respects: a preliminary and tentative indication of a causal relation between viewing violence on television and aggressive behavior; an indication that any such causal relation operates only on some children (who are predisposed to be aggressive); and an indication that it operates only in some environmental contexts. (Surgeon General's Scientific Advisory Committee on Television and Social Behavior, 1972, p. 11)

Some critics said this is a watered-down conclusion, heavily influenced by the network members of the committee, and that the research done for the committee really justifies a stronger conclusion. Some researchers have objected particularly to the statement that the causal relationship applies only to those children already predisposed to be aggressive. In the overview to one of the five volumes summarizing the research done for the committee, researcher Robert Liebert concludes that television violence may be contributing to the aggressive behavior "of many normal children" (Liebert, 1972, p. 30).

In 1982, the National Institute of Mental Health issued a report updating the 1972 surgeon general's study. The report offered this conclusion:

> What is the effect of all this violence? After 10 or more years of research, the consensus among most of the research community is that violence on television does lead to aggressive behavior by children and teenagers who watch the programs. This conclusion is based on laboratory experiments and field studies. Not all children become aggressive, of course, but the correlations between violence and aggression are positive. In magnitude, television violence is as strongly correlated with aggressive behavior as any other behavioral variable that has been measured. The research question has moved from asking whether or not there is an effect to seeking explanations for the effect. (1983, p. 28)

Recent research has looked at how violence is presented on television. A study that examined cable television as well as the major networks found that very few violent programs show long-term negative consequences of violence, that most violent scenes show the violence unpunished, and that most violent interactions show no pain or long-term negative consequences of the violence (National Television Violence Study, 1996). The researchers recommended that producers be more creative in showing more violent acts being punished, more negative consequences of violent acts, and more alternatives to the use of violence in solving problems.

SOCIAL LEARNING THEORY

One theory that is useful in studying the effects of the mass media is Albert Bandura's social learning theory (Bandura, 1977). This theory can be particularly useful in analyzing the possible effects of television violence, but it is also a general theory of learning that can be applied to other areas of mass media effects.

Reinforcement theory, one of the earlier formulations of learning theory, states that learning takes place when a behavior is reinforced with some reward. If this were the only way that learning could take place, people would have to try all kinds of behaviors themselves and then keep the ones that were rewarded and abandon the ones that led to punishment. Social learning theory recognizes that people can bypass this rather inefficient approach to learning and can acquire some behaviors simply by observation and storing the observations as a guide to future behavior.

Social learning theory acknowledges that human beings are capable of cognition or thinking and that they can benefit from observation and experience. Social learning theory recognizes that much human learning takes place through watching other people model various behaviors. For instance, a ballet student can learn certain movements by watching the instructor demonstrate those movements. This kind of learning can also obviously take place through the mass media. Someone can observe another person engaged in a certain behavior on television and can then practice that behavior in his or her own life.

Many of the effects of the mass media might take place through a process of social learning. These effects could include such things as people learning how to wear new fashions, people learning how to interact on dates, and people learning behaviors identified with being male or female. Of course, another example of social learning could be people learning new kinds of aggressive behavior from watching movies or television entertainment programs.

THE POWERFUL-EFFECTS MODEL

The powerful-effects model was first presented by Elisabeth Noelle-Neumann in her article "Return to the Concept of Powerful Mass Media" (1973). Her spiral of silence theory would fit under the powerful-effects model. Three other studies that also indicate a powerful effect due to the mass media have been conducted by Mendelsohn (1973), Maccoby and Farquhar (1975), and Ball-Rokeach, Rokeach, and Grube (1984a, 1984b).

Mendelsohn describes his own participation in three projects. The first, the CBS "National Drivers Test," resulted in 35,000 viewers enrolling in driver training courses. A second project involved a six-minute film called "A Snort History" that dealt with drinking and driving. The film was entertaining enough to be shown in a first-run motion picture theater along with the Clint Eastwood film *Dirty Harry*. The result of showing the film was that 3 out of 10 viewers said they would consider changing some of their previously held ideas regarding safe driving. A third project, an informational soap opera series aimed at Mexican-Americans in Los Angeles, led to 6 percent of the viewers (13,400 persons) reporting they had joined a community organization, one of the prime objectives of the series.

Mendelsohn says the three campaigns were successful because they were based on certain steps: (1) Spell out clearly the objectives of the campaign. (2) Pinpoint the target audience. (3) Work to overcome indifference of the audience toward the particular issue. (4) Find relevant themes to stress in messages.

Maccoby and Farquhar undertook an ambitious program that attempted to use mass communication to reduce heart disease. The study was conducted in three towns, with one (Gilroy) receiving an eight-month mass media campaign, another (Watsonville) receiving the same mass media campaign plus intensive group instruction for a sample of high-risk adults, and the third (Tracy) serving as a control and receiving neither type of communication. Pretests in all three towns before the campaign included measures of information, attitudes, and reported behaviors as well as a physical examination. Both the mass media campaign and the intensive instruction were aimed at producing behavior changes that would reduce the risk of coronary disease. These behaviors included reducing or stopping smoking, improving diets (particularly by eliminating foods high in cholesterol), and increasing amounts of exercise. Results showed that both types of communication campaigns were effective in reducing the amounts of egg consumed and the number of cigarettes smoked and in lowering the cholesterol level as well as an overall measure of heart disease risk, the Cornfield risk score. The greatest effects were in Watsonville, the town with the mass media campaign and the intensive instruction for a selected group, but there were also significant effects in Gilroy, the town with mass media only.

Another example of what might be considered a powerful effect achieved through mass communication comes from The Great American Values Test of Ball-Rokeach, Rokeach, and Grube (1984a, 1984b). These researchers developed a model for changing people's values—not an easy task, since our values are usually deeply held and a basic part of our personality. Their model states that people change their values and attitudes—and even their behavior—when they are forced to face inconsistencies in their basic values. This is a theory with some relationship to the consistency theories (see Chapter 8). The researchers argue that people who are forced to recognize inconsistencies in their belief systems experience a sense of dissatisfaction with themselves and that this can lead to reassessment and change.

These researchers designed an extensive experiment to test their theory for changing values. They produced a half-hour television program called "The Great

American Values Test." They obtained the cooperation of Ed Asner, former star of "The Mary Tyler Moore Show" and "The Lou Grant Show," and Sandy Hill, the former anchor of "Good Morning America," who both agreed to be the hosts for the program. The program begins by discussing results of some public opinion polls that assessed the values of the American people. Then Asner and Hill begin to challenge the audience by pointing out some inconsistencies in the rankings of values. For instance, they point out that the public ranks "freedom" third as a value, but "equality" is ranked twelfth. Asner asks what this means, and suggests the possibility that people are interested in freedom for themselves but not for other people. The hosts go on to a similar discussion of the value "a world of beauty," ranked seventeenth by the public. They contrast that with "a comfortable life," which is ranked much higher. They suggest that the low ranking for "a world of beauty" might explain why so many people are willing to live with pollution and ugliness.

The television program was shown on all three network stations in the Tri-Cities area of eastern Washington at the same time one evening. The program was heavily promoted beforehand, both on the television stations and in publications like *TV Guide*. The program was blacked out in Yakima, a city 80 miles away, so that the city could serve as a control.

The researchers studied the impact of the programming by comparing samples from the Tri-Cities area and Yakima. A random sample of residents of each city was selected from the phone book. The 1,699 respondents in the Tri-Cities area were called immediately after the broadcast of the program to see whether they had watched it and whether or not they were interrupted while watching it. Respondents in both cities received a questionnaire in which they were asked to rank 18 basic values, as well as to indicate their attitudes on racism, sexism, and environmental conservatism. They also answered some questions measuring their dependency on television. Then, to measure the effects of the program on behavior, respondents received three solicitations to send money to actual organizations. These came 8, 10, and 13 weeks after the program was broadcast. The solicitations came from a group aimed at providing opportunities for black children, the women's athletic program at Washington State University, and an environmental group attempting to promote antipollution measures.

Because the researchers were able to eliminate competing programs by scheduling the program on all three network stations, the program received an impressive Nielsen rating of 65 percent, meaning that 65 percent of the viewers watching television at that time were watching this program. Results showed that the program had an effect on donating money to organizations—the Tri-Cities respondents gave significantly more money than the Yakima respondents. Furthermore, viewers who watched without interruption gave more money than viewers who were interrupted.

Viewers of the program also changed their value rankings. They significantly increased their ranking of two of the target values, freedom and equality. They also increased, but less dramatically, their ranking of a third value, a world of beauty. The attitudes related to these values were also affected. Viewers became more antiracist and proenvironment in their attitudes. The authors also found that the viewers' dependency on television was an important factor in producing effects. Those persons who scored higher in dependency on television were more likely to watch the program, and when they did watch, they were more likely to change their values, change their attitudes, and contribute money to causes related to values discussed on the program.

The Great American Values Test experiment had a striking result: a single half-hour television program was able to change viewers' attitudes, their rankings of basic values, and their willingness to engage in behavior of a political nature. And all of this was done in a real-world setting, eliminating any question of whether these results apply outside of the laboratory.

THE SIZE OF EFFECTS

The numerous theories or research approaches that have been presented during the half-century or so of mass communication research have provided a number of different answers to the question of the size of mass communication effects. These theories can be presented in a time-line diagram that shows the time for each theory and the size of effect that it attributed to the media (see Figure 14.4, p. 317). The bullet theory, one of the earliest and most simplistic notions about mass communication, attributed quite strong effects to mass communication. After some time had passed, however, this conception was replaced by the limited-effects model. Eventually, though, research began to suggest that the limited-effects model might have swung the pendulum too far in the other direction. Research on a number of topics, including the knowledge gap, agenda setting, and the effects of television violence, indicated that mass communication was having more than limited effects. This position might be called the moderate-effects model. And finally, as we have discussed, a number of recent studies, including those by Noelle-Neumann, Mendelsohn, Maccoby and Farquhar, and Ball-Rokeach, Rokeach, and Grube, have shown mass communication to have powerful effects. It appears, however, that the powerful-effects model will be much more subject to qualifications than the bullet theory. "Powerful effects" do not occur universally or easily, but only when the right communication techniques are used under the right circumstances.

NEW DIRECTIONS IN EFFECTS RESEARCH

The Social Construction of Reality

One of the effects of mass communication may be to alter people's perceptions of reality, or, more broadly, their view of the world. This is a different effect from changes in attitudes, behavior, or knowledge. In fact, one of the criticisms of much communications effects research is that much of it has concentrated

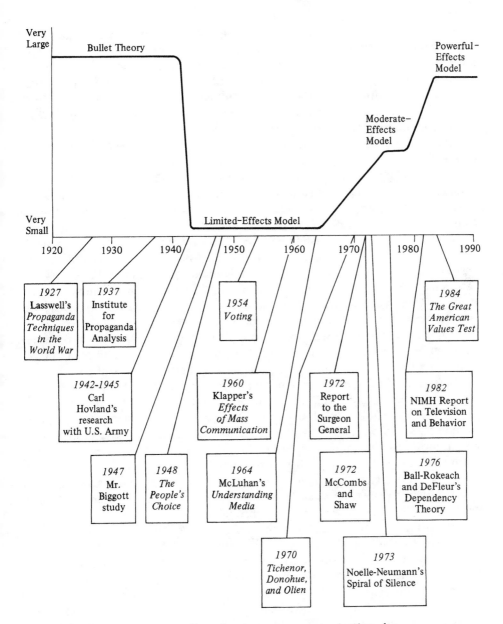

FIGURE 14.4 Size of effect due to mass communication, for various theories

on short-term effects on variables that are easy to measure through the experimental paradigm. Feminist theorists have argued that the effects of pornography range beyond the simple and isolated behavioral and attitudinal changes produced in laboratory studies and include the shaping of gender and sexual stereotypes (Preston, 1990). Gerbner (1990) stated that cultivation theory stemmed partly from the "narrowly conceived tactical emphasis of post-World War II communications research" (p. 249).

The process by which a person develops his or her views of the world can be described as the social construction of reality.

The social construction of reality has been a popular topic recently in mass communication theory, as well as in other academic fields. Perhaps it is worth noting that the phrase might better be stated as the "construction of social reality." As John Searle (1995) points out in his book *The Construction of Social Reality*, it is important to distinguish between mountains, which exist whether or not we believe in them, and money, which has the meaning that it does because we agree to treat it that way. Searle makes a distinction between brute facts, such as the existence of mountains, and institutional (or humanly constructed) facts, such as the value of money. The brute facts become the raw material for the construction of social facts.

Cultivation theory provides one approach to empirical research on the social construction of reality, but there are other approaches. Adoni and Mane (1984) proposed a three-part model of the process of the construction of social reality. The parts are "objective reality" (the reality experienced as the objective world existing outside the individual and made up of facts), "symbolic reality" (any form of symbolic expression of objective reality including art, literature, and media contents), and "subjective reality" (the reality constructed by the individual on the basis of objective and symbolic reality). Adonie and Mane recommend that research attempting to investigate the social construction of reality should include all three types of reality. Elliott, Kelly, and Byrd (1992) used a "social construction of reality" approach to study the effects of Oliver Stone's film *JFK*. Many in the press saw the film as a propagandistic attempt to influence an audience to a particular point of view. Part of the concern with *JFK* was that it blended real documentary film with reconstructed scenes.

Drawing upon the work of Adoni and Mane (1984), Elliott, Kelly, and Byrd developed a model of the possible effects of the film *JFK* on individuals' subjective reality (see Figure 14.5). They begin with the assumption that people attempt to construct a "subjective reality" based on information from objective reality and symbolic reality. Information used to construct a subjective reality is evaluated in terms of its perceived reality. The greater the perceived reality, the greater the likelihood that the information will be incorporated into an individual's subjective reality. People go through greater or lesser degrees of message elaboration, as described in Petty and Cacioppo's (1986) elaboration likelihood model. The greater the elaboration, the greater the likelihood of changes in images. In the case of *JFK*, the authors have broken symbolic reality into three components: unsanctioned symbolic reality (made up of conspiracy theories,

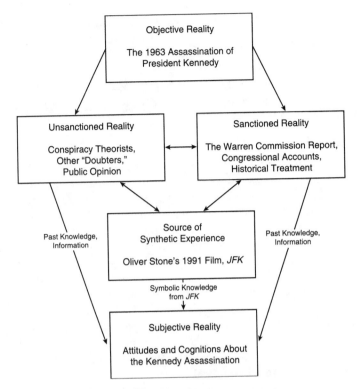

FIGURE 14.5 The construction of subjective reality based on the movie *JFK*

SOURCE: From W. R. Elliott, J. D. Kelly, and J. T. Byrd, "Synthetic History and Subjective Reality: The Impact of Oliver Stone's *JFK*," paper presented to the Communication Theory and Methodology Division, Association for Education in Journalism and Mass Communication, Montreal, August 1992. Reprinted by permission.

etc.), sanctioned symbolic reality (made up of official governmental reports, etc.), and synthetic experience (the film *JFK*).

The authors predicted that exposure to the film *JFK* would have effects on both first-order beliefs and second-order beliefs. First-order beliefs are the "facts" about the Kennedy assassination, including those that most people accept (such as the time of the assassination) and those that the film presents but which are not universally accepted (such as the existence of three assassination teams). Second-order beliefs are generalizations from "facts" to perceptions about more general processes. Examples of second-order beliefs would be political mistrust or acceptance of the idea of a "shadow government" that actually runs the United States.

Elliott, Kelly, and and Byrd conducted a field experiment in which a "film" group of students was offered free passes to attend the motion picture *JFK* while a control group was not. The students were surveyed shortly after exposure to the film and then again three weeks later. The results showed that viewing *JFK* did have an effect on first-order beliefs, or the "facts" of the assassination, including even the synthetic facts, where the movie differed from widely accepted accounts. The movie had an effect on one of the second-order beliefs, belief in a shadow government, but not the other, political mistrust.

Media Framing

In a dispute over a controversial issue, it is common to see each side struggling to define—or frame—the issue in its own terms. For instance, in the debate over abortion, one side may spend a great deal of energy in attempting to present the argument as one concerning the life of an unborn child. At the same time, another side may attempt to say the dispute is really about a woman's right to choose what happens to her and her body. To a certain extent, the advocates that succeed in making others accept their framing of the debate have already won the debate. Research on survey questionnaires has shown that public opinion on abortion can shift radically depending upon just how the question is worded.

The news media also tend to frame issues in various ways. A frame can be defined as "a central organizing idea for news content that supplies a context and suggests what the issue is through the use of selection, emphasis, exclusion, and elaboration" (Tankard et al., 1991).

Media scholars have found the concept of framing useful for examining media coverage of news. To a certain extent, the concept of media framing presents a new paradigm to replace the older paradigm of studying the "objectivity and bias" of the media (Hackett, 1984). Bias studies tended to focus on whether news coverage was positive, neutral, or negative toward a candidate, idea, or institution. Once one begins to think of news coverage in terms of framing, the old concept of bias seems somewhat narrow and simplistic.

The framing of news stories may also have more subtle—and powerful—influences on audiences than bias in news stories. Audience members may be able to detect that a story is biased against a particular political candidate. But they may not detect as easily that a news event is being packaged as a certain type of story.

Frames are sometimes defined by those in power and then picked up and transmitted by the news media. For instance, during the Reagan administration much of the news from Latin America was framed in terms of a Communist threat to the United States. Certainly the occurrences in that region could have been framed in other ways—for instance, that these were developing nations in which many people were leading lives of hardship. But the news coverage tended to reflect the framing that the U.S. government was giving to the situation. Examination of much coverage of international events for the 40 years after World War II suggests that the cold war often provided an overriding frame.

The concept of framing may have other advantages besides allowing more sophisticated analyses of news coverage. Framing may help us to understand how people process news. For instance, the framing of a news story may have important effects on the way the information in the story is processed and stored (Bleske, 1995). Some ways of framing the news may "hook up" better than others with existing ideas or schemas about a topic that people already have in their minds.

Sometimes the framings of news stories are suggested by particular devices that are accessed early in the processing of the stories. These devices include headlines, leads (beginning paragraphs of news stories), pull quotes (quotes taken from an article and set in large type), and nut graphs (key paragraphs in articles telling what they are about). These devices sometimes fit in the category of Advanced Organizers. The concept of Advanced Organizers is based on the idea that the information stored in people's heads is organized in a hierarchy, with specific information grouped under broader principles (Ausubel, 1960). An Advanced Organizer provides some of the general structure by which specific information can be organized before the specific information is presented.

Research has shown that media framing can have an effect on the way audience members end up interpreting an issue. For instance, Shah and Domke (1995) conducted an experiment in which one group received a news story presenting health care in an ethical frame and another group received a news story presenting health care in a societal frame. The story with the ethical frame emphasized rights and morals associated with health care. The story with the societal frame emphasized costs and benefits to society, and, indirectly, to individuals. The results showed that individuals receiving the story framing health care as an ethical issue were later more likely to interpret health care as an ethical issue than individuals receiving the story framing health care as a societal issue. Furthermore, there was some tendency for the ethical framework to extend to totally different issues the individuals were asked to interpret.

One researcher (Iyengar, 1991) argued that some of the most important framing done by the media has to do with suggesting who is responsible for a problem and who can help provide a remedy for the problem. His research indicates that much television news, by focusing on discrete events out of context, causes viewers to assign responsibility for social problems to individuals rather than to society as a whole. For instance, coverage of terrorism could focus on scenes of aircraft hijackings, hostage situations, and bombings. Or it could deal with analyzing terrorism as a general political problem influenced by economic and political oppression, global politics, and local political turmoil. The former would probably lead audience members to assign causal responsibility for terrorism to particular individuals and groups, while the latter might lead to assigning responsibility to factors in society as a whole.

Maher (1995) examined the possible effects of newspaper framing of the causes of environmental problems. He determined the media framing of causes of a local environmental problem in Austin, Texas, by conducting a content analysis of the local daily newspaper. He then surveyed a sample of the public

TABLE 14.1   Media framing and public opinion concerning causes of the Barton Creek environmental controversy

	Media Framing of Causes*	Public Opinion about Causes**
Cause		
Developers	89.2	56.1
Polluters	57.3	16.3
Growth	53.7	9.3
Population growth	2.4	7.6
Other	—	11.1

*Percentage of newspaper stories mentioning this cause. Numbers add to more than 100% because many stories mentioned more than one cause.
**Percentage of survey respondents mentioning this cause. The percentages are based on those who mentioned some cause in response to an open-ended question: "What do you think are the underlying causes of the environmental problems at Barton Creek?"
SOURCE: From Thomas Michael Maher, "Media Framing and Salience of the Population Issue: A Multimethod Approach," unpublished Ph.D. dissertation, The University of Texas at Austin, 1995. Reprinted by permission.

to assess their perception of causes for the problem. It was Maher's thesis that media framing ignores a link between population growth and environmental problems, and that the public, under the influence of the media coverage, would also fail to make that link. Results of his analysis are shown in Table 14.1. The table shows a rather close correspondence between the weight assigned to various causes by the news coverage and the percentage of the public mentioning those factors as underlying causes of the environmental problems at Barton Creek.

CONCLUSIONS

Communication researchers have not yet come up with a unified theory that will explain the effects of mass communication. Instead we have a number of theories, each attempting to explain some particular aspect of mass communication. As communication research advances, perhaps we shall see several of these mini-theories combined into one overall theory of mass communication effects. Or, perhaps some of these theories will not survive the test of empirical research and will be winnowed out, while others survive.

The most recent theorizing about mass media effects seems to be suggesting that most mass media effects do not occur "across the board," but are contingent on other variables (Chaffee, 1977). Perry (1988) argues that the truth of a hypothesis differs in different circumstances, and puts in a plea for placing research findings in their context.

Deutsch (1986), discussing the social sciences in general, commented:

> Probably the structure of society and most social outcomes are the result of a plurality or multiplicity of relatively weak forces and processes. The search for single causes and single models, which has been pursued for a long time, turns out to be less fruitful than once was thought. Outcomes of a particular kind seem to occur most often when "all systems are "go"—that is, when all the weak factors, or at least a critical number of them, point in the same direction. Step by step, more of these weak factors are being identified. (pp. 11–12)

Thus, the statement that "it depends" is an accurate description of the answer to many questions about media effects. The answer "it depends" should not be met with despair and a throwing up of the hands, however. The answer "it depends" does not mean that we do not know what is going on. In contrast to what we knew 40 or 50 years ago, we now have some more definite ideas of what "it" depends on. As Elihu Katz has noted, the factors of selective perception and interpersonal relations are two important variables that the effects of mass communication depend on.

The newer approaches of the social construction of reality and media framing also extend our thinking about the effects of mass communication in subtle and sophisticated ways that offer promise for greater understanding.

DISCUSSION

1. Which of the theories of the effects of mass communication are most relevant to Senator Bob Dole's charges against the media? What would these theories say about his charges?
2. Which version of cultivation theory do you think is more likely to be correct—the original hypothesis suggesting "across the board" effects or the revised hypothesis suggesting effects for particular types or genres of programs?
3. What are some examples of the third-person effect at work? Can you think of examples in which people have taken some action on the basis of the effect they thought a message would have on others?
4. One possible implication of the third person effect is that people may be underestimating the effect of messages on themselves. What are some examples of situations in which you or others may be under-estimating the effects of mass communication on yourself or themselves?
5. What role do the mass media play in the spiral of silence? What are some examples of the mass media playing that role?
6. What is meant by the "social construction of reality"? How is the concept useful in the study of mass communication?

7. Some writers have suggested that the media framing of events can have more powerful effects than biased coverage of events. Why might this be true?

8. Several theories of the effects of mass communication suggest that the effects might be contingent or dependent on other variables. What are two or three of the most important of these variables?

REFERENCES

Adoni, H., and S. Mane (1984). Media and the social construction of reality: Toward an integration of theory and research. *Communication Research* 11: 323-340.

Altheide, D. L. (1984). Media hegemony: A failure of perspective. *Public Opinion Quarterly* 48: 476-490.

Ausubel, D. P. (1960). The use of advance organizers in the learning and retention of meaningful verbal material. *Journal of Educational Psychology* 51: 267-272.

Ball-Rokeach, S. J., M. Rokeach, and J. W. Grube (1984a). The Great American Values Test. *Psychology Today,* Nov., pp. 34-41.

Ball-Rokeach, S. J., M. Rokeach, and J. W. Grube (1984b). *The Great American Values Test: Influencing Behavior and Belief through Television.* New York: Free Press.

Bandura, A. (1977). *Social Learning Theory.* Englewood Cliffs, N.J.: Prentice-Hall.

Bleske, G. L. (1995). Schematic frames and reader learning: The effect of headlines. Paper presented at the annual meeting of the Communication Theory and Methodology Division of the Association for Education in Journalism and Mass Communication, Washington, D.C., August.

Chaffee, S. H. (1977). Mass media effects: New research perspectives. In D. Lerner and L. M. Nelson (eds.), *Communication Research—a Half-Century Appraisal*, pp. 210-241. Honolulu: University Press of Hawaii.

Chaffee, S. H., and J. L. Hochheimer (1985). The beginnings of political communication research in the United States: Origins of the "limited effects model." In M. Gurevitch and M. R. Levy (eds.), *Mass Communication Review Yearbook*, vol. 5, pp. 75-104. Beverly Hills, Calif.: Sage.

Davison, W. P. (1983). The third-person effect in communication. *Public Opinion Quarterly* 47:1-15.

DeFleur, M. L., and S. Ball-Rokeach (1982). *Theories of Mass Communication*, 4th ed. New York: McKay.

Deutsch, K. W. (1986). What do we mean by advances in the social sciences? In K. W. Deutsch, A. S. Markovits, and J. Platt (eds.), *Advances in the Social Sciences, 1900-1980: What, Who, Where, How?* pp. 1-12. Cambridge, Mass.: Abt Books.

Dobrow, J. R. (1990). Patterns of viewing and VCR use: Implications for cultivation analysis. In N. Signorielli and M. Morgan (eds.), *Cultivation Analysis: New Directions in Media Effects Research*, pp. 71-83. Newbury Park, Calif.: Sage.

Dole, B. (1995). Text of remarks by Senator Bob Dole, Los Angeles, Calif., May 31, 1995.

Elliott, W. R., J. D. Kelly, and J. T. Byrd (1992). Synthetic history and subjective reality: The impact of Oliver Stone's *JFK*. Paper presented at the annual meeting of the Communication Theory and Methodology Division of the Association for Education in Journalism and Mass Communication, Montreal, Canada, August.

Gamson, W. A., D. Croteau, W. Hoynes, and T. Sasson (1992). Media images and the social construction of reality. *Annual Review of Sociology* 18: 373-393.

Gerbner, G. (1990). Epilogue: Advancing on the path or righteousness (maybe). In N. Signorielli and M. Morgan (eds.), *Cultivation Analysis: New Directions in Media Effects Research*, pp. 249-262. Newbury Park, Calif.: Sage.

Gerbner, G., and L. P. Gross (1976a). Living with television: The violence profile. *Journal of Communication* 26 (no. 2): 172-199.

Gerbner, G., and L. P. Gross (1976b). The scary world of TV's heavy viewer. *Psychology Today*, Apr., pp. 41-45, 89.

Gerbner, G., L. Gross, M. Morgan, and N. Signorielli (1980). The "mainstreaming" of America: Violence profile no. 11. *Journal of Communication* 30 (no. 3): 10-29.

Gerbner, G., L. Gross, M. Morgan, and N. Signorielli (1986). Living with television: The dynamics of the cultivation process. In J. Bryant and D. Zillman (eds.), *Perspectives on media effects*, pp. 17-40. Hillsdale, N.J.: Lawrence Erlbaum.

Gerbner, G., L. Gross, M. Morgan, and N. Signorielli (1994). Growing up with television: The cultivation perspective. In J. Bryant and D. Zillmann (eds.), *Media Effects: Advances in Theory and Research*, pp. 17-41. Hillsdale, N.J.: Lawrence Erlbaum.

Gunther, A. (1991). What we think others think: Cause and consequence in the third-person effect. *Communication Research* 18: 355-372.

Gunther, A. C. (1995). Overrating the X-rating: The third-person perception and support for censorship of pornography. *Journal of Communication* 45 (no. 1): 27-38.

Hackett, R. A. (1984). Decline of a paradigm? Bias and objectivity in news media studies. In M. Gurevitch and M. R. Levy (eds.), *Mass Communication Review Yearbook*, vol. 5, pp. 251-274. Beverly Hills, Calif.: Sage.

Hawkins, R. P., and S. Pingree (1990). Divergent psychological processes in constructing social reality from mass media content. In N. Signorielli and M. Morgan (eds.), *Cultivation Analysis: New Directions in Media Effects Research*, pp. 35-50. Newbury Park, Calif.: Sage.

Hirsch, P. (1980). The "scary world" of the nonviewer and other anomalies: A reanalysis of Gerbner et al.'s findings on cultivation analysis. *Communication Research* 7: 403-456.

Iyengar, S. (1991). *Is Anyone Responsible? How Television Frames Political Issues*. Chicago: The University of Chicago Press.

Klapper, J. T. (1960). *The Effects of Mass Communication*. New York: Free Press.

Lang, K., and G. E. Lang (1968). *Politics and Television*. Chicago: Quadrangle.

Lasorsa, D. L. (1991). Political outspokenness: Factors working against the spiral of silence. *Journalism Quarterly* 68: 13-140.

Lefkowitz, M. M., L. D. Eron, L. O. Walder, and L. R. Huesmann (1972). Television violence and child aggression: A followup study. In G. A. Comstock and E. A. Rubinstein (eds.), *Television and Social Behavior*, vol. 3, pp. 35-135. Washington, D.C.: U.S. Government Printing Office.

Liebert, R. M. (1972). Television and social learning: Some relationships between viewing violence and behaving aggressively (overview). In J. P. Murray, E. A. Rubinstein, and G. A. Comstock (eds.), *Television and Social Behavior*, vol. 2, pp. 1-42. Washington, D.C.: U.S. Government Printing Office.

Liebert, R. M., and R. A. Baron (1972). Short-term effects of televised aggression on children's aggressive behavior. In J. P. Murray, E. A. Rubinstein, and G. A. Comstock (eds.), *Television and Social Behavior*, vol. 2, pp. 181-201. Washington, D.C.: U.S. Government Printing Office.

Maccoby, N., and J. W. Farquhar (1975). Communication for health: Unselling heart disease. *Journal of Communication* 25 (no. 3): 114-126.

McLeod, J. M., K. Daily, W. Eveland, Z. Guo, K. Culver, D. Kurpius, P. Moy, E.Horowitz, and M. Zhong (1995). The synthetic crisis: Media influences on perceptions of crime. Paper presented at the annual meeting of the Communication Theory and Methodology Division of the Association for Education in Journalism and Mass Communication, Washington, D.C., August.

McLuhan, M. (1965). *Understanding Media: The Extensions of Man.* New York: McGraw-Hill.

McLuhan, M. (1978). The brain and the media: The "western" hemisphere. *Journal of Communication* 28 (no. 4): 54-60.

Maher, M. (1995). Media framing and salience of the population issue: A multimethod approach. Unpublished dissertation, The University of Texas at Austin.

Manheim, J. B. (1976). Can democracy survive television? *Journal of Communication* 26 (no. 2): 84-90.

Mendelsohn, H. (1973). Some reasons why information campaigns can succeed. *Public Opinion Quarterly* 37: 50-61.

Meyrowitz, J. (1985). *No Sense of Place.* New York: Oxford University Press.

Morgan, M., and N. Signorielli (1990). Cultivation analysis: Conceptualization and methodology. In N. Signorielli and M. Morgan (eds.), *Cultivation Analysis: New Directions in Media Effects Research,* pp. 13-34. Newbury Park, Calif.: Sage.

National Assessment of Educational Progress (1975). *Writing Mechanics, 1969-75: A Capsule Description of Changes in Writing Mechanics.* Washington, D.C.: U.S. Government Printing Office.

National Institute of Mental Health (1983). Television and behavior: Ten years of scientific progress and implications for the eighties. In E. Wartella and D. C. Whitney (eds.), *Mass Communication Review Yearbook,* vol. 4, pp. 23-35. Beverly Hills, Calif.: Sage.

National Television Violence Study. (1996). Studio City, Calif.: Mediascope.

Noelle-Neumann, E. (1973). Return to the concept of powerful mass media. In H. Eguchi and K. Sata (eds.), *Studies of Broadcasting: An International Annual of Broadcasting Science,* pp. 67-112. Tokyo: Nippon Hoso Kyokai.

Noelle-Neumann, E. (1980). Mass media and social change in developed societies. In G. C. Wilhoit and H. de Bock (eds.), *Mass Communication Review Yearbook,* vol. 1, pp. 657-678. Beverly Hills, Calif.: Sage.

Noelle-Neumann, E. (1993). *The Spiral of Silence: Public Opinion—Our Social Skin,* 2nd ed. Chicago: University of Chicago Press.

Perry, D. K. (1988). Implications of a contextualist approach to media-effects research. *Communication Research* 15: 246-264.

Perse, E. M., D. A. Ferguson, and D. M. McLeod (1994). Cultivation in the newer media environment. *Communication Research* 21: 79-104.

Potter, W. J. (1993). Cultivation theory and research: A conceptual critique. *Human Communication Research* 19: 564-601.

Preston, E. H. (1990). Pornography and the construction of gender. In N. Signorielli and M. Morgan (eds.), *Cultivation Analysis: New Directions in Media Effects Research,* pp. 107-122. Newbury Park, Calif.: Sage.

Rimmer, T., and M. Howard (1990). Pluralistic ignorance and the spiral of silence: A test of the role of the mass media in the spiral of silence hypothesis. *Mass Comm Review* 17: 47-56.

Rubin, A. M., E. M. Perse, and D. S. Taylor (1988). A methodological examination of cultivation. *Communication Research* 15: 107–134.

Saito, S. (1995). Cultivation theory revisited: Another look at the theory and implications for future research. Paper presented at the annual meeting of the Communication Theory and Methodology Division of the Association for Education in Journalism and Mass Communication, Washington, D.C., August.

Sallach, D. L. (1974). Class domination and ideological hegemony. *Sociological Quarterly* 15 (no. 1): 38–50.

Salwen, M. B., C. Lin, and F. R. Matera (1994). Willingness to discuss "Official English": A test of three communities. *Journalism Quarterly* 71: 282–290.

Searle, J. (1995). *The Construction of Social Reality*. New York: Free Press.

Shah, D., and D. Domke (1995). Manipulating the media frame of electoral issues: An examination of voters' issue interpretations and decision-making. Paper presented at the annual meeting of the Communication Theory and Methodology Division of the Association for Education in Journalism and Mass Communication, Washington, D.C., August.

Shapiro, M. (1995). Discussant's remarks at the annual meeting of the Communication Theory and Methodology Division of the Association for Education in Journalism and Mass Communication, Washington, D.C., August.

Shoemaker, P. J., and E. K. Mayfield (1984). Mass media content as a dependent variable: Five media sociology theories. Paper presented at the annual meeting of the Communication Theory and Methodology Division of the Association for Education in Journalism and Mass Communication, Gainesville, Fla., August.

Signorielli, N. (1990). Television's mean and dangerous world: A continuation of the cultural indicators perspective. In N. Signorielli and M. Morgan (eds.), *Cultivation Analysis: New Directions in Media Effects Research*, pp. 85–106. Newbury Park, Calif.: Sage.

Steinfeld, J. L. (1973). TV violence is harmful. *Reader's Digest*, Apr., pp. 7–38, 40, 43, 45.

Surgeon General's Scientific Advisory Committee on Television and Social Behavior (1972). *Television and Growing Up: The Impact of Televised Violence*. Washington, D.C.: U.S. Government Printing Office.

Tankard, J. W., L. Hendrickson, J. Silberman, K. Bliss, and S. Ghanem (1991). Media frames: Approaches to conceptualization and measurement. Paper presented at the annual meeting of the Communication Theory and Methodology Division of the Association for Education in Journalism and Mass Communication, Boston, August.

Walters, R. H., and E. Llewellyn-Thomas (1963). Enhancement of punitiveness by visual and audiovisual displays. *Canadian Journal of Psychology* 17: 244–255.

chapter **15**

Uses of the Mass Media

Previous chapters have dealt, for the most part, with what the media do to their audiences. Indeed, many of us, both in the media and out of the media, tend to think of the media "acting" upon their viewers, listeners, and readers. Subconsciously we often continue to accept the model of the media as a hypodermic needle or a bullet directed to a passive target. But audiences are not always passive; indeed, one classic study, titled "The Obstinate Audience," pointed out that the audience is often quite active (Bauer, 1964). Other researchers echo the statement: "The notion of 'the active communicator' is rapidly achieving preeminent status in the communication discipline" (Bryant & Street, 1988, p. 162). Rubin (1994) has argued that audience activity is the core concept of the uses and gratifications approach.

Along similar lines, one group of authors suggested that the term "audience" be replaced with the idea of an active "reader" of mass communication content (Gamson, Croteau, Hoynes, & Sasson, 1992). These authors stress that much mass media content is rich in meaning and open to multiple readings.

In this chapter we shall examine some research concerning what the audience does with the media, as we take up an area of research often referred to as "the uses and gratifications approach." The uses and gratifications approach involves a shift of focus from the purposes of the communicator to the purposes of the receiver. It attempts to determine what functions mass communication is serving for audience members. In at least one respect the uses and gratifications approach to the media fits well with the Libertarian theory and John Stuart Mill's notions of human rationality. Both stress the potential of the individual for self-realization.

BEGINNINGS OF THE USES
AND GRATIFICATIONS APPROACH

The uses and gratifications approach was first described in an article by Elihu Katz (1959) in which he was reacting to a claim by Bernard Berelson (1959) that the field of communication research appeared to be dead. Katz argued that the field that was dying was the study of mass communication as persuasion. He pointed out that most communication research up to that time had been aimed at investigating the question "What do media do to people?"

Katz suggested that the field might save itself by turning to the question "What do people do with the media?" He cited a few studies of this type that were already done. One of them was, curiously enough, by Berelson. It was his What 'Missing the Newspaper' Means," a 1949 study conducted by interviewing people during a newspaper strike about what they missed in their newspapers (Berelson, 1965).

During this two-week strike of deliverymen, most readers were forced to find other sources of news, which is what they overwhelmingly said they missed the most. Many read because they felt it was the socially acceptable thing to do, and some felt that the newspaper was indispensable in finding out about world affairs. Many, however, sought escape, relaxation, entertainment, and social prestige. These people recognized that awareness of public affairs was of value in conversations. Some wanted help in their daily lives by reading material about fashion, recipes, weather forecasts, and other useful information.

Another example cited by Katz was Riley and Riley's study (1951) showing that children well integrated into groups of peers "use" adventure stories in the media for group games while children not well integrated use the same communications for fantasizing and daydreaming. This example illustrates a basic aspect of the uses and gratifications approach—different people can use the same mass communication message for very different purposes. Another study examined the functions radio soap operas fulfilled for regular listeners. Some listeners found emotional release from their own problems. For others, listening provided escape, while a third group sought solutions to their own problems (Herzog, 1944).

USES AND GRATIFICATIONS
IN AN ELECTION CAMPAIGN

Blumler and McQuail (1969) used the uses and gratifications approach as the overall research strategy in a study of the 1964 general election in Britain. The central aim of their study was "to find out why people watch or avoid party broadcasts; what uses they wish to make of them; and what their preferences are between alternative ways of presenting politicians on television" (pp. 10-11). Part of their aim was to answer the challenging question posed by earlier election studies that indicated mass media election campaigns had little effect on voters: if voters are not influenced by mass media election programming,

TABLE 15.1   Reasons for watching party broadcasts in the British general election of 1964, as endorsed by TV owners

	Percent
To see what some party will do if it gets into power	55
To keep up with the main issues of the day	52
To judge what political leaders are like	51
To remind me of my party's strong points	36
To judge who is likely to win the election	31
To help make up my mind how to vote	26
To enjoy the excitement of the election race	24
To use as ammunition in arguments with others	10

Note: Respondents could endorse more than one reason.
SOURCE: From Jay G. Blumler and Denis McQuail, *Television in Politics: Its Uses and Influence.* Chicago: University of Chicago Press, 1969. Copyright by Jay G. Blumler and Denis McQuail. Reprinted by permission of Faber and Faber Ltd. and the University of Chicago Press.

why do they follow it at all? Also, the researchers expected that classifying viewers according to their motives for viewing might disclose some previously undetected relationships between attitude change and campaign exposure, and thus might tell us something about effects after all.

Blumler and McQuail began the task of determining people's motives for watching political broadcasts by using open-ended questions to interview a small sample. On the basis of the responses to these questions, they drew up a list of eight reasons for watching political broadcasts. This list was used in subsequent interviewing with a large sample survey. On the basis of this interviewing, the researchers determined the frequency with which each reason was cited, as shown in Table 15.1. The three most frequently mentioned reasons reflect a desire for what Blumler and McQuail call "surveillance of the political environment." These reasons, each cited by more than half the respondents, indicate that people used the political broadcasts as a source of information about political affairs. Other data from the survey indicated that one of the specific purposes of this surveillance was to find out about campaign promises and pledges. Only about a third of the respondents chose "To remind me of my party's strong points," a reason that would indicate the political broadcasts were being used for reinforcement of existing attitudes. This casts some doubt on the indication from some earlier research that people turn to the mass media primarily for reinforcement.

CLASSIFYING INDIVIDUAL NEEDS AND MEDIA USES

A few years later, in a paper that summarized work in the field to that time, Katz, Blumler, and Gurevitch (1974) pointed out that the studies are concerned with:

(1) the social and psychological origins of (2) needs, which generate
(3) expectations of (4) the mass media or other sources, which lead to
(5) differential patterns of media exposure (or engagement in other
activities), resulting in (6) need gratifications and (7) other consequences, perhaps mostly unintended ones. (p. 20)

They cite two Swedish researchers who in 1968 proposed a "uses and
gratifications model" that included the following elements:

1. The audience is conceived of as active, that is, an important part of
   mass media use is assumed to be goal directed.
2. In the mass communication process much initiative in linking need
   gratification and media choice lies with the audience member.
3. The media compete with other sources of need satisfaction. (pp.
   22-23)

The uses and gratifications literature has provided several ways of classifying
audience needs and gratifications. Some have spoken of "immediate" and "de-
ferred" gratifications (Schramm, Lyle, & Parker, 1961); others have called them
"informational-educational" and "fantasist-escapist" (entertainment) (Weiss, 1971).

McQuail, Blumler, and Brown (1972), working in England, suggested the
following categories:

1. Diversion (escape from routine and problems; emotional release)
2. Personal relationships (social utility of information in conversations;
   substitute of the media for companionship)
3. Personal identity or individual psychology (value reinforcement or
   reassurance; self-understanding; reality exploration, etc.)
4. Surveillance (information about things which might affect one or will
   help one do or accomplish something)

In 1975, Mark R. Levy (1978b) examined the cross-national applicability of
the McQuail, Blumler, and Brown typology with a sample of 240 adults living
in Albany County, New York. He was not able to duplicate their classification of
television news uses and gratifications but found that their four groupings or
clusters of items in England were reduced to three substantially overlapping
dimensions. All three clusters contained surveillance items, and the other two
clusters were equally mixed. Levy speculated that the differences may be caused
by several factors, including the greater availability of television news in the
United States, the fact that Americans may rely on it for a greater variety of needs,
and the differences in style and presentation of television news.

In a more complete report of the same research Levy (1978a) concluded
that besides informing viewers, television news also tests their perceptions and
attitudes on "fresh" events and personalities. However, the participation is at a
distance with reality "sanitized" and made safe by the celebrity newsreader. Many

TABLE 15.2 Percentage of respondents citing specific criteria for news program choice

Reasons for Watching	Newscast		
	6 P.M.	*11 P.M.*	*Network*
Active			
News quality	12.0	12.4	7.9
Program format	18.1	6.0	1.8
Newscasters	21.3	29.1	41.8
Subtotal	51.4	47.5	51.5
Passive			
"Habit"	8.8	4.8	2.2
Channel	24.3	31.2	27.9
Don't know	5.1	5.8	7.2
Subtotal	38.2	41.8	37.3
Miscellaneous	10.4	10.7	11.2
	(N = 189)	(N = 140)	(N = 125)

SOURCE: From Mark R. Levy, "The Audience Experience with Television News," *Journalism Monographs* 55, April 1978, p. 7. Reprinted by permission.

viewers, he says, "actively" choose between competing newscasts, "arrange their schedules to be near a television set at news time, and pay close, albeit selective, attention to the program" (p. 25). The reasons reported for selection of news programs are shown in Table 15.2.

Katz, Gurevitch, and Haas (1973) see the mass media as a means used by individuals to connect themselves with others (or disconnect). They listed 35 needs taken "from the (largely speculative) literature on the social and psychological functions of the mass media" and put them into five categories:

1. Cognitive needs (acquiring information, knowledge, and understanding)
2. Affective needs (emotional, pleasurable, or aesthetic experience)
3. Personal integrative needs (strengthening credibility, confidence, stability, and status)
4. Social integrative needs (strengthening contacts with family, friends, etc.)
5. Tension release needs (escape and diversion) (pp. 166–167)

The researchers interviewed 1,500 respondents in Israel "on the assumption that people are aware of their needs and able to identify their sources of satisfaction" (p. 179) and reached the following conclusions, among others:*

---

* From E. Katz, M. Gurevitch, and H. Haas, "On the Use of the Mass Media for Important Things." *American Sociological Review* 38 (1973): 164–181. Reprinted by permission.

1. For all needs examined, the nonmedia sources (combined) were deemed more gratifying than the mass media. Friends, holidays, lectures, and work were nonmedia sources of gratification.

2. The greater the "distance" from a referent—social, physical, or psychological—the more important the role of the media. Yet, interpersonal communication—formal and informal—competes even in areas relating to political leadership and negative reference groups.

3. Certain comparative processes—such as striving for a higher standard of living, or satisfying oneself that one's time is well spent or that one's country is a good place to live in—seem well served by the media. So are "escapist needs." On the whole, however, friends are more important than the mass media for needs having to do with self-integration, even the need "to be entertained."

4. For individuals who say that matters of state and society are important to them, the rank order of media usefulness in serving these needs is entirely consistent, regardless of the respondent's educational level. Newspapers are the most important medium, followed by radio, then television. Books and films fall far behind. Altogether, the centrality of the newspaper for knowledge and integration in the sociopolitical arena cannot be overstated.

5. Needs having to do with self are associated with different kinds of media, depending on the specific functions involved. Knowing oneself is best served by books; enjoying oneself is associated with films, television, and books; while the newspaper contributes to self-regulation and self-confidence. (p. 180)

Perse and Courtright (1993) identified 11 needs that can be satisfied by communication, either mass or interpersonal: to relax, to be entertained, to forget about work or other things, to have something to do with friends, to learn things about myself and others, to pass the time away (particularly when bored), to feel excited, to feel less lonely, to satisfy a habit, to let others know I care about their feelings, to get someone to do something for me.

CRITICISMS OF THE USES
AND GRATIFICATIONS THEORY

The uses and gratifications approach has drawn some criticism, particularly for being nontheoretical, for being vague in defining key concepts (for example, "needs"), and for being basically nothing more than a data-collecting strategy (see Elliott, 1974; Swanson, 1977, 1979; Lometti, Reeves, & Bybee, 1977). Very little has been done to explore the antecedents of gratifications sought (Palmgreen & Rayburn, 1982). Often needs that people seek to fulfill through media use are inferred from questions about why they use the media, leading to the suspicion that the need was created by the media, or is a rationalization for media use.

In light of the research since Freud indicating the complexity and obscurity of human motivation, there is also something a little simplistic or naïve about using self-reports to determine motives. A 1983 critique of uses and gratification studies and an attempt to link them to psychological value expectancy theory criticizes the confounding of operational definitions and the analytical model, questions internal consistency, cites the lack of theoretical justification for a model offered, and says "the discussion ranges far from the results, which do not support their theoretical underpinnings" (Stanford, 1983, pp. 247-250).

One criticism of the uses and gratifications approach is that it is focused too narrowly on the individual (Elliott, 1974). It relies on psychological concepts such as need, and it neglects the social structure and the place of the media in that structure. One answer to that criticism has come from Rubin and Windahl (1986), who have proposed a synthesis of the uses and gratifications approach and dependency theory (Ball-Rokeach & DeFleur, 1976). Their "uses and dependency model" places individuals within societal systems, which help shape their needs.

The uses and gratifications perspective has also been criticized by media hegemony advocates. They say it goes too far in claiming that people are free to choose the media fare and the interpretations that they want (White, 1994). According to the media hegemonists, mass media messages tend to reinforce the dominant world view of the culture, and audiences find it difficult to avoid this "preferred reading."

Finally, the finding from some studies that exposure to mass communication may not always be highly deliberate or purposeful challenges some of the basic notions of the uses and gratifications approach. People often seem to be making their way through the mass communication environment while on a kind of "automatic pilot" (Donohew, Nair, & Finn, 1984). This view suggests that much use of mass communication might involve a low level of attention, and, in fact, might be appropriately labeled ritualistic or habitual. Many people much of the time might not be interested in surveillance or personal guidance as much as they are just interested in some mildly pleasant stimulation.

In a similar point, a massive study of television viewing (Kubey & Csikszentmihalyi, 1990) suggested that the concept of an active audience is misleading when applied to television watching. This study of television viewing by different demographic groups and with respondents ranging in ages from 10 to 82 found that people consistently report their experiences with television as being passive, relaxing, and involving relatively little concentration. They also argue that television and films, in comparison with print, are likely to produce much more uniform cognitive and affective responses in an audience due to their pictorial nature. Uniform effects are not the kind of thing a uses and gratifications approach would predict.

EMPIRICAL TESTS OF THE USES
AND GRATIFICATIONS THEORY

Bryant and Zillmann (1984) conducted an experimental study of whether an individual's mood influences the selection of television programs. These researchers investigated the selection of exciting and relaxing television programming by students who, prior to an opportunity to choose their viewing, had been purposely either stressed or bored (see Table 15.3):

> Stressed subjects watched nearly six times as much relaxing television as did bored subjects, [while] bored subjects watched nearly twice as much exciting fare as did stressed subjects. . . . Looked at another way, whereas subjects under stress selected approximately the same amount of exciting and relaxing television, bored subjects exposed themselves to exciting programming about 10 times longer than to relaxing fare. (pp. 12–13)

The researchers concluded that "the findings lend strong support to the utility of the selective exposure propositions" and that "subjects make intelligent program choices . . . when using television exposure as a means for alleviating boredom and stress" (p. 20).

The Bryant and Zillmann research, although not called a uses and gratification study, clearly falls into this area. It was a controlled experiment and provided data that did not rely on self-report, one of the criticisms of much of the earlier work in uses and gratifications. In general, it provided some support for uses and gratifications theory.

Lometti and Addington (1992) tested two competing views of the television audience. One was the uses and gratifications perspective, which suggests that an active audience seeks out programs to satisfy psychological and social needs.

TABLE 15.3 Selective exposure to relaxing and exciting programs as a function of boredom and stress

	Experimental Condition	
Program Type	*Boredom*	*Stress*
Exciting	793	441
Relaxing	74	427
Combined	867	868

Note: Exposure time is in seconds. Maximally possible time was 900 seconds, or 15 minutes.
SOURCE: From Jennings Bryant and Dolf Zillmann, "Using Television to Alleviate Boredom and Stress: Selective Exposure as a Function of Induced Excitational States," *Journal of Broadcasting* 28 (Winter 1984): 13. Reprinted with permission.

The other was the passive audience perspective, which contends that people first decide to watch television and then find a program from what is available. Their results from a national probability survey found little support for the passive audience perspective, with only 9 percent of program decisions involving people watching whatever comes on next.

Several other studies provide less support for basic tenets of the uses and gratifications approach. Elliott and Rosenberg (1987), following the example of the pioneering newspaper strike study of Berelson 40 years earlier, were able to study media use during a newspaper strike in Philadelphia in September 1985. The researchers took advantage of the strike to look at the relationship between newspaper gratifications sought and media use during the strike. Basically, they were investigating whether readers of the Philadelphia newspapers would turn to other media during the strike to fulfill the functions of surveillance and social contact, killing time, entertainment, and advertising. The results showed mild tendencies for readers seeking surveillance and social contact to turn to other newspapers, to newsmagazines, and to local and national TV news, but the correlations were not large. The seeking of the gratifications of killing time, entertainment, and advertising were not associated with increases of use of other media. The researchers interpret these results as indicating that "media gratifi-cations are primarily the result of the social situation and background factors and may depend more on habit than on internalized need states" (p. 687).

Further evidence that at least some media use may be a matter of habit comes from a study by Stone and Stone (1990). They carried out a telephone survey in which people indicated their reasons for watching evening television soap operas by expressing their extent of agreement with eight statements. One of the statements was "It's an enjoyable habit I like doing." The results showed the respondents rated the habit statement as the reason closest to why they watched continuing evening television dramas.

NEW TECHNOLOGY AND THE ACTIVE AUDIENCE

Researchers have only begun to study the ways that cable television and other new media offering expanded user choices relate to the user's pursuit of uses and gratifications. A few studies done so far provide clues concerning the impact of new technology on how people use the mass media.

Cable television provides new and diverse opportunities for the audience to become active. With cable, the number of channels can increase from the 10 or fewer available with broadcast television to as many as 108. Cable viewers adopt various strategies to cope with this increased number of choices. One strategy is to narrow one's regular watching to a subset of the available channels that correspond to one's interests. This subset has been called an individual's "channel repertoire" (Heeter & Greenberg, 1985). Viewers differ in their aware-ness of available cable options. To some extent, viewers appear to be over-whelmed by the number of programs and channels now available. One survey of users of a 35-channel cable system found viewers were able to correctly identify an average of only nine channels by their number or location on the channel selector (Heeter & Greenberg, 1985).

About half the time, cable viewers have a program in mind when they turn on the television set. The other half of the time, programs are chosen at the time of viewing. Viewers use a variety of scanning strategies to decide which programs to watch. These strategies differ in whether they are automatic (going from channel to channel in the order that they appear) or controlled (going from one selected channel to another on the basis of some desired goal), elaborated (involving all or most channels) or restricted (involving a limited number of channels), and exhaustive (searching all channels before returning to the best choice) or terminating (stopping when the first acceptable option is located). The most active viewers of cable television tend to use controlled, elaborated, and exhaustive searching strategies. They tend to be young adults (Heeter & Greenberg, 1985).

The videocassette recorder also gives the television viewer opportunities to be a more active viewer. It offers the user greater flexibility in terms of times for viewing and it increases the choices of available content. Levy (1980) argues that using a VCR to time-shift programs is a demanding task and that viewers who take the trouble to do it must be among the most active members of the television audience.

Further evidence that VCR users are essentially an active audience comes from additional research by Levy (1987). In a study conducted in Israel, he gave VCR owners questionnaires that measured nine different types of activity. The measuring instrument was the Levy-Windahl typology of audience activity that had been tested previously with television news viewers. The typology measures these nine kinds of activity: selectivity before exposure, during exposure, and after exposure; involvement before exposure, during exposure, and after exposure; and utility before exposure, during exposure, and after exposure. The VCR owners showed higher degrees of activity for most of the items than the television news viewers had shown in earlier research.

Several studies looked at the uses to which people put computers as communication devices. Perse and Courtright (1993) found in a 1988 survey that computers ranked lowest among 12 types of mediated and interpersonal communication for satisfying communication needs such as relaxation, entertainment, self-awareness, and excitement. The picture changed a few years later, however. Another survey (Perse and Dunn, 1995) looked particularly at the use of computers to communicate with others through information services and the Internet, or what the authors called *computer connectivity*. People using computers for electronic communication were satisfying the following needs: learning, entertainment, social interaction, escapism, passing the time, and out of habit. Use of computers hooked to networks or information services for reasons of passing time or out of habit suggests a ritualistic use, not a use aimed at the gratifications provided by specific content. The authors suggest that this ritualistic use of computers for connectivity might actually lead some users of computer networks or information services to become addicted.

RECENT DEVELOPMENTS IN USES
AND GRATIFICATIONS RESEARCH

One recent development has been a movement away from conceptualizing audiences as active or passive to treating activity as a variable (Rubin, 1994). That is, sometimes media users are selective and rational in their processing of media messages, but at other times they are using the media for relaxation or escapism. These differences in type and level of audience activity might also have consequences for media effects. For instance, cultivation effects of the type proposed by Gerbner and his associates might be most likely to occur when audience members are viewing television for diversion or escape.

Another new direction has been to focus on media use for satisfying particular needs. For instance, one possible use of the mass media is to relieve loneliness. Canary and Spitzberg (1993) found evidence supporting this use, but the relationship depended on the extent of loneliness. They found the heaviest use of the media to relieve loneliness in the situationally lonely, or those who were temporarily lonely. They found less use of the media to relieve loneliness in the chronically lonely, or those who have felt lonely for a period of years. The explanation seems to be that the chronically lonely attribute their loneliness to internal factors, and so do not believe that communication in itself will provide relief.

CONCLUSIONS

The uses and gratifications approach reminds us of one very important point— people use the media for many different purposes. This approach suggests that to a large extent, the user of mass communication is in control. The uses and gratifications approach can serve as a healthy antidote to the emphasis on passive audiences and persuasion that has dominated much earlier research.

Empirical research testing basic tenets of uses and gratifications theory has so far come up with mixed results. Bryant and Zillmann found evidence that stressed subjects would choose relaxing content while bored subjects would choose exciting content, supporting the idea that viewers choose media content to provide gratifications they are seeking. But Elliott and Rosenberg, in their replication of Berelson's classic newspaper strike study, did not find that readers deprived of their newspapers did a great deal of shifting to other media to fulfill the functions they may have been missing. Elliott and Rosenberg concluded that much of mass media use might be merely a matter of habit. The study by Stone and Stone also suggests the importance of habit in explaining media use.

Despite these mixed results, the uses and gratifications approach may have a chance to come into its own as we move into the information age and media users are confronted with more and more choices. It is obvious that the media user dealing with cable television with as many as 500 channels or with a videocassette recorder that allows time-shifting, archiving, and repeated viewing of television content is a much more active audience member than the traditional media consumer of a few years ago. The uses and gratifications approach should eventually have some things to say about the users of these new media. After all, it is the single area of theory that has attempted most directly to deal with the active audience.

At the very least, the uses and gratifications approach should direct our attention to the audience of mass communication. Brenda Dervin (1980) recommended that the development of information campaigns should begin with study of the potential information user and the questions that person is attempting to answer in order to make sense of the world. The same lesson probably applies to the producers of much of the content of the mass media. Media planners in many areas should be conducting more research on their potential audiences, and the gratifications those audiences are trying to obtain.

DISCUSSION

1. What is the evidence that audience members are active rather than passive?
2. Which of the lists of the possible uses and gratifications obtained from the mass media do you find most useful? Why?
3. Researchers have come up with lists of uses and gratifications that people obtain from the media which range from as few as 2 to as many as 35. What are the advantages and disadvantages of having a short versus a long list?
4. There are probably a number of ways that an audience member can be active. Name as many as you can.
5. Researchers have suggested that the concept of audience activity should be treated as a variable, with levels ranging from low to high. What are the advantages of thinking about audience activity this way?
6. What are the major criticisms of the uses and gratifications approach?
7. Are new communication media such as the Internet providing uses and gratifications that the old media did not, or are they just meeting the old needs in different ways?
8. How can the uses and gratifications approach be used to help our understanding of mass communication effects?

REFERENCES

Ball-Rokeach, S. J., and M. L. DeFleur (1976). A dependency model of mass-media effects. *Communication Research* 3: 3–21.

Bauer, R. A. (1964). The obstinate audience: The influence process from the point of view of social communication. *American Psychologist* 19: 319–328.

Berelson, B. (1959). The state of communication research. *Public Opinion Quarterly* 23: 1-6.

Berelson, B. (1965). What "missing the newspaper" means. In W. Schramm (ed.), *The Process and Effects of Mass Communication*, pp. 36-47. Urbana: University of Illinois.

Blumler, J. G., and D. McQuail (1969). *Television in Politics: Its Uses and Influence*. Chicago: University of Chicago Press.

Bryant, J., and R. L. Street, Jr. (1988). From reactivity to activity and action: An evolving concept and Weltanschauung in mass and interpersonal communication. In R. P. Hawkins, J. M. Wiemann, and S. Pingree (eds.), *Advancing Communication Science: Merging Mass and Interpersonal Processes*, pp. 162-190. Newbury Park, Calif.: Sage.

Bryant, J., and D. Zillmann (1984). Using television to alleviate boredom and stress: Selective exposure as a function of induced excitational states. *Journal of Broadcasting* 28: 1-20.

Canary, D. J., and B. H. Spitzberg (1993). Loneliness and media gratifications. *Communication Research* 20: 800-821.

Dervin, B. (1980). Communication gaps and inequities: Moving toward a reconceptualization. In B. Dervin and M. J. Voight (eds.), *Progress in Communication Sciences*, vol. 2, pp. 73-112. Norwood, N.J.: Ablex.

Donohew, R. L., M. Nair, and S. Finn (1984). Automacity, arousal, and information exposure. In R. N. Bostrom (ed.), *Communication Yearbook 8*, pp. 267-284. Beverly Hills, Calif.: Sage.

Elliott, P. (1974). Uses and gratifications research: A critique and a sociological alternative. In J. G. Blumler and E. Katz (eds.), *The Uses of Mass Communications: Current Perspectives on Gratifications Research*, pp. 249-268. Beverly Hills, Calif.: Sage.

Elliott, W. R., and W. L. Rosenberg (1987). The 1985 Philadelphia newspaper strike: A uses and gratifications study. *Journalism Quarterly* 64: 679-687.

Gamson, W. A., D. Croteau, W. Hoynes, and T. Sasson (1992). Media images and the social construction of reality. *Annual Review of Sociology* 18: 373-393.

Heeter, C., and B. Greenberg (1985). Cable and program choice. In D. Zillmann and J. Bryant (eds.), *Selective Exposure to Communication*, pp. 203-224. Hillsdale, N.J.: Lawrence Erlbaum.

Herzog, H. (1944). Motivations and gratifications of daily serial listeners. In W. Schramm (ed.), *The Process and Effects of Mass Communication*, pp. 50-55. Urbana: University of Illinois Press.

Katz, E. (1959). Mass communication research and the study of popular culture: An editorial note on a possible future for this journal. *Studies in Public Communication* 2: 1-6.

Katz, E., J. G. Blumler, and M. Gurevitch (1974). Utilization of mass communication by the individual. In J. G. Blumler and E. Katz (eds.), *The Uses of Mass Communications: Current Perspectives on Gratifications Research*, pp. 19-32. Beverly Hills, Calif.: Sage.

Katz, E., M. Gurevitch, and H. Haas (1973). On the use of the mass media for important things. *American Sociological Review* 38: 164-181.

Kubey, R., and M. Csikszentmihalyi (1990). *Television and the Quality of Life: How Viewing Shapes Everyday Experience*. Hillsdale, N.J.: Lawrence Erlbaum.

Levy, M. R. (1978a). The audience experience with television news. *Journalism Monographs* 55, April.

Levy, M. R. (1978b). Television news uses: A cross-national comparison. *Journalism Quarterly* 55: 334-337.

Levy, M. R. (1980). Home video recorders: A user survey. *Journal of Communication* 30 (no. 4): 23-25.

Levy, M. R. (1987). VCR use and the concept of audience activity. *Communication Quarterly* 35: 267-275.

Lometti, G. E., B. Reeves, and C. R. Bybee (1977). Investigating the assumptions of uses and gratifications research. *Communication Research* 4: 321-338.

Lometti, G. E., and Addington, T. (1992). Testing opposing views of the audience: How the active television viewer seeks programs. Paper presented at the annual meeting of the Communication Theory and Methodology Division of the Association for Education in Journalism and Mass Communication, Montreal, Canada, August.

McQuail, D., J. G. Blumler, and J. R. Brown (1972). The television audience: A revised perspective. In D. McQuail (ed.), *Sociology of Mass Communications*, pp. 135-165. Harmondsworth, Eng.: Penguin.

Palmgreen, P., and J. D. Rayburn, II (1982). Gratifications sought and media exposure: An expectancy value model. *Communications Research* 9: 561-580.

Perse, E. M., and J. A. Courtright (1993). Normative images of communication media: Mass and interpersonal channels in the new media environment. *Human Communication Research* 19: 485-503.

Perse, E. M., and D. G. Dunn (1995). The utility of home computers: Implications of multimedia and connectivity. Paper presented at the annual meeting of the Communication Theory and Methodology Division of the Association for Education in Journalism and Mass Communication, Washington, D.C., August.

Riley, M. W., and J. W. Riley, Jr. (1951). A sociological approach to communications research. *Public Opinion Quarterly* 15: 445-460.

Rubin, A. M. (1994). Media uses and effects: A uses-and-gratifications perspective. In J. Bryant and D. Zillmann (eds.), *Media Effects: Advances in Theory and Research*, pp. 417-436. Hillsdale, N.J.: Lawrence Erlbaum.

Rubin, A. M., and S. Windahl (1986). The uses and dependency model of mass communication. *Critical Studies in Mass Communication* 3: 184-199.

Schramm, W., J. Lyle, and E. B. Parker (1961). *Television in the Lives of Our Children.* Stanford, Calif.: Stanford University Press.

Stanford, S. W. (1983). Comments on Palmgreen and Rayburn, "Gratifications sought and media exposure." *Communication Research* 10: 247-258.

Stone, G., and D. B. Stone (1990). Lurking in the literature: Another look at media use habits. *Mass Comm Review* 17 (nos. 1 and 2): 25-33, 46.

Swanson, D. L. (1977). The uses and misuses of uses and gratifications. *Human Communication Research* 3: 214-221.

Swanson, D. L. (1979). Political communication research and the uses and gratifications model: A critique. *Communication Research* 6: 37-53.

Weiss, W. (1971). Mass communication. *Annual Review of Psychology* 22: 309-336.

White, R. A. (1994). Audience "interpretation" of media: Emerging perspectives. *Communication Research Trends* 14 (no. 3): 3-36.

part VI

The Media as Institutions

$\mathbf{M}$ass communication products are now typically produced by organizations that are complex businesses employing large numbers of people. It is no longer sufficient, if it ever was, to attempt to theorize about mass communication at the level of the individual receiver as an information processor, at the level of the audience as made up of members of groups, or even at the level of individuals linked through interpersonal communication. Certain aspects of mass communication begin to become apparent only when we shift our focus from the individual as a unit of analysis to the society as a whole. Once we do this, we can begin to think about the roles that mass communication plays in society, and the functions that mass communication serves for a society as a whole. Chapter 16 takes this more macro perspective and looks at the relationships between the mass media and society. Chapter 17 deals with an important aspect of the mass media viewed as institutions—the patterns of ownership of the media and the possible consequences of those patterns.

Mass Media in Modern Society

Modern society is nearly unimaginable without the mass media: newspapers, magazines, paperbacks, radio, television, and film. The mass media are many things to many people and serve a variety of functions, depending on the type of political and economic system in which the media function, the stage of development of the society, and the interests and needs of specific individuals. In this chapter we will examine several views of what the media should be and do in several types of societies and some observations of how the media actually function.

Some understanding of the role of mass communication in society is necessary for a complete theory of mass communication. One of the goals of communication theory is to make possible accurate predictions of the effects of the mass media. Political, social, and economic forces directly affect media content. Media ownership and control affect media content, which in turn determines media effects.

FOUR THEORIES OF THE PRESS

One well-known classification of the press systems of the world is presented in the book *Four Theories of the Press* (Siebert, Peterson, & Schramm, 1956). Its authors divided the world's press into four categories: authoritarian, libertarian, social responsibility, and Soviet-totalitarian (see Table 16.1). These are "normative theories" derived from observation, not from hypothesis testing and replication using social science methods as described in Chapter 2.

TABLE 16.1 Four rationales for the mass media

	Authoritarian	Libertarian	Social Responsibility	Soviet-Totalitarian
Developed	in 16th and 17th century England; widely adopted and still practiced in many places	adopted by England after 1688, and in U.S.; influential elsewhere	in U.S. in the 20th century	in Soviet Union, although some of the same things were done by Nazis and Italians
Out of	philosophy of absolute power of monarch, his government, or both	writings of Milton, Locke, Mill, and general philosophy of rationalism and natural rights	writing of W. E. Hocking, Commission on Freedom of Press, and practitioners; media codes	Marxist-Leninist-Stalinist thought, with mixture of Hegel and 19th century Russian thinking
Chief purpose	to support and advance the policies of the government in power; and to service the state	to inform, entertain, sell—but chiefly to help discover truth, and to check on government	to inform, entertain, sell—but chiefly to raise conflict to the plane of discussion	to contribute to the success and continuance of the Soviet socialist system, and especially to the dictatorship of the party
Who has right to use media?	whoever gets a royal patent or similar permission	anyone with economic means to do so	everyone who has something to say	loyal and orthodox party members
How are media controlled?	government patents, guilds, licensing, sometimes censorship	by "self-righting process of truth" in "free market place of ideas," and by courts	community opinion, consumer action, professional ethics	surveillance and economic or political action of government
What is forbidden?	criticism of political machinery and officials in power	defamation, obscenity, indecency, wartime sedition	serious invasion of recognized private rights and vital social interests	criticism of party objectives as distinguished from tactics
Ownership	private or public	chiefly private	private unless government has to take over to ensure public service	public
Essential differences from others	instrument for effecting government policy, though not necessarily government owned	instrument for checking on government and meeting other needs of society	media must assume obligation of social responsibility; and if they do not, someone must see that they do	state-owned and closely controlled media existing solely as arm of state

SOURCE: From F. S. Siebert, T. B. Peterson, and W. Schramm, *Four Theories of the Press* (Urbana: University of Illinois Press, 1956), p. 7. Reprinted with permission of the University of Illinois Press.

Authoritarian Theory

In the West, the invention of the printing press and movable type came at a time when the world was under authoritarian rule by monarchs with absolute power. It is no surprise that the first rationale or theory of the press was that of a press supporting and advancing the policies of the government in power and serving the state. A printer was required to get permission and, in some cases, a patent from the monarch or the government in order to publish. Through the use of patents, licensing, direct censorship, and often self-regulation through printers' guilds, individuals were prevented from criticizing the government in power. In authoritarian systems the press may be either publicly or privately owned; nevertheless it is regarded as an instrument for furthering government policy.

Censorship, both government and private, is alive and well today in many parts of the world, including countries which often profess to be democracies. The CBS newsmagazine "60 Minutes" felt compelled to withdraw a program critical of the tobacco industry because of the possibility of legal action. Their chief source, a former tobacco industry executive, had signed an agreement not to disclose internal company matters. The CBS lawyers feared that the network could be sued, not for having libeled the tobacco company by a false report, but rather because "60 Minutes" could be held liable for having induced the employee to break a contract, which could lead to a multi-billion-dollar lawsuit against CBS (*New York Times*, Nov. 12, 1995, p. E14; Carter, 1995). Many see this as a dangerous precedent which could undercut most investigative reporting. (CBS later broadcast much of the program.)

Journalists have had frequent clashes with the government of Singapore, known for its tight control of media content where officials censor or edit programs and publications. The *Asian Wall Street Journal,* the *Far Eastern Economic Review,* and the *International Herald Tribune* (the latter owned jointly by the *New York Times* and the *Washington Post*) have all, at one time or another, run afoul of the Singapore government, paying fines and facing tight controls. The city-state has allowed *Vogue* and *Elle* to start local editions, but not *Cosmopolitan.* According to George Yeo, the Minister of Information and Arts, "Cosmopolitan was not allowed because they are advocating or celebrating fringe lifestyles" (Reuter, Nov. 1, 1994). Singapore has maintained tight control on the ownership of satellite dishes and hopes the introduction of state-controlled cable television will make ownership of satellite dishes a meaningless issue.

To deal with the perceived threat of a free wheeling Internet, the Minister of Information has decided the government should embrace and monitor it. The *New York Times* observed editorially (Nov. 8, 1995):

> The catch is the Government will be able to monitor use of the Internet that goes through local servers, and is already intervening to block material it considers pornographic. The Government has blunted an uncensored Internet forum on Singapore political life by assembling a group of users who make sure the Government's views are represented.

The editorial concludes, "In Singapore, a little democracy can be a dangerous thing." (p. A14)

Singapore's neighbor to the north, Malaysia, which also tightly controls ownership of television satellite dishes, is concerned about Malaysian students studying abroad who are "smearing" the country's name on the Internet. Information Minister Mohamed Rahmat said the country is considering laws to curb such abuses (Reuter, Sept. 10, 1995). In Myanmar (Burma) a member of the ruling military junta, Lt. Gen. Myo Nyunt, in an effort to stamp out "alien culture," lashed out at entertainers wearing decadent outfits incompatible with Burmese culture (Associated Press, Feb. 25, 1995).

Satellite television in Asia has been forced to self-censorship in order to woo sensitive viewers and curry favor with nervous governments. Ted Turner's TNT & Cartoon Network has dropped Porky Pig in deference to Moslem viewers. Rupert Murdoch's STAR TV dropped BBC news broadcasts over North Asia when Communist officials found uncensored Western news threatening, and edited heavily its pop-music Channel V to be accepted for use by Singapore's government-controlled media (Reuter, Jan. 18, 1995).

Libertarian Theory

Out of the Enlightenment and the general theories of rationalism and natural rights developed a libertarian theory of the press to counter the authoritarian view. From the writings of Milton, Locke, and Mill came the notion that the press was to serve the function of helping to discover truth and checking on government as well as informing, entertaining, and selling. Under the libertarian theory the press is chiefly private, and anyone who can afford to do so can publish. The media are controlled in two ways. With a multiplicity of voices, the "self-righting process of truth" in the "free market place of ideas" would enable individuals to differentiate between truth and falsehood. Also, the legal system makes provision for the prosecution of defamation, obscenity, indecency, and wartime sedition. Under the libertarian theory the press is chiefly private and the media are instruments for checking on government as well as meeting the other needs of the society.

The libertarian theory of the press developed in England during the 18th century but was not permitted in the British colonies in North America until the break with the mother country. After 1776 it was implemented in areas not under control of colonial governors and was formally adopted with the First Amendment to the new Bill of Rights appended to the Constitution.

Mill's **On Liberty.** One of the best concise articulations of the arguments favoring a "free press" was set forth in the mid-19th century by John Stuart Mill in Chapter 2 of *On Liberty.* Mill argues that to silence an opinion we may silence the truth. It is here that we find this oft-quoted passage (1859/1956):

If all mankind minus one were of one opinion, mankind would be no more justified in silencing that one person than he, if he had the power, would be justified in silencing mankind. . . . If the opinion is right, they [mankind] are deprived of the opportunity of exchanging error for truth; if wrong, they lose, what is almost as great a benefit, the clearer perception and the livelier impression of the truth produced by its collision with error. (p. 21)

Mill argues that since no person is infallible, the question of truth or falsehood of an opinion should be left to every person to judge. He adds that when one lacks trust in one's own opinion, an individual usually relies on the prevailing or majority opinion for support or guidance. (Chapter 10 discusses the findings of modern social psychology on the effects of group judgments on individual judgments.)

Mill quickly points out that the opinions of "the world" in general are no more infallible than those held by an individual because of the limited experiences of groups and entire societies as well as individuals (p. 22). Mill adds:

Ages are no more infallible than individuals, and every age having held many opinions which subsequent ages have deemed not only false but absurd; and it is as certain that many opinions, now general, will be rejected by future ages, as it is that many, once general, are rejected by the present. (p. 23)

Mill argues that assuming an opinion to be true because every opportunity to disprove it has failed is far different from assuming it to be true and not permitting its refutation. The only justification we have for assuming an opinion to be true is that it has withstood every opportunity to prove it false and this is the only way in which a human being has any rational assurance of being right.

The libertarian theory holds that human beings are capable of correcting their errors, but only when there is the possibility of discussion and argument to bring forth fact and truth eventually. Mill argues that the only way a human being can approach knowing the whole of any subject is by hearing what persons of all varieties of opinions and character of mind may have to say about it (p. 25). (A discussion of abstraction is found in Chapter 5.)

Later Mill argues not only that opinions must be tested and defended to be held on rational grounds but also that opinions not challenged lose their vitality and effect. He says that however true an opinion may be, it will become dead dogma rather than living truth "if it is not fully, frequently and fearlessly discussed." He adds that it is seldom possible to shut out discussion entirely and that once it begins, beliefs not grounded on conviction give way before the slightest argument (p. 43). (McGuire's immunization to counterpersuasion in Chapter 9 relates directly to this point.)

The libertarian theory, with its notion of truth eventually winning out in the marketplace of ideas, was useful and viable before the industrial revolution made itself felt in publishing and later in broadcasting. As technology made possible ever-faster and ever-wider distribution of newspapers, the economies of mass production became more and more important. Larger newspapers began buying out or merging with smaller newspapers until today very few cities have competing newspapers. This caused thoughtful individuals, both inside and outside the media, to question the usefulness of the libertarian theory in a democratic society. It was argued that with fewer and fewer media voices, it was becoming more and more difficult for significant and sometimes unpopular views to gain a hearing.

In addition, 20th-century psychology has demonstrated that human beings do not always deal with information in seemingly rational ways. Rationalization is itself an attempt to provide a rational explanation for an irrational act. These findings undercut the "rational man" philosophies upon which the libertarian theory is based.

Social Responsibility Theory

In the 20th century in the United States, the notion developed that the media, the only industry singled out for protection in the Bill of Rights, must meet a social responsibility. This social responsibility theory, evolving from media practitioners, media codes, and the work of the Commission on Freedom of the Press (Hutchins Commission), holds that while the media inform, entertain, and sell (as in the libertarian theory), they must also raise conflict to the plane of discussion.

The social responsibility theory holds that everyone who has something of significance to say should be allowed a forum and that if the media do not assume their obligation, somebody must see to it that they do. Under this theory, the media are controlled by community opinion, consumer action, professional ethics, and, in the case of broadcasting, governmental regulatory agencies because of technical limits on the number of channels or frequencies available (Siebert et al., 1956). (In the United States, as of this writing, there has been a trend for many years to "deregulate" broadcasting. The argument put forth is that with the new technologies such as cable television and low-power broadcasting, enough channels are now available in each community to make regulation unnecessary.)

The social responsibility theory has generated considerable discussion over who should see to it that the media act in a socially responsible manner and how decisions should be made as to what is or is not a significant opinion worthy of media space or time.

Other recommendations of the Hutchins' Commission dealt with the training of journalists. The commission observed that besides making frequent errors, the media seldom relate the day's news with larger issues affecting their audiences. Many of the problems were attributed to the education of reporters and editors and poor preparation before undertaking assignments. The commission's concern appears to have been well founded, both then and now.

Reporters and editors frequently make mistakes when dealing with the most basic facts involving math, science, history, and geography. Obvious factual errors lead to questioning the accuracy of an entire report. If reporters and editors cannot get obvious facts correct, can the viewer or reader trust them to get the more obscure facts correct? This leads, in turn, to questioning the credibility of the media, which is now probably at or near an all-time low.

One report cited the "1,540-kilometer (2,480-mile) Sino-Russian border" (Associated Press, Feb. 22, 1995). A kilometer is *shorter* than a mile—it is about 5/8 of one mile. The number of kilometers is always greater than the equivalent distance in miles. A report about the Alaskan 1,200-mile Iditarod Sled Dog Race cited, among the dangers, "sub-zero temperatures, howling winds, snowstorms, and bears" (National Public Radio, Morning Edition, March 3, 1993). Many listeners would know that bears hibernate in sub-zero temperatures. A map of Russia accompanying a story about a pipeline explosion carried the heading "Fire *Cited*" (italics added, ABC-TV, April 27, 1995). A front page story was headed, "I.R.S. Workers Were *Peaking* at Returns" (italics added, *New York Times*, July 19, 1994, p. A1). One local weather forecaster announced the days are getting longer because we just passed the winter *equinox* (Channel 24, Austin, Texas, Dec. 23, 1995).

The media often refer to the "battle of Wounded Knee," in 1890, when 350 American Indians, mainly women and children, were shot to death by troopers of the Seventh Cavalry. The late attorney William M. Kunstler wrote to one newspaper, "Your caption makes this massacre appear a battle and not wanton murder." (*New York Times*, March 10, 1993, p. A14)

A local television anchor and graduate of a major university broadcast journalism program, in a report about Columbus Day, said that Columbus proved the world isn't flat (Austin, Texas, Channel 24, Oct. 13, 1991). One of *Magellan's* ships returned to Spain in 1522, completing the first circumnavigation of the globe, thus proving the world isn't flat.

During coverage of the 50th anniversary of D-Day in Normandy, France, one commercial network anchor, during a fly-over by World War II B 17 bombers, reported that they had dropped paratroopers on the morning of D-Day (ABC News, June 6, 1994). Another correspondent reported that "pathfinders" marked targets for bombers (National Public Radio, June 6, 1994). Actually, the paratroopers were dropped from transport aircraft while other airborne troops landed with gliders and the pathfinders marked landing zones for the paratroopers and gliders (Ryan, 1959).

A radio host, in the introduction to an interview with the British actor Richard Todd said, "Richard Todd was a British soldier who took part in holding the Orne Bridge in France for allied forces in World War II. The effort was memorialized in the film *A Bridge Too Far*" (National Public Radio, Weekend Edition, Nov. 13, 1993). Actually, the Orne bridge was taken and held during the Normandy invasion on June 6, 1944 while the bridge memorialized in the film *A Bridge Too Far* was the bridge at Arnhem, Holland, taken, and held briefly, by the British First Airborne Division during Operation Market Garden in

September 1944. The introduction, confusing two events, may have been added after the interview was concluded.

A radio anchor reported that the Branch Davidians at Waco, Texas, had a "50-*millimeter* machine gun" (National Public Radio, Morning Edition, March 1, 1993). Guns are measured by the diameter of their bores, and a 50-millimeter machine gun would have to have a bore diameter of about two inches. A 50-*caliber*, which is one-half inch in diameter, is the common designation of a heavy machine gun.

A photo caption referred to a U.S. Marine Corps "*Lieut. Comdr,*" which is a U.S. Navy rank (*New York Times,* Oct. 11, 1994, p. A9). Probably the caption writer had confused it with *Lieutenant Colonel,* a Marine Corps rank, and a quick check with a reference book would have cleared up any confusion.

Sometimes the media rely on "experts," who themselves demonstrate ignorance of the topics in which they claim expertise. One military "expert" from a Washington "think tank," commenting on our intervention in Somalia said, "Twenty-eight thousand people total is less than one division" (National Public Radio, Weekend Edition, Dec. 6, 1992). An Army or Marine division is about 10,000 to 14,000 people, depending on the type of division (infantry, armor, airborne). A knowledgeable media person would catch and question such errors.

Some have observed that most reporters and editors are unfamiliar with military and weapons terminology, because probably most have never served in the military and are unfamiliar with weapons. Given the vast expenditures on the military, the rising crime rates in our society, and the increasing media coverage of weapons, the much-maligned National Rifle Association has published a firearms glossary of terms for the media (Dickey, 1994, and on the Internet at: http://www.nra.org/pub/general/gun_glossary).

Soviet-Totalitarian Theory

In the meantime, the authoritarian theory of the press had, in many parts of the world, evolved into the Soviet-totalitarian theory of the press. The Soviets viewed the chief purpose of the media to be that of contributing to the success and continuance of the Soviet system. The media are controlled by the economic and political actions of the government as well as by surveillance, and only loyal and orthodox party members can use the media regularly. The tactics of the party may be criticized, but the objectives or goals may not. The media in the Soviet system are state-owned and state-controlled and exist solely as an arm of the state to further the state.

Since *Four Theories of the Press* was written, there have been many changes in the socialist countries. In the People's Republic of China private ownership of newspapers was allowed on a limited scale during the 1980s. More criticism has been tolerated, especially if it is criticism of individuals or local policies that undermine the goals of the nation's "four modernizations" program. Today more changes of political direction are again taking place in the People's Republic of China.

Pravda, the Communist party daily, began publishing criticisms of the special privileges enjoyed by the political elite in the Soviet Union (Kimelman, 1986; Keller, 1989a, 1989b; Fein, 1989).

During 1989 press restrictions were also lifted in the East European satellite nations. (Kamm, 1989; Bohlen & Haberman, 1990).

The functions and role of the mass media in the new states of the former Soviet Union and in Eastern Europe are probably best described as being in a state of flux. China, North Korea, Vietnam, and Cuba are the only countries to still follow the Soviet model of the press expressly serving the wishes of the government.

THE NEWS MEDIA AS AGENTS OF POWER

J. Herbert Altschull, in the first edition of his book *Agents of Power* (1984), argued that the categories in *Four Theories of the Press,* which were formulated during the cold war, are no longer relevant. He maintained that the analysis is an "us-versus-them" approach that reflects the hostility of the period. Altschull says, "One of the most critical of all difficulties we face in efforts to avoid the perils of global confrontation lies in labeling and in the language of conflict" (p. 108). He maintains that an independent press cannot exist and that the mass media are the agents of those who hold the economic, political, and social power in any system.

After a sweeping review of the history and functioning of the world's press systems, much of it based on personal experience, Altschull concludes that today there are three models of the press. These are: the market (or capitalist) model; the communitarian (or socialist) model; and the advancing (or, less accurately, developing countries) model (1995, Chap. 22). Altschull's comparisons of articles of faith, purposes, and views on press freedom of the three models appear in Tables 16.2, 16.3, and 16.4 (pp. 354–355).

Altschull reaches the following conclusions (1995):

1. In all press systems, the news media are agents of the people who exercise political and economic power. Newspapers, magazines, and broadcasting outlets thus are not independent actors, although they have the potential to exercise independent power.
2. The content of the news media always reflects the interests of those who finance the press.
3. All press systems are based on a belief in free expression, although free expression is defined in different ways.
4. All press systems endorse the doctrine of social responsibility, proclaim that they serve the needs and interests of the people, and state their willingness to provide access to the people.
5. In each of the three press models, the press of the other models is perceived to be deviant.

TABLE 16.2 Articles of faith

Market Nations	Communitarian Nations	Advancing Nations
The press is free of outside interference.	The press transforms and educates people to class and cultural consciousness.	The press is a unifying and not a divisive force.
The press serves the public's right to know.	The press provides for the objective needs of the people.	The press is a device for beneficial social change.
The press reports fairly and objectively.	The press reports objectively about the realities of experience.	The press is meant to be used for two-way exchanges between journalists and readers.

From J. H. Altschull, *Agents of Power: The Media and Public Policy,* 2nd ed. (White Plains, NY: Longman, 1995), p. 427. Reprinted by permission of Longman.

TABLE 16.3 Purposes of journalism

Market Nations	Communitarian Nations	Advancing Nations
To seek truth.	To search for truth.	To serve truth.
To be socially responsible.	To be socially responsible.	To be socially responsible.
To inform (or educate) neither politically nor culturally.	To educate the people and enlist allies politically and culturally.	To educate politically and culturally.
To serve the people impartially; to support capitalist doctrine.	To serve the people by demanding support for correct doctrine.	To serve the people by seeking, in partnership with government, change for beneficial purpose.
To serve as a watchdog of government.	To mold views and behavior.	To serve as an instrument of peace.

From: J. H. Altschull, *Agents of Power: The Media and Public Policy,* 2nd ed. (White Plains, NY: Longman, 1995), p. 429. Reprinted by permission of Longman.

6. Schools of journalism transmit ideologies and value systems of the society in which they exist and inevitably assist people in power in maintaining their control of the news media.

7. Press practices always differ from theory. (pp. 440-441)

In his first edition Altschull summed up his views thus:

The history of the press demonstrates that newspapers and the more modern variations of the press have tended to serve the selfish interests of the paymasters, while at the same time perpetuating the image of a

TABLE 16.4 Views on press freedom

Market Nations	Communitarian Nations	Advancing Nations
A free press means journalists are free of all outside control.	A free press means all opinions are published, not only those of the rich and powerful.	A free press means freedom of conscience for journalists.
A free press is one in which the press is not servile to power and not manipulated by power.	A free press is required to counter oppression of legitimate communities.	Press freedom is less important than the viability of the nation.
No national press policy is needed to ensure a free press.	A national press policy is required to guarantee that a free press takes the correct form.	A national press policy is needed to provide legal safeguards for freedom.

From J. H. Altschull, *Agents of Power: The Media and Public Policy*, 2nd ed. (White Plains, NY: Longman, 1995), p. 435. Reprinted by permission of Longman.

press operating in the service of the consumers of the news. To expect that the news media will make a dramatic U-turn and scoff at the wishes of the paymasters is to engage in the wildest kind of utopian fantasies. (1984, p. 299)

FUNCTIONS OF THE MEDIA

Harold Lasswell and Charles Wright are among the early scholars who have seriously considered the functions and role of the mass media in society. Wright (1959) defines mass communication in terms of the nature of the audience, the nature of the communication experience, and the nature of the communicator.

Lasswell (1948/1960), scholar of communication and professor of law at Yale, noted three functions of the mass media: surveillance of the environment, the correlation of the parts of society in responding to the environment, and the transmission of the social heritage from one generation to the next. To these three functions Wright (1959, p. 16) adds a fourth, entertainment. In addition to functions, the media may also have dysfunctions, consequences that are undesirable for the society or its members. A single act may be both functional and dysfunctional.

Surveillance, the first function, informs and provides news. In performing this function the media often warn us of expected dangers such as extreme or dangerous weather conditions or a threatening military situation. The surveillance function also includes the news the media provide that is essential to the economy, the public, and society, such as stock market reports, traffic reports, weather conditions, and so on.

The surveillance function can also cause several dysfunctions. Panic may result through the overemphasis of dangers or threats to the society. Lazarsfeld and Merton (1948/1960) have noted a "narcotizing" dysfunction when individuals fall into a state of apathy or passivity as a result of too much information to assimilate. Besides that, too much exposure to "news" (the unusual, abnormal, extraordinary) may leave many audience members with little perspective of what is the usual, normal, or ordinary in a society.

In an article titled "Awareness Overdose," the writer asks, "Have we crammed so many health sound bites down our throats that we just don't care anymore?" (MacNair, 1993)

News is often defined as the unusual. When the abnormal or unusual become normal or usual the activity frequently drops from the news, even if it is murder. Following the murder of several foreign tourists in Florida, *New York Times* columnist Russell Baker wrote (Sept. 11, 1993):

> It's a sign of the American decline that eight tourists murdered in Florida capture national headlines when the thousands and thousands of Americans routinely murdered cause such little splash. . . . When it comes to murder, it's now Americans who don't matter. (p. A21)

Correlation, the second function, is the selection and interpretation of information about the environment. The media often include criticism and prescribe how one should react to events. Correlation is thus the editorial and propaganda content of the media. The correlation function serves to enforce social norms and maintain consensus by exposing deviants, confers status by highlighting selected individuals, and can operate as a check on government. In carrying out the correlation function the media can often impede threats to social stability and may often monitor or manage public opinion.

The correlation function can become dysfunctional when the media perpetuate stereotypes and enhance conformity, impede social change and innovation, minimize criticism, enforce majority views at the expense of minority opinions that are not aired, and preserve and extend power that may need to be checked.

One of the frequently cited major dysfunctions of media correlation is the creation of what Daniel Boorstin has termed "pseudo events" or the manufacture of "images" or "personalities"—much of the stock in trade of the public relations industry. Products and corporations are given "images," and individuals have public "personalities" manufactured for them through the creation of "events" contrived to gain media exposure. Aspiring politicians and entertainers seek exposure for public recognition and acceptance, and corporations seek a respected image and sought-after products and services.

John Wayne, known to the world as the stereotypical macho man and all-around tough guy, was filmed in dozens of western shoot-outs and military battles, yet he never served a day in the armed forces. Bing Crosby was a cool, reserved man whose image as a bright, friendly, cheerful movie star was projected and defended by Hollywood publicists (Scott, 1986).

As *transmitters of culture*, the media function to communicate information, values, and norms from one generation to another or from the members of a society to newcomers. In this way they serve to increase social cohesion by widening the base of common experience. They aid the integration of individuals into a society by continuing socialization after formal education has ended as well as by beginning it during the preschool years. It has been noted that the media can reduce an individual's sense of estrangement (anomie) or feeling of rootlessness by providing a society to identify with.

However, because of the impersonal nature of the mass media, it has been charged that the media contribute to the depersonalization of society (a dysfunction). Mass media are interposed between individuals and remove personal contact in communication.

It has also been charged that the media serve to reduce the variety of subcultures and help augment mass society. This is the notion that because of the mass media, we tend more and more to speak the same way, dress the same way, think the same way, and act and react the same way. It is based on the idea that thousands of hours of media exposure cause millions of people to accept role models presented by the media. Along with this tendency for standardization goes the charge that the mass media impede cultural growth.

Probably most media content is intended as entertainment, even in newspapers, if one considers the many columns, features, and fillers. Media entertainment serves to provide respite from everyday problems and fills leisure time. The media expose millions to a mass culture of art and music, and some people contend that they raise public taste and preference in the arts. However, there are others who argue that the media encourage escapism, corrupt fine art, lower public taste, and prevent the growth of an appreciation for the arts. The various functions and dysfunctions of the media are summarized in Table 16.5.

VALUES AND IDEOLOGY IN SUPPORT OF THE SOCIETY

Harold Lasswell (1948/1960) pointed out that in every society, values that are shaped and distributed constitute an ideology in support of the network as a whole (1960, p. 123). He notes that in the ideological conflict of world politics, "the ruling elites view one another as potential enemies . . . [and] the ideology of the other may appeal to disaffected elements at home and weaken the internal power position of each ruling class" (1960, p. 124).

Lasswell adds that "one ruling element is especially alert to the other, and relies upon communication as a means of preserving power" (1960, p. 124). Discussing barriers to efficient communication in a society, Lasswell notes:

Some of the most serious threats to efficient communication for the community as a whole relate to the values of power, wealth, and respect. Perhaps the most striking examples of power distortion occur when the content of communication is deliberately adjusted to fit an

TABLE 16.5   Functional analysis of mass communication, based on Lasswell and Wright

Function	Dysfunction
1. Surveillance: informs, provides news	
Warning—natural dangers	Possibility of panic, overemphasis
Instrumental—news essential to economy, public, society	Narcotization—apathy, passivity, too much to assimilate
Exposure to norms—personalities, events	Overexposure, little perspective
2. Correlation: selects, interprets, criticizes	
Enforces social norms—consensus, exposes deviants	Enhances conformity, perpetuates stereotypes
Status conferral—opinion leaders	Creates pseudo events, images, "personalities"
Impedes threats to social stability, panic	Impedes social change, innovation
Monitors, manages public opinion	Minimizes criticism, tyranny of majority
Checks on government, safeguards	Preserves, extends power
3. Transmission of culture: teaches	
Increases social cohesion—widens base of common experience	Reduces variety of subcultures, augments mass society
Reduces anomie—sense of estrangement	Depersonalizes, lack of personal contact
Continue socialization—before/after education, aids, integration	Tendency for standardization, impedes cultural growth
4. Entertainment	
Private respite, escapism, fills leisure time	Encourages escapism, preoccupation with leisure
Creates mass culture—art, music—mass exposure	Corrupts fine art
Raises taste, preference	Lowers taste, impedes growth

SOURCE: Adapted from Charles W. Wright (1960). "Functional Analysis in Mass Communication." *Public Opinion Quarterly* 24: 605–20 (Winter). Also see: Charles R. Wright, *Mass Communication: A Sociological Perspective* (3rd ed.), pp. 4–6. New York: Random House (1986); and Harold D. Lasswell, "The Structure and Function of Communication in Society," in Wilbur Schramm, ed., *Mass Communication* (Urbana: University of Illinois Press, 1960, pp. 117–130).

ideology or counter ideology. Distortions related to wealth not only arise from attempts to influence the market, for instance, but from rigid conceptions of economic interest. A typical instance of inefficiencies connected with respect (social class) occurs when an upper class person mixes only with persons of his own stratum and forgets to correct his perspective by being exposed to members of other classes. (pp. 126–127)

Ever larger segments of the U.S. mass media now strive for more "upscale" audiences (those with higher educations and incomes and more prestigious occupations) in order to attract the advertisers of "high-ticket" consumer products.

In the process these media tailor their content to meet the interests of the upscale audiences they seek and, it is charged, fail to acknowledge the concerns, views, and perspective of other classes that Lasswell refers to. Often cited as a major cause of the urban riots that swept U.S. cities in the mid- and late 1960s were the frustrations of minority members over their inability to communicate their grievances to the general population.

At the annual convention of the American Society of Newspaper Editors, their president Loren Ghiglione scolded editors for "looking at the world increasingly through the eyes of the comfortable." He said, "We often think of ourselves as Davids, fighting the establishment, but the public sees us more as status-quo, establishment Goliaths" (Jones, 1990).

As the media use more "upscale" content, reporters, editors, camera operators, and news anchors are also more frequently drawn from the upper middle class, or aspire to it, and identify with the officials they cover. It is often charged that this identification and these aspirations bias their perspective on the society they report, often unconsciously. Media people usually vehemently deny this charge, but too often their reporting and editing betray them.

In the past, television network officials strongly denied that the sponsors had any voice in the type and content of the programs that were aired. Either procedures have changed, or the industry has become much more candid in discussing its operations. The lead of a syndicated column about the season's forthcoming entertainment on one network read: "The nation's television critics are months away from reviewing the new fall shows, but CBS has been given an enthusiastic nod from the group whose criticism counts most: the sponsors" (Gendel, 1986).

The former network morning news, once produced by their news divisions, is now a group of shows under the jurisdiction of the entertainment divisions. These "infotainment" programs have very little of what has traditionally been regarded as news; instead they feature entertainment designed to attract the "upscale" audience that advertisers demand. The difference between hard realities and the content of the new infotainment "shows" is sometimes glaring.

Speaking of the flow of information within a society, Lasswell says:

When the ruling classes fear the masses, the rulers do not share their picture of reality with the rank and file. When the reality picture of kings, presidents, and cabinets is not permitted to circulate through the state as a whole, the degree of discrepancy shows the extent to which the ruling groups assume that their power depends upon distortion. Or to express the matter another way: If the "truth" is not shared, the ruling elements expect internal conflict, rather than harmonious adjustment to the external environment of the state. Hence the channels of communication are controlled in the hope of organizing the attention of the community at large in such a way that only responses will be forthcoming which are deemed favorable to the power position of the ruling classes. (1960, p. 129)

The revelations contained in the Pentagon Papers of truths about the Vietnam War not shared with the American public are a good example of the point Lasswell makes. Another example is the continuing struggle for economic and political control of the Corporation for Public Broadcasting. In violation of the basic principles established in the 1967 act that created the corporation, Congress, presidents, and a number of economic and political groups have used a wide variety of methods to influence content and eliminate views different from their own. These have included attempts to eliminate all government funding for public broadcasting (Wicklein, 1986). Corporate sponsors select many of PBS's programs (Wicklein, 1986, pp. 32–33).

OUR MENTAL PICTURE OF THE WORLD

The distinguished political columnist Walter Lippmann, writing in his classic *Public Opinion* (1922), discussed the discrepancy between the world and the "realities" we perceive and act upon. He pointed out that most of what we know of the environment we live in comes to us indirectly, but "whatever we believe to be a true picture, we treat as if it were the environment itself" (p. 4). Lippmann pointed out that although we find it hard to apply this notion to the beliefs upon which we are now acting, it becomes easy to apply it to other people and other ages and to the ludicrous pictures of the world about which they were in dead earnest.

Fictions and symbols, aside from their value to the existing social order, are important to human communication. Nearly every individual deals with events that are out of sight and hard to grasp. Lippmann observes, "The only feeling that anyone can have about an event he does not experience is the feeling aroused by his mental image of that event." He adds that at certain times we respond as powerfully to fictions as to realities, and often we help create those fictions. In every case there has been inserted between us and the environment a pseudo environment, and it is to this pseudo environment that we respond. If these responses are acts, they are in the real environment, not the pseudo environment that stimulated them. For this reason, Lippmann says, "what is called the adjustment of man to his environment takes place through the medium of fictions" (pp. 13, 15).

Lippmann does not mean that these fictions are lies but rather that we react to a representation of an environment that we manufacture ourselves. We do this because the real environment is too big, too complex, and too fleeting for direct experience. (See Chapter 5 on abstraction.) To act on the environment we must reconstruct it as a simpler model before we are able to deal with it.

Lippmann then discusses "the world-wide spectacle of men acting upon their environment, moved by stimuli from their pseudo-environments" (p. 20). These actions can result in commands

. . . which set armies in motion or make peace, conscript life, tax, exile, imprison, protect property or confiscate it, encourage one kind of enterprise and discourage another, facilitate immigration or obstruct it, improve communication or censor it, establish schools, build navies, proclaim "policies," and "destiny," raise economic barriers, make property or unmake it, bring one people under the rule of another, or favor one class against another." (pp. 20, 21)

What we do, then, is not based on certain and direct knowledge but on our pictures of the world, usually provided by someone else. The way we imagine the world determines what we do, our efforts, feelings, and hopes, but not our achievements or results. Propaganda, Lippmann points out, is an effort to alter the pictures to which we respond. In *Public Opinion*, Lippmann deals with the reasons why pictures inside our heads often mislead us in our dealings with the outside world. Among the factors that limit our access to the facts, he lists the following: censorship, limitations of social contact, meager time available each day for paying attention to public affairs, distortions as a result of compressing events into short messages (abstraction), the use of a small vocabulary to describe a complex world (Chapter 5), and the fear of facing facts that threaten our lives (Chapter 8).

POPULAR TASTE AND SOCIAL ACTION

In an article titled "Mass Communication, Popular Taste, and Organized Social Action" (1948/1960), two well-known and respected communication researchers and sociologists, Paul F. Lazarsfeld and Robert K. Merton, raise several important questions about the use of the media in our society. One of their major concerns is the use of the mass media by powerful interest groups to exercise social control. They point out that organized business, which "occupies the most spectacular place" among the chief power groups, has replaced the more direct means of control of mass publics through the use of propaganda called "public relations." The authors say:

Economic power seems to have reduced direct exploitation, achieved largely by disseminating propaganda through the mass media of communication. . . . The radio program and the institutional advertisement serve in place of intimidation and coercion . . . media have taken on the job of rendering mass publics conformative to the social and economic status quo. (1948, pp. 96–97; 1960, pp. 493–494)

A good example of this occurred in late 1990 when the Exxon Corporation gave the Alaska Visitors Association $7 million to win back potential tourists still scared away by the 1989 oil spill. Had Exxon run commercials claiming that

Prince William Sound is "nearly recovered" and "nearly restored" it would have invited skepticism. Instead, Exxon gave tax-deductible dollars, written off as a business expense, to the Alaska Visitors Association, an innocuous-sounding group with greater credibility (Creed, 1990).

The National Public Radio program "Nightly Business Report" is, understandably, pro business. Unfortunately, the program fails to identify the personal financial interests of at least one of its commentators. Carla Anderson Hills argues for more open and liberalized trade, reforming tax policies, decreasing federal spending, and "fast track" procedures for approving trade agreements. She advocates more open trade policies with China and China's entry into the World Trade Organization (Nightly Business Report, Dec. 19, Nov. 21, Oct. 26, Sept. 26, Aug. 22, July 25, 1995).

On the "Nightly Business Report," Mrs. Hills is identified only as the "Chairman of Hills and Company." In fact, Mrs. Hills led the U.S. negotiations on the North American Free Trade Agreement. The company of which she is now chairwoman and CEO is an international trade consulting firm in Washington, D.C. She helps solve trade and investment problems for major U.S. companies. She helped convince the Canadian government to withdraw a plan to discourage smoking. She shares an office suite with her husband, Roderick, the former chairman of the Securities and Exchange Commission, who now heads Hills Enterprises, which sets up investment funds in emerging markets. Mrs. Hills serves on the boards of directors of AT&T, AIG, Chevron, and Time-Warner (Alm, 1995; Dunne, 1995; Stopa, 1995).

Some might contend that her activities and her financial interests and affiliations should be known to her viewers. At the least, she could be identified as an international trade consultant in Washington, D.C.

Lazarsfeld and Merton then go on to discuss several of the functions of the media: status conferral; enforcement of social norms; and the narcotizing dysfunction.

Status conferral, or recognition by the mass media, indicates that one is important enough to single out from the mass and that one's behavior and opinions are significant enough to demand media attention. By legitimating the status of individuals and groups the media confer status and prestige.

The mass media may enforce social norms as a result of their "exposure" of conditions that deviate from professed public morality. Publicity forces members of a group to acknowledge that these deviations have occurred and requires that individuals take a stand. A person is forced to choose between repudiating the norm and being identified as outside the moral framework or supporting the norms, whatever his or her private beliefs. Lazarsfeld and Merton say, "Publicity closes the gap between 'private attitudes' and 'public morality'" (1948, p. 103). By preventing continued evasion of an issue, publicity brings about pressure for a single rather than a dual morality. The mass media reaffirm social norms by publicly exposing deviations from them.

The authors observe that another consequence of the mass media is a "narcotizing" of the average reader or listener as a result of the flood of media stimuli. They call this the "narcotizing dysfunction" on the assumption that it is not in society's best interest to have a large portion of the population apathetic and inert. The authors suggest that the result of a flood of communications may be a superficial concern with problems and that this superficiality may cloak mass apathy. The interested and informed individual may know about the problems of the society without recognizing that he or she has failed to make decisions and do something about them. In this way, the authors say, mass media are among the most respectable and efficient of social narcotics, and increasing dosages may be transforming our energies from active participation to passive knowledge (pp. 105–106).

SOCIAL CONFORMISM

In much of Western society the media are supported by the corporate business world as a result of the social and economic system. The media, in turn, support that system. Lazarsfeld and Merton note that this support comes not only in the form of advertising but also in the content of the media, which usually confirms and approves the present structure of society. In their words, "this continuing reaffirmation underscores the duty to accept" (1948, p. 107).

The authors charge that this comes about not only through what is said but, more important, through what is not said, for the media "fail to raise essential questions about the structure of society." The authors say that the commercially sponsored media provide little basis for the critical appraisal of society and "restrain the cogent development of a genuinely critical outlook" (p. 107). They note that there are occasional critical articles or programs but that they are so few that they are overwhelmed by the tide of conformist materials.

They note that social objectives are abandoned by commercial media when those objectives interfere with profits and that this economic pressure results in conformity by omitting sensitive issues (p. 108).

George F. Kennan, former U.S. ambassador to the Soviet Union, charged that the media caused a prolongation of the cold war through their lack of critical analysis because they had become bland as a result of the influence of advertising ("MacNeil/Lehrer NewsHour," Dec. 23, 1988).

CONDITIONS OF MEDIA EFFECTIVENESS

Lazarsfeld and Merton say three conditions are required for media effectiveness: monopolization; canalization rather than change of basic values; and supplementary face-to-face contact.

Monopolization occurs in the absence of mass media counterpropaganda. It exists not only in authoritarian societies but also in any society in which there is an absence of countering views on any issue, value, policy, or public image. Sometimes this near or complete absence is illustrated by the fact that when a "sacred" institution is questioned by the media, the article or program becomes the center of a storm of controversy and is remembered years later as an outstanding exception to the norm.

Critics observe that the commercial television networks have, in their quest for higher ratings and upscale audiences, largely abandoned the controversial hard-hitting documentaries of the past.

Bill Moyers, known nationally for his television documentaries, said (*Newsweek,* Sept. 15, 1986):

> Our center of gravity shifted from the standards and practices of the news business to show business. . . . It is no coincidence that in an era when the president says, "America's back," CBS News's promotional campaign is "We keep America on top of the world." That's what happens when you decide not to examine your culture but to flatter it. (p. 53)

The spread of cable and videocassettes has caused a decline in network audience shares and a loss of revenue. As a result the networks have cut expenditures, including those for documentaries. An article about network cost cutting observes (Boyer, 1986):

> Back when the networks were fat and happy . . . [there] was a strong commitment to news and public affairs programming. CBS used to maintain two-dozen full-time documentary makers; they now have one. In the place of thoughtful, sometimes ponderous and usually low-rated documentaries have come magazine shows . . . and snappy instant documentaries . . . specifically designed to perform in the ratings. (pp. 1, 28)

Many other underlying assumptions, issues, policies, and values are dealt with only peripherally, if at all. The television documentary "The Business of Religion" questioned some aspects of some religions, but the larger question of the overall value of religion in society is seldom, if ever, discussed in the major media. During recent years the media have increasingly questioned business methods without ever questioning the underlying assumptions—for example, the private ownership of natural resources. Whatever the intent of the framers of the First Amendment, whatever the arguments of the Enlightenment that truth will win out in the marketplace of ideas, whatever the logic of Mill in his arguments for the liberty of thought and discussion—including the idea that beliefs not vigorously defended lose their vitality—many basic assumptions that underlie society are never questioned or challenged in any meaningful way.

Lazarsfeld and Merton point out that advertising usually attempts to *canalize* existing patterns of behavior or attitudes. It often attempts to get the consumer to switch brands of a product he or she is already habituated to use, be it toothpaste or automobiles. Once a pattern of behavior or an attitude has been established, it can be canalized in one direction or another. Propaganda, in contrast, usually deals with more complex matters. Its objectives may be at odds with deep-seated attitudes that must be reshaped, rather than the simple canalizing of existing value systems. The authors conclude that although the mass media have been effective in canalizing basic attitudes, there is little evidence of their bringing about attitude change by themselves.

Lazarsfeld and Merton cite a third condition: *supplementation* through face-to-face contacts. Here mass media that are neither monopolistic nor canalizing may, nevertheless, prove effective. The authors cite Father Coughlin, who combined propagandistic radio talks with local organizations. Members listened to him and then followed his radio talks with group discussions of the views he had expressed. The combination of radio talks, the distribution of newspapers and pamphlets, and the coordinated locally organized small discussion groups, all reinforcing one another, proved especially successful. ("Media forums" were discussed in Chapter 11.)

Such combinations of the mass media and reinforcing discussion groups are expensive and are usually found only in cases of planned change in the service of the status quo or in the case of the diffusion of innovation in developing countries. Often such combinations of mass media and discussion groups are used in political systems where central authorities have almost total control. These systems are then used to implement policies and directives from the central leadership. As Lazarsfeld and Merton point out, such media and discussion group collaboration has seldom been achieved by groups trying to bring about social change in modern industrial society. They say, "The forward looking groups at the edges of the power structure do not ordinarily have the large financial means of the contented groups at the center" (1948, p. 117).

The authors add, "Organized business does approach a virtual 'psychological monopoly' of the mass media. Radio commercials and newspaper advertisements are, of course, premised on a system which has been termed free enterprise." They close by saying, "Face-to-face contacts with those who have been socialized in our culture serve primarily to reinforce the prevailing culture patterns." (Indeed, when those contacts do not do so, we often suffer the psychological discomfort of dissonance discussed in Chapter 8.) "Thus," the authors conclude, "the very conditions which make for the maximum effectiveness of the mass media of communication operate toward the maintenance of the ongoing social and cultural structure rather than toward its change" (p. 118).

One has only to look critically at the myriad of "special sections" that bloat most metropolitan dailies or fill local newscasts to see that the media are designed for merchants, not consumers. The only exceptions seem to be those that critique books, films, the performing arts, and restaurants. The largest single purchase for most people is a house. The real estate or housing section of most Sunday newspapers is filled not only with ads but with "editorial" content that is, more often than not, puffery for local developers, builders, and real estate agents. One finds here articles that are, in fact, public relations handouts extolling the virtues of various housing developments or the benefits of using agents in home purchases and sales. Rare indeed is the housing section that critiques designs, floor plans, quality of construction, subdivision planning, cost compared to value offered, financing available, or other relevant matters. The same can be said for the automotive, food, fashion, and travel sections. One is hard pressed to find a travel article in which the waiters were not unfailingly prompt, the natives uniformly cheerful, the service completely efficient, the accommodations totally comfortable, the costs entirely reasonable, and the skies ever sunny and blue.

ENDURING VALUES IN THE NEWS

Sociologist Herbert J. Gans argues that "the news does not limit itself to reality judgments; it also contains values, or preference statements" (Gans, 1979, p. 40). He says that underlying the news in the United States is a picture of the nation and society as the media think it ought to be. These values are rarely explicit and must be inferred because journalists do not, in most instances, insert these values into the news.

Gans calls these *enduring values* and says they can be found in many different kinds of news stories over a long period of time. Often, he says, they help define news and affect what activities become news.

From a continual scrutiny of the news he identified eight enduring values (see Table 16.6). They emerged from the way events were described, the tone used in stories, and the connotations of verbs, nouns, and adjectives commonly used by journalists. The first of Gans's enduring values is *ethnocentrism* (the attitude that one's own race, nation, or culture is superior to all others), as, he observes, is the case for other countries. This, he says, is most explicit in foreign news, which evaluates others by the extent to which they follow American values and practices. He adds that the news carries many stories critical of domestic conditions, but only as deviations from American ideals.

The clearest expression of ethnocentrism in all countries, says Gans, is war news. For example, atrocities committed by one's own forces do not often get into the news. For nearly two years the American mass media did not use the pictures of the Mylai massacre in which American soldiers were later found guilty of having murdered at least 109 unarmed civilian prisoners. Only after a former GI, Ron Ridenhour, began a letter-writing campaign to members of Congress and an investigation into the massacre was opened were the pictures finally given national exposure, 20 months after the actual event (*Life*, Dec. 5, 1969). Seymour M. Hersh, the reporter who finally broke the story, detailed the refusals he got at the magazines *Life* and *Look* as well as Ron Ridenhour's earlier refusal by *Life* before the story was finally made public, even though photographs were available (Hersh, 1969). Finally, the story and photos of the Mylai massacre were first published on Nov. 20, 1969, in the *Cleveland Plain Dealer*, a daily newspaper.

Domestic news stresses *altruistic democracy*, according to Gans. Domestic news indicates how American democracy should perform by frequently citing deviations from unstated ideals. This can be seen in stories of corruption,

TABLE 16.6 Gan's enduring values in the news

Ethnocentrism	to value one's own nation above all others (most explicit in foreign news)
Altruistic Democracy	news implies that politics should be based on the public interest and service
Responsible Capitalism	news implies that business people will refrain from unreasonable profits and gross exploitation of workers or customers
Small-Town Pastoralism	favoring of small towns over other types of settlements (including the desirability of nature and smallness per se)
Individualism	preservation of the freedom of the individual against the encroachments of nation and society
Moderatism	discouragement of excess or extremism (violations of the law; the dominant mores; or enduring values)
Order	respect for authority and of relevant enduring values; concern for social cohesion
Leadership	moral and otherwise competent leadership, honest and candid, with vision, physical stamina and courage

SOURCE: Adapted from Herbert J. Gans, "The Messages behind the News," *Columbia Journalism Review,* Jan.–Feb. 1979, pp. 40–45.

conflict, protest, and bureaucratic malfunctioning. However, Gans says, the news is selective when it keeps track of violations of official norms. While the media have been concerned with freedom of the press and related civil liberties, it has not been as concerned with the violations of the civil liberties of radicals, of due process, of habeas corpus, and of other constitutional protections, particularly for criminals.

Although the media are consistent in reporting political and legal failures in achieving altruistic and official democracy, the press concerns itself much less with the economic barriers that prevent its realization, according to Gans. The media, he says, pay little attention to the relationship between poverty and powerlessness or to the difficulty that middle-class Americans have in gaining political access. There is an assumption, according to Gans, that the polity and the economy are separate and independent of each other. Private industry's intervention in the government is, typically, not viewed as seriously as government intervention in the economy. As a result, the news rarely notes the extent of public subsidy to private interests.

The enduring news value of *responsible capitalism* is, according to Gans, "an optimistic faith that, in the good society, businessmen and women will compete with each other . . . but that they will refrain from unreasonable profits and gross exploitation of workers or customers" (1979, p. 41). He says that there is little explicit or implicit criticism of the oligopolistic nature of much of today's economy.

Gans points out that " 'welfare cheaters' are a continuing menace and are more newsworthy than people, other than the very rich, who cheat on their taxes" (1979, p. 42). A recent exception to this are the scandals in the financial industries in 1990, although some critics claim the media reported them only after they were exposed by government agencies.

Other enduring values that Gans cites are *small-town pastoralism*, or a favoring of small towns over other types of settlements; *individualism*, the preservation of the freedom of the rugged individualist against the encroachments of society and the nation; *moderatism,* the discouragement of excess or extremism; order, both moral and social, including disapproval of any rejection of prevailing ethics or rules; and *leadership*, the method of maintaining moral and social order.

Gans contends that the news contains not only values but also ideology, even if it consists of ideas that are only partly thought out. He calls "this aggregate of values and the *reality judgments* associated with it paraideology, partly to distinguish it from the deliberate, integrated, and more doctrinaire set of values usually defined as ideology; it is ideology nevertheless" (1979, p. 45) (emphasis added). He says that the beliefs that are reflected in the news are neither liberal nor conservative but actually professional values, especially the reformist value or the belief "in honest, fair, and competent public and private institutions and leaders." Reports of violations of this value anger those in power, whether they be liberal or conservative (Gans, 1985, p. 32).

MAKING NEWS: THE SOCIAL
CONSTRUCTION OF REALITY

Sociologist Gaye Tuchman, in her book *Making News* (1978), contends that news is the social construction of reality. The book is based on a series of participant observations in media newsrooms and interviews of newspeople over a period of 10 years. The act of making news, Tuchman says, is the act of constructing reality itself rather than a picture of reality (p. 12). She asserts that the news is an ally of legitimated institutions and that it also legitimates the status quo. Tuchman links news professionalism and news organizations to the emergence of corporate capitalism. She argues that news is a social resource whose construction limits an analytic understanding of contemporary life (p. 215). She contends that "through its routine practices and the claims of news professionals to arbitrate knowledge and to present factual accounts, news legitimates the status quo" (p. 14).

CONTROLLING THE NEWS STAFF
AND MAINTAINING THE STATUS QUO

Why and how media maintain news and editorial policy was explored in two articles by Warren Breed, former newspaper reporter, Columbia Ph.D., and long-time faculty member at Tulane University. In "Social Control in the Newsroom"

(1955), Breed explored the areas in which news and editorial policy are usually maintained and where they are bypassed. Breed observed that the newspaper publisher, as owner or a representative of ownership, has the right to set and enforce the newspaper's policy. However, conformity is not automatic.

By policy Breed means the orientation shown by a newspaper in its editorials, news columns, and headlines regarding certain issues and events. "Slanting" almost never means prevarication, Breed points out, but rather it is the "omission, differential selection, and preferential placement, such as 'featuring' a pro-policy item, 'burying' an anti-policy story, etc." (1955, p. 327). Breed contends that every newspaper, whether it admits it or not, has a policy. Politics, business, and labor are the major areas of policy, much of which results from considerations of class. Breed points out that policy is usually covert because it is often against the ethical norms of journalism and media executives want to avoid being embarrassed by accusations that they have ordered the slanting of a news story.

Martin Feldstein, president of the National Bureau of Economic Research, observed on the "Nightly Business Report" that local newspapers were not reporting on the riskiness of local savings and loans (March 20, 1989). He added that if there were no 100 percent depositor's insurance (i.e., coinsurance) in an institution's failure, individuals would have some of their own money at risk and would be more interested in the management of local savings and loan companies.

Because of the covert nature of policy a new reporter cannot be told what the policy is but must learn to anticipate what is expected in order to win rewards and avoid punishments. Since policy is never made explicit, a new reporter learns policy in a number of indirect ways. First, the staffer reads the newspaper every day and learns to diagnose its characteristics. Usually his or her own output is patterned after that of newsroom colleagues. The newcomer's stories tend to reflect what is defined as standard procedure. The editing of a newcomer's copy is another guide to what is or is not acceptable. Occasionally a staffer may, in an oblique way, be reprimanded. The implication is that punishment will follow if policy is not adhered to.

Through gossip among staffers and by other means the new reporter learns of the interests, affiliations, and characteristics of the executives. Conferences at which the staffer outlines findings and executives discuss how to shape a story offer insight through what the executives say and do not say. Again, policy is not stated explicitly. Other sources of information for staffers about executives are house organs, observation of executives in meetings with various leaders, and opinions executives voice in unguarded moments.

In 1990, the publisher of the *Austin American-Statesman,* Roger Kintzel, was also the chairman of the Greater Austin Chamber of Commerce. Observers commented on the seeming lack of objective reporting about the drive to woo the computer chip-making consortium U.S. Memories to Austin with large tax concessions and other inducements (Forrest, 1989). Apparently stung by criticism, the newspaper ran a long article defending this seeming conflict of interest (Ladendorf, 1990). Among other things, the article said:

A conflict would not occur, Kintzel maintained, because he would not allow one to exist. . . .

"It's very easy for me to keep those things separate," he said. "I'm surprised that people should think that I would feel the need to manage the news because of a one-year volunteer job at the chamber."

There is no compromising the integrity of the newspaper." (p. H1)

Two years earlier, a veteran high-tech reporter, Kathleen Sullivan, who was a skeptic, not a booster, at that same Austin daily, lost her job. When Sullivan reported about worker safety and health problems at a big Austin semiconductor chip manufacturer after an unreported fire and a chemical leak, she angered a local power broker. When she reported the public and private incentives used to lure Sematech, a federally funded consortium to improve the manufacture of computer chips, the power broker reportedly complained to the publisher, Kintzel, who had been deputy vice chairman of the chamber of commerce's economic development council that the power broker chaired. As she was finishing a story critical of another Austin high-tech company, Sullivan was forced to resign for reasons the paper won't explain and "was offered $8,000 if she would promise not to criticize the paper, sue it, use the notes she had gathered at the *Statesman* for future stories" (Curtis, 1988). Three weeks after she left the *Statesman,* Sullivan was hired for the high-tech beat for the *San Francisco Examiner* (Shahin, 1988). One of Sullivan's early stories for the *Examiner,* that the Austin Dell Computer Company's top-selling computer did not comply with Federal Communications Commission standards for radio frequency emissions, is one she claims was squelched by the *Statesman* (Shahin & Forest, 1988).

Breed lists a number of reasons a staffer conforms to policy. The publisher's power to fire or demote is one. However, editors have many opportunities to prevent a situation from reaching this point. Editors can ignore stories that allow for deviation from policy, or, if the story cannot be ignored, it can be assigned to a "safe" reporter. Should a story reach an editor in an unacceptable form, it can be edited, and reasons other than policy—such as pressures of time and space—can be given.

New reporters may feel obligation and esteem toward the people who hired them, helped show them the ropes, or did them other favors. Breed says that these "obligations and warm personal sentiments toward superiors play a strategic role in the pull to conformity" (1955, p. 330). This factor seems to determine not only conformity to policy but morale and good news policy as well.

The desires that most young staffers have for status achievement are another reason for conforming to policy. Many reporters noted that a good path for advancement is to get big page one stories, and this means stories that do not oppose policy. Many staffers view newspapering as a stepping stone to more lucrative positions, and a reputation as a "troublemaker" is a serious hurdle.

Among the other reasons for conformity to policy that Breed notes are the absence of conflicting group allegiance, the pleasant nature of the activity (e.g., the in-groupness in the newsroom, the interesting nature of the work, nonfinancial perquisites), and the fact that news becomes a value and is a continuous challenge.

Through these many factors the new staffer identifies with veteran staffers and executives. Because of shared norms, the newcomer's performance soon emulates theirs. The new staffer usually learns rapidly to put aside personal beliefs or ethical ideals brought to the job and to conform to policy norms.

POSSIBILITIES FOR POLICY DEVIATION

There are situations that permit deviations from policy. Because policy is covert, its norms are not always entirely clear. If policy were spelled out explicitly, motivations, reasons, alternatives, and other complicating material would have to be provided. Because policies are not spelled out, a reporter often has an undefined zone that allows a certain amount of freedom.

Staffers who gather the news can use their superior knowledge of a story to subvert policy because executives may be ignorant of particular facts. Staffers are in a position to make decisions at many points. If a staffer cannot get "play" for a story because it violates policy, the story can be "planted" through a friendly staffer with a competitor. The reporter can then argue that the story has become too big to ignore.

Staffers covering "beats" (police, fire, city hall, courts, etc.) have greater leeway in deciding which stories to cover and which to ignore than those working on individual assignments from the editor. Beat reporters can sometimes ignore stories that would support policies they dislike or that they feel run counter to professional codes. Of course, this is possible only if potential competitors cooperate. And as one might expect, reporters who are considered "stars" can more often violate policy than others.

Breed contends that to the extent that policy is maintained, the existing system of power relationships is maintained. He says, "Policy usually protects property and class interests, and thus the strata and groups holding these interests are better able to retain them" (1955, p. 334). Although much news is printed objectively so that the community can form opinions openly, important information is often denied the citizenry when policy news is buried or slanted.

An item headlined, "Huge U.S. Loss on Pensions," reporting corporate underfinancing of pension plans in one year of more than $1-billion, was buried on page C17 (*New York Times*, Feb. 20, 1992).

A report that a Federal District Court found a former city business loan director guilty of stealing $250,000 in city loan money and trying to hide his use of the funds for personal and business expenses was relegated to page B1. The front page carried a story headlined, "Volunteers Share Valentine Spirit" (*Austin American-Statesman*, Feb. 15, 1992).

Breed concludes that because the newsperson's source of rewards is from colleagues and superiors rather than from readers, the staffer abandons societal and professional ideals in favor of the more pragmatic level of newsroom values. The staffer thereby gains both status rewards and group acceptance. Breed says (1995):

> Thus the cultural patterns of the newsroom produce results insufficient for wider democratic needs. Any important change toward a more "free and responsible press" must stem from various possible pressures on the publisher, who epitomizes the policy making and coordinating role. (p. 335)

One of the often-stated reasons for the urban riots by minorities in the 1960s was the feeling that their grievances were not being communicated to the general public. They recognized correctly, of course, that before one can hope for change the problem must be recognized. Since that time this has come to be called "consciousness raising."

Thirteen years after the publication of Breed's article, the Report of the National Advisory Commission on Civil Disorders (the *Kerner Report*) said this about media coverage of urban minority grievances (NACCD, 1968):

> Our second and fundamental criticism is that the news media have failed to analyze and report adequately on racial problems in the United States and, as a related matter, to meet the Negro's legitimate expectations in journalism. By and large, news organizations have failed to communicate to both their black and white audiences a sense of the problems America faces and the sources of potential solutions. The media report and write from the standpoint of the white man's world. The ills of the ghetto, the difficulties of life there, the Negro's burning sense of grievance, are seldom conveyed. Slights and indignities are part of the Negro's daily life, and many of them come from what he now calls "the white press"—a press that repeatedly, if unconsciously, reflects the biases, the paternalism, the indifference of white America. This may be understandable, but it is not excusable in an institution that has the mission to inform and educate the whole of our society. (p. 366)

SOURCES RATING REPORTERS

Most news sources have probably always tried to control or influence the way they are portrayed by the media. That, after all, is much of the stock-in-trade of the public relations industry and one of the reasons for press releases. Commercial firms now offer corporations systems to evaluate reporters, especially reporters who cover business. One such firm offers profiles of more than 400 reporters for an annual subscription (Gladstone, 1995). Usually the emphasis is on how well a journalist reports a corporation's message. (In 1995 the U.S. Secretary of Energy paid a company more than $40,000 to rate the reporters who cover that department.)

Skeptics claim that critical reporters are being denied access and that coverage is becoming more sycophantic. Those critics claim that corporations try to find the reporters who uncritically present the corporate message.

MASS COMMUNICATION AND SOCIOCULTURAL INTEGRATION

In a second article, Warren Breed (1958) looked at the ways in which the media function to maintain the status quo. He points out that in a conflict of values the mass media sometimes sacrifice accurate reporting of significant events for the virtues of respect for convention, public decency, and orderliness. Breed observes that newspapers generally speak well of the hometown and its leaders. Most of his examples are concerned with protecting the dominant values and interests of American society.

Breed begins by observing that a major problem for any society is the maintenance of order and social cohesion, including consensus over a value system. He quotes E. C. Devereau: "Such head-on conflicts are prevented also by various barriers to communication embedded in the social structure; taboo'd areas simply are not to be discussed, and hence the conflict need not be 'faced'" (1958, p. 109).

A rather dramatic example of "taboo'd areas" can be seen in the paucity of media discussion about the inequities of the draft during the Vietnam War, even after the war ended. In most cases the sons of the middle class went to college while the sons of the poor went to Asia.

A generation later, when the United States was deploying the largest army abroad since the Vietnam War, the issue was raised again when President Bush announced that an additional 100,000 troops would be sent to the Middle East to augment the 225,000 already there. *Washington Post* columnist Mark Shields, speaking on the "MacNeil/Lehrer NewsHour" (Nov. 2, 1990), expressed his "anger and disappointment" that the people in Washington making decisions on the Persian Gulf were out of contact with the American people. He said:

> The reality is that at any Washington dinner party whether it's a Democrat or Republican, or conservative or liberal, there is nobody there who knows anybody of the 1.8 million American enlisted personnel. Because they come from a different America. They don't come from the journalistic establishment. There are no sons of senators, there are no sons of CEO's, there are no sons of anchormen or syndicated columnists there. There's something desperately wrong when people talk about policy abstractions, about sending people there to the very likelihood of death. . . . If the U.S. national interest is really involved here, then the President of the United States and the leaders of this country have the responsibility to say that it's everybody's fight.

Shields observed that nobody mentions the draft and he called for exposing everybody to the risk of war in the Middle East.

Five days later (Nov. 7, 1990), John Kenneth Galbraith, in an article on the op-ed page of the *New York Times*, expanded on this criticism. After pointing out that the young men and women deployed in Saudi Arabia and facing possible extinction are drawn from the poorer families of America, he suggested, facetiously:

> Instead, let us establish a special volunteer service corps for the duration of the Middle Eastern troubles. These battalions, recruited at the universities and in the better suburbs, and from among the numerous young men and women now or recently at work in Wall Street, would provide opportunity for military service for those now so undemocratically exempted by their wealth or comparative affluence. . . . A large response . . . would show that we are not risking the lives only of the poor for the gasoline the economically more fortunate consume and, in the words of President Bush, for the "way of life" which those with higher incomes especially enjoy.
>
> A limited response, which is not entirely to be ruled out, would drive home the fact that we are, indeed, asking the poor to protect the rich. (p. A21)

While other writers have said that the media maintain consensus through the dramatization of proper behavior, Breed set out to demonstrate that they also do this by omission. He says that the media "omit or bury items which might jeopardize the sociocultural structure and man's faith in it" (1958, p. 111).

It took biographer Robert Caro (1990) to reconstruct the wartime service of Lyndon Johnson, which consisted of "a total of 13 minutes" of action while a passenger in a B-26 on a bombing mission over New Guinea that drew fire from Japanese Zeros. Caro says Johnson had promised Texas voters in 1941 that if the United States entered the war he would "be in the front line, in the trenches, in the mud and blood." Caro adds, Johnson spent "the first five months of the war trying to further his political future while ensconcing himself in precisely the type of bureaucratic 'safe, warm naval berth' he had promised to avoid." Only an upcoming election compelled Johnson to fly to a Pacific combat zone, not to fight but as an observer. After his one combat mission Johnson "left the combat zone on the next plane out," Caro wrote. Neither the pilot nor the corporal who shot down a Zero was decorated for the mission, but Johnson was awarded the Silver Star, the Army's third-highest combat award. In later years, Johnson often wore the miniature of the award in the buttonhole of his lapel. A Texas newspaperman, Horace Busby, who occasionally worked for Johnson from 1948 to 1968, said, "for about 40 years I have been wondering when this story would be told. It's just been there waiting for somebody to find it" (Trueheart, 1989).

Breed found that items in the political and economic areas were most frequently omitted. Typically they involved "an elite individual or group obtaining privilege through nondemocratic means." He notes that the most striking fact is that the word *class* is seldom mentioned in the media: "class, being social inequality, is the very antithesis of the American creed," Breed observes (1958, p. 114). Other sacrosanct areas that Breed identifies are religion, the family, patriotism, the community, medicine, and law and justice.

Religion.   Of religion Breed says, "It should be noted that religion is of double significance to social integration: It is not only a value in itself but it justifies and rationalizes other sentiments which bring order to a society" (1958, p. 112). Clergymen are rarely sentenced to prison. More rare, however, is prominent display of this uncommon event. Several cases of sexual abuse by clergy in Chicago, Santa Fe, and Boston have been publicized recently (Steinfels, 1992; Steinfels, 1993; Anon, 1993).

Family.   Breed contends that the media portray the family as an institution without which society would perish. It may be true that in recent years the media have devoted some time and space to alternate life-styles, but in general it seems difficult to dispute Breed's contention.

Patriotism.   Breed observes that patriotism is another value protected by the media. He says, "When an individual is accused of disloyalty, favorable discussion of him by the media is sharply checked. He cannot be dramatized as an individual or a leader, only as a 'controversial' person under suspicion" (1958, p. 113).

Of the press and its policy regarding patriotism and national ethnocentrism, Breed says:

> American soldiers overseas may violate norms involving persons and property for which they would be publicly punished in the country, but the press here minimizes overseas derelictions. In other countries, they are "representatives" of our nationality and thus in a quasi-sacred position. (1958, p. 113)

Community.   Of the media's coverage of their communities Breed says, "The progress, growth, and achievements of a city are praised, the failures buried" (1958, p. 113). Breed notes the "chamber of commerce" attitude on the part of the media.

One newspaper, with a blurb on page one headed "Still Growing," touted an article headlined "Austin's Bright Future," a story describing the city's growth in construction, trade, manufacturing, finance, insurance, real estate, services, government, transportation, communication and utilities (Breyer, 1995). Nowhere did the story mention the accompanying increases in crime, traffic jams, air and water pollution, and taxes, or the increasingly crowded schools.

When NBC correspondent Linda Ellerbee traveled to San Antonio to do a story as part of the Texas Sesquicentennial, she did one report from the Alamo (Feb. 24, 1986). In her report she stated that not all of those at the Alamo were

Texans, that not all present chose to "fight and die" at the Alamo (at least one went over the wall before the battle started), that at that time Texas was a part of Mexico, and that the southerners who immigrated into Texas wanted to keep slaves, which were not allowed under Mexican law. This report created considerable dissonance and the Daughters of the Texas Revolution threatened to boycott the local network affiliate.

Medicine.   "Physicians are almost never shown in a bad light by the press, and the treatment of doctors in other media such as daytime serials is often worshipful," says Breed (1958, p. 113). Even rarer are stories showing "doctors acting in selfish rather than professional fashion" (p. 114).

This is another topic where media coverage has changed considerably since Breed wrote nearly four decades ago. With rising costs of medical care, greater awareness of health issues and increasing numbers of lawsuits for medical malpractice, the media have covered the medical professions to a much greater extent and with greater depth than heretofore.

Law and Justice.   Breed contends that the media function to protect "power" and "class." He observes that "critics have for centuries noted the disproportionate power of elites and the winking by the media at their actions" (1958, p. 111).

Many would argue that things have changed considerably in the nearly four decades since Breed made these observations, especially when the national media cover widely known figures.

When the Chief Judge of New York State was indicted for extortion and then sentenced to 15 months in prison, the media give the story extensive coverage for nearly a year (Barbanel, 1992; Verhovek, 1992; Schemo, 1993).

Nor did the presidents of charities and other "non-profit" organizations escape media attention for their thefts of funds. The president of the United Way, with a salary of $390,000, plus benefits, was sentenced to seven years in prison with an added three years' probation for stealing hundreds of thousands of dollars from the charity and spending it on himself and on girlfriends (Barringer, 1992b; Arenson, 1995; Facts on File, 1995). The director of the American Parkinson's Disease Association confessed to embezzling more than $800,000 over a period of 10 years and was arrested for mail and wire fraud (Walsh, 1995). The SEC charged the founder of the Foundation for New Era Philanthropy with fraud that cost other charities more than $100 million in a pyramid scheme, and Unicef accused Kenyan staffers of defrauding the organization of $10 million through various schemes (*Fortune,* 1995). The venerable NAACP had its moments in the media spotlight for a number of scandals which resulted in the ousting of its executive director (Shepard, 1995). The Episcopal Church was not immune to scandal either, when it was found that its former treasurer misappropriated $2.2 million of church funds, mainly for her own personal use (Niebuhr, 1995).

The United Way scandal of 1992 spurred the media to investigate the salaries of its presidents in 16 major cities and found that United Way chiefs were paid twice the salary of their median donor (Barringer, 1992a). Later that year a study found that more than one-third of the 100 largest charities paid their chief executives $200,000 or more in salary and benefits in 1991, with seven paying their chief executives more than $400,000 that year (Associated Press, 1992).

Public officials have fared no better, with one former U.S. Treasurer found guilty of three felonies—evasion of $47,000 in federal income taxes, conspiracy to make false statements to the government about her finances, and obstruction of a federal grand jury (Johnston, 1994). One recent cabinet member (Agriculture) has been forced to resign and at least three others are, or have been, under scrutiny (Elliott, 1995; Stein, 1995).

After the former Interior Secretary James G. Watt, in a plea bargain, pleaded guilty to a single misdemeanor charge of trying to influence a federal grand jury, one newspaper used a four-column headline in the A-section, pointing out that he had avoided a trial on 18 perjury and influence-peddling felony charges (Johnston, 1996).

Breed says that when television dramas portray a businessman as a villain, for example, they focus on the individual, not on the institution. When newspapers report investigations detailing the structural faults of campaign financing, lobbying, concentrations of economic power, or the like, Breed contends that they are usually not featured. He says that the media "do not challenge basic institutions by exploring the flaws in the working of institutions" (p. 116).

CONCLUSIONS

The world has changed considerably since the end of World War II. Many media systems no longer fit the old classifications of *Four Theories of the Press*, especially in the developing countries. Moreover, the late 1980s have seen radical and continuing changes in media functions and control in the socialist countries.

It is apparent that in the West, the ideal functions of the mass media, as defined by the libertarian and social responsibility theories of the press and the rationale so logically developed by John Stuart Mill, are at considerable variance with actual practice. Wright, Lasswell, Lippmann, Lazarsfeld, Merton, Breed, Altschull, Gans, and Tuchman are but a few of the many who have made such observations. Although it is true that the media omissions cited by Warren Breed four decades ago are still present, they are probably much less prevalent today than they were at the time he wrote. However, the gap between the ideal and the reality remains a major problem for a democratic society.

DISCUSSION

1. For each of the four theories of the press give an example of a nation that follows that system.
2. Are any of the nations you named (above) "pure" examples of the system which you ascribe to them?

3. If a society claims a system of social responsibility for the press, who should "watch the watchdog" (the media)?
4. What steps might be taken to improve accuracy in the media?
5. Are the mass media "agents of power"? Explain.
6. Are Altschull's categorizations of the media more useful than those of *Four Theories of the Press*? Why, or why not?
7. Give examples of some of the functions and dysfunctions of the mass media.
8. What are some media "fictions" (as Lippmann used the term) to which large numbers of people have responded in recent years?
9. Name a recent "pseudo event." Why was it a pseudo event?
10. In Herbert Gans's terms, can you think of an enduring value in the news?

REFERENCES

Alm, Richard (1995). Defending NAFTA; former envoy says don't blame treaty for problem with peso. *Dallas Morning News*, May 6, p. 1F.

Altschull, J. Herbert (1984). *Agents of Power: The Role of the News Media in Human Affairs*. New York: Longman.

——— (1995). *Agents of Power: The Media and Public Policy*. New York: Longman.

Anon. (1993). Former priest pleads guilty to molesting 28 children in the 1960s. *New York Times*, Oct. 5, p. A13.

Arenson, Karen W. (1995). Former United Way president is sentenced to 7 years for fraud. *New York Times*, June 23, p. A14.

Associated Press (1995). Top salaries at foundations reported. *New York Times*, Sept. 8, p. 14D.

Barbanel, Josh (1992). Arrested, a judge prepares to step down in New York. *New York Times*, Nov. 9, p. A13.

Barringer, Felicity (1992a). Charity presidents' generous salaries and benefits raise uneasy questions. *New York Times*, Mar. 16, p. C10.

——— (1992b). United Way stops paying ex-leader. *New York Times*, Mar. 18, p. C20.

Bohlen, C., and C. Haberman (1990). How the Ceausescus fell: Harnessing popular rage. *New York Times*, Jan. 7, pp. 1, 11.

Boyer, P. J. (1986). Trauma times on network TV. *New York Times*, Nov. 2, Sec. 3, pp. 1, 28.

Breed, W. (1955). Social control in the newsroom. *Social Forces*, May: 326-335. Also in W. Schramm (ed.) (1960), *Mass Communication*, 2nd ed. Urbana: University of Illinois Press.

——— (1958). Mass communication and sociocultural integration. *Social Forces* 37: 109-116. Reprinted in L. Dexter and D. White (eds.) (1964), *People, Society and Mass Communications*. New York: Free Press.

Breyer, R. Michelle (1995). Austin's bright future. *Austin American-Statesman*, Mar. 25, pp. A1, E1, E5.

Caro, R. (1990). *Means of Ascent*. New York: Knopf.

Carter, Bill (1995). "60 Minutes" says it held story due to management pressure. *New York Times*, Nov. 13, p. C8.

Creed, J. (1990). Exxon's slick trick. *New York Times*, Nov. 4, Sec. 4, p. 19.

Curtis, T. (1988). Altered statesman. *Texas Monthly*, Apr., p. 176.

Dickey, Pete (1994). Helping the media get it right! *American Rifleman*, Jan., pp. 50–51; 78.

Dunne, Nancy (1995). People. *Financial Times,* Aug. 28, p. 7.

Elliott, Deni (1995). Private lives of public people; dividing line blurred by erosion of principles. *Arizona Republic*, June 4, p. E1.

Facts on File (1995). United Way ex-chief sentenced. *World News Digest*, June 29, p. 471 D1.

Fein, E. (1989). Ending long silence, Soviets report big increase in crime. *New York Times*, Feb. 15, p. 46.

Forrest, H. (1989) Media clips. *Austin Chronicle*, Nov. 17, p. 4.

Fortune (1995). Less than charitable behavior. Oct. 30, p. 24.

Gans, H. J. (1979). The messages behind the news. *Columbia Journalism Review*, Jan.–Feb.: 40–45.

———— (1985). Are U.S. journalists dangerously liberal? *Columbia Journalism Review*, Nov.–Dec.: 29–33.

Gendel, M. (1986). CBS's new lineup pleases sponsors. *Austin American-Statesman,* May 18, Show World (insert), p. 15.

Gladstone, Brooke (1995). Reporters give corporate reportcards a low grade. National Public Radio, Morning Edition, Dec. 18, Transcript 1761-8.

Hersh, S. M. (1969). Notes on the art: The story everyone ignored. *Columbia Journalism Review,* Winter, pp. 55–58.

———— (1970). How I broke the Mylai 4 story. *Saturday Review,* July 11, pp. 46–49.

———— (1972). The story everyone ignored. In M. Emery and T. Smythe (eds.), *Readings in Mass Communications*, 1st ed. Dubuque, Iowa: Wm. C. Brown.

Johnston, David (1994). U.S. Treasurer under Bush pleads guilty to 3 felonies. *New York Times*, Feb. 18, p. A11.

———— (1996). Former Interior Secretary avoids trial with a guilty plea. *New York Times*, Jan. 3, p. A7.

Jones, A. S. (1990). At U.S. newspaper editors' talks, criticism and 1960's headliners. *New York Times*, April 6, p. A12.

Kamm, H. (1989). Hungarians shocked by news of vast poverty in their midst. *New York Times*, Feb. 6, p. 3.

Keller, B. (1989a). Another Soviet taboo is broken: Paper attacks Communist party. *New York Times*, Feb. 9, 1989, p. 1.

———— (1989b). A proposed Soviet law limits press censorship. *New York Times*, Sept. 27, p. 8.

Kimelman, D. (1986). Soviet newspaper prints criticism of privileges. *Austin American-Statesman*, Feb. 16, p. C5.

Ladendorf, K. (1990). Controversy greets chamber tenure of publisher Kintzel. *Austin American-Statesman*, Mar. 4, pp. H1, H5.

Lasswell, H. (1948, 1960). The structure and function of communication in society. In L. Bryson (ed.), *The Communication of Ideas* (1948). New York: Institute for Religious and Social Studies. Reprinted in W. Schramm (ed.) (1960), *Mass Communications*. Urbana: University of Illinois Press.

Lazarsfeld, P., and R. Merton (1948). Mass communication, popular taste and organized social action. In L. Bryson (ed.), *The Communication of Ideas*. New York: Institute for Religious and Social Studies. Reprinted in W. Schramm (ed.) (1960), *Mass Communications*. Urbana: University of Illinois Press.

Lippmann, W. (1922). *Public Opinion*. New York: Macmillan. Chap. 1 reprinted in W. Schramm (ed.) (1960), *Mass Communications*. Urbana: University of Illinois Press.

MacNair, Jenny (1993). Awareness overdose. *U. Magazine: The National College Magazine*. October, p. 12.

Mill, J. (1859, reprinted 1956). *On Liberty*. Indianapolis, Ind.: Bobbs-Merrill.

National Advisory Commission on Civil Disorders (1968). Report of the National Advisory Commission on Civil Disorders (The Kerner Report). New York: Bantam Books.

Niebuhr, Gustav (1995). Episcopal Church says former treasurer misappropriated $2.2 million. *New York Times*, May 2, p. A17.

Ryan, Cornelius (1959). *The Longest Day, June 6, 1944*. New York: Simon & Schuster.

Schemo, Diana Jean (1993). 15-month prison term for New York's ex-chief judge. *New York Times*, Sept. 10, p. A16.

Scott, W. (1986). Personality Parade. *Parade*. Apr. 27.

Shahin, J. (1988). Austin redux: The Kathleen Sullivan mystery. *Columbia Journalism Review*, July–Aug., p. 14.

Shahin, J., and H. Forest (1988). *Austin Chronicle*, July 1, p. 4.

Shepard, Paul (1995). NAACP convention hampered by scandal. (Cleveland) *Plain Dealer*, July 8, p. 6A.

Siebert, F. S., T. B. Peterson, and W. Schramm (1956). *Four Theories of the Press*. Urbana: University of Illinois Press.

Stein, Jacob A. (1995). Four probes endanger the executive branch. *National Law Journal*, June 19, p. A21.

Steinfels, Peter (1992). Inquiry in Chicago breaks silence on sex abuse by Catholic priests. *New York Times*, Feb. 24, p. A1.

———— (1993). Archbishop of Santa Fe quits amid accusations about sex. *New York Times*, March 20, p. A6.

Stopa, Marsha (1995). Q & A: World trade. *Crain's Detroit Business*, May 29, pp. 1, 8.

Trueheart, C. (1989). LBJ embroidered scanty record in war, his biographer says. *San Francisco Chronicle*, Nov. 2, p. A22.

Tuchman, G. (1978). *Making News: A Study in the Construction of Reality*. New York: Free Press.

Verhovek, Sam Howe (1992). Top New York judges won't seek to oust court's chief over arrest. *New York Times*, Nov. 11, p. A1.

Walsh, Sharon (1995). Parkinson's Association director accused of embezzling $800,000. *Washington Post*, Oct. 31, p. D1.

Wicklein, J. (1986). The assault on public television. *Columbia Journalism Review*, Jan.–Feb.: 27–34.

Wright, C. (1959). *Mass Communication*. New York: Random House.

chapter 17

Media Chains and Conglomerates

The Gerbner verbal model (see Chapter 3) recognizes that communication takes place "through some means, to make available materials." For these two aspects of the communication process—means and availability—Gerbner lists as areas of study "investigation of channels, media, controls over facilities" and "administration; distribution; freedom of access to materials."

As mentioned in Chapter 16, Warren Breed (1955) points out that the media "omit or bury items which might jeopardize the sociocultural structure" and that "policy usually protects property and class interests" (p. 334). Closely related to this and also cited in Chapter 16 are Lazarsfeld and Merton's discussion of "social conformism," Gans's "responsible capitalism," Tuchman's comments concerning "the social construction of reality," and Altschull's observations that the news media are agents of the people who exercise political and economic power and that the content of the news media always reflects the interests of those who finance the press. If these observations are correct, some knowledge of mass media ownership is necessary to understand fully the workings of mass communication.

MEDIA CHAINS

ABC, the third largest U.S. television network, was bought by Capital Cities Communications for $3.5 billion in March 1985. At that time ABC owned television stations in New York, Chicago, Detroit, Los Angeles, and San Francisco, as well as 12 radio stations in major markets, a publishing business, and a film company. ABC reported revenues in 1984 of $3.7 billion and profits of $195 million. Capital Cities, which reported 1984 profits of $135.2 million on revenues of $939.7 million, owned 7 television stations (including stations in Philadelphia and Houston), 12 radio stations, 8 daily newspapers, 9 weeklies, and several cable television systems.

In August 1995, Walt Disney Company purchased Capital Cities/ABC for $19 billion, making it the world's most powerful media and entertainment company (Fabrikant, 1995). In 1993 Capital Cities/ABC ranked first in the nation with $4.6 billion in electronic communication revenues (broadcasting, programming, cable, and technology) (*Broadcasting & Cable Yearbook*, 1995, p. C-221). The move combined filmed entertainment, cable television, broadcasting, and telephone wires through joint ventures with three regional phone companies.

Pending is the purchase of Turner Broadcasting by Time-Warner for $7.5 billion, which would once again make it the world's largest media and entertainment concern. The Federal Trade Commission, however, wants to give the merger close scrutiny for several reasons (Haddad, 1995). Time-Warner led the nation with $4.1 billion cable revenue in 1993 (*Broadcasting & Cable Yearbook*, 1995, p. C-223).

Time Inc. and Warner Communications had merged in 1989 to become the then largest media corporation in the world. Time Inc. published not only *Time, Life, Fortune, Sports Illustrated, Money*, and *People* magazines but also Time-Life Books; Little, Brown books; and weekly newspapers. It was heavily into films, broadcasting, cable television, investment corporations, and forest products (pulp, paperboard, packaging, building materials, interior wall products, bedroom furniture, timberland, etc.). The new Time Inc.–Warner Communications became the largest magazine publisher in the United States and had a total worldwide readership of more than 120 million. As the world's largest video company, second largest cable company, and one of the largest book publishers, it conducted operations on five continents (Bagdikian, 1990, p. 240).

In 1995 Westinghouse purchased CBS for $5.4 billion. CBS ranked second and Westinghouse ranked sixth in electronic communications revenue with $3.5 billion for the former and $705 million for the latter in 1993 (*Broadcasting & Cable Yearbook,* 1995, p. C-221). The purchase, involving the merger of 16 television stations and 21 FM and 18 AM stations, needed waivers from the Federal Communications Commission. The total number of broadcasting stations owned by the new company exceeded the current limits because of a rule preventing a company from owning two television stations in the same or overlapping market (Andrews, 1995; Wharton & Flint, 1995). After 10 years of already deep cuts and layoffs at CBS, Westinghouse announced to Wall Street analysts that it planned to slash at least $70 million more in costs and to increase profits by $300 million in two years with job cuts and by squeezing more out of its network-owned stations (Lowry, 1995).

Gannett, the nation's largest newspaper chain, which publishes *USA Today* and 82 other dailies, with a total circulation of 5.8 million, spent $1.7 billion for Multimedia Inc. (Bendavid, 1995; Anon, 1995). It acquired an additional 11 dailies, 49 weeklies or semi-weeklies, five network-affiliated television stations (to add to the ten it already owned), cable systems with 450,000 subscribers, two radio stations (in addition to the 11 it already owned), and the syndicated television talk shows of Rush Limbaugh, Phil Donahue, and Sally Jessy Raphael.

Before the purchase, Gannett ranked eighth in the nation in broadcasting revenues ($397 million in 1993) and Multimedia ranked seventh that year among cable companies ($481 million). Gannett also owns the largest outdoor advertising company in North America (Anon, 1995; Harwood, 1995). (For other details on Gannett, see Bagdikian, 1992, Chap. 4; Winski, 1981; and Tate, 1981.)

In August 1995 the Miami-based Knight-Ridder chain, with a reputation for excellence and second in number of dailies after Gannett, purchased four dailies owned by the Lesher family, in suburban San Francisco, for $360 million (Hall & Hallissy, 1995). It owned 27 dailies before the Lesher purchase. By year's end the chain was pressing its biggest newspaper combination, the *Philadelphia Inquirer* and the *Philadelphia Daily News,* to double profits by increasing newsstand prices, cutting 230 to 250 jobs, cutting features, and cutting local news by about 20 percent. The goal is to increase profits from 8 percent to 15 percent within two years, to satisfy investors (Glaberson, 1995d). In 1993 Knight-Ridder also ranked sixth in the nation with cable revenues of $491 million (*Broadcasting & Cable Yearbook*, 1995, p. C-223). In a geographic reversal, the Sacramento, California, based McClatchy Newspapers Inc. bought the respected News and Observer (N & O) Publishing Co. of Raleigh, North Carolina, for $373 million (Koonce, 1995). McClatchy bought the N & O for 75 times its net income (high by any measure) and the new owners immediately announced their intent to recoup their high purchase price by increasing the paper's operating margin (which was already well within industry standards). In the offing are personnel cuts, elimination of the company's traditional 5 percent annual contribution to charity, and reduction in amounts earmarked for employee pensions. The Raleigh company's pioneering on-line N and O net, with its potential to give McClatchy a head start in electronic media, was one of the factors reported to make the purchase so attractive to McClatchy.

By 1987, twelve large chains, many of which are also involved in broadcasting, cable, magazine and book publishing, and other media, controlled nearly half of the nation's daily newspaper circulation (Table 17.1).

While chains have been buying up small media chains and individual newspapers, many newspapers have been merged with their local competitors or eliminated entirely. Those that survive are often subjected to deep personnel cuts and other cost-cutting measures, as investors demand ever higher returns on their investments.

Between 1960 and 1995 the number of evening papers dropped by a third, from 1,459 to 947, reflecting the changing habits of Americans who are turning more and more from newspapers to television during their after-work time. Some of the evening papers changed to morning publication, as reflected in the nearly doubling in number of morning dailies from 312 to 611 during the same period (Glaberson, 1995a). Nevertheless, the total number of dailies in the nation dropped from 1,771 in 1960 to 1,558 in 1994, for a loss of more than 200 dailies during a period when the population of the United States increased from 180 million to 263 million.

Of greater concern is the fact that the number of cities with competing dailies dropped from 552 in 1920 to 28 in 1986 (Table 17.2, p. 385). As John C.

TABLE 17.1 Proportion of total daily circulation controlled by largest chains

Chain	Number of Dailies	Circulation	Percentage of Total Circulation	Cumulative Percentage
1. Gannett	90	5,887,787	9.43%	9.43%
2. Knight-Ridder	33	3,848,495	6.16	15.59
3. Newhouse	27	3,034,836	4.86	20.45
4. Times Mirror	9	2,714,165	4.35	24.80
5 Tribune	9	2,685,124	4.30	29.10
6. Dow Jones	23	2,519,287	4.03	33.13
7. New York Times	26	1,768,209	2.83	35.96
8. Scripps Howard	20	1,531,200	2.45	38.41
9. Thomson	96	1,481,047	2.37	40.78
10. Hearst	15	1,456,093	2.33	43.11
11. Cox	20	1,287,363	2.06	45.17
12. News America	3	1,256,941	2.01	47.18

SOURCE: From 1987 *Editor & Publisher International Yearbook,* as cited in J. C. Busterna, "Trends in Daily Newspaper Ownership," *Journalism Quarterly* 65 (1988): 836. Reprinted with the permission of The Association for Education in Journalism and Mass Communication.

Busterna points out, between 1960 and 1986 the number of cities with competing dailies declined from 4.2 percent to 1.9 percent. In 1960 those cities with competing dailies constituted 42 percent of total daily circulation, but by 1986 the 28 cities that still had competition accounted for only 21 percent of total daily circulation (1988, p. 833).

Since 1986 at least 21 dailies, including some of the biggest, have either closed or been merged, leaving several more cities without daily newspaper competition. Among newspapers which have either closed or been merged since 1986 are: the *Houston Post;* the *Milwaukee Journal* and the *Milwaukee Sentinel;* the *San Antonio Light; San Diego Tribune;* the *Anchorage* (Alaska) *Times;* the *Pittsburgh Press;* the *Dallas Times Herald;* the *Kansas City Times;* the *Miami News; Los Angeles Herald-Examiner; Baltimore News American; Baltimore Evening Sun;* and the *St. Louis Globe-Democrat* (Hendren, 1995; Verhovek, 1995). Houston, the nation's fourth most populous city (1.6 million), became the largest city without daily newspaper competition when the *Houston Post* closed in April 1995 (Fitzgerald, 1995).

In 1995, of the ten most populous cities in the United States, only four, New York, Los Angeles, Chicago, and Detroit, had competing general-circulation daily newspapers. Four others, Houston, San Diego, Dallas, and San Antonio, have one daily each, while Philadelphia and Phoenix have two dailies each, under single ownerships in each of the cities (Table 17.3).

TABLE 17.2 Trends in ownership of daily newspapers: 1920–1986

	1920	1940	1960	1986
Circulation (000)	27,791	41,132	58,881	62,453
Total dailies	2,042	1,878	1,763	1,657
Total daily cities	1,295	1,426	1,461	1,513
One-daily cities	716	1,092	1,222	1,389
Percentage of total	55.3	76.6	83.6	91.8
Joint monopoly cities	27	149	160	75
Joint operating cities	0	4	18	21
Total non-competitive	743	1,245	1,400	1,485
Percentage of total	57.4	87.3	95.8	98.1
Competing daily cities	552	181	61	28
Newspaper chains	31	60	109	127
Chain newspapers	153	319	560	1,158
Average dailies per chain	4.9	5.3	5.1	9.1
Independent newspapers	1,889	1,559	1,203	499
Percentage of total	92.5	83.0	68.2	30.1
Newspaper owners	1,920	1,619	1,312	626

SOURCE: From 1987 *Editor & Publisher International Yearbook* for 1986 figures. All earlier figures from Raymond B. Nixon and Jean Ward, "Trends in Newspaper Ownership and Inter-Media Competition," *Journalism Quarterly* 38:3–14 (Winter 1961), p. 5. As cited in J. C. Busterna, "Trends in Daily Newspaper Owership," *Journalism Quarterly* 65 (1988): 833. Reprinted with the permission of The Association for Education in Journalism and Mass Communication.

TABLE 17.3 General circulation daily newspapers in the ten most populous U.S. cities

City	1990 Population (in Millions)	Daily Newspapers
New York	7.32	*News; Post; Times; Wall St. Journal*
Los Angeles	3.48	*News; Times*
Chicago	2.78	*Sun Times; Tribune*
Houston	1.63	*Chronicle*
Philadelphia	1.58	*Inquirer; News*[a]
San Diego	1.11	*Union-Tribune*
Detroit	1.02	*Free Press; News*[b]
Dallas	1.00	*Morning News*
Phoenix	.98	*Republic; Gazette*[c]
San Antonio	.94	*Express-News*

[a] Both the *Philadelphia Inquirer* and *Philadelphia News* are owned by the Knight-Ridder chain.
[b] The *Detroit Free Press* is owned by Knight-Ridder and the *Detroit News* is owned by Gannett. They are in a joint operating agreement for business, production, and distribution facilities.
[c] The *Phoenix Republic* and the *Phoenix Gazette* are both owned by Phoenix Newspapers, Inc.
SOURCE: Adapted from 1990 U.S. Census, and *Editor & Publisher International Yearbook*, 1995.

Busterna says:

> The decline in head-to-head daily newspaper competition can be ex-
> plained in terms of a few economic factors. There is little product
> differentiation among daily newspapers. The content of typical com-
> peting dailies is very similar giving readers no reason to purchase more
> than one. This similarity is a product of a decline of the partisan press
> and the establishment of objectivity in presenting news and balance in
> selecting editorial page features. The lack of different content typically
> creates homogeneous audiences for advertisers. As a result, advertisers
> flock disproportionately to the larger circulation daily. With no special
> content to attract readers and a smaller audience for advertisers,
> competition is often doomed. (pp. 833–834)

Busterna adds that other media complement daily newspapers rather than
provide substantial competition for news, opinion, and advertising. He concludes
that other media don't appear to be good substitutes for the loss of competing
daily newspapers (p. 835).

The number of chain-owned newspapers doubled from 1960 to 1986,
reducing the proportion of independently owned dailies during the same period
from 68 percent to 30 percent, and the trend has continued. The 1995 purchase
of the family-owned *Raleigh* (N.C.) *News and Observer* by the McClatchy chain
is one of the more recent examples.

Busterna also points out that the number of chains peaked in 1978 with
169, and since then there has been a sharp decline in their number, suggesting
that chains are merging with other chains (p. 835). Indeed, the average number
of dailies per chain almost doubled from 1960 to 1986, at a time when the total
number of dailies declined by 106 (Table 17.2). Busterna points out that this
has "caused a large jump in the proportion of absentee-owned chain dailies. . . .
the foreseeable future should find the continuing consolidation of daily newspapers into the hands of a small number of distant firms" (p. 838). The 1995
Knight-Ridder purchase of the four-newspaper Lesher chain in California is a
recent example.

Earlier, James N. Rosse (1980) attributed the dramatic decline in newspaper
competition to several factors, including these:

1. Loss of effective newspaper market segmentation, or an inability to
   find an audience for which a newspaper could differentiate itself from
   competitors and for which advertisers were willing to pay enough to
   make publication profitable
2. Competition for advertising revenue from the broadcast media
3. Decline in readership of newspapers per household
4. Population shifts from inner cities with great population diversity to
   more homogeneous suburbs with individual suburban newspapers that
   serve the more homogeneous population more efficiently.

Declining circulations have helped hasten the demise of many daily newspapers in recent years. The circulation losses have, in part, been attributed to the skyrocketing cost of newsprint, resulting in increasing newsstand prices and subscription costs. In the six months that ended in September 1995, seven of the country's 10 largest metro dailies lost circulation (Glaberson, 1995c).

Many reasons exist for the growth of media conglomerates. This phenomenon is, of course, part of the larger economic trend in our society that favors concentration in general with the advantages of large-scale operation. Another factor is the inheritance tax laws, which make it difficult for a family-owned media to be passed on to heirs when large sums are needed to pay taxes. There is also the inability to challenge chain ownership under current antitrust laws.

The tremendous real or potential profitability of many of the media is another factor in the growth of media conglomerates. Profit figures in the newspaper industry are hard to come by since few nonchain dailies sell public stock and issue public business reports. Even in recession years and in the face of long strikes, newspapers have traditionally shown growth in profits exceeding that in most other industries, although in recent years that has changed somewhat.

An article about the buying up of independent newspapers by chains referred to papers "that either earn or have the potential to earn pretax profit margins of 25% to 30% or higher. The Speidel chain [of 13 newspapers] acquired by Gannett [for $178 million], had pretax margins of 34%" (*Business Week*, 1977, p. 57). Such rates in the banking industry would be usurious in most states. Chains have the expectation that their local managers will produce high profits. Usually these profits are not put back into the community to improve local media but are returned to the corporate headquarters to enable the conglomerate to purchase additional media elsewhere, called by some a form of economic colonialism.

Otis Chandler of the Times-Mirror Company stressed local media competition as one of the biggest considerations in any prospective acquisition. The choicest property is one that has a market almost to itself. Chandler was quoted as saying, "In these markets [large metropolitan areas] you worry about cost per thousand, or the other media buys that an advertiser could make. All that doesn't mean a thing in smaller media markets because the advertiser has no competitive buys." He added that if a newspaper is noncompetitive, "it gives you a franchise to do what you want with profitability. You can engineer your profits. You can control expenses and generate revenue almost arbitrarily." Times-Mirror Company bought *Newsday* in 1970 and increased profits by 72 percent in the first year, in part by doubling the price of the paper (*Business Week*, 1977, pp. 58–59).

During the past decade the Los Angeles Times-Mirror Company has fallen on harder times. Although in 1993 it ranked eighth in the nation in cable and other electronic information revenues, it has, during the past decade, taken deep cost-cutting measures. Its second-quarter profits for 1995 dropped by 19 percent compared with the same period a year earlier (Williams, 1995). Three days after Times-Mirror closed *New York Newsday,* the company announced that it would eliminate about 700 jobs from its flagship newspaper the *Los Angeles Times* and about 300 more from six of its East Coast newspapers, including the *Hartford*

(Conn.) *Courant*. It also announced that it would close its consumer multimedia group, reduce its investment in several cable television programming ventures, close its Washington office, and no longer finance its prestigious Times Mirror Center for the People and the Press (Landler, 1995). In September 1995 it closed the renowned *Evening Sun* of Baltimore, the newspaper of H. L. Mencken (Glaberson, 1995a).

Concern about "chain-store news," the maintenance of a "diverse and competitive press," and the effects of "massive business empires" on our media have been voiced for at least 50 years. A nationally known and highly regarded media critic pointed out that residents of most American cities have access to competing automobile dealerships, even though we have only four manufacturers of automobiles in the United States. Not so with newspapers—most U.S. cities have no competition in newspapers (Bagdikian, 1978, p. 31).

Defenders of newspaper chains and monopoly newspaper cities reply that other sources of news, including newsmagazines, radio, and television, are available. The fact is that much of the news in all the media comes from the Associated Press which, in turn, relies very heavily on its local members. The members most apt to gather news are the daily newspapers, which are, increasingly, in one-owner cities.

National newsmagazines are of little help to the individual who wants and needs information about his or her own community—the actions of the city council and county commissioners on tax increases and zoning ordinances, school board policies, fire and police protection, maintenance and construction of roads, water and sewage treatment facilities, and the myriad of other local issues that affect a person's everyday life.

Although local television evening news programs now often run one hour, in reality that hour is usually split into two highly redundant half-hour segments, preceding and following the national evening news. After making allowances for commercials, weather, sports, "fillers," network feeds of items not used on the national news, PR handouts, and "happy talk," most local evening news programs, with a few exceptions, probably contain less than five minutes of local news.

Significant local news coverage on radio is so unusual that when it does occur the rare exception merits special recognition.

Trying to Hold and Gain Readers

Newspapers have tried a variety of methods in recent years to hold and gain readers.

The Gannett chain instituted "News 2000" to determine what readers want to see. Using surveys, public forums, reader panels, and other feedback methods, the chain required its newspapers to tailor their contents to readers' wishes. The reader-driven newspapers are "designed to reconnect newspapers to their communities by involving readers in the entire news production process" (Underwood, 1993, p. 42).

The *Olympian* (Olympia, Washington) had its news pages redesigned, its beat system restructured, and a new system of editor oversight instituted to insure "that Gannett's concept of community-based news dominates the news columns." The editors contend that the newspaper is now more responsive to community interests, and circulation has increased. Reporters say the emphasis on brief stories has resulted in a lack of depth in news coverage. Most stories run no longer than six to ten inches. Also, in ten years five top editors, all from outside the newspaper and the community, have come and gone. Some claim more and more news ideas are generated from the meetings of transient editors than from reporters working in the community. Newsroom staff now meet with business department employees to come up with schemes to sell more ads. As part of Gannett's effort to get more minority views into the news, reporters are to include as many minority sources as possible. Reporters claim that this results in minority sources often ending up in stories even if they are unqualified to comment on the matter at hand. Editors claim the changes are the reason the *Olympian* is one of Gannett's top growth newspaper. Critics say that in a fast-growing community like Olympia, circulation should be rising under any circumstances. And Gannett's vice president for news told journalism educators at their annual convention in 1993 that they should teach the fundamentals of "News 2000" (reader-driven news) as part of their programs.

The *Miami Herald*'s publisher told his staff to "focus its newsroom resources on nine subject areas that readers have told us are especially important and useful" (Glaberson, 1995b). Several *Herald* journalists noted that among items not on the list of reader preferences are: national politics, religion, economics, investigative reporting, and world affairs. The publisher said the newspaper's focus on reader preferences was an attempt to respond to sinking circulation. The Knight-Ridder newspaper has been cutting its staff and closing bureaus for some time.

Another approach is called "civic journalism," "public journalism," or "community journalism." While definitions vary, most seem to want journalists to end their neutrality on certain questions in order to make public life work (Hoyt, 1995). Editor Buzz Merritt of the *Wichita Eagle,* which has been experimenting with public journalism the longest, says public journalism consists of framing news

> in a way that facilitates people thinking about solutions, not just problems and conflict. The most crucial thing is to figure out how you frame stories in a way that accomplishes that end. (Hoyt, 1995, p. 27)

Critics of public journalism have called it:

> the latest substitute for a healthy editorial budget and solid journalistic instincts;
> an end to journalistic neutrality and objectivity;
> an attempt to shape or direct events or outcomes;

an overuse of marketing techniques, polls, surveys, and focus groups instead of actually spending time reporting on citizens;

an excellent cover for pandering, often to build circulation;

"kissing up to the chamber of commerce" (Aug, 1995); and

public relations practice (*PR News,* May 16, 1994).

Some critics have called the new directions taken by journalism "market-driven" journalism, which argues for providing content that will get and hold an audience in order to sell more advertising space or time. The content provided is, of course, determined by feedback from readers or viewers. John H. McManus (1994), among others, believes that news operations are becoming too market-driven. His book, *Market Driven Journalism,* which concentrates on television, is subtitled, "Let the citizen beware?"

The media have always had to get and hold audiences in order to survive, but the new emphasis on paying more attention to audience wishes has called into question the balance between the need to make a profit and the duty to perform public service.

In general, "reader-driven," "civic," "community," "public," or "market-driven" journalism are all attempts by the various media to capture and hold the attention of readers and viewers. With addtional channels of information and entertainment available—broadcasting, cable, videocassettes, and now the Internet, and with generally declining newspaper readership, all of the media are trying to be more visually attractive and more accessible. Journalists are redefining what is news to focus on what really has an impact on people and writing in more appealing ways, often by "humanizing" the news. The critics charge that often these innovations lead to pandering to readers and "dummying down" the news.

Concentration of Broadcasting

Ownership of broadcasting is equally concentrated. In 1989 nearly four of every five television stations in the 100 largest markets in the United States were group-owned (Table 17.4). The total number of regular commercial TV stations (exclusive of low-power stations) in the 100 largest markets increased from 420 in 1982 to 677 in 1989. Of these 677 TV stations in the 100 largest population centers, 529 or 78.1 percent were licensed to groups. On the basis of the Federal Communications Commission's market reach formula, only three groups (the network owned-and-operated stations of ABC, CBS, and NBC) reach more than 20 percent of the nation's TV households. However, these three networks are also able to reach more than 95 percent of the nation's households when their affiliated stations are included.

Howard (1989) observes that the number of television stations under group ownership (two or more stations under single ownership) has increased since 1982, and the number of groups has increased from 158 in 1982 to 205 in 1989 (p. 791). However, five groups reached the limit of twelve TV stations each, and

TABLE 17.4 Multiple ownership of TV stations by market rank, January 1, 1989

Market Ranking	Number of Stations			Number of Stations Group-Owned			Percentage of Stations Group-Owned		
	VHF	UHF	All TV	VHF	UHF	All TV	VHF	UHF	All TV
1–10	43	80	123	42	47	89	97.7	58.8	72.4
11–25	58	66	124	53	50	103	91.4	75.8	83.1
26–50	70	87	157	64	62	126	91.4	71.3	80.3
51–75	73	80	153	64	56	120	87.7	70.0	78.4
76–100	60	60	120	51	40	91	85.0	66.7	75.8
Total (1–100)	304	373	677	274	255	529	90.1	68.4	78.1

SOURCE: From H. H. Howard, "Group and Cross-Media Ownership of TV Stations: A 1989 Update," *Journalism Quarterly* 66 (1989): 788. Reprinted with the permission of The Association for Education in Journalism and Mass Communication.

twenty-four groups now own more than the former limit of seven stations each (p. 791). In 1989 the overwhelming number of group-owned stations, 189 or 92 percent, could reach fewer than 5 percent of the nation's television homes (p. 789).

MEDIA CROSS-OWNERSHIP

From the standpoint of the individual citizen, probably one of the greatest threats to diversity of news and opinion about local issues is media cross-ownership or joint ownership (a newspaper and a television station under single ownership in one community).

If one accepts the notions of the libertarian and social responsibility theories of the press, the arguments put forth by Mill regarding the liberty of thought and discussion, and the position of Judge Learned Hand, who wrote in *U.S. v. Associated Press* that "right conclusions are more likely to be gathered out of a multitude of tongues," one must agree that when cross-ownership reduces diversity in news and opinions, it also threatens truth and understanding.

As of early 1989, nearly one-fourth of the television stations in the nation's 100 largest population centers were affiliated with newspaper publishers (Table 17.5). Of the 677 TV stations in the 100 most populous cities, 167 were newspaper-related, an increase of 27 stations between 1982 and 1989. However, because of the large increase in the number of new stations in the 100 largest markets (especially UHF), the actual percentage of newspaper affiliated TV stations declined from 33.3 percent in 1982 to 24.7 percent in 1989 (Howard, 1989, p. 790).

Howard also reported a steady decline in both percentage and number of local newspaper-television cross-ownerships in the top 100 markets. They had dropped from 16.1 percent (60 stations) at the beginning of 1973, to 8.3 percent (35 stations) in 1982, to 3.7 percent (25 stations) at the beginning of 1989 (1989, p. 790).

Howard wrote (1989):

Three reasons seem to account for the increase in the number of newspaper-affiliated television stations:

1. Although the FCC has sought to eliminate local cross-media ownerships of newspaper and TV properties, it has not objected to newspaper ownership of broadcast stations in markets where a publisher does not engage in the newspaper business.
2. Media companies with holdings in both the publishing and broadcast fields (and often cable as well) have experienced rapid growth during recent years.
3. Finally, existing media companies have added new television stations to their broadcast holdings. (pp. 790–791)

TABLE 17.5 Newspaper-affiliated television stations, January 1, 1989

Market Rank	VHF		UHF		Both VHF and UHF	
	Number	Percentage	Number	Percentage	Number	Percentage
1–10	25	58.1	8	10.0	33	26.8
11–25	19	32.8	5	7.5	24	19.4
26–50	31	44.3	9	10.3	40	25.5
51–75	30	41.1	7	8.8	37	24.2
76–100	26	43.3	7	11.7	33	27.5
Total (1–100)	131	43.1	36	9.6	167	24.7

SOURCE: From H. H. Howard, "Group and Cross-Media Ownership of TV Stations: A 1989 Update," *Journalism Quarterly* 66 (1989): 791. Reprinted with the permission of The Association for Education in Journalism and Mass Communication.

393

MEDIA CONGLOMERATES

One of the most rapidly expanding areas of media ownership is that of media conglomerates. A parent corporation may own newspapers, magazines, book publishing houses, news services, public opinion polling organizations, radio and television stations, cable TV, broadcasting networks, and companies that produce records and tapes and the associated "clubs" that promote, sell, and distribute those records and tapes.

Often a conglomerate derives only a fraction of its annual revenue from media activities, the bulk of its operations being in manufacturing and sales. These include such diverse activities as international telecommunications, the manufacture of electronic systems for defense and space, musical instruments, frozen foods, investment corporations, paper and wood products, timberlands, furniture manufacturing, vehicle rental agencies, cement, sugar, citrus, livestock, cigars, and candy. If these seem like a varied mixture, indeed that is, after all, the definition of conglomerate. A number of these conglomerates involved in the mass media rank well up among the Fortune 500 listings of the largest corporations in the United States.

The dean of Columbia's graduate school of journalism, Osborn Elliott, speaking at the presentation of the Alfred I. du Pont–Columbia University broadcast journalism awards in 1986, said (Boyer, 1986):

> News divisions, which once may have enjoyed some kind of special standing within their companies, may now be perceived as just another chicken in the corporate henhouse, to be stuffed or starved as may serve the corporate purpose. (p. 46)

In 1993 General Electric reported the third highest revenues in the nation in electronic communication income—$3.1 billion (*Broadcasting & Cable Yearbook*, 1995, p. C-221). The General Electric Company bought Radio Corporation of America in 1985 for $6.28 billion. RCA, in turn, owned NBC and seven television stations in the nation's largest cities. However, only a fraction of RCA's total revenues were derived from broadcasting; twice as much came from electronic products and services, much of it from defense and space contracts. The rest of RCA's revenues came from its publishing houses and such diverse operations as frozen foods and vehicle rental.

After the sale of RCA to General Electric, one could not help but speculate on the kind of news coverage RCA's subsidiary NBC might provide should GE become involved in another conspiracy and price-fixing scandal. Between 1911 and 1967 GE was the defendant in 65 antitrust actions. One resulted in jail sentences for three GE officials and fines and settlements reaching more than $58 million (Moskowitz, Katz, & Levering, 1980, p. 178.)

In 1995, while the purchase of CBS by Westinghouse was in progress, the nationally acclaimed television newsmagazine "60 Minutes" was pressured by the CBS legal staff to "pull" a story highly critical of the tobacco industry (Carter, 1995).

Apparently management at CBS feared that a possible lawsuit by the tobacco company in question would jeopardize the Westinghouse-CBS deal (Walker, 1995). In addition, the then owner of CBS also had holdings in a cigarette manufacturer. Only a few months earlier ABC had lost a sixteen-month long lawsuit, which cost ABC several million dollars in legal fees, over an award-winning investigation ABC did about the manipulation of nicotine in cigarettes (Weinberg, 1995).

Television's Bill Moyers, commenting on CBS pulling the tobacco story, said (Walker, 1995):

> More and more, corporations that have no feel for journalism, and no interest in journalism, are dominating what used to be the outlets for journalism. I think the best thing a school of communications or a journalism school can do today is to somehow endow young people with the steely resolve to be independent, to be mavericks, to be guerrilla journalists, to be prepared for a life on the run (p. D5).

He added:

> I think we'll return to the days of the pamphleteer, Moyers said, and the *Internet* holds more hope than broadcasting. (emphasis added)

Paramount Communications Inc. (before mid-1989 it was called Gulf + Western) deals, or has dealt, in insurance, manufacturing, zinc, cement, apparel, paper, building products, auto replacement parts (both in the United States and overseas), rocket engineering, jet engines and missile parts, nuclear power plants, sugar, citrus and frozen juices, mining (on four continents), livestock, cigars, candy, and a host of other industries. It also produces prime-time television shows, and owns Paramount Pictures and Simon & Schuster book publishers (Bagdikian, 1992, pp. 28–30). It took a full-page ad in the *New York Times* to list its many entertainment and publishing activities (June 5, 1989, p. 29). It operates in all 50 states and 50 other countries.

Ben Bagdikian, dean emeritus of journalism at Berkeley and formerly the first ombudsman at the *Washington Post*, relates in his book *The Media Monopoly* the fate of a book manuscript critical of big corporations that was submitted to Simon & Schuster, a subsidiary of Gulf + Western (now Paramount Communications Inc.). Although one of Simon & Schuster's editors and her staff were unanimous in supporting publication of the book, the corporation president opposed its publication, even though it never mentioned Gulf + Western, because he felt it made all corporations look bad (Bagdikian, 1992, pp. 27–30). The book in question, *Corporate Murders*, was not published.

Bagdikian cites other similar examples.

When the first edition (1983) of Bagdikian's book *The Media Monopoly* was about to be published, Simon & Schuster asked Beacon Press to delete criticism of it from the book and asked to see the manuscript. When Beacon Press refused, Simon & Schuster threatened the publisher with a libel suit. Beacon Press stood firm, and the incident has been related in Bagdikian's book through four editions (1992, pp. 27-30). (Beacon Press, the Boston-based publishing arm of the Unitarian Church, published the Pentagon Papers in 1971 over the objections of the Nixon administration. They described the origins of U.S. intervention in Vietnam [*Wall Street Journal*, April 7, 1983, p. 10; McDowell, 1983].)

Before Bagdikian sent the manuscript of *The Media Monopoly* to Beacon Press the manuscript had been turned down by twelve major commercial publishing houses, including the publisher of most of his earlier books. None of the publishers were ones he had written about, and none provided reasons for their rejections of the manuscript (Rips, 1988, p. 16).

Ben Bagdikian has called for a series of changes (1977, p. 22; 1978, p. 34) whereby the professional staffs of newspapers and broadcasting stations can choose their own top editors, to have representatives on the board of directors, and have a voice in determining the annual news budget. He points out that this is done on a number of quality European papers including *Le Monde,* often cited as one of the best newspapers in the world. Bagdikian gets to the heart of the matter when he says (1977):

> Broadcast and newspaper news is too important an ingredient in the collective American brain to be constantly exposed to journalistically irrelevant corporate policy. . . . Staff autonomy in the newsroom has not been the ordinary way of running business, even the news business. But there is no reason to expect that a person skilled at building a corporate empire is a good judge of what the generality of citizens in a community need and want to know. Today, news is increasingly a monopoly medium in its locality, its entrepreneurs are increasingly absent ones who know little about and have no commitment to the social and political knowledge of a community's citizens. More and more, the news in America is a by-product of some other business, controlled by a small group of distant corporate chieftains. If the integrity of news and the full information of communities are to be protected, more can be expected from autonomous news staffs than from empire builders mainly concerned with other businesses in other places. (p. 22)

More recently, Bagdikian (1992) explored at book length the accelerating concentration of media ownership, now in the hands of 23 corporations who control the majority of U.S. media (p. 4); interlocking directorates and the corporate desire for only positive information; the trend to mass advertising directed at "upscale" audiences and its impact on media content, especially as it affects minorities and the poor; media monopoly and the myth of media competition; the use of media power to obtain, through political means, special economic considerations; the reduction of local media coverage in favor of cheaper syndicated material and its impact on citizen knowledge of local affairs; the result of maintaining the status quo when news is not put into its social, economic, and political context; and a series of other media issues.

Among the remedies Bagdikian suggests are:

1. A limit on the number of broadcasting stations, newspapers, magazines, and book publishers under a single ownership (During the 1980s the FCC nearly doubled the limit on broadcasting stations allowed under single ownership, and seems to be moving toward eliminating limits on ownership altogether. Of course, there has never been a limit in the print media.)
2. Limits on the cross ownership of media
3. Free broadcasting time for political candidates to help prevent their having to become beholden to large financial contributors
4. A progressive tax on advertising
5. The selection of top editors by professional newspaper staffs
6. Mandated free prime-time for the representatives of all political parties in political campaigns. (pp. 223–237)

Other suggestions that have been made include divestiture of cross-owned media in single communities, divestiture of network-owned and operated stations, reductions in the amount of programming originated by the network, and more autonomy for news staffs, including employee ownership.

CONCLUSIONS

Several media scholars have pointed out that media ownership determines media control, which, in turn, determines media content, probably the major cause of media effects. Media ownership is an important concern of communication theorists dealing with media effects.

A number of reasons have been advanced opposing the increasing concentration of ownership in the U.S. media. Nearly all are concerned with the effects of ownership on media content and its ultimate effects on society. This chapter has discussed some of the many possible remedies that have been suggested.

DISCUSSION

1. The three most powerful national television networks are now owned by industrial conglomerates. What are some of the disadvantages or possible threats to society of such combinations? Can you name some benefits?

2. What are some of the advantages to a community to be a one-newspaper town? Some of the disadvantages?
3. What advantages and disadvantages are there in newspaper chain ownership, to both the newspaper and the community?
4. Are media attempts to get and hold an audience (civic, community, public, reader and market-driven journalism) good or bad? What can be said for and against such journalism?
5. What is media cross-ownership? What are some of its advantages? Its dangers?
6. What might be done to offset or correct some of the problems you see concerning media ownership and control of content today? Why do you suggest these steps?
7. Compare the earlier definition of propaganda as "symbol-manipulation designed to produce action in others" with the definition of "civic journalism" as framing news "in a way that facilitates people thinking about solutions, not just problems and conflict. The most crucial thing is to figure out how you frame stories in a way that accomplishes that end."

REFERENCES

Andrews, Edmund L. (1995). F.C.C. approval seen today for Westinghouse-CBS deal. *New York Times*, Nov. 22, p. D2.

Anon. (1995). Gannett, Multimedia will merge Monday. *Palm Beach Post*, Dec. 2, p. B7.

Aug, Lisa (1995). New paths or old? *Columbia Journalism Review*, Nov.–Dec.: 5.

Bagdikian, B. (1978). The media monopolies. *Progressive*, June: 31-37.

——— (1990). *The Media Monopoly*. Boston: Beacon Press.

——— (1992). *The Media Monopoly*. Boston: Beacon Press.

Bendavid, Naftali (1995). Gannett Co./ Multimedia Inc. *Legal Times,* Aug. 7, p. 17.

Boyer, P. (1986). Nightline wins journalism prize. *Austin American-Statesman*, Feb. 9, p. 46.

Breed, W. (1955). Social control in the newsroom. *Social Forces*, May: 326-335.

Broadcasting & Cable Yearbook (1995). Washington, D.C.: Broadcasting Publications, Inc.

Business Week (1977). The big money hunts for independent newspapers. Feb. 21, pp. 56-60; 62.

Busterna, J. C. (1988). Trends in daily newspaper ownership. *Journalism Quarterly* 65: 831-838.

Carter, Bill (1995). Tobacco company sues former executive over CBS interview. *New York Times*, Nov. 22, p. A14.

Fabrikant, Geraldine (1995). Walt Disney to acquire ABC in $19 billion deal to build a giant for entertainment. *New York Times*, Aug. 1, p. A1.

Fitzgerald, Mark (1995). Houston Post Closes. *Editor and Publisher*, Apr. 22, p. 14.

Glaberson, William (1995a). Times Mirror will close the Baltimore Evening Sun. *New York Times*, May 26, p. D4.

——— (1995b). The Miami Herald's ninefold path to reader enlightenment raises some journalist's eyebrows. *New York Times,* Oct. 23, p. C7.

———— (1995c). Circulation drops at many large papers. *New York Times,* Oct. 31, p C7.
———— (1995d). Another city faces cuts at its papers. *New York Times,* Nov. 6, pp. C1, C6.
Haddad, Charles (1995). FTC asks Turner, Time Warner for more information. *Atlanta Constitution,* Nov. 10, p. 3F.
Hall, Carl T., and Erin Hallissy (1995). East bay newspaper chain sold, Knight-Ridder buys Contra Costa Times. *San Francisco Chronicle,* Aug. 29, p. A1.
Harwood, Richard (1995). The media's healthy dinosaurs. *Washington Post,* Sept. 13, p. A19.
Hendren, John (1995). Baltimore evening newspaper will close. Associated Press, in *Austin American-Statesman,* May 26, p. D8.
Howard, H. H. (1989). Group and cross-media ownership of TV stations: A 1989 update. *Journalism Quarterly* 66: 785-792.
Hoyt, Mike (1995). Are you now, or will you ever be, a civic journalist? *Columbia Journalism Review,* Sept.–Oct.: 27.
Koonce, Burke, III (1995). Change signaled by N&O owner. *Triangle Business Journal* (Raleigh, N.C.), Sept. 1, Sec. 1, p. 1.
Landler, Mark (1995). Times Mirror sets more cuts and closings. *New York Times,* July 20, p. D5.
Lowry, Tom (1995). Westinghouse plans heavy cuts at CBS. New York Daily News Service, in *Austin* (Texas) *American-Statesman,* Nov. 17, p. C7.
McDowell, E. (1983). Censorship raised in book dispute. *New York Times,* April 9, p.19.
McManus, John H. (1994). *Market Driven Journalism: Let the Citizen Beware?* Thousand Oaks, Calif.: Sage.
Moskowitz, M., M. Katz, and R. Levering (eds.) (1980). *Everybody's Business.* New York: Harper & Row.
Rips, G. (1988). All the news that's fit to print. *Texas Observer,* Feb. 12, pp. 12-16.
Rosse, J. (1980). The decline of direct newspaper competition. *Journal of Communication* 30: 65-71.
Tate, C. (1981). Gannett in Salem: Protecting the franchise. *Columbia Journalism Review,* July–Aug.: 51-56.
Underwood, Doug (1993). The very model of the reader-driven newsroom? How the Olympian got to the pinnacle of Gannett's News 2000 pyramid. *Columbia Journalism Review,* Nov.–Dec.: 42.
Verhovek, Sam Howe (1995). Houston Post bought and closed by rival. *New York Times,* April 19, p. C6.
Walker, Dave (1995). Corporations dangle media on a string, Bill Moyers says. *Arizona Republic,* Nov. 14, p. D5.
Weinberg, Steve (1995). Smoking guns: ABC, Philip Morris and the infamous apology. *Columbia Journalism Review,* Nov.–Dec., p. 29.
Wharton, Dennis and Joe Flint (1995). Kidding aside, FCC OKs eye deal. *Variety,* Nov. 27-Dec. 3, p. 96.
Williams, Stephen M. (1995). Times Mirror to cut 1,000 newspaper jobs. *New York Times,* July 20, p. F1.
Winski, J. (1981). Case study: How Gannett took Oregon. *Advertising Age* 52, July 6, p. 1. Reprinted in M. Emery and T. Smythe, *Readings in Mass Communication: Concepts and Issues in the Mass Media,* 6th ed. (1986), pp. 50-61; 5th ed. (1983), pp. 69-79. Dubuque, Iowa.: Wm. C. Brown.

part **VII**

Bringing It All Together

Throughout this book we have approached the process of mass communication from several different perspectives, including that of the individual as a receiver, as a member of a group, as a recipient of mass media effects, as a user of the mass media, and the mass media as institutions in society. In covering these perspectives, we have summarized a large number of theories and a great deal of research dealing with mass communication.

There is probably no framework or model that would successfully bring all these diverse perspectives, theories, and research findings together. In the final chapter of the book, Chapter 18, we attempt to bring together as much as we can of this material through the use of one particular communication model—the Westley-MacLean model.

The search for a more unified theory of mass communication goes on, but in the meantime, communication research and theory have produced a rich body of findings that can help us to communicate better and perhaps even to live better lives.

chapter 18

The Overall Picture

Early in this book we discussed the need for research and theory in communication and their application to the fields of journalism, advertising, radio, television, film, and public relations. After discussing the scientific method, a number of models of the communication process were presented and discussed. We now attempt to bring most of the material discussed in earlier chapters together by relating it to an overall model, the Westley-MacLean model.

The Westley-MacLean model (Figure 3.4[d] in Chapter 3, reprinted here as Figure 18.1) expanded the Newcomb model of interpersonal symmetry (Chapters 3 and 8) to include a communicator role (C) and to accommodate a number of "objects of orientation" (X).

When they presented their model in 1957, Westley and MacLean said:

> Communications research and theory have blossomed from a variety of disciplinary sources in recent years. People probing the communications area have here focused on theoretical issues and there on "practical" concerns. Thus, one finds today a jungle of unrelated concepts and systems of concepts on the one hand and a mass of undigested, often sterile empirical data on the other. (p. 31)

They added:

> In this paper, we are trying to develop a single communication model which may help to order existing findings. It also may provide a system of concepts which will evoke new and interrelated research directions, compose old theoretical and disciplinary differences, and in general bring some order out of a chaotic situation. . . . Can a simple,

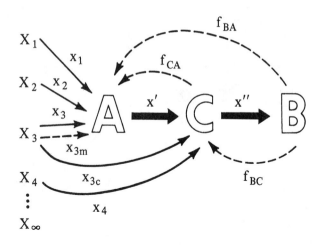

The messages C transmits to B (x″) represent his selections from both messages to him from As (x′) and C's selections and abstractions from Xs in his own sensory field (x_{3c}, x_4), which may or may not be Xs in A's field. Feedback not only moves from B to A (f_{BA}) and from B to C (f_{BC}) but also from C to A (f_{CA}). Clearly, in the mass communication situation, a large number of Cs receive from a very large number of As and transmit to a vastly larger number of Bs, who simultaneously receive from other Cs.

FIGURE 18.1 Steps in the progression of the Westley-MacLean model

SOURCE: From B. H. Westley and M. MacLean, "A Conceptual Model for Communication Research," *Journalism Quarterly* 34 (1957): 31–38. Reprinted with the permission of The Association for Education in Journalism and Mass Communication.

parsimonious model be built capable of drawing together many of the existing approaches to mass communications without serious loss in utility? (p. 31)

THE MODEL AND COMMUNICATION RESEARCH

Communicators

In the Westley-MacLean model, the A roles (advocacy roles) or communicators select and transmit messages purposively. Information theory, explored in Chapter 3, deals with sources that select messages out of all those possible and produce suitable signals for transmission over whatever channel is used. Chapter 3 also discussed the role of gatekeepers and coupling. Chapter 5 dealt with the effects of language on perception, including assumptions built into languages about the nature of reality, and abstraction and the misuses of language, including over-generalization, two-valued thinking, and unconscious projection. Consistency theories have equal meaning for both communicators and receivers. To a greater or lesser extent, depending on the issue, we all practice selective attention and perception. Persuasion research (Chapter 9) indicates the active role of the receiver and that single messages are unlikely to change strongly held attitudes. Research about the communication of innovation indicates that attitudes are probably best changed with a combination of interpersonal and media messages used as "media forums" (Chapters 9 and 11). Communicators who promote the adoption of a new technology need to be aware of the constraints on an innovator's ability to foresee the impact of an innovation (Chapter 11). The studies dealing with the credibility of the source (Chapter 9) or communicator are, of course, of direct application here.

The concept of agenda setting (Chapter 12) raises important questions for the communicator. Will the public pay attention to issues connected with an event because of labels a journalist applies to the event? Newsmakers have long sought to place items on the media agenda, and there is evidence of intermedia agenda setting, whereby certain media systematically influence other media. We now have some evidence that interactions between media, officials, events, and the public all play a part in agenda setting. Abstract issues may not be as tractable to agenda setting as concrete issues. Time-related issues in agenda setting (how long it takes for the effect to develop and how long it will last) and how frequency of exposure affects agenda setting are also now being investigated. The effects of agenda setting on attitudes and behaviors are areas of recent research. Public or civic journalism is closely related to agenda setting.

The channel roles (C) provide the behavioral system roles (B) with a more extended environment by selecting and transmitting the information Bs require, especially information that is beyond Bs' immediate reach. Cs make abstractions from objects (X) appropriate to satisfying Bs' needs or solving Bs' problem. We have already mentioned information theory, semantics, and selective attention as they relate to abstraction in connection with A roles. In a like manner they apply to C roles.

In the Westley-MacLean model, Cs select and transmit nonpurposively the information Bs require. (Nonpurposively means without intent to influence.) However, as gatekeepers, Cs often engage in transmitting messages designed to engender attitude change, as in the case of advertising and public relations campaigns and in more general ways. Cs also serve different roles in various types of societies and may have several functions as well as dysfunctions. Lasswell has pointed to distortions of media content as a method of achieving or main-taining social control. Breed discusses news policy and slanting, areas omitted or seldom dealt with by communicators, and the distortions brought about by civic boosterism. Media chains, conglomerates, and cross ownership in single communities can all result in distortions and omissions of news and a reduction in the diversity of news—a threat to truth and understanding. This becomes increasingly important as large chains are merged with still larger conglomerates and often the number of individual media voices in a community is drastically reduced (Chapter 17). Some researchers suggest that the communicator is often in a position to exercise great influence as to what readers and viewers will think about (the agenda-setting function), even if not the conclusions they will reach about an issue. Agenda-setting research suggests that the media shape people's views about the major problems facing society. However, the problems emphasized by the media may not be those that are in reality the most pressing. Recently some major corporations have controlled media agendas by threatening lawsuits if news unfavorable to their interests were aired (Chapter 17).

Conversely, new forms of media (online services, the Internet, e-mail, newsgroups and mailing lists, and the Web) are intended for smaller groups and for individuals. These new media may undercut the power of large corporate media to influence people's views. As individuals, including political candidates, and businesses set up Web sites (pages) they bypass the control traditional mass media have had over the content of their messages. However, these new forms of media are not without their disadvantages. Critics have charged that heavy users of the new media are falling into "plainspeak," are removed from the "real" world, and accept information which has not been checked for accuracy by traditional media editors.

The so-called New News often combines information and entertainment, using talk shows and MTV to deliver its messages with speed and vividness while avoiding the intervention of journalists. This, of course, is appealing to most politicians.

The mass media can help close the knowledge gaps (Chapter 13) that exist in society, including those brought about by the disparities of home computer ownership between various income and ethnic groups.

Studies have shown that the more educated are more likely to get information from newspapers while the less educated rely more on television, a finding especially useful to planners of information campaigns. Unfortunately, many of the media have not been interested in reaching the lower-status segments of society because these are unwanted by advertisers. On the other hand, stagnant or declining circulation has led many newspapers to try a variety of methods in recent years to hold and gain readers (Chapter 17).

Receivers

The Bs in the Westley-MacLean model are the behavioral system roles or the "receivers." They can be an individual (a personality system), a primary group, or a social system. B needs "transmissible messages as a means of orienting itself in its environment and as a means of securing problem solutions and need satisfactions."

Uses and gratifications research helps to explain to communicators some selective behavior in media use by receivers and the reasons for it. The findings should help communicators better tailor their messages for their audiences.

Bs can select from a number of Cs, as diffusion studies have shown, which is why C remains an agent of B only so long as C fulfills B's needs. Bs are the destination in information theory terms and must decode the messages. Bs bring their backgrounds to the messages to provide connotative meanings. As pointed out in Chapter 4, "meaning is something invented, assigned, given, rather than something received." Bs exercise selective perception and often make information fit an existing schema as a result of their past experiences, cultural expectations, needs, moods, and attitudes. The Keck and Mueller study (Chapter 4) of U.S. Army commercials is a good recent example of making messages fit expectations and needs. Another example is the findings that men and women have different reasons for watching televised sports, and gratify different needs by doing so (Chapter 8).

The receiver is given more of an active role as an information-processing agent in the newer models of persuasion, which view persuasion more as a process (Chapter 9).

Receiver's attitudes may serve many functions and different messages may be needed to reach different types of individuals (Chapter 9). Bs use selective exposure, attention, and retention when dealing with messages. There is also evidence (Chapter 4) that much mass communication use may be ritualistic or habitual and it may involve a low level of attention.

As Chapter 10 points out, how we interpret and act on message content is often the result of the groups we are members of, identify with, or aspire to. More recent research has focused on the interactions among group members and the formation of norms, the formation of attitudes toward political parties and candidates, and the use of ethnic groups as reference groups. Some applied research has dealt with the effectiveness of antismoking and AIDS information campaigns.

Consistency theories predict that when messages that cause psychological discomfort are directed to Bs (receivers), they will use selective attention, perception, and retention or fall back on rationalization, incredulity, or attacks on source credibility to avoid or reduce the psychological discomfort. The research on the use of fear appeals in messages (Chapter 9) is another related area of inquiry. However, if the messages offer rewards (utility, novelty, etc.) great enough to offset the discomfort, Bs may not avoid them. Communicators who wish to change attitudes held by receivers must first understand the functions of those attitudes for receivers if any measure of success is to be achieved. Inoculation theory provides the other side of the coin, making attitudes resistant to persuasion.

The Axelrod schema theory of information processing (Chapter 3) integrates much of what we know about how receivers deal with information. It diagrams how a receiver (B) decides if a message is worth processing, if it relates to already stored concepts, and how it is transformed to complement existing knowledge. Leveling and sharpening separate essential elements from non-essential details. When receivers process information it may be given various slants that make it less accurate, because often only the conclusions drawn from the evidence are stored.

A somewhat different approach to how individuals (Bs) process information is that of psychologist John F. Kihlostrom (Chapter 4). He compares individual information processing with the way a computer processes information.

In recent years mass communication theory has shifted its focus to put greater emphasis on audience activity and the uses an individual makes of information. Researchers find that individuals choose varying media, including computer networks, for reasons that vary as their needs vary (Chapter 15). Some information theorists have moved toward cognitive science or information processing with an emphasis on cognitions rather than attitudes, and how cognitions are restructured, rather than how change is effected. Scott (Chapter 4) stresses that pictures can act as symbols and are processed cognitively just like other forms of information. This is an area of human information processing that is just beginning to be explored. Others have looked at the effects of receiver involvement and picture relevance on attitudes toward products and purchase intentions (Chapter 9).

If receivers are to be reached through opinion leaders, two-step flow and communication of innovation research indicate that media appropriate to the particular sphere of influence must be carefully selected.

While the media serve many functions for receivers they can also have a number of dysfunctions. Walter Lippmann, more than a half-century ago, discussed the gap between reality and the pictures of reality we carry around in our heads. For the receiver the media supply information, gratify needs, and have other uses. The effects of mass communication are contingent on many other variables, as much recent research has shown (Chapter 14). These areas need further research along with the effects of the media on political behavior and the effects of viewing violence on television.

Messages

In the model, "messages" about Xs (objects or events "out there" that have characteristics capable of being transmitted in some abstracted form) are transmitted through channels from As and/or Cs to Bs. These messages can inform, persuade, and educate. Information theory introduces the concepts of channel capacity, the notion that in one sense information is not meaning, the important use of redundancy to offset noise, and the use of entropy as a measure of the difficulty of a message. General semantics sheds light on the problems we encounter in using language to communicate abstractions about reality.

Readability measures provide a way of judging the difficulty of textual materials. Chapter 7 discusses the Catalano research, which indicates that most news agency and newspaper leads fall into the "difficult" or "very difficult" reading categories. This suggests an area which may need improvement for newspapers with declining readerships. Broadcasters might well want to check some of their material with Fang's Easy Listening Formula. The chapter cites several studies that indicate some mass media campaigns have used language far too difficult for their intended audiences. More recent approaches to readability look at the text along with reader characteristics (Brinkley) and cognitive processing factors (Zakaluk and Samuels). Those working with languages other than English might consult the work of Rabin. As was noted, more research is needed on the effects of organization of material, directness of approach, and the conceptual difficulty of textual materials, and probably on the "listenability" of spoken messages.

Messages often contain the techniques identified in studies of propaganda, an area that provided the roots for attitude-change research and the general studies of the effects of mass communication. An understanding of these techniques for designing messages is of considerable value to the receiver as well as the communicator.

MASS MEDIA RESEARCH

Communication research is the application of social science research methods to the problems communicators deal with. It is an attempt to replace as much guesswork as possible with verified theories. Theories and research methods in the social sciences are not as accurate or refined as those used in the physical sciences. Understanding and predicting human behavior is extremely difficult; nevertheless, the imperfect statements that can be made about human behavior as a result of research are better than the guesswork upon which much of communication has been based.

Research provides the information to help plan communication and evaluate its results. To sum up what we have learned about the uses of research in mass communication, we offer the following survey:

1. *Audience studies* are usually survey-type research designed to measure the amount of interest in various mass media content and the reasons for it. With print media, audience studies are usually in the form of "one-time" surveys, whereas television ratings most often use an adaptation of the "panel" method where samples of the audience are repeatedly measured over a period of years. Studies of media use and media credibility, reader interest surveys, and broadcast "ratings" are examples of this type of research.

2. *Message content and design* immediately brings to mind the content analysis of messages, but content analysis can often be used in conjunction with other research methods to great advantage. Experimental designs in a laboratory setting are often used to determine the most effective version of a message to achieve a desired objective with a specific population. Research on the advantages of presenting one side of an issue or two sides of an issue, the use of fear appeals, the optimum levels of repetition (both in Chapter 9), the uses of language, and the various methods of counterpersuasion are examples of message content and design studies. So are field studies done by advertising agencies and public relations firms to determine the most effective form or versions for their commercials and advertisements.

3. *Effect studies* involve the planning and evaluation of the effects of media campaigns as well as the choice of media used. Studies involving the diffusion of innovations, the functions and dysfunctions of the media, the agenda-setting function of the media, and the effects of viewing television violence are obvious examples. In the commercial world, advertisers are interested in the most effective means of increasing sales, public relations practitioners seek the best ways to improve a corporate image, campaign managers need the means to get a candidate elected, and statesmen want the best ways to win acceptance for a policy or a program. Effect studies can use many research methods: experimental designs, survey research, content analysis, and case studies, as well as combinations of these.

4. *Communicator analysis* has traditionally been linked with "gatekeeper" studies (case studies). Studies dealing with the effects of language on perception and abstraction can also be classified as communicator analysis. The effects of source credibility on the acceptance of a message are also directly related to communicator studies. One such example is the research done on celebrity sources who have become associated with a number of media messages (Chapter 9). Research into the effects of media chains, conglomerates, and cross-ownership on the content of the media are all examples of communicator analysis.

As can be seen, any listing of research in mass communication contains a great deal of overlap. One cannot separate media effects from message content, or communicator analysis from message content. Communicators, messages, audiences, and effects are all interrelated—that interrelation is necessary for communication. Research methods are tools to aid communicators in understanding the communication process and predicting the effects of their efforts.

CONCLUSION

As we pointed out in our preface, this book is intended as an introduction to the development of mass communication theory. It provides the reader with a grounding in the beginnings of an ongoing field of research.

By now you are aware that communications theory and research stands at the crossroads of many other fields. The student seeking related courses and the practitioner seeking related reading might wish to consider some of the following, which is by no means an exhaustive list:

Psychology: social psychology, perception, psychology of language, sensory psychology, information processing, human learning

Sociology: public opinion, collective behavior, formal organizations, social change, communication

Government: public opinion, theory construction, empirical theory and modeling, research design

Philosophy: philosophy of science, science and the modern world, communication and culture

Linguistics: study of language, language and society

Computer sciences: computer application courses

Also, research methods (survey research, experimental design, content analysis, case studies, etc.) and statistics in a number of fields, especially psychology, educational psychology, sociology, government, and communications.

The student or practitioner who wishes to keep abreast of the most recent developments in this field can find them in a number of publications. Found in academic and other libraries, these journals regularly publish articles about the most recent advances in communication theory and research, and the function, effects, and role of the mass media. Among the best of them are (in alphabetical order): *Columbia Journalism Review; ETC.: A Review of General Semantics; Journal of Broadcasting and Electronic Media; Journal of Communication; Journalism Quarterly;* and *Public Opinion Quarterly.*

We wish our readers well in their ongoing quest to understanding the functions, effects, and role of the mass media in modern society.

REFERENCE

Westley, B., and M. MacLean (1957). A conceptual model for communication research. *Journalism Quarterly* 34: 31-38.

Index

About The Authors

Werner J. Severin was invited in 1984 to the People's Republic of China as the first Fulbright professor of journalism to that country. He has made six trips to Asia in recent years.

James W. Tankard, Jr., is a professor in the Department of Journalism at the University of Texas. He is the author of *The Statistical Pioneers* and the coauthor with Michael Ryan of *Basic News Reporting*.